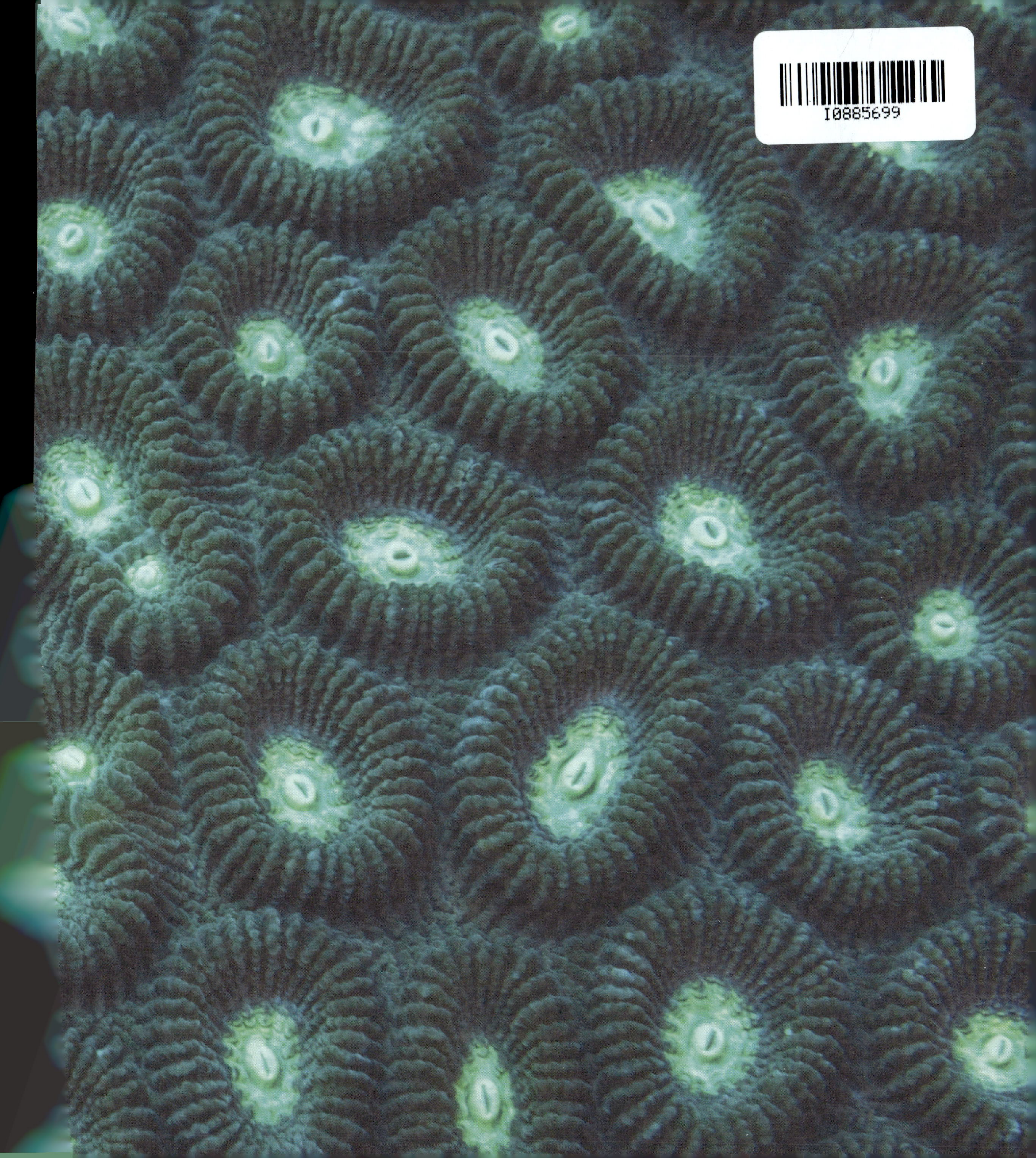

O C E A N S

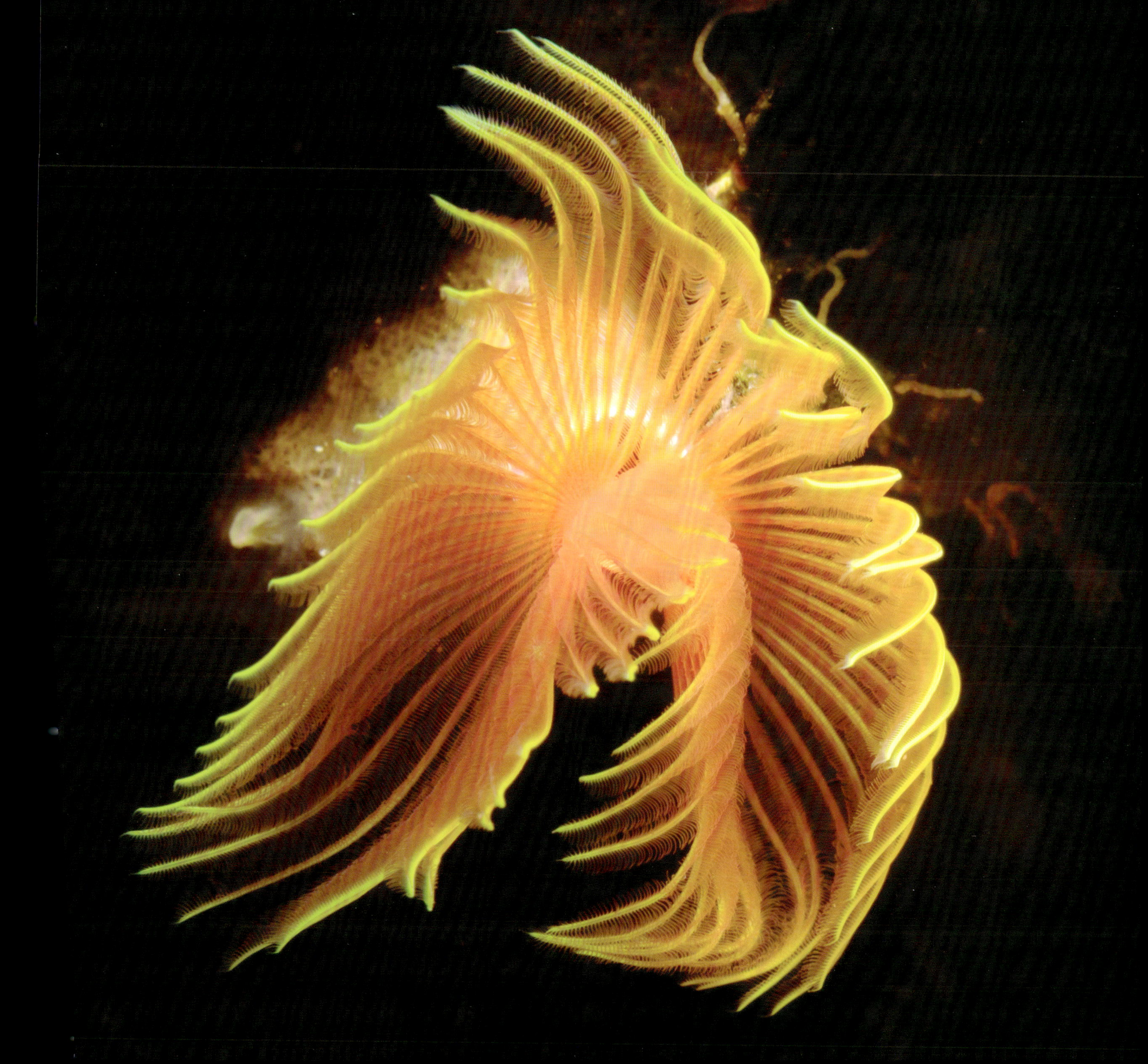

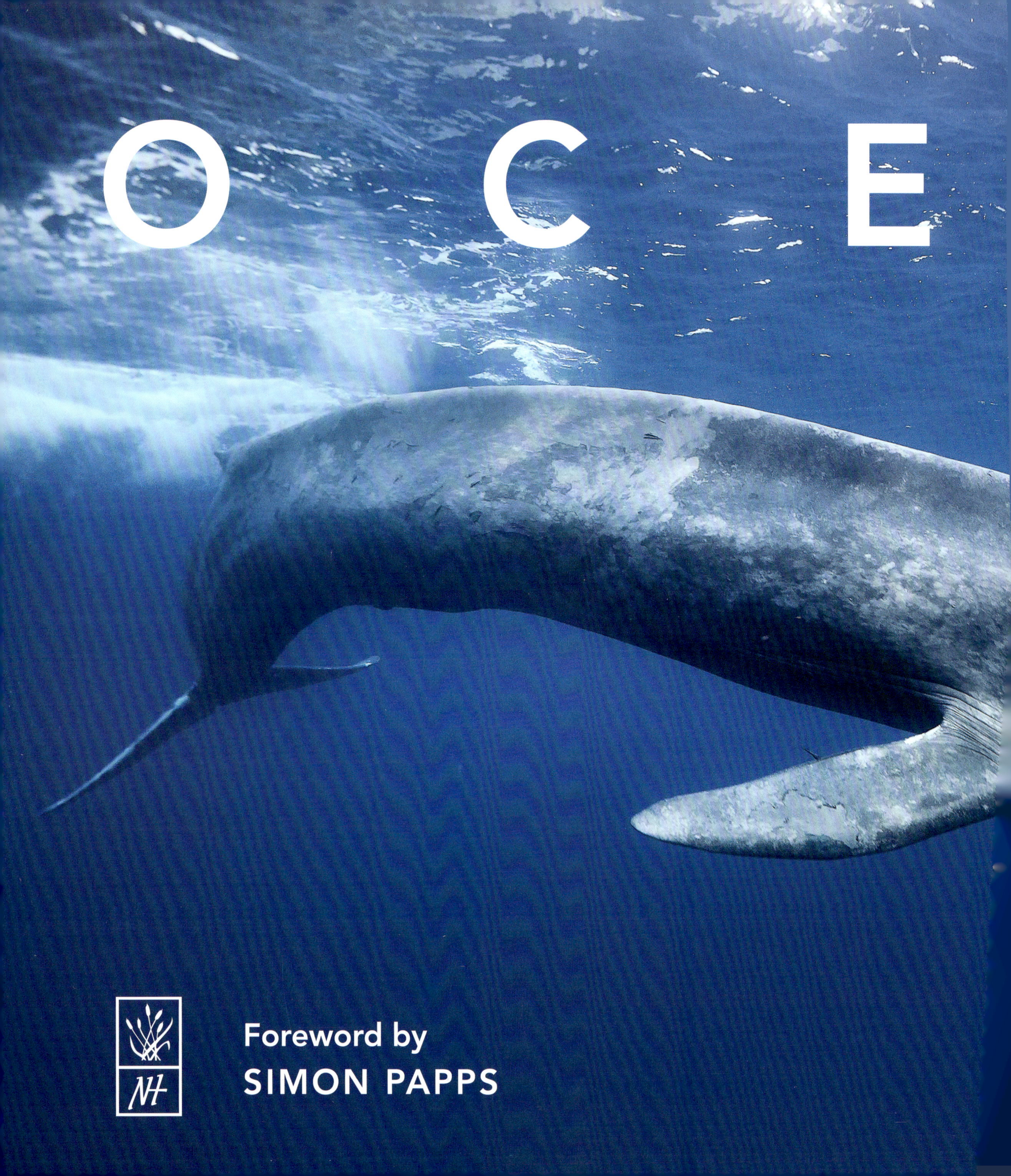

O C E

Foreword by
SIMON PAPPS

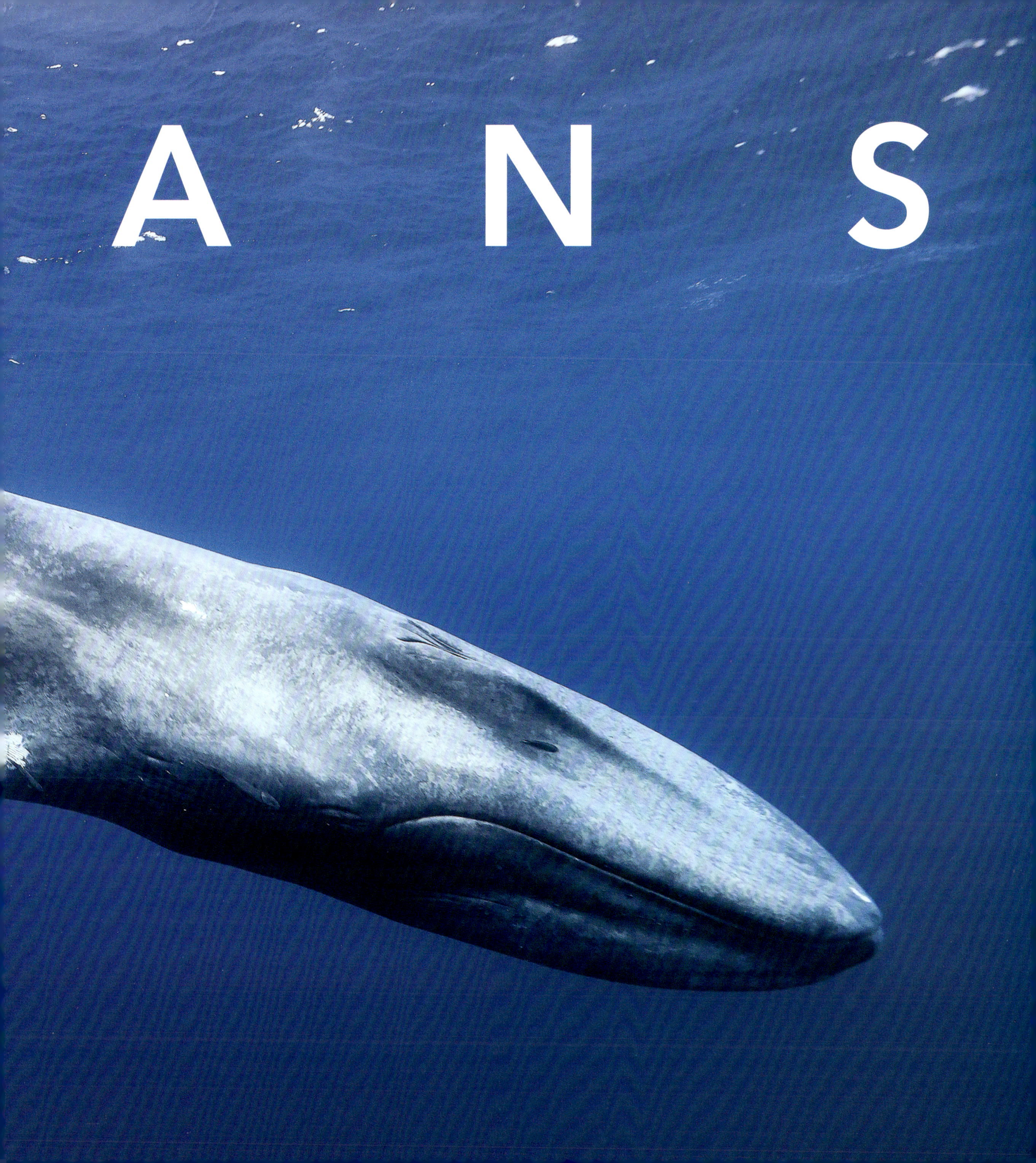
A N S

AMAZING OCEANS

From the surface, the ocean can appear an almost lifeless place, perhaps save for seabirds such as terns or petrels skimming over the surface and cetaceans such as whales and dolphins breaching from the depths. But look beneath the waves and there are myriad creatures that find a home anywhere from the shallow shores to the depths of the deepest ocean chasm. As this book illustrates, marine life comes in all shapes, forms and patterns, and some of the creatures out there look as though they have been dreamed up by a sci-fi film director with an over-active imagination.

HIDDEN TREASURES

The world's oceans are home to biodiversity hot-spots that can rival anything on land. The greatest diversity of species can be found in tropical oceans. For example, the Caribbean Sea is home to 12,000 marine species, Australia's Great Barrier Reef holds more than 9,000 known species, the 'Coral Triangle' in the Indo-Pacific is home to more than 3,000 species of fishes and 500 corals, and the Red Sea hosts more than 2,000 species of fishes, about 10 per cent of which are endemic and occur nowhere else. All of these figures are works in progress as new species are continually being discovered.

As we head from the tropics towards the poles, the diversity of species is not so great but the colder waters support a staggeringly large biomass, with billions of tiny organisms such as krill underpinning a food chain that supports fishes, seabirds, great whales and much more besides.

UNBELIEVABLE DIVERSITY

So far nearly a quarter of a million different species have been found and identified in oceans around the world, and there are doubtless many more waiting to be discovered, particularly in the deepest and most remote areas.

Some of the greatest oceanic wildlife spectacles include the 'sardine run' off South Africa, where billions of pilchards gather together in huge shoals and attract a feeding frenzy of predators including sharks and other fishes, seabirds, whales and dolphins.

Divers will be familiar with world-famous attractions such as swimming with alien-looking Hammerhead Sharks in the Bahamas or Colombia, with gigantic Whale Sharks in Mexico or the Philippines, or with awe-inspiring Great White Sharks in Australia or South Africa, and these special sites have produced some of the most iconic images of underwater wildlife over the years. It is not just the oceanic 'megafauna' that fascinates, though – the little critters are equally if not more intriguing and engaging, whether it's the many outlandish species of nudibranchs (or 'sea slugs') that can be encountered around the world, tiny cryptic pygmy seahorses that can hide in plain sight on coral, or the charismatic Coconut Octopus encountered during a 'muck dive'. The list is seemingly endless, with many of the highlights from around the world depicted in this book.

THE WORLD'S TRASH CAN

Perhaps because much of this spectacular wildlife is out of our sight, hidden under the surface of the ocean, humans in general seem to have scant regard for marine ecosystems. It's a case of 'out of sight, out of mind', with millions of tonnes of non-biodegradable plastic waste being disposed of in the oceans over the years, resulting in widespread pollution, including famously a vortex of plastic the size of Texas in the Pacific Ocean. Of course, such waste is ingested by marine creatures such as turtles and seabirds and is a killer for millions.

It is not just pollution that is harming our seas. Overfishing has been a problem for centuries – take the utter depletion of stocks in the North Atlantic as an example. However, today a combination of a relentlessly growing human population and the advent of much more widespread and unsustainable industrial-scale fishing methods are resulting in the depletion and destruction of ocean ecosystems on a more far-reaching and serious scale than ever before. Often the victims are termed 'bycatch', with animals such as dolphins, turtles and albatrosses, which aren't even targeted by the methods, being so seriously hard hit that some are threatened with extinction.

THE FUTURE

With the climate crisis gathering pace it is imperative for our own sake that we look after the world's oceans, which act as the world's biggest and most effective carbon sink – in this respect they are more important even than the world's forests. Hopefully the growing urgency of the situation will lead to humans treating the world's oceans with greater care and respect. As this beautiful book illustrates, there is so much amazing, astonishing life still out there, and the more we can do to protect it, the better.

Simon Papps

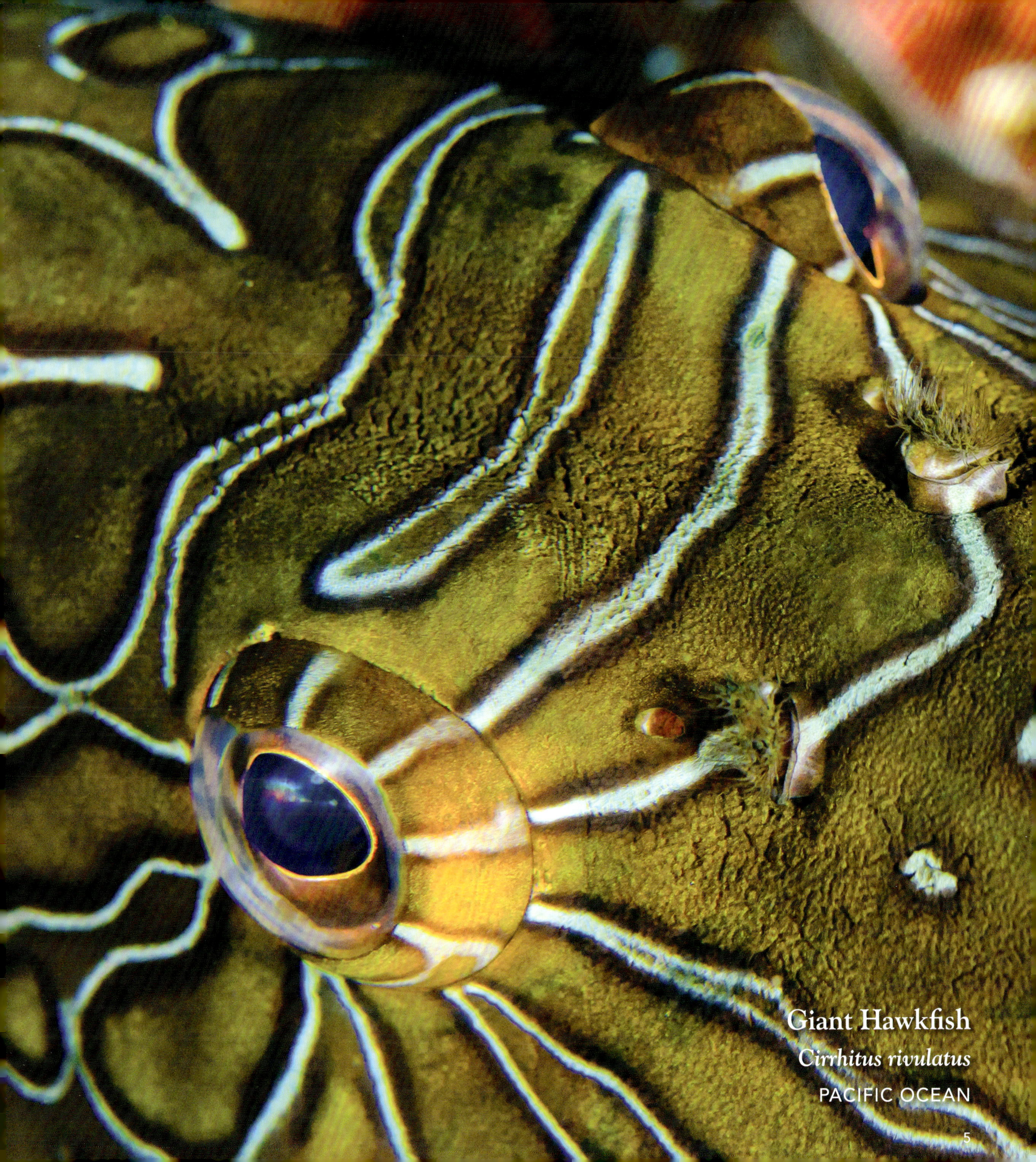

Giant Hawkfish
Cirrhitus rivulatus
PACIFIC OCEAN

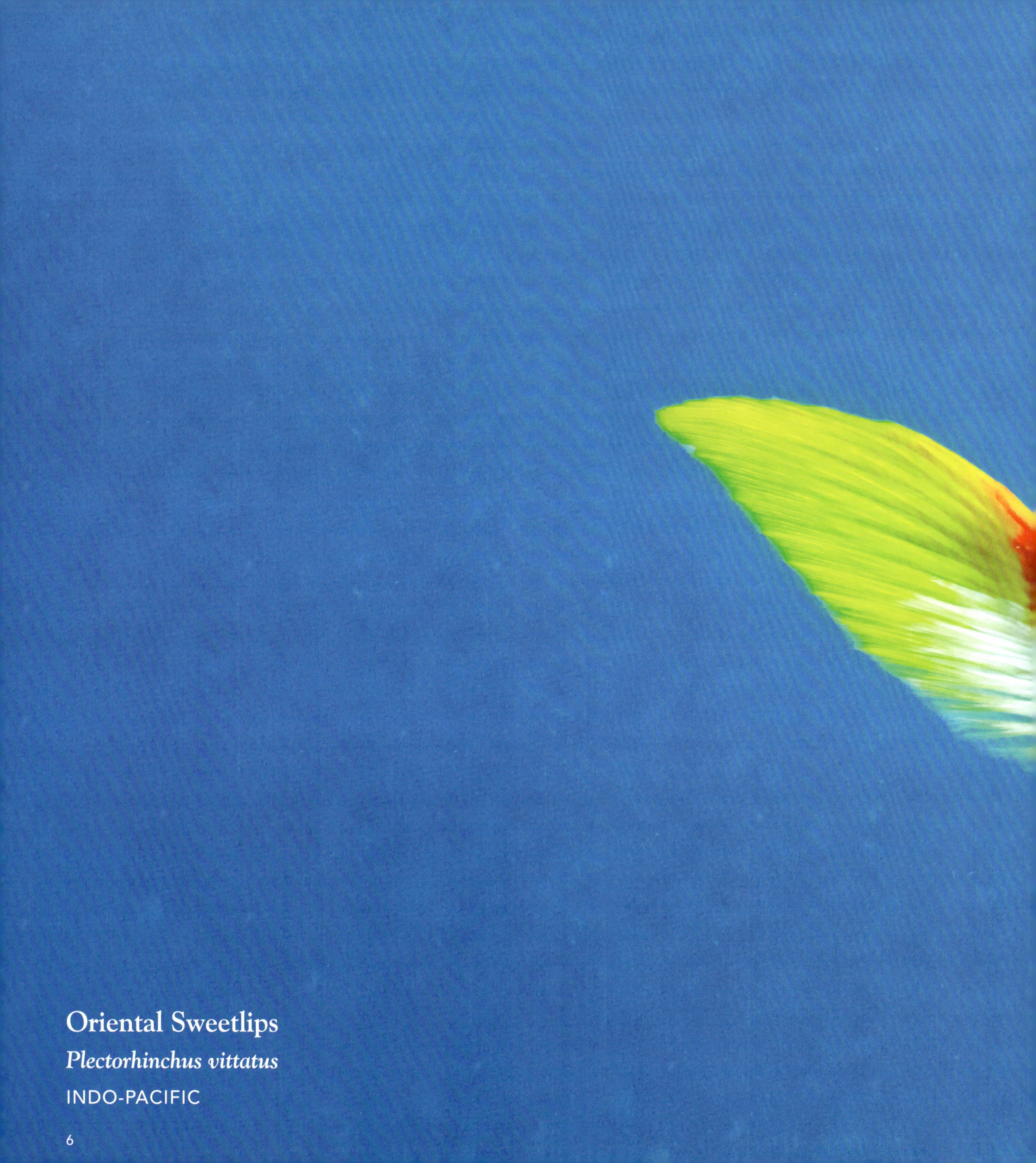

Oriental Sweetlips

Plectorhinchus vittatus

INDO-PACIFIC

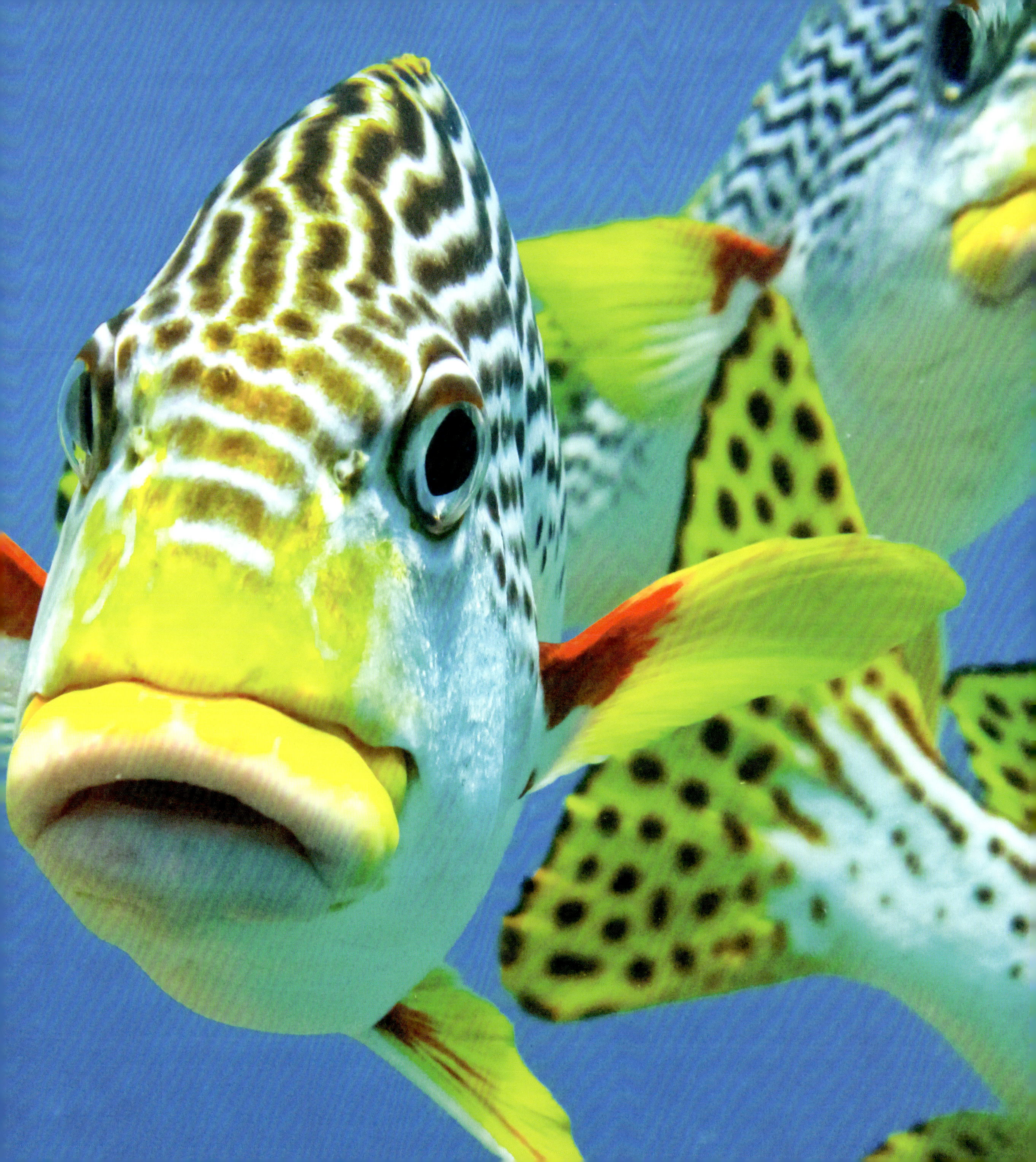

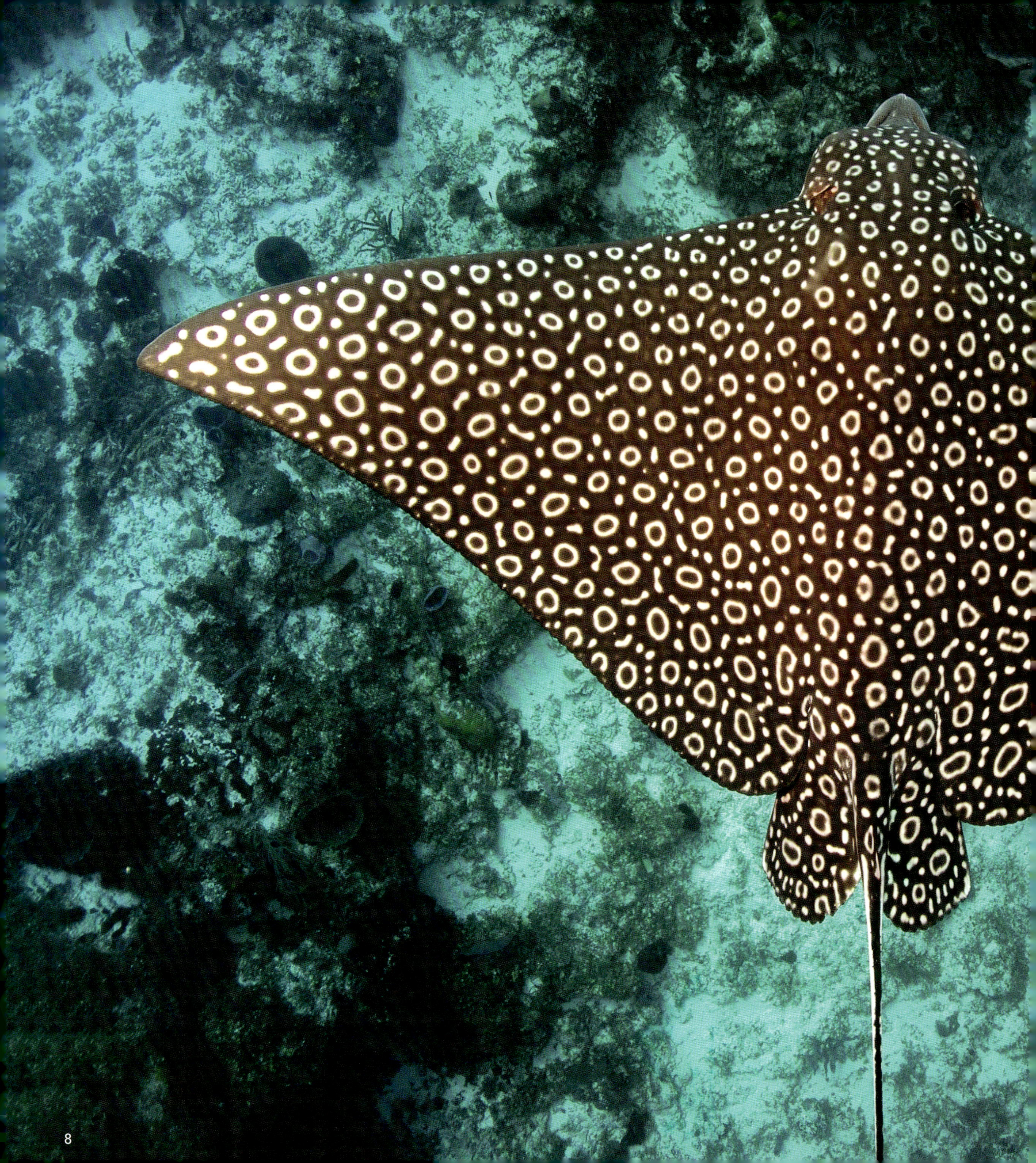

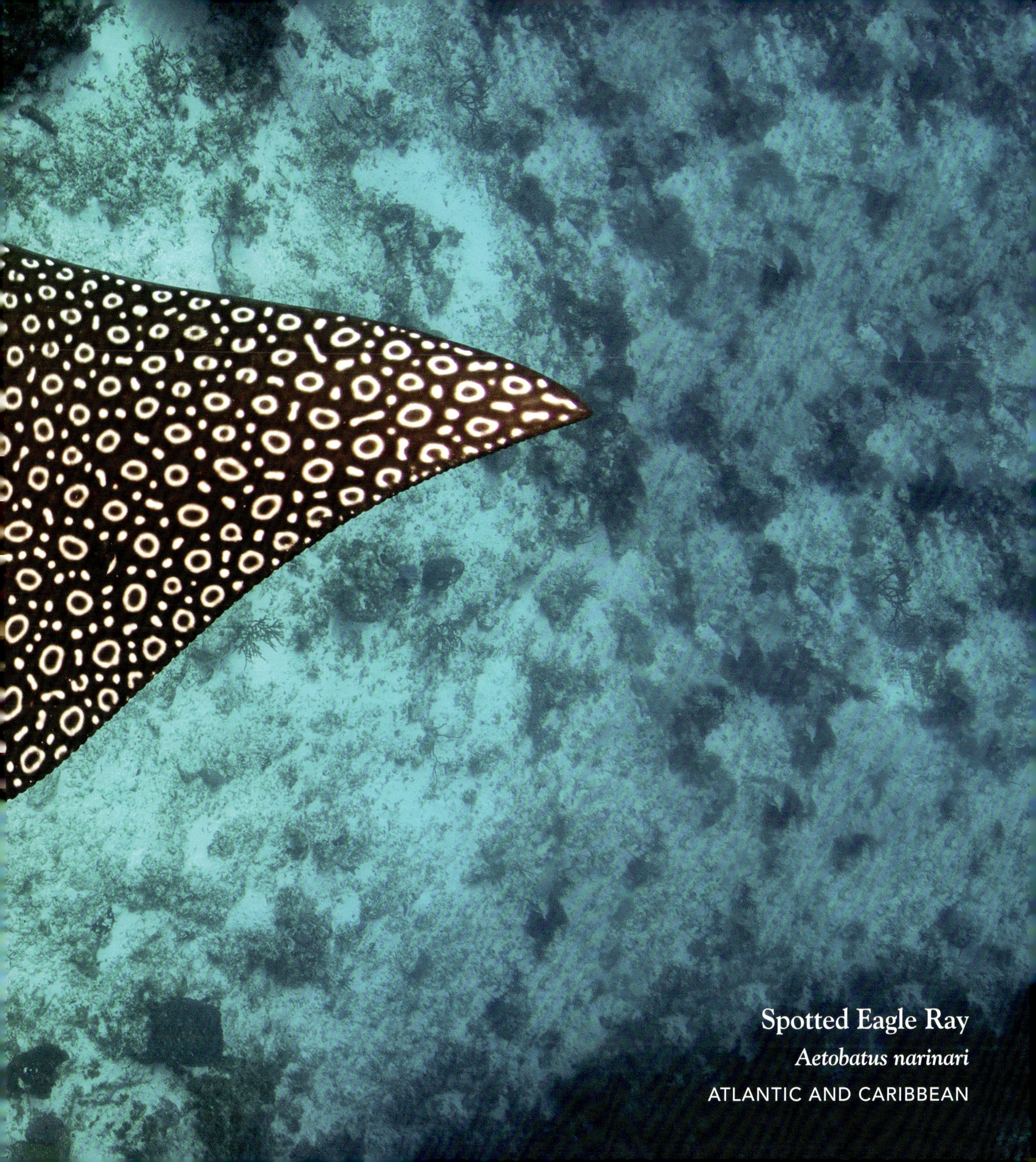

Spotted Eagle Ray

Aetobatus narinari

ATLANTIC AND CARIBBEAN

Goby species

Gobiidae

INDO-PACIFIC

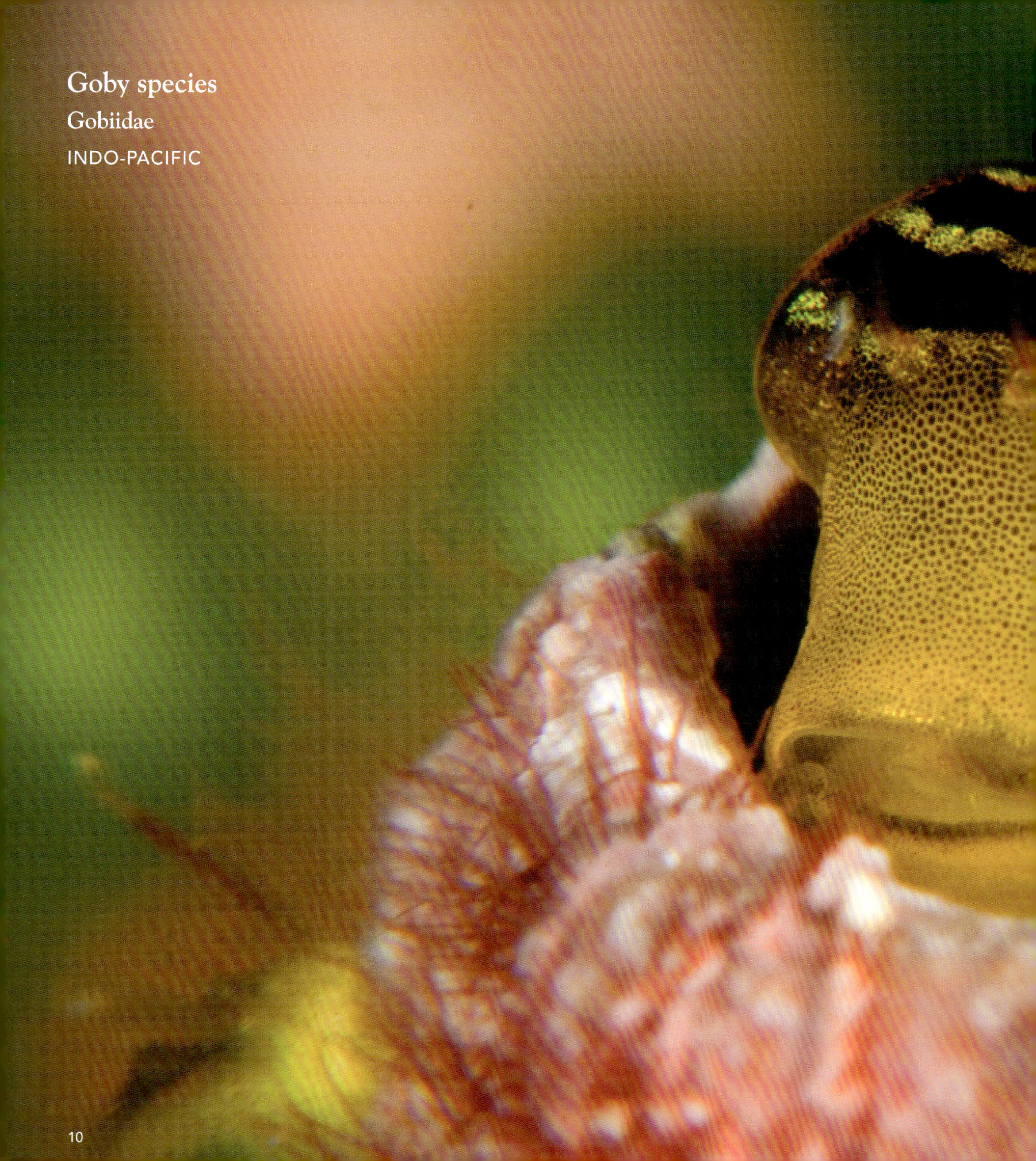

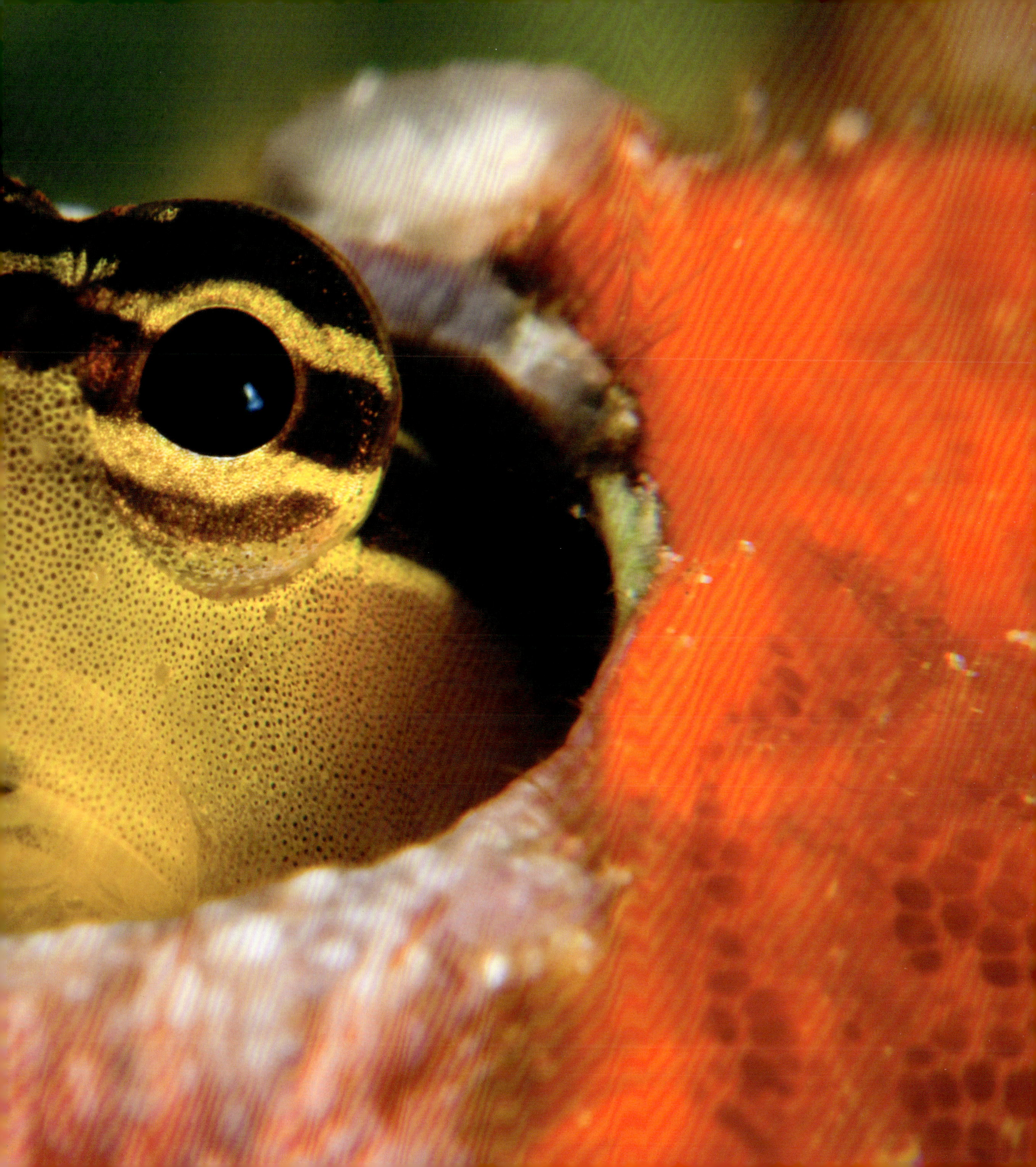

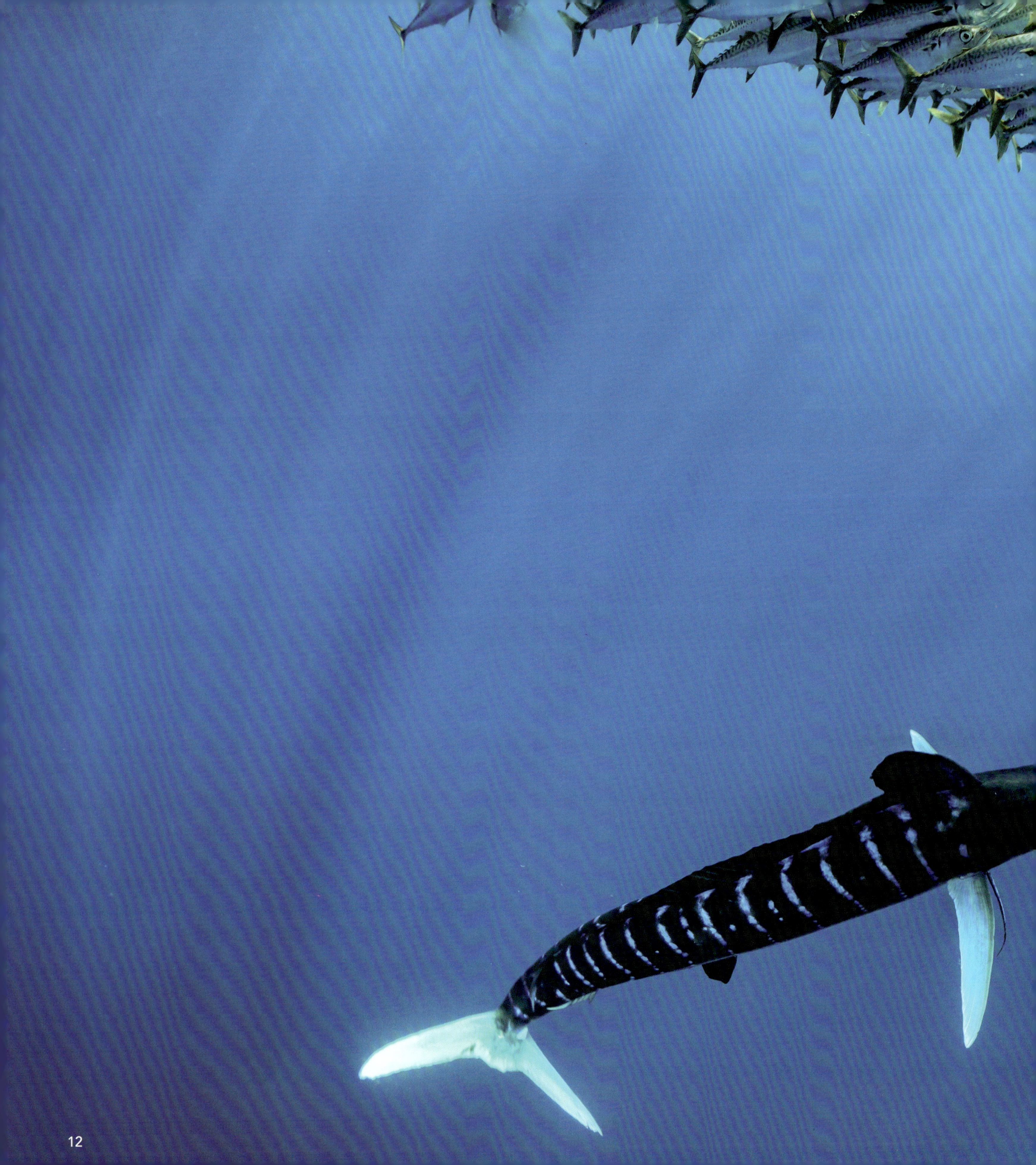

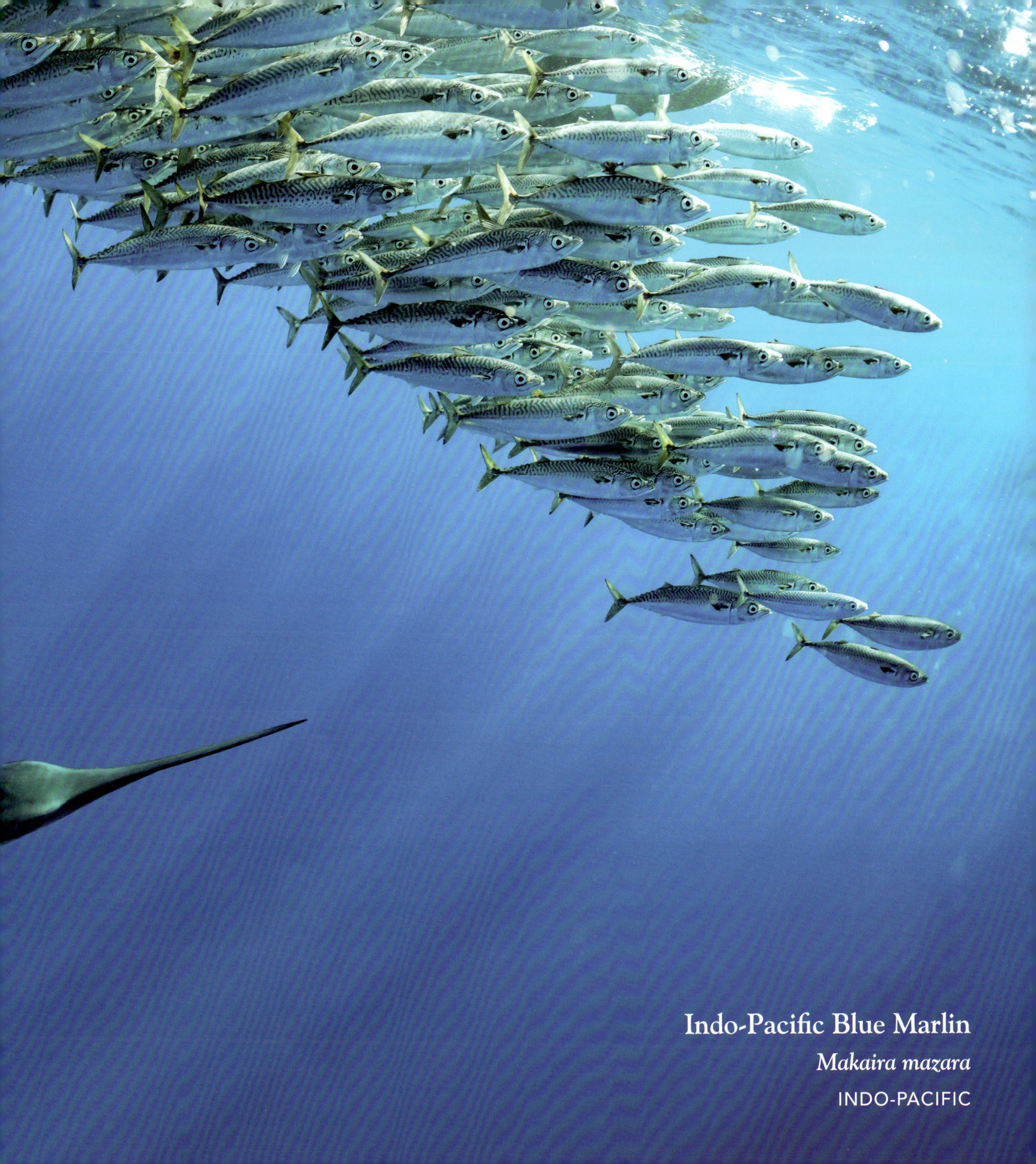

Indo-Pacific Blue Marlin

Makaira mazara

INDO-PACIFIC

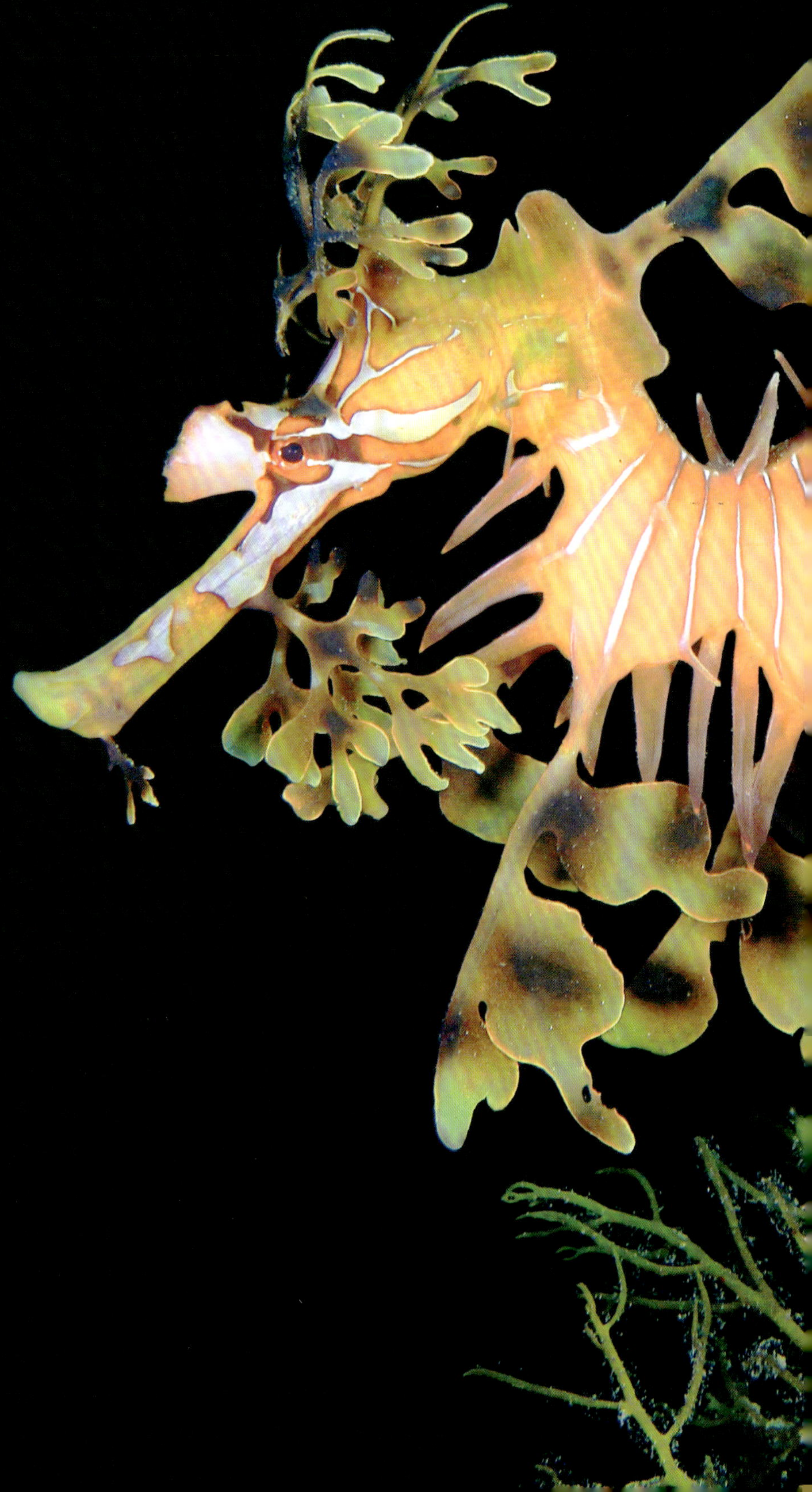

Leafy Seadragon

Phycodurus eques

SOUTHERN AUSTRALIA

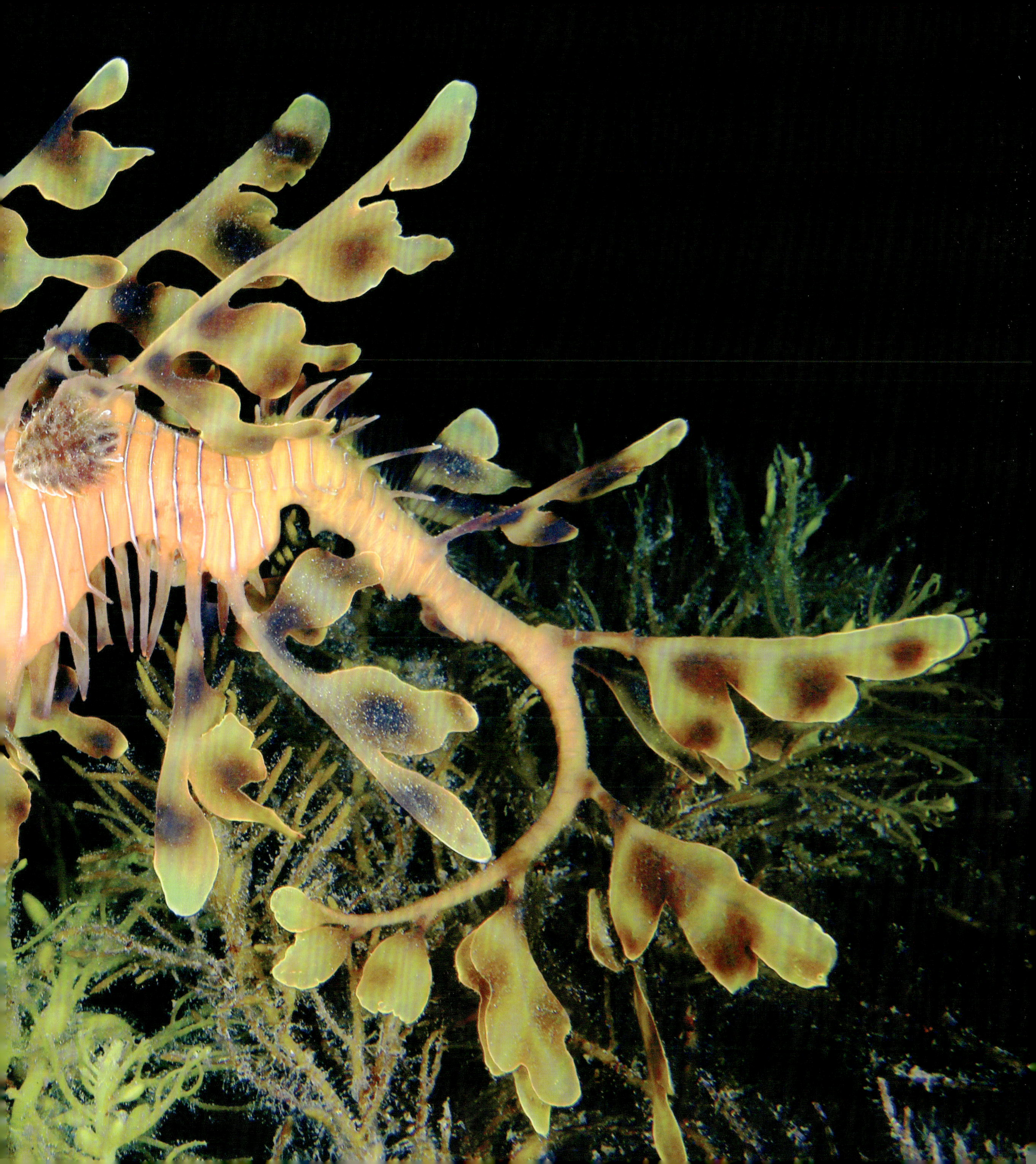

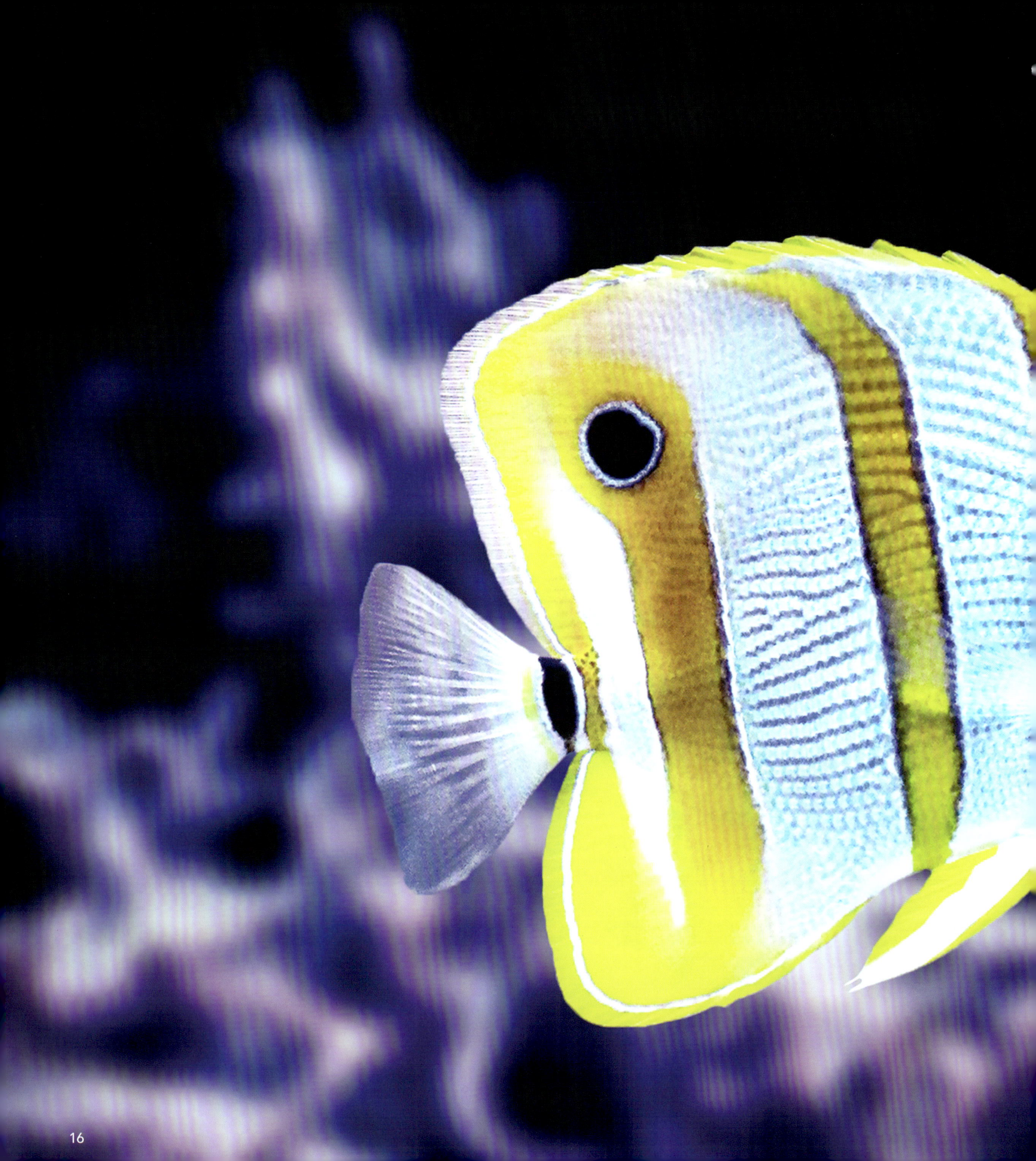

Copperband Butterflyfish

Chelmon rostratus

INDO-PACIFIC

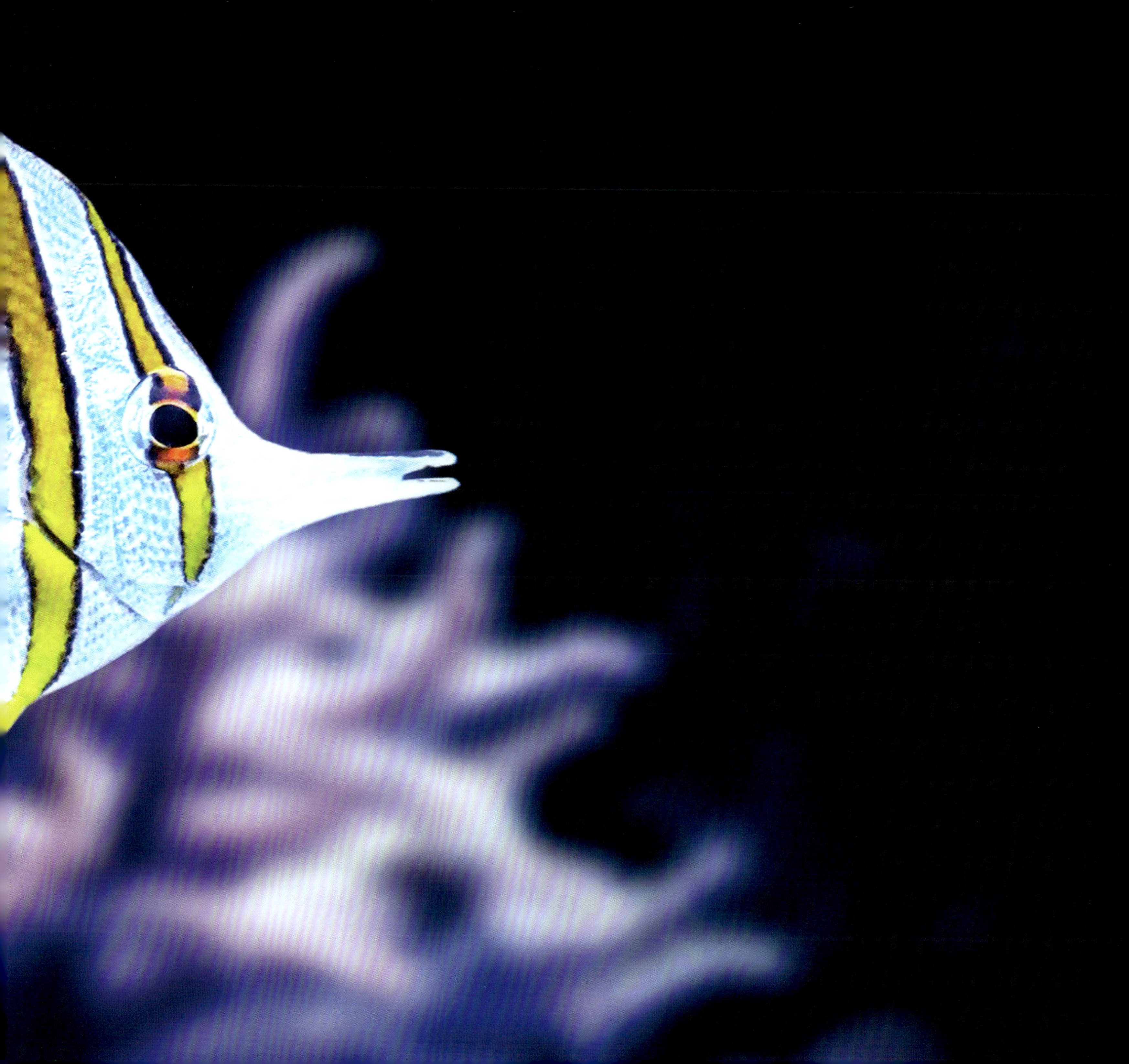

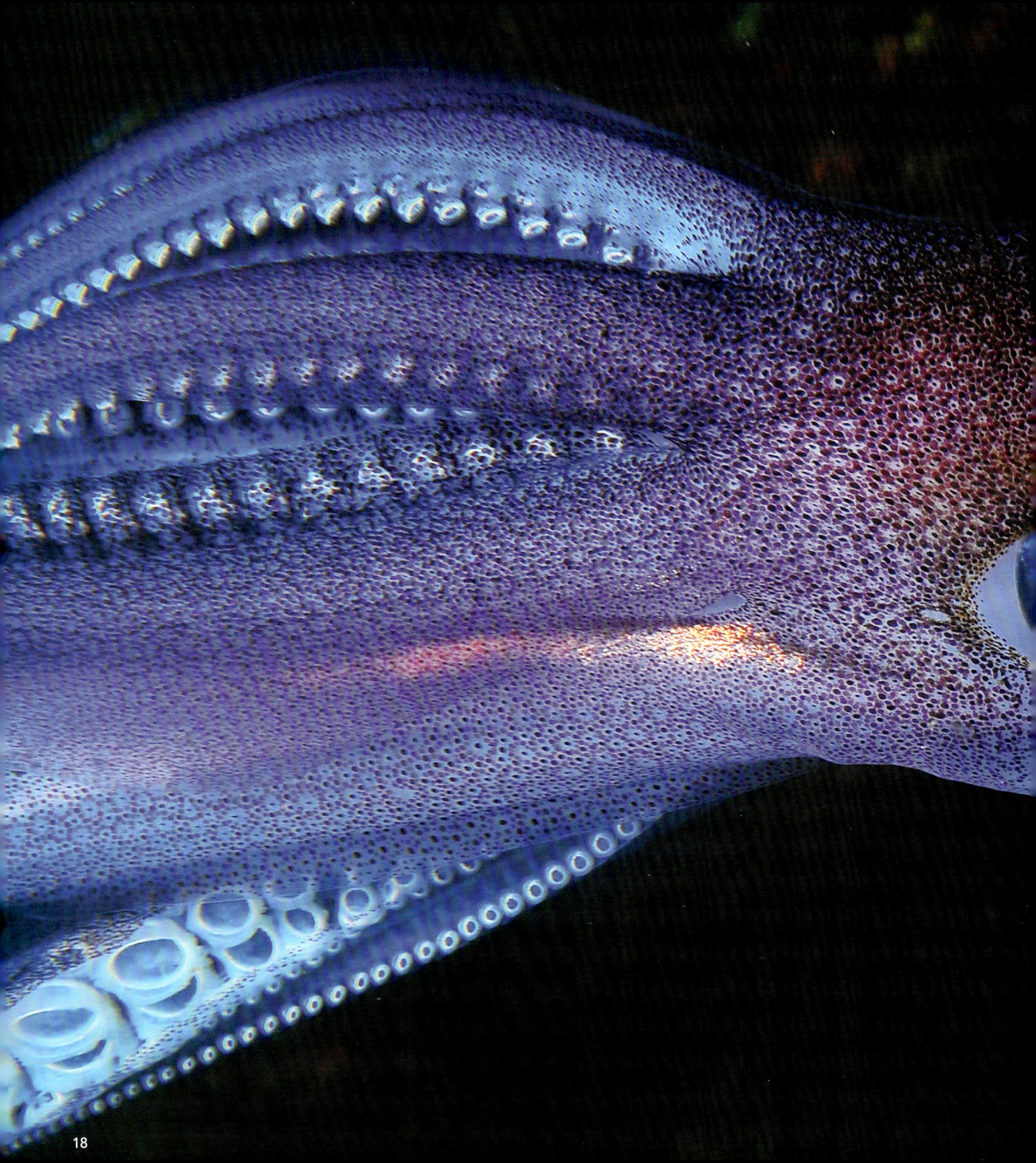

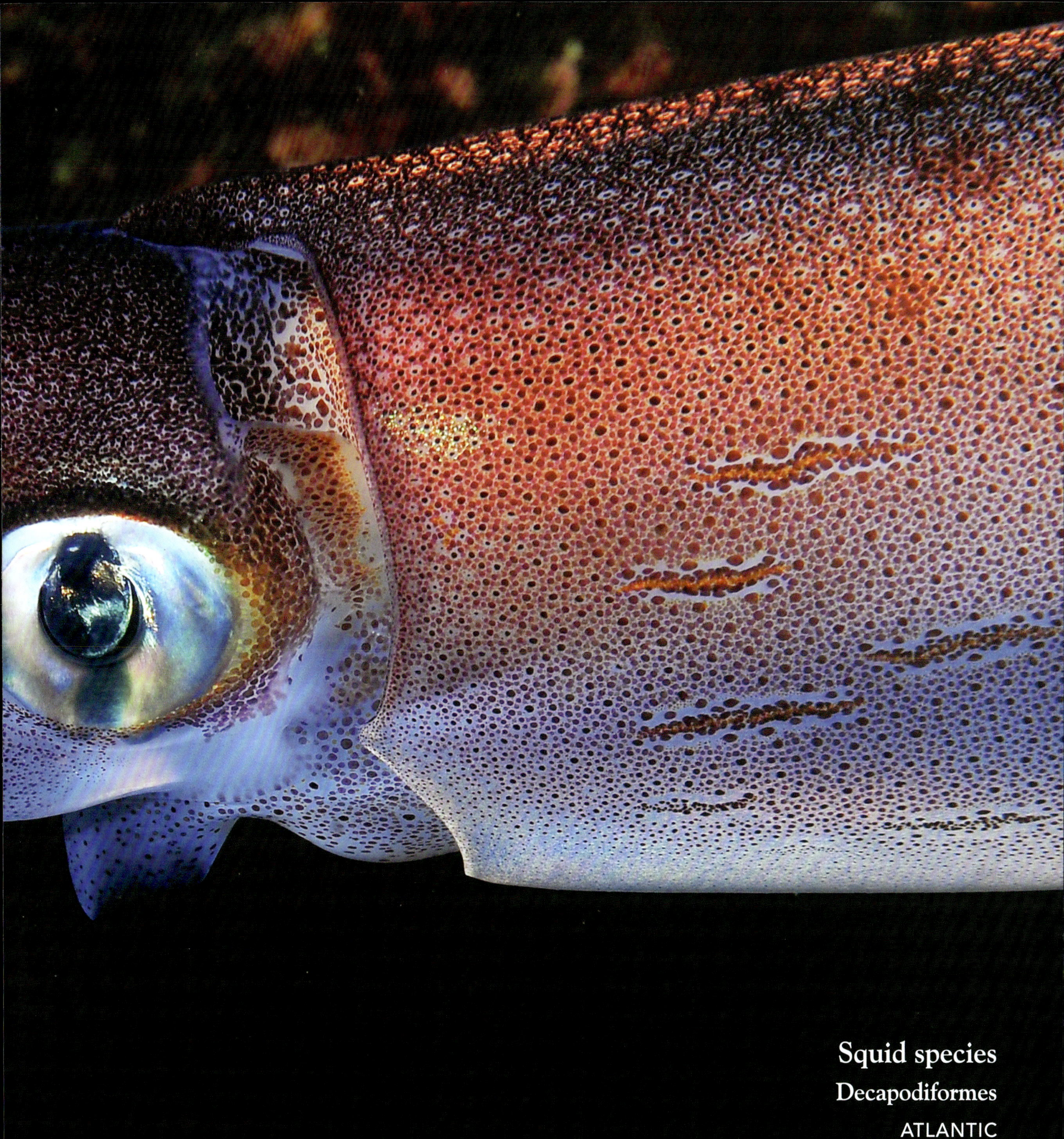

Squid species

Decapodiformes

ATLANTIC

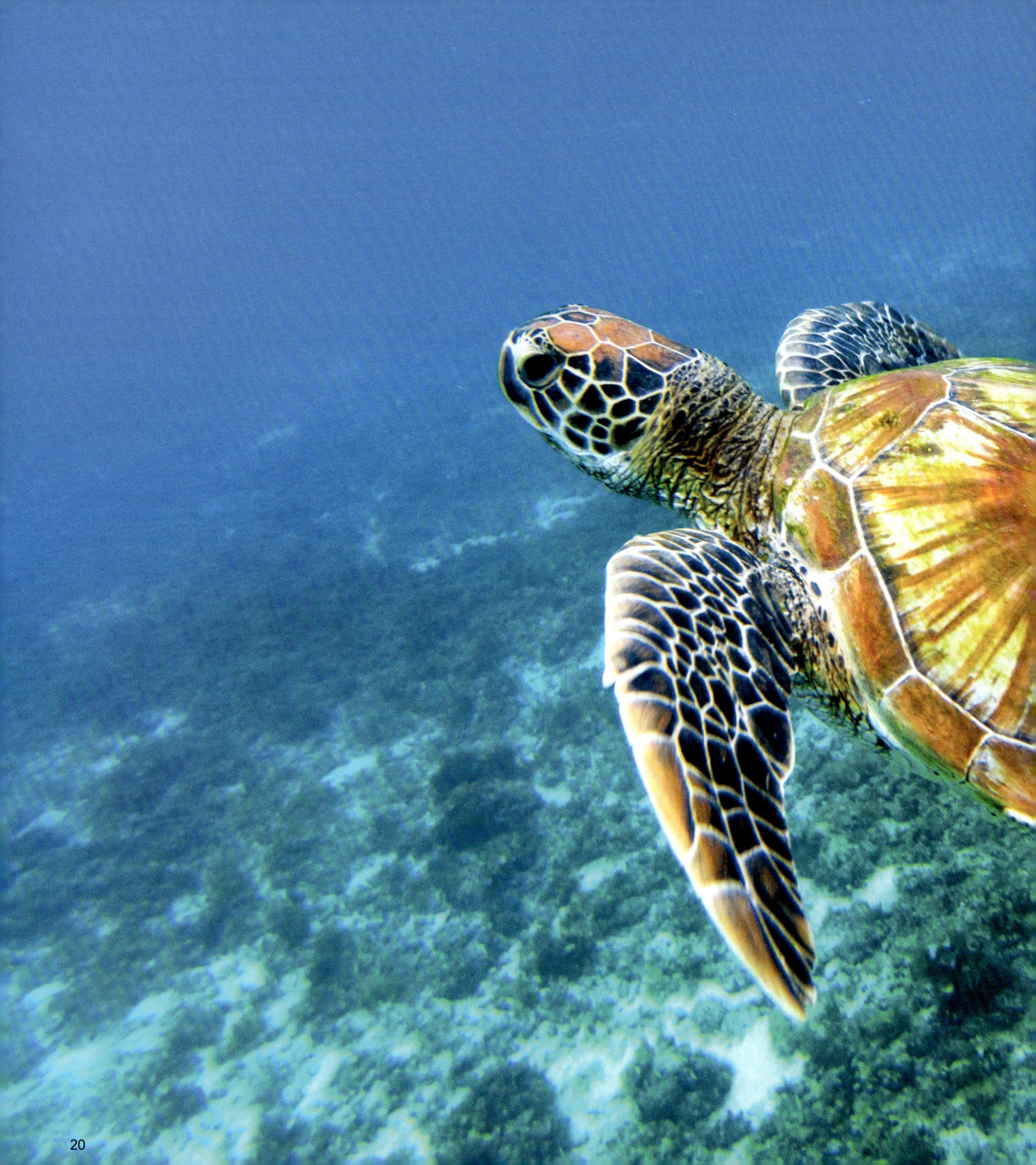

Hawksbill Turtle

Eretmochelys imbricata

TROPICAL AND SUBTROPICAL OCEANS WORLDWIDE

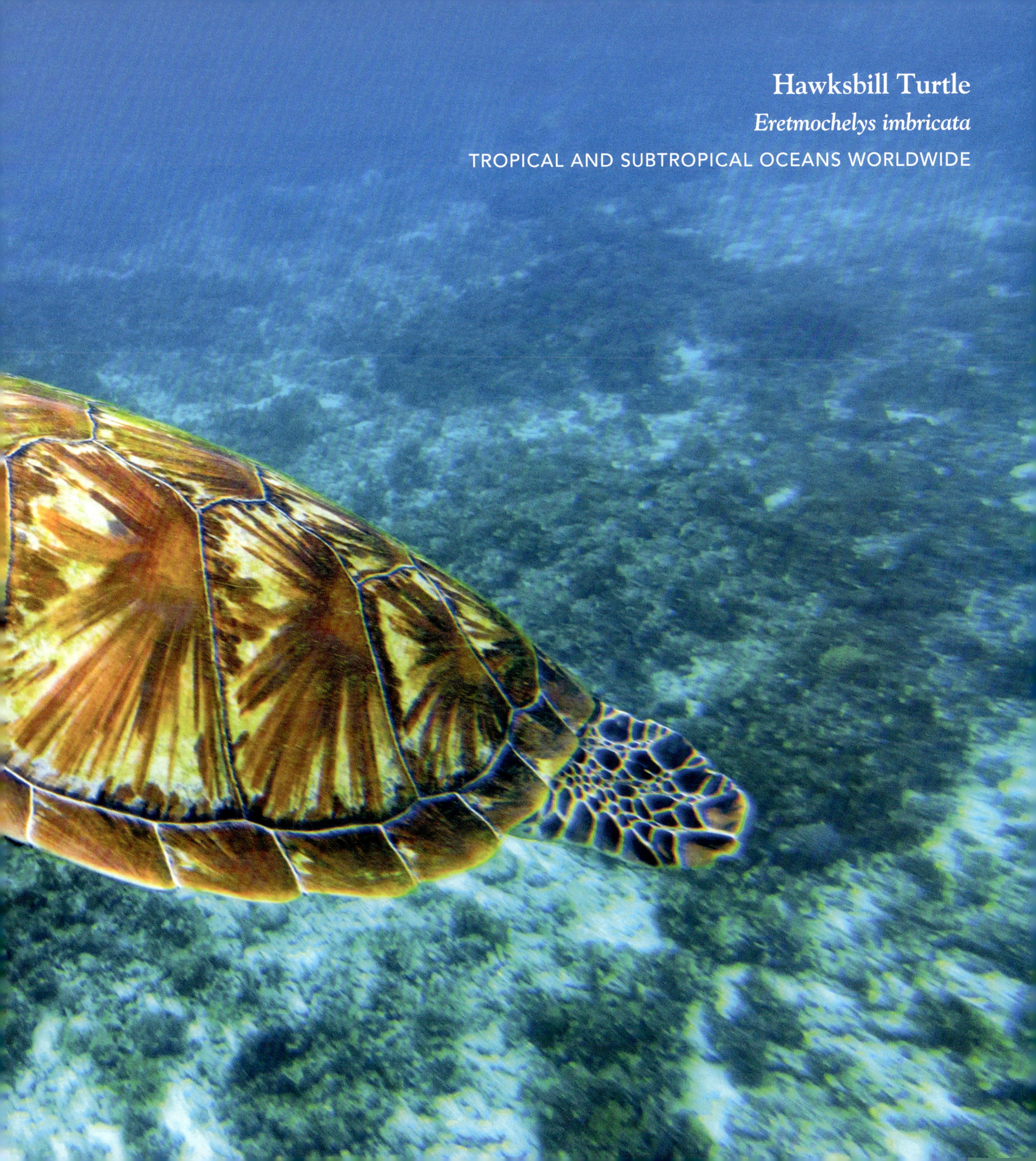

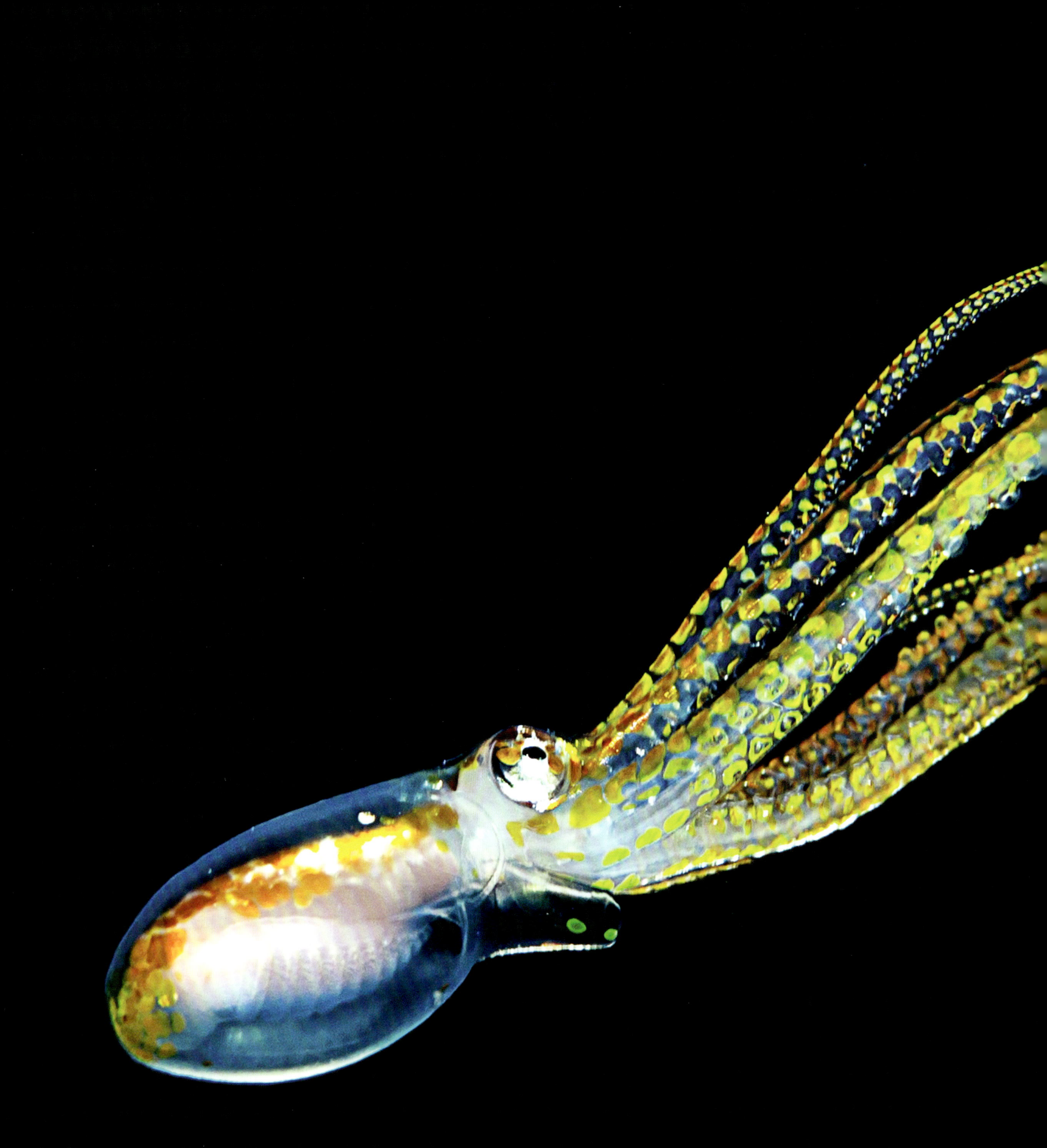

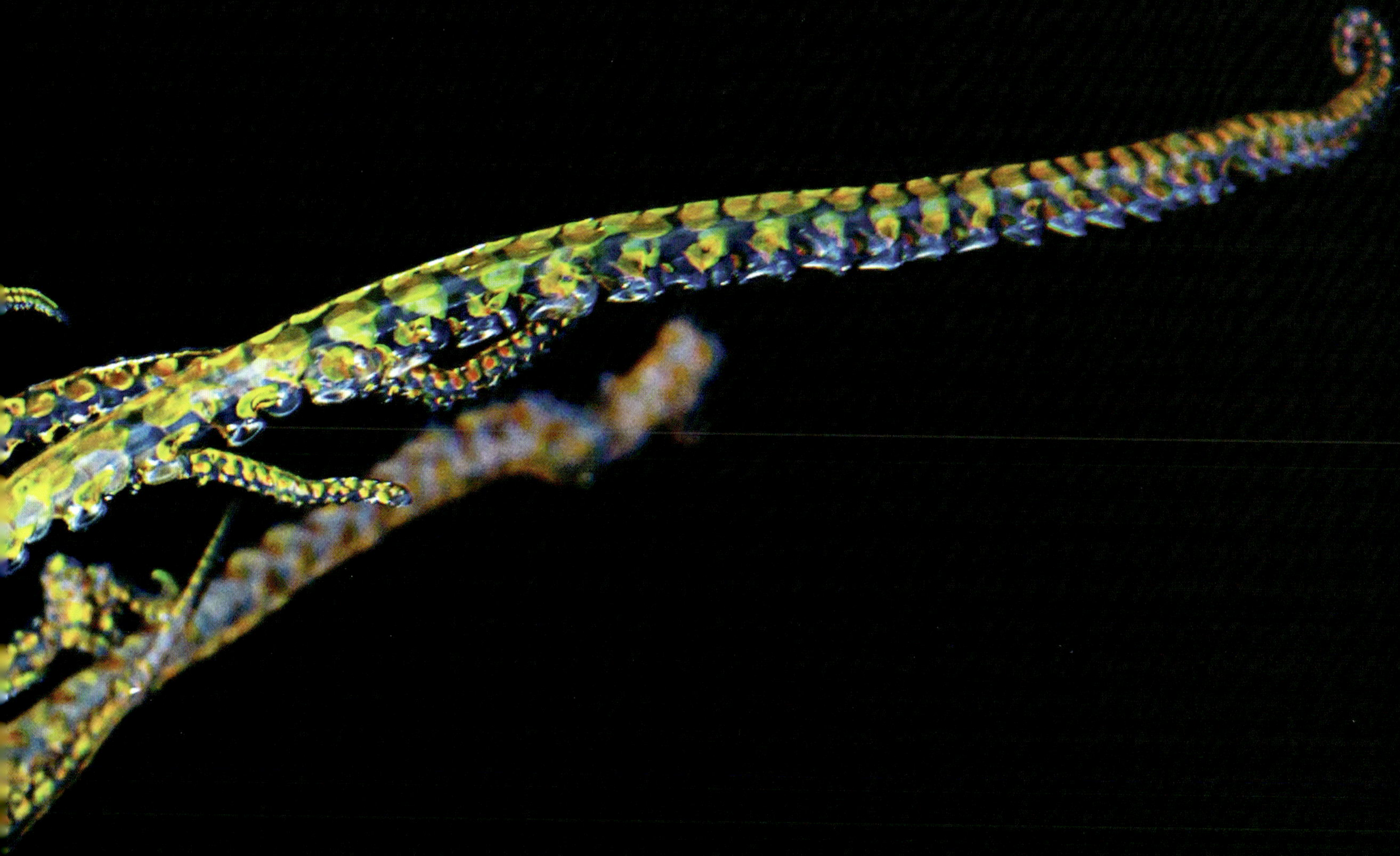

Octopus species

Octopoda

OCEANS WORLDWIDE

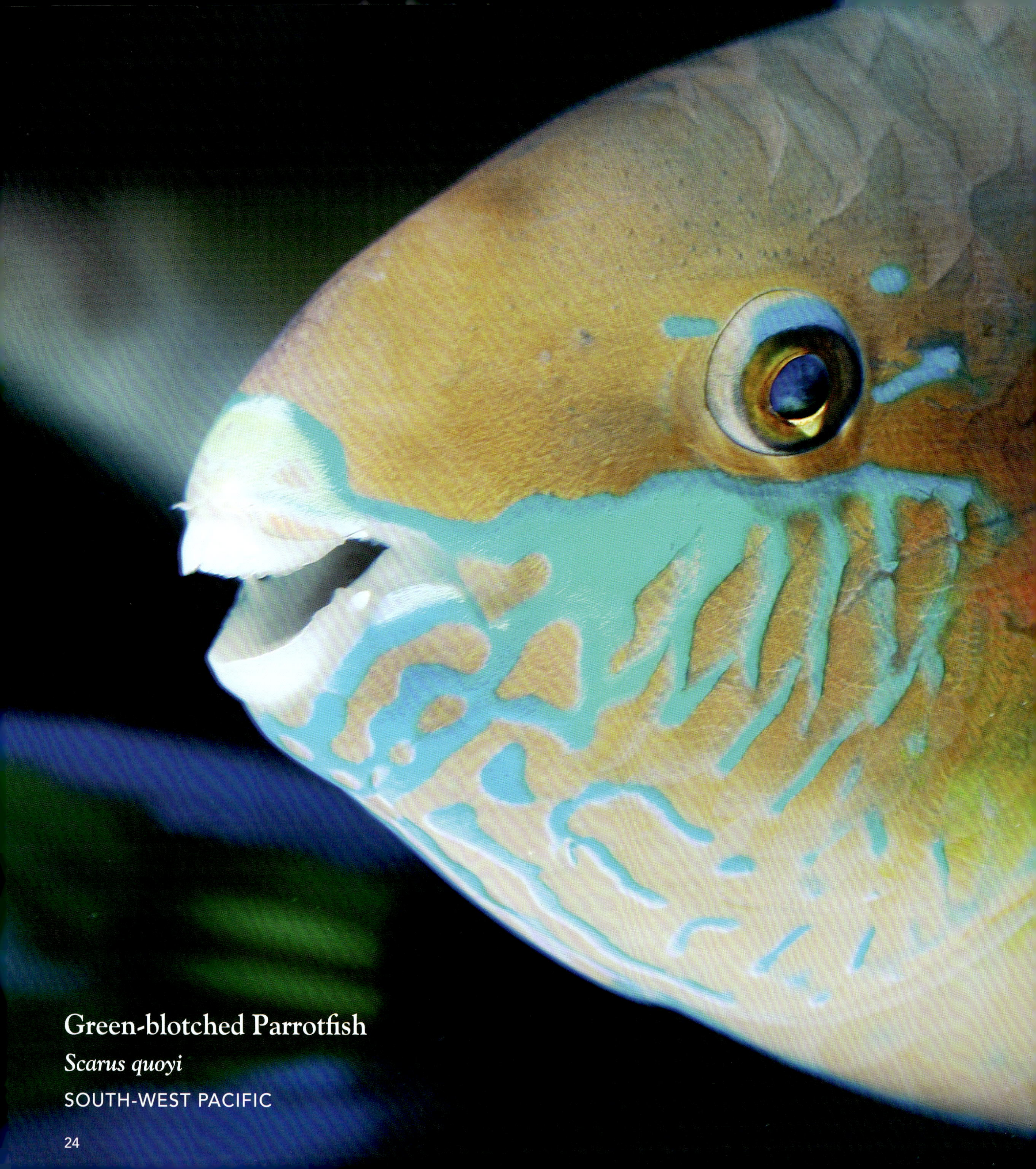

Green-blotched Parrotfish

Scarus quoyi

SOUTH-WEST PACIFIC

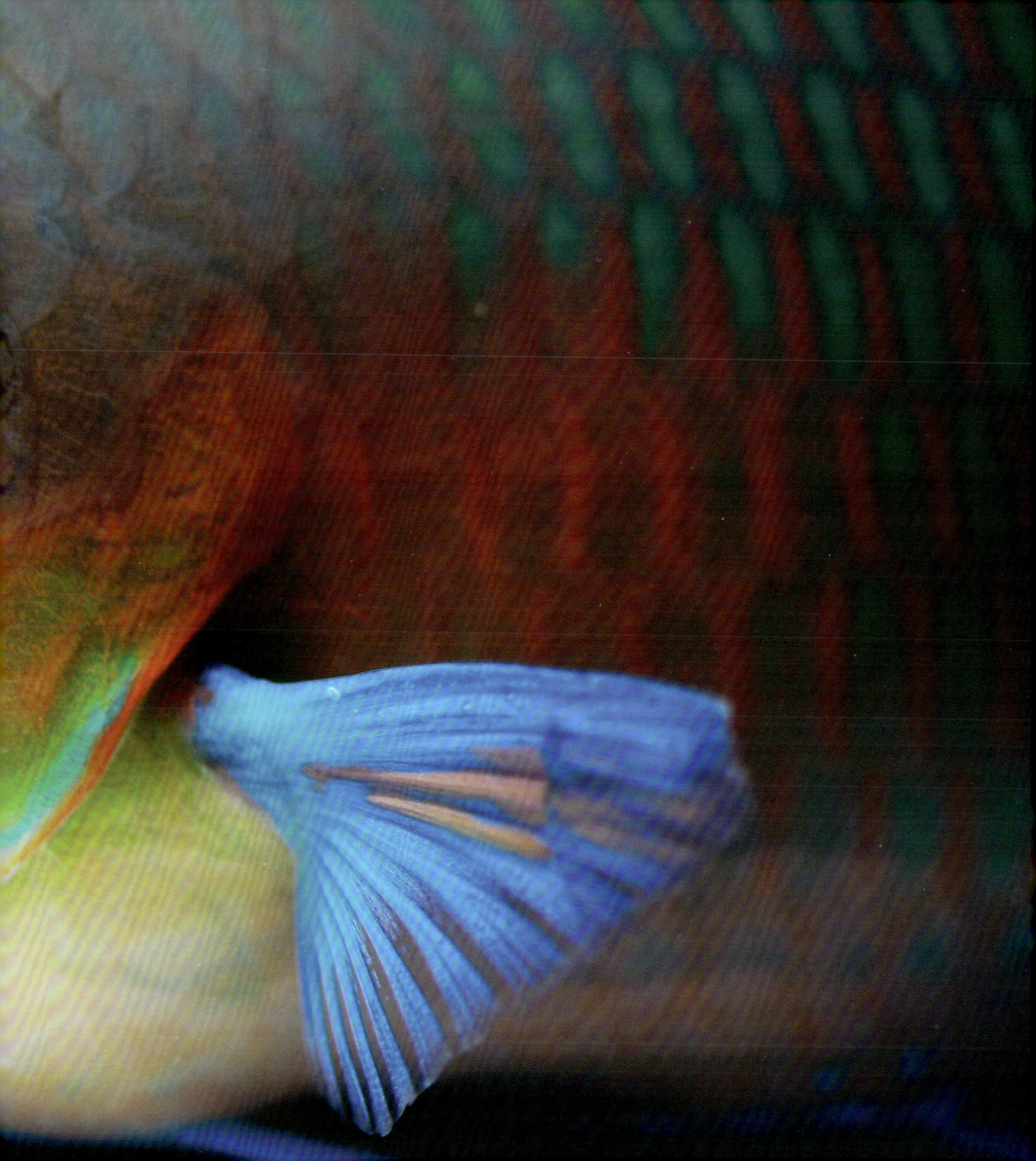

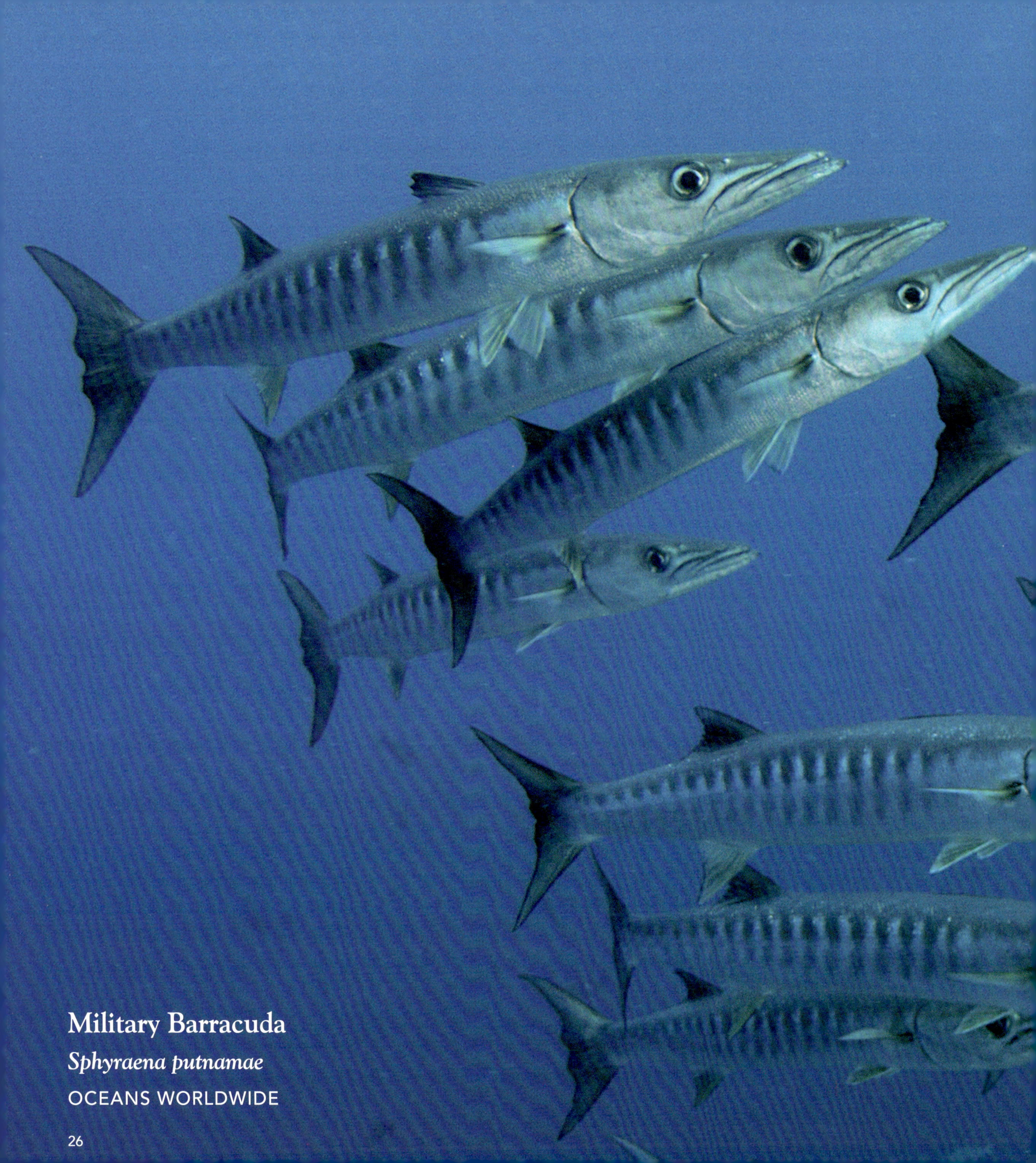

Military Barracuda

Sphyraena putnamae

OCEANS WORLDWIDE

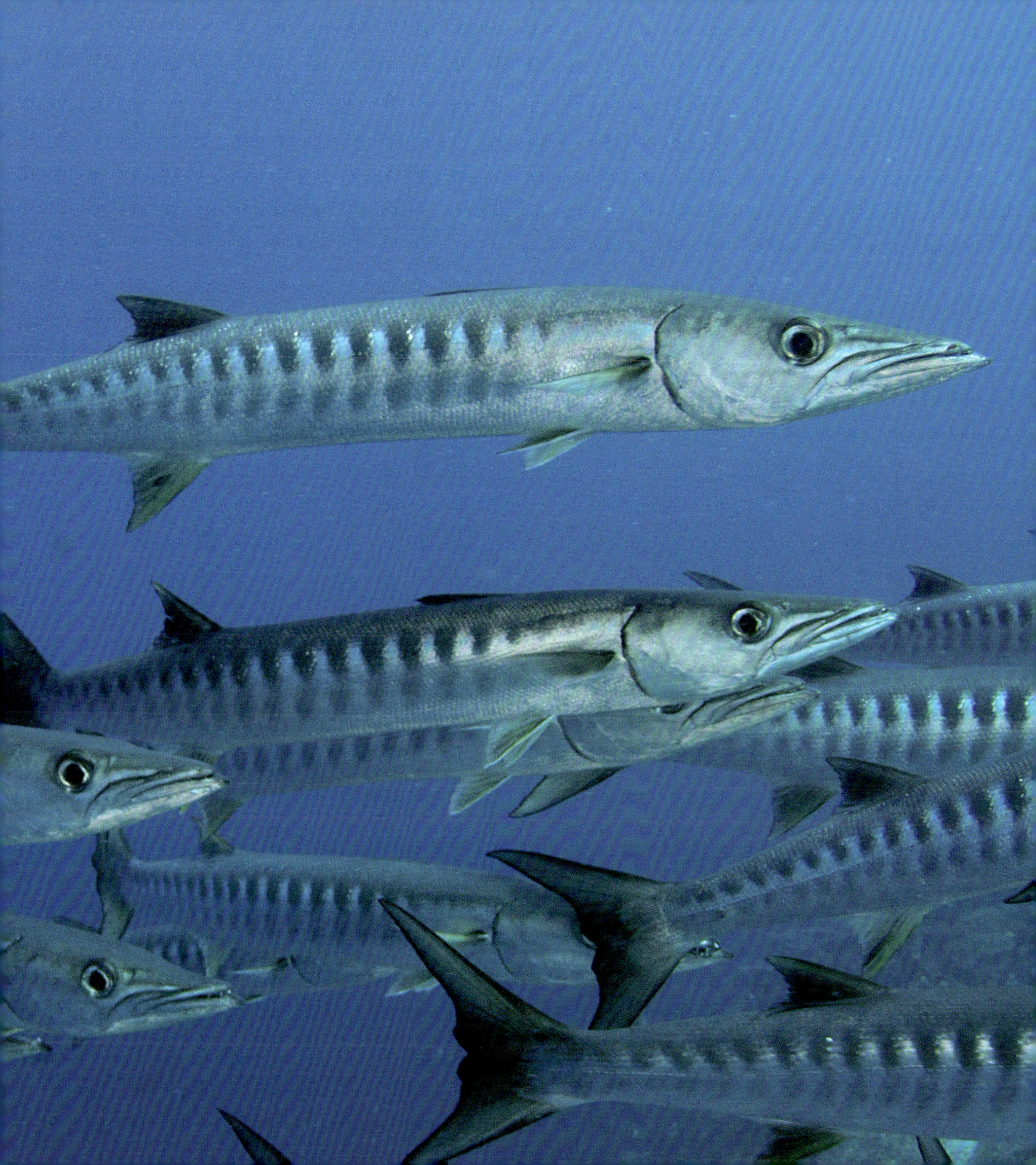

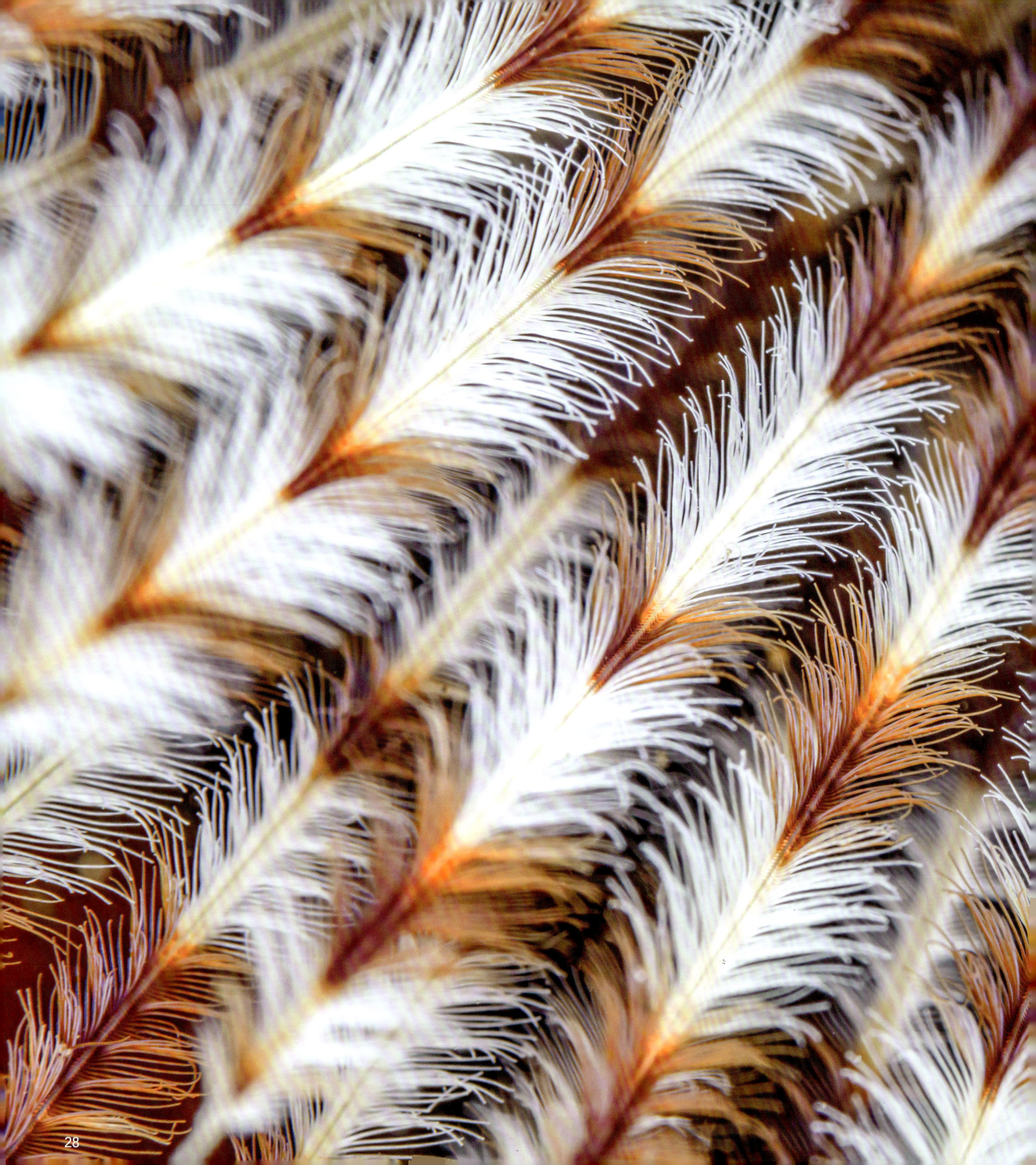

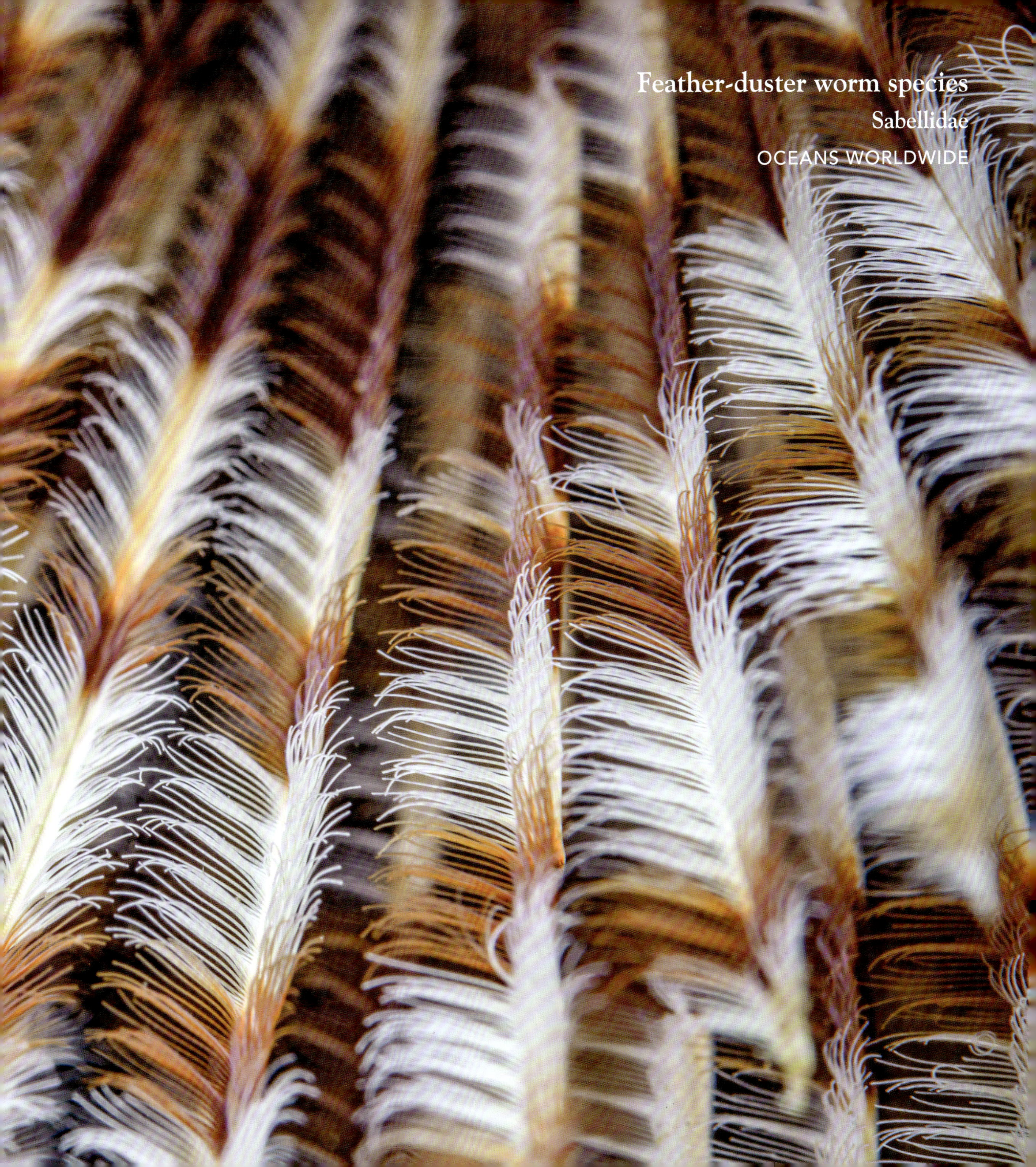

Feather-duster worm species

Sabellidae

OCEANS WORLDWIDE

Ribbon Eel

Rhinomuraena quaesita

INDO-PACIFIC

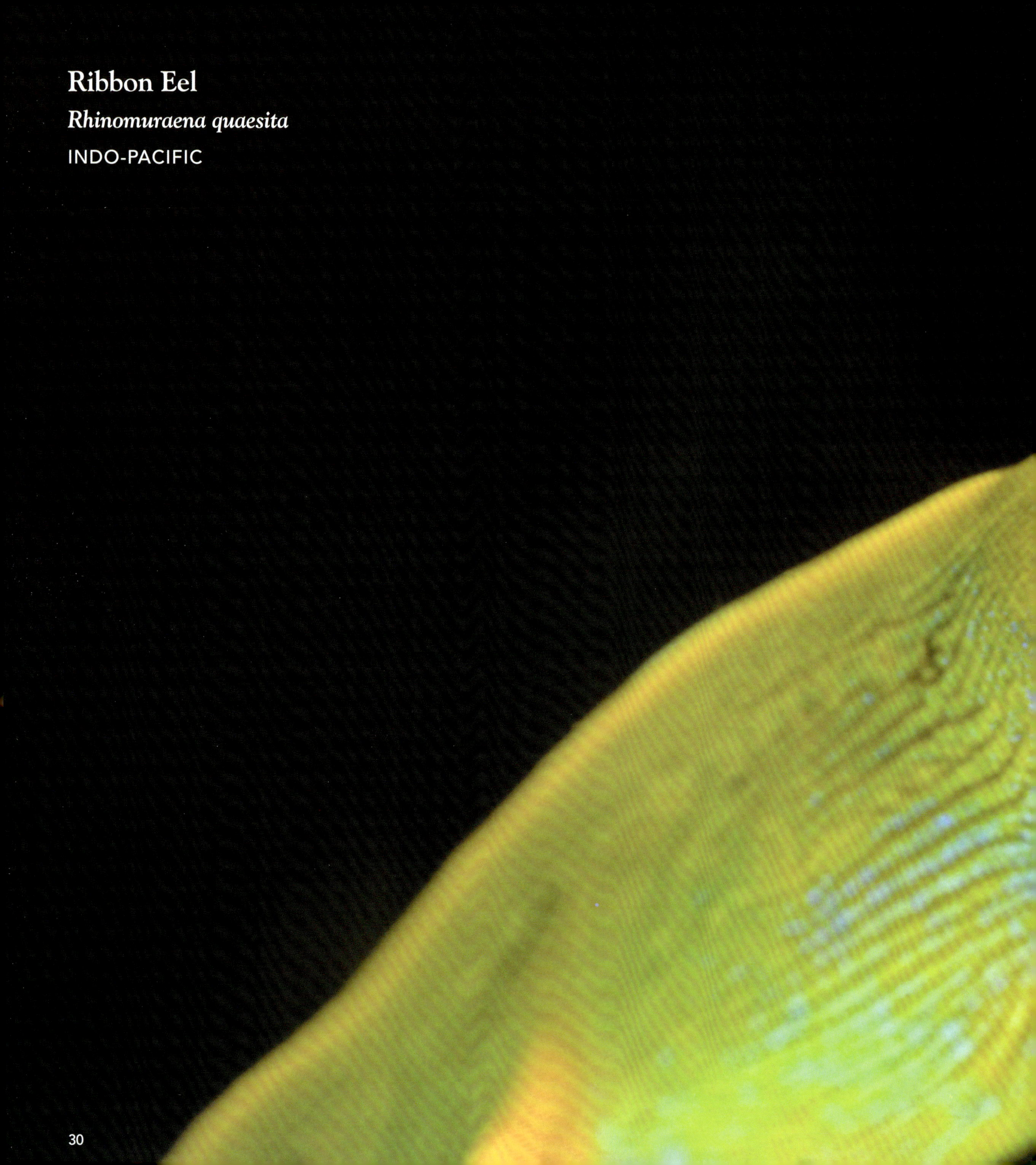

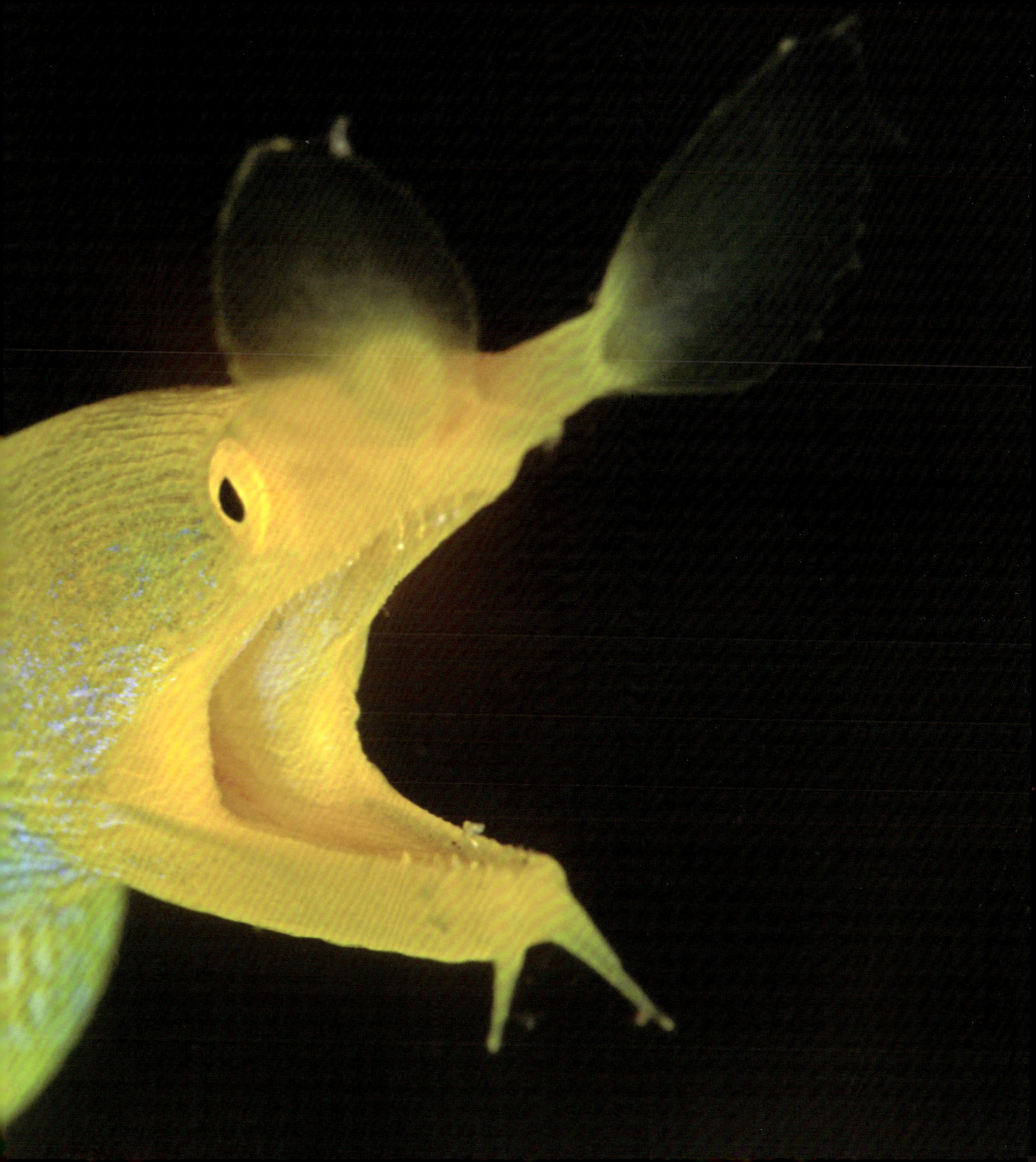

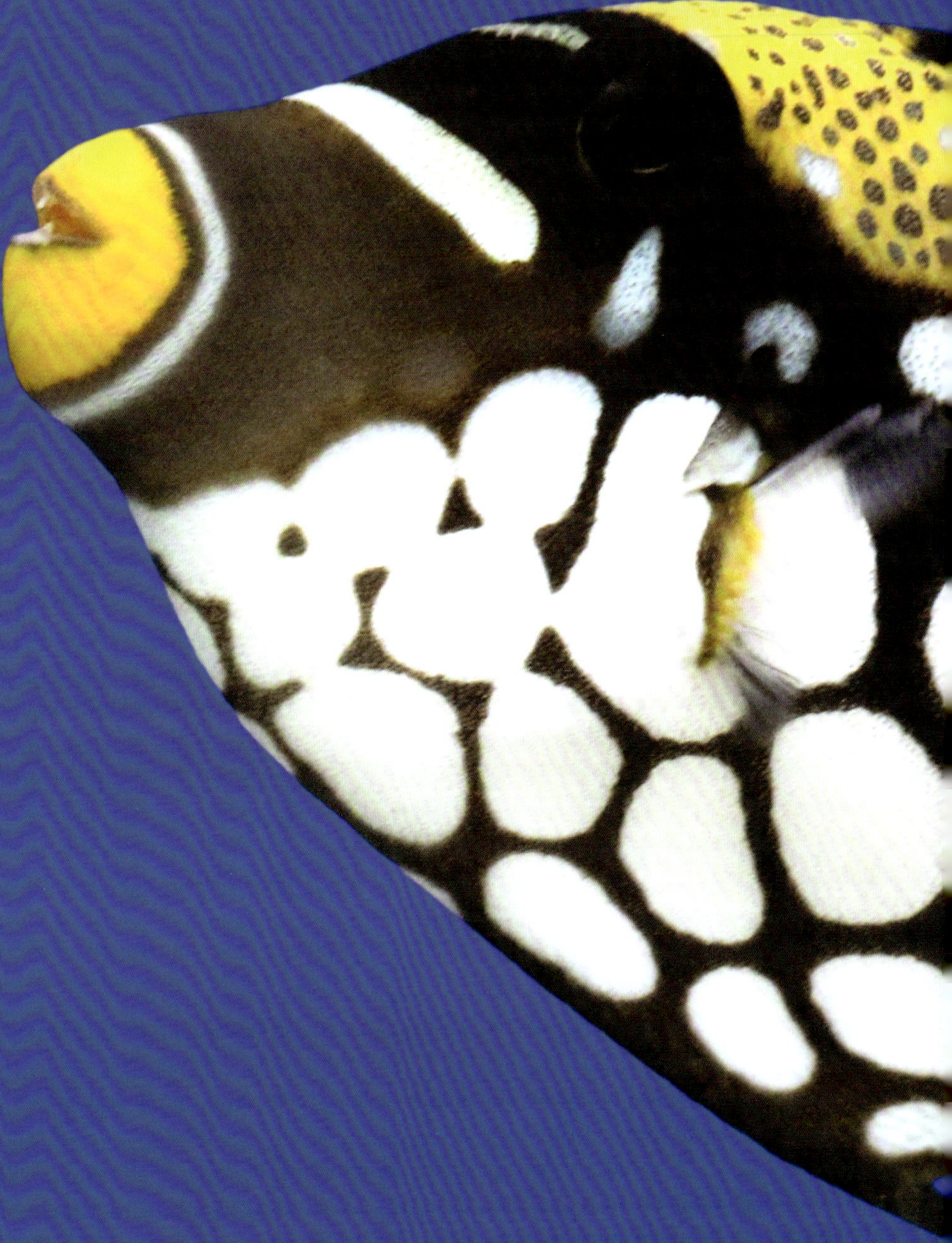

Clown Triggerfish

Balistoides conspicillum

INDO-PACIFIC

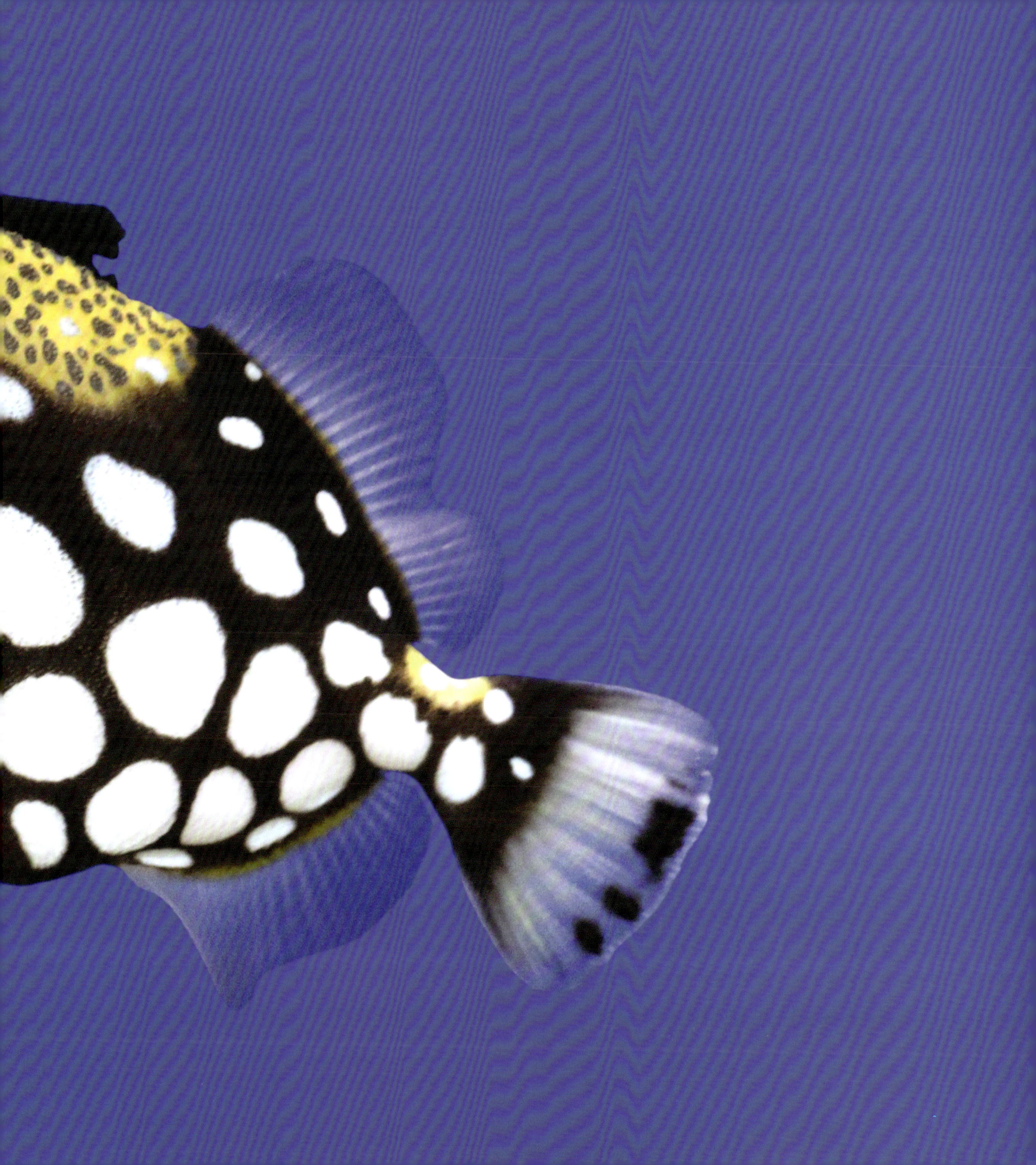

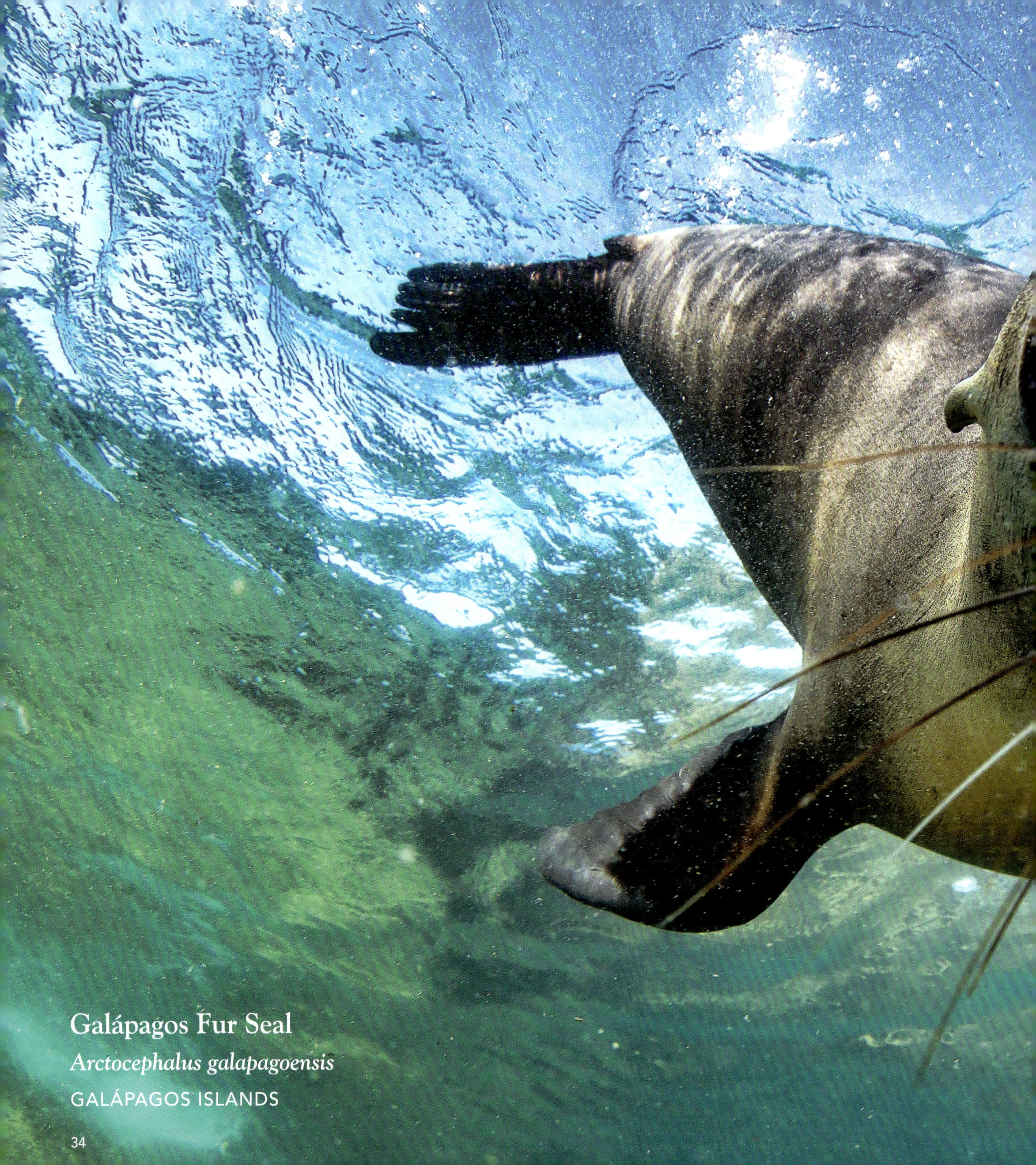

Galápagos Fur Seal

Arctocephalus galapagoensis

GALÁPAGOS ISLANDS

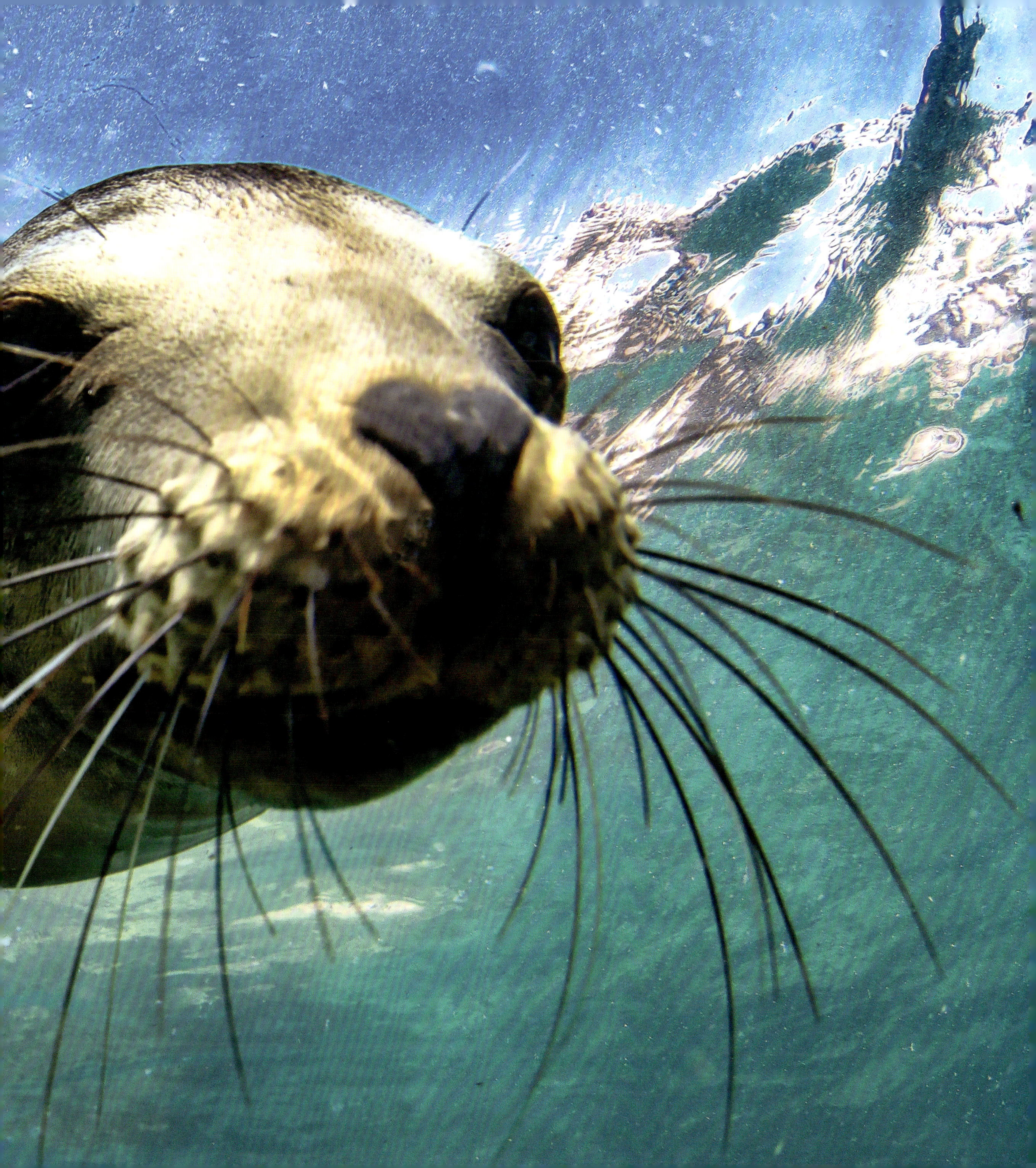

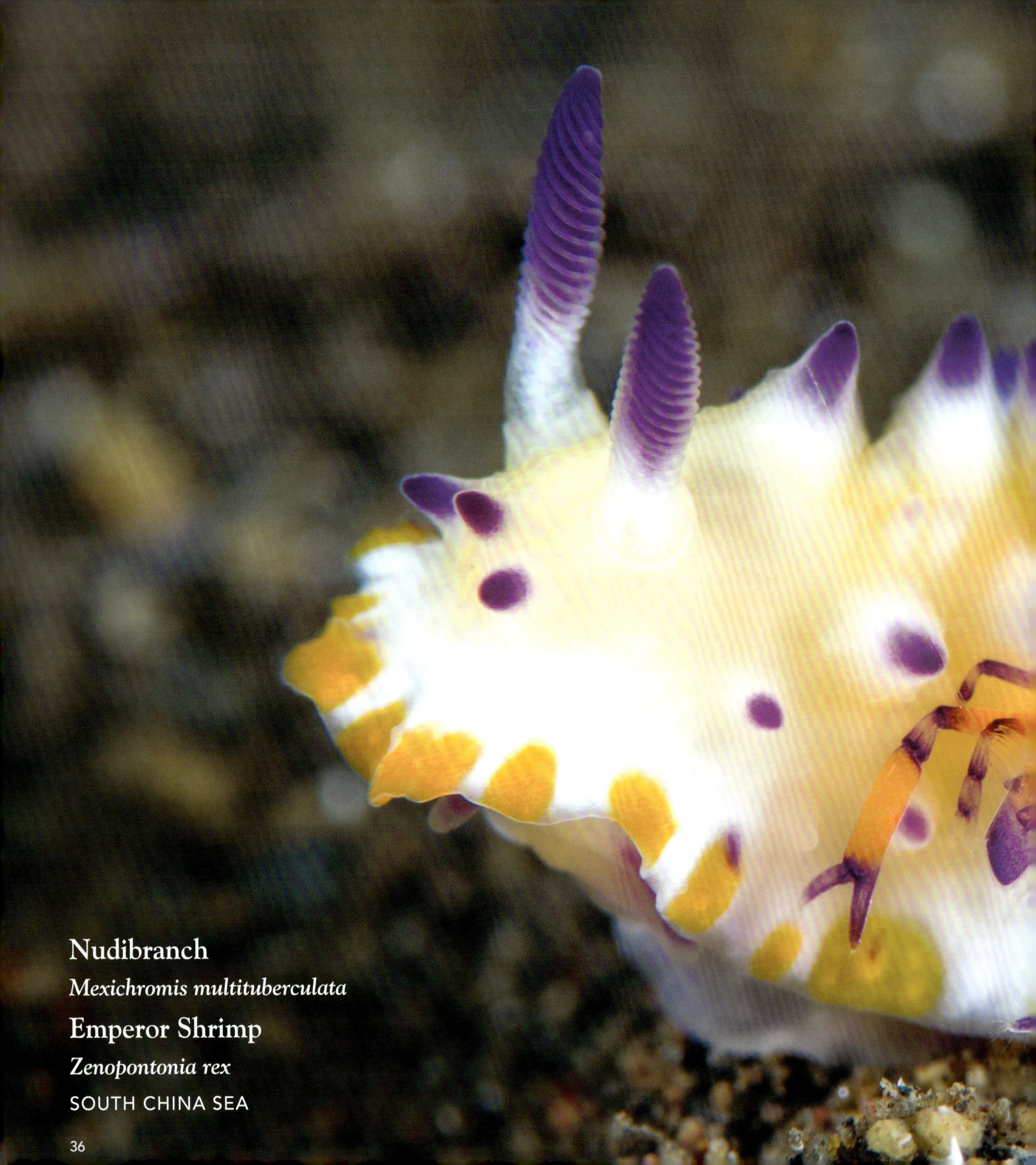

Nudibranch

Mexichromis multituberculata

Emperor Shrimp

Zenopontonia rex

SOUTH CHINA SEA

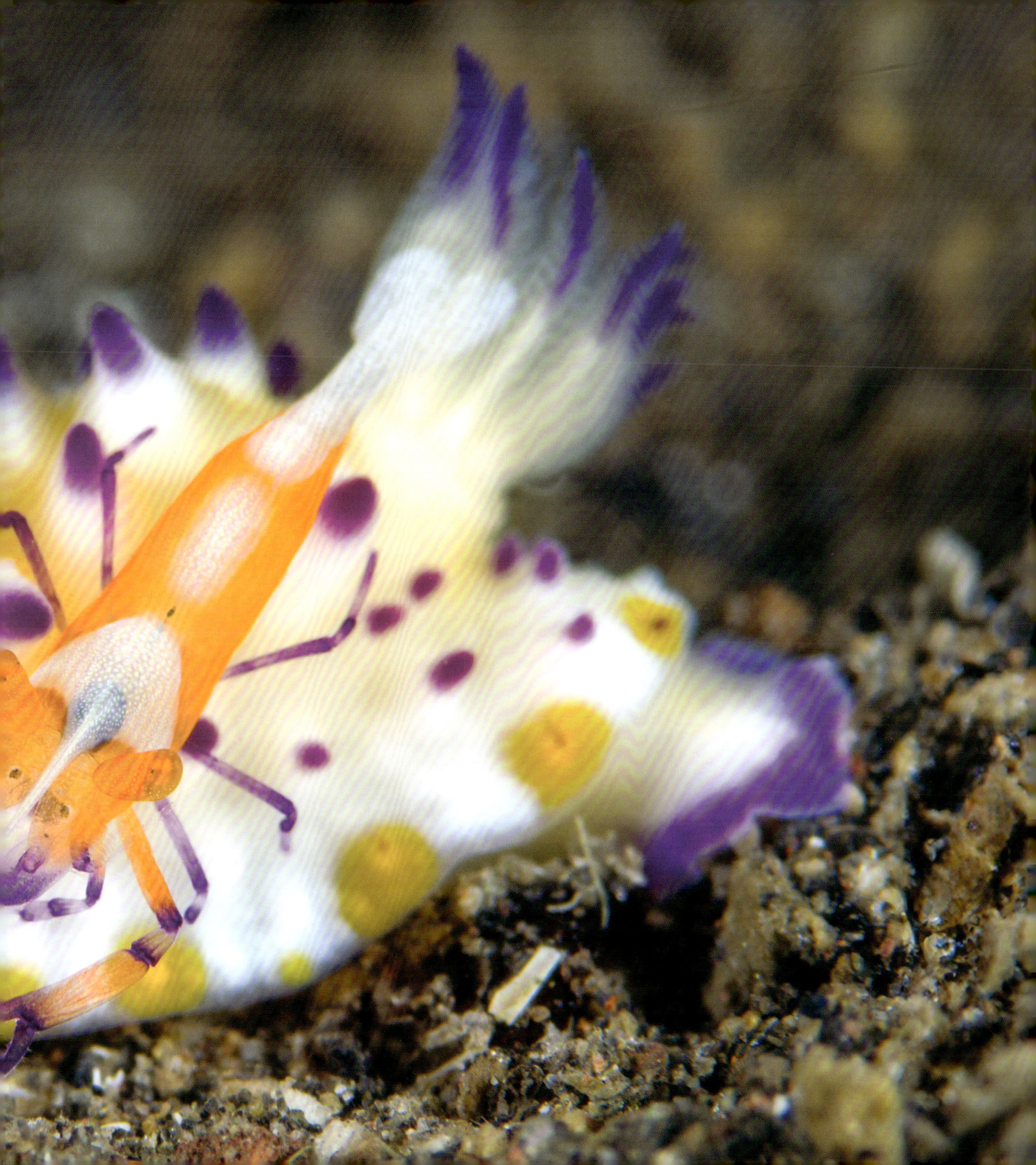

Ribbon Sawtail Fish

Idiacanthus fasciola

OCEANS WORLDWIDE

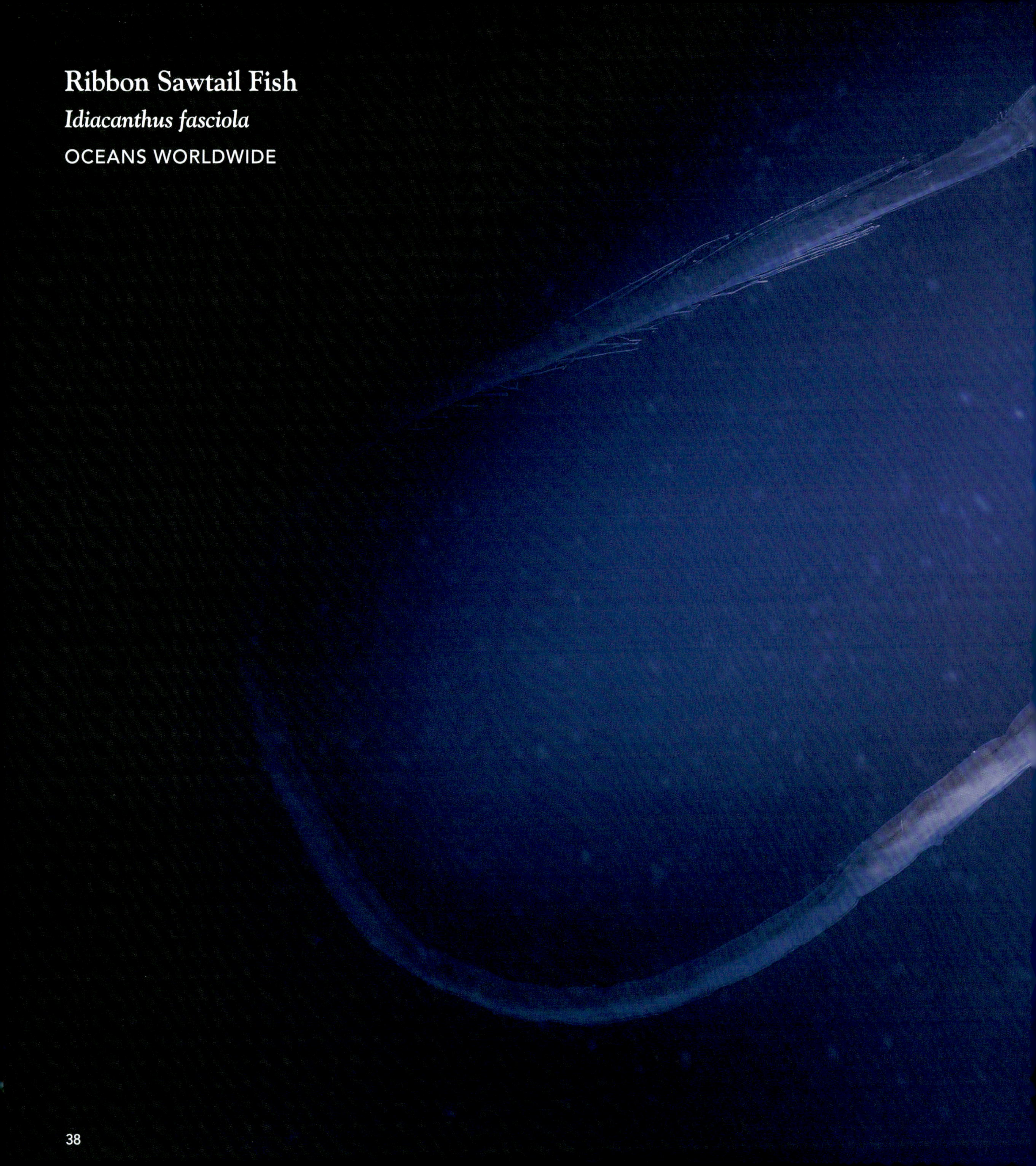

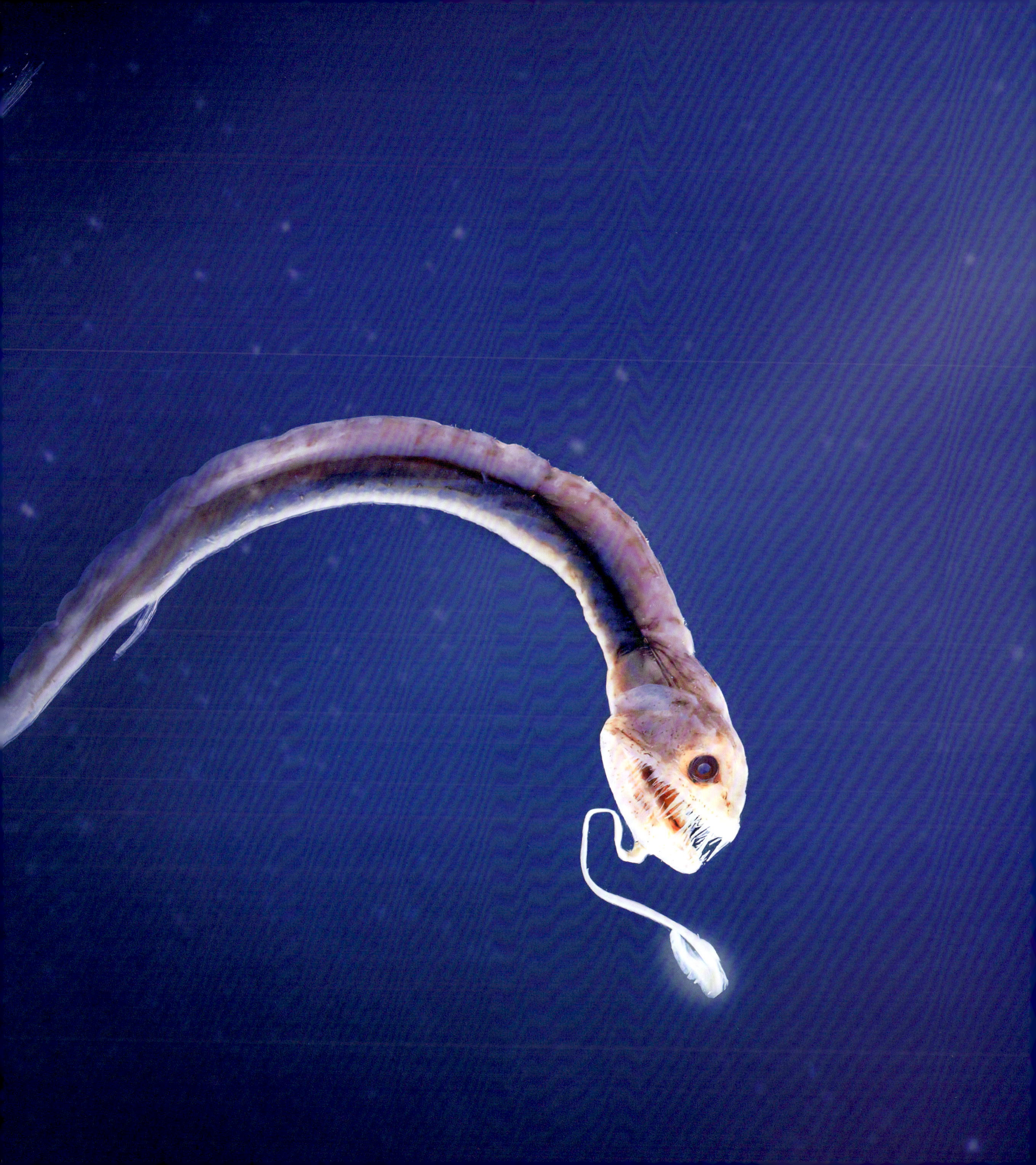

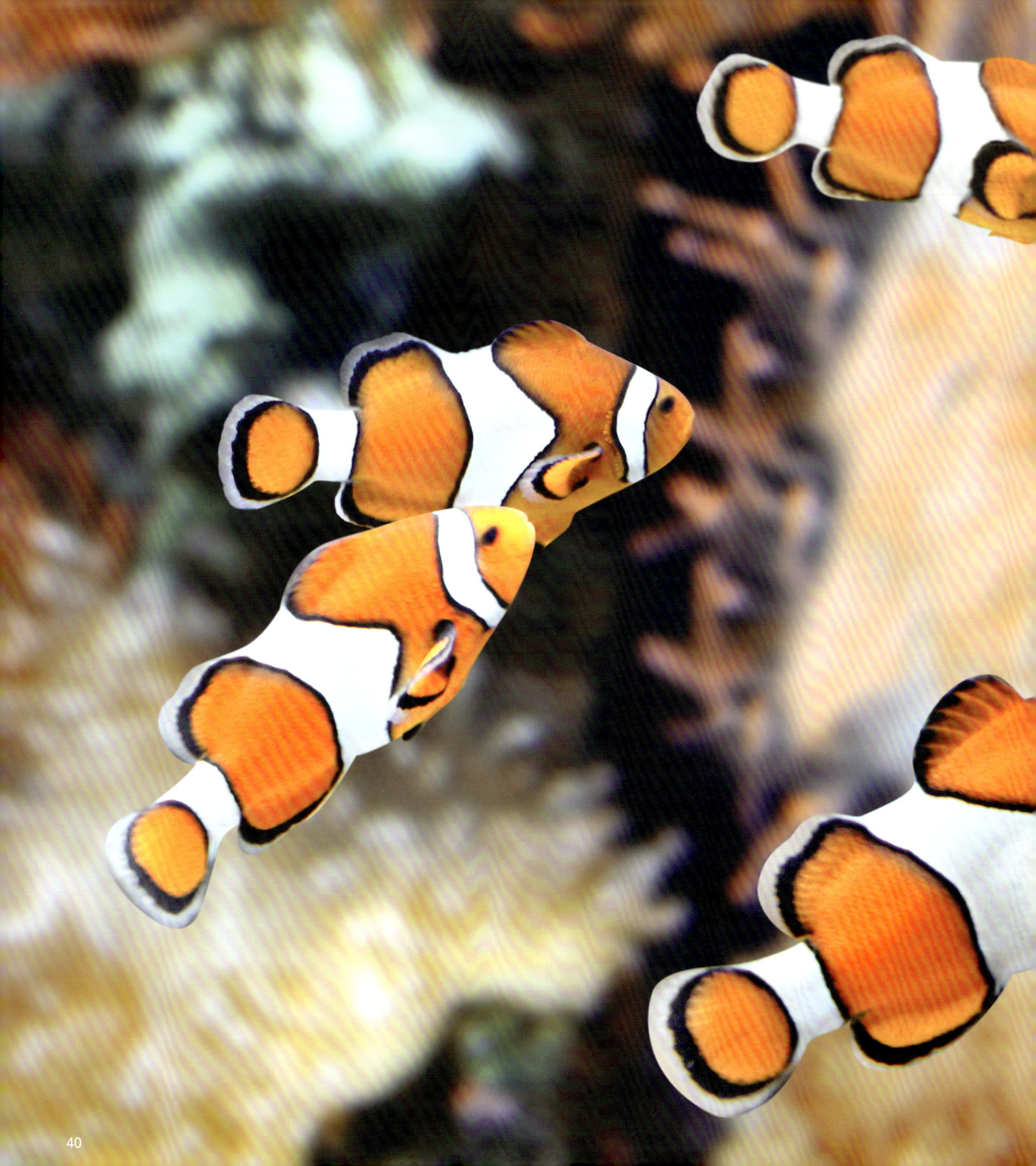

Ocellaris Clownfish

Amphiprion ocellaris

INDO-PACIFIC

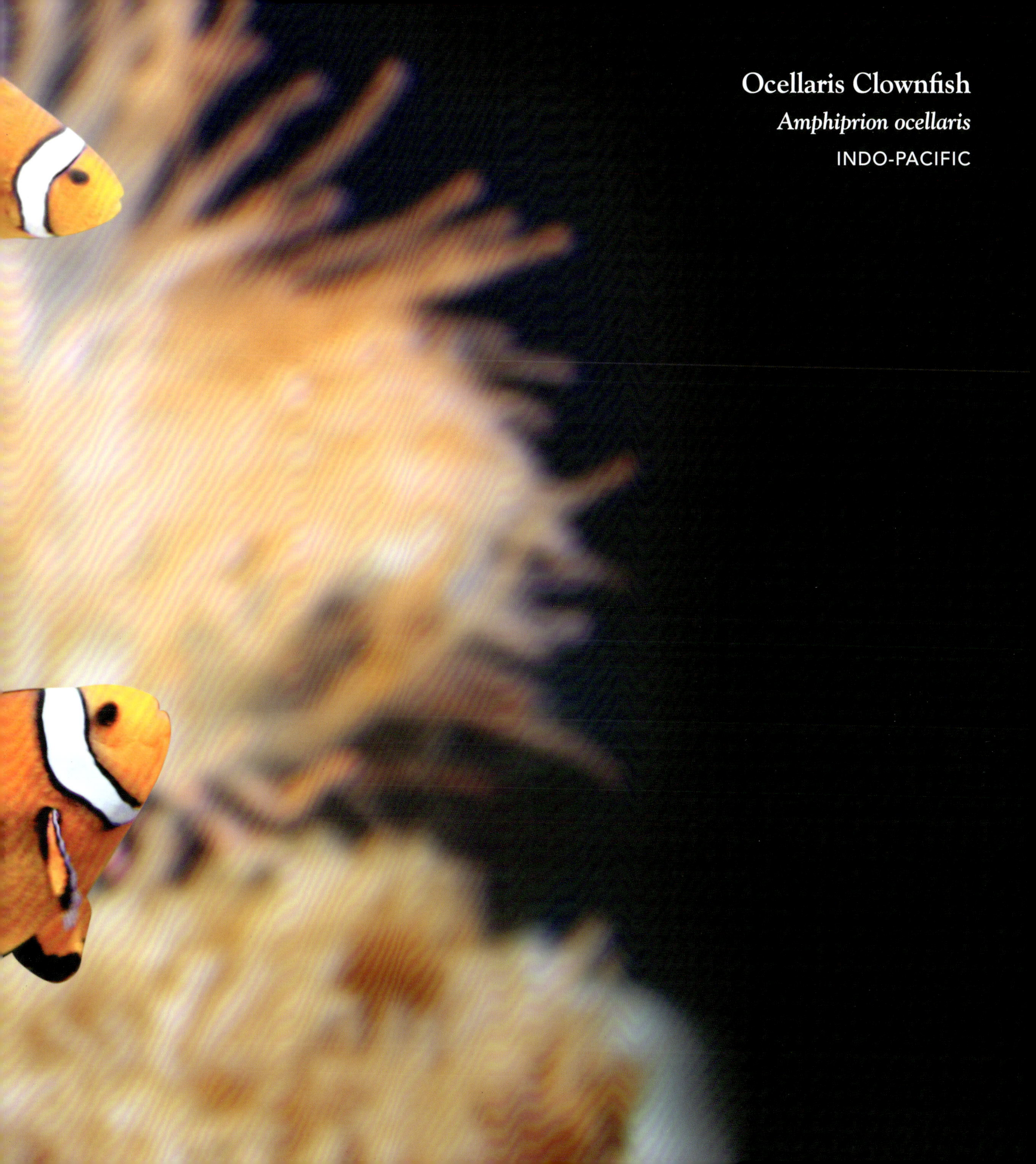

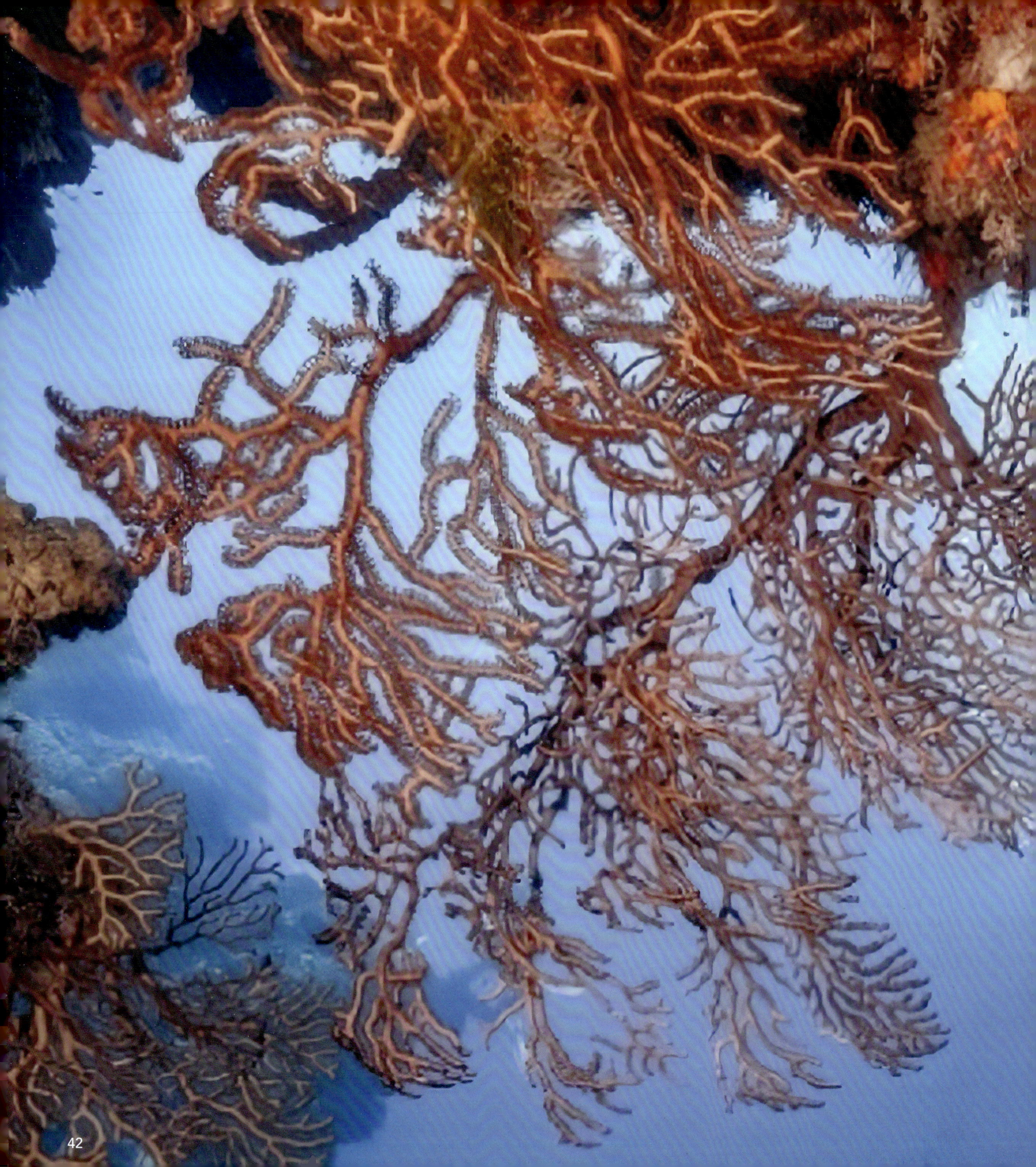

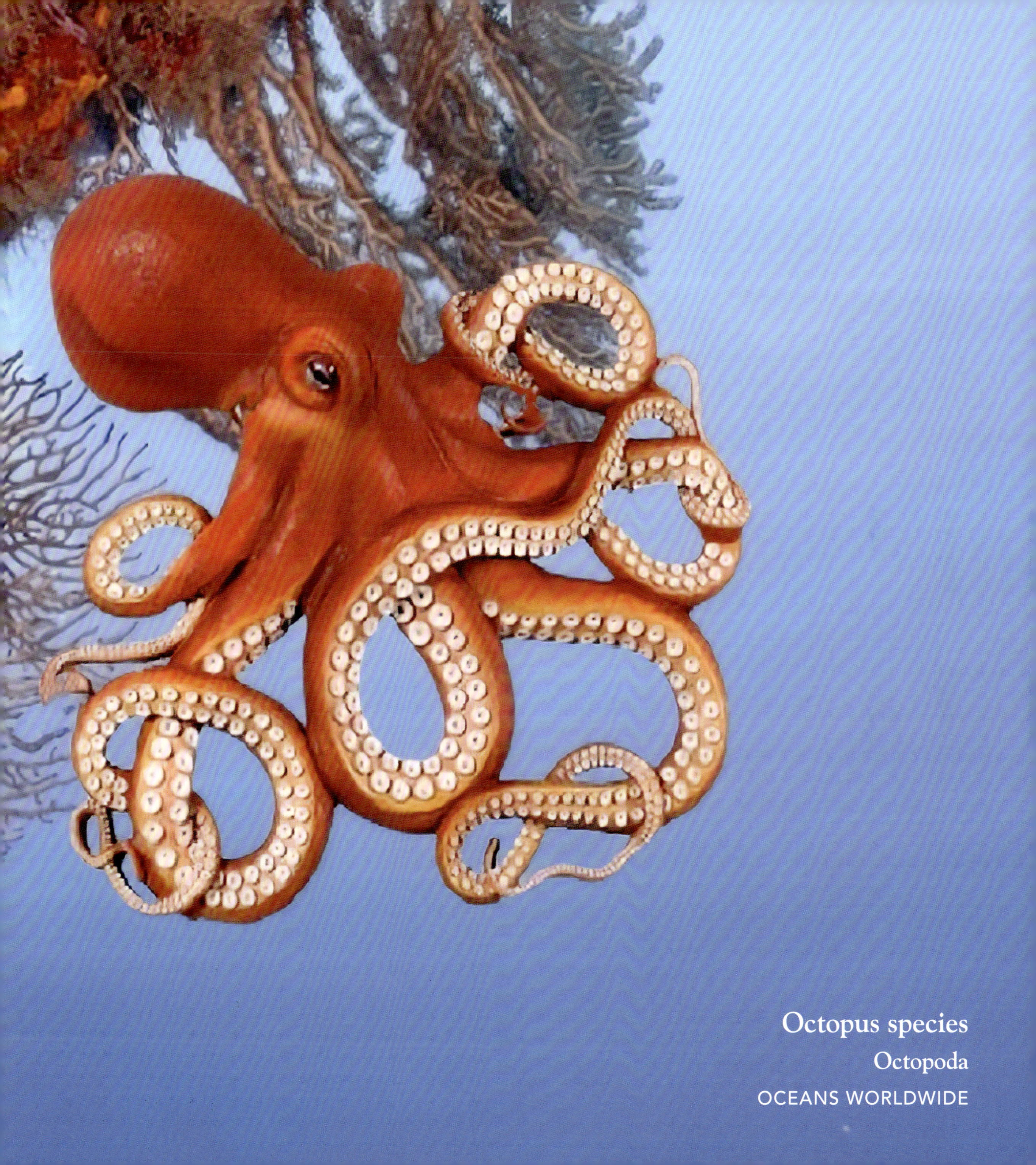

Octopus species

Octopoda

OCEANS WORLDWIDE

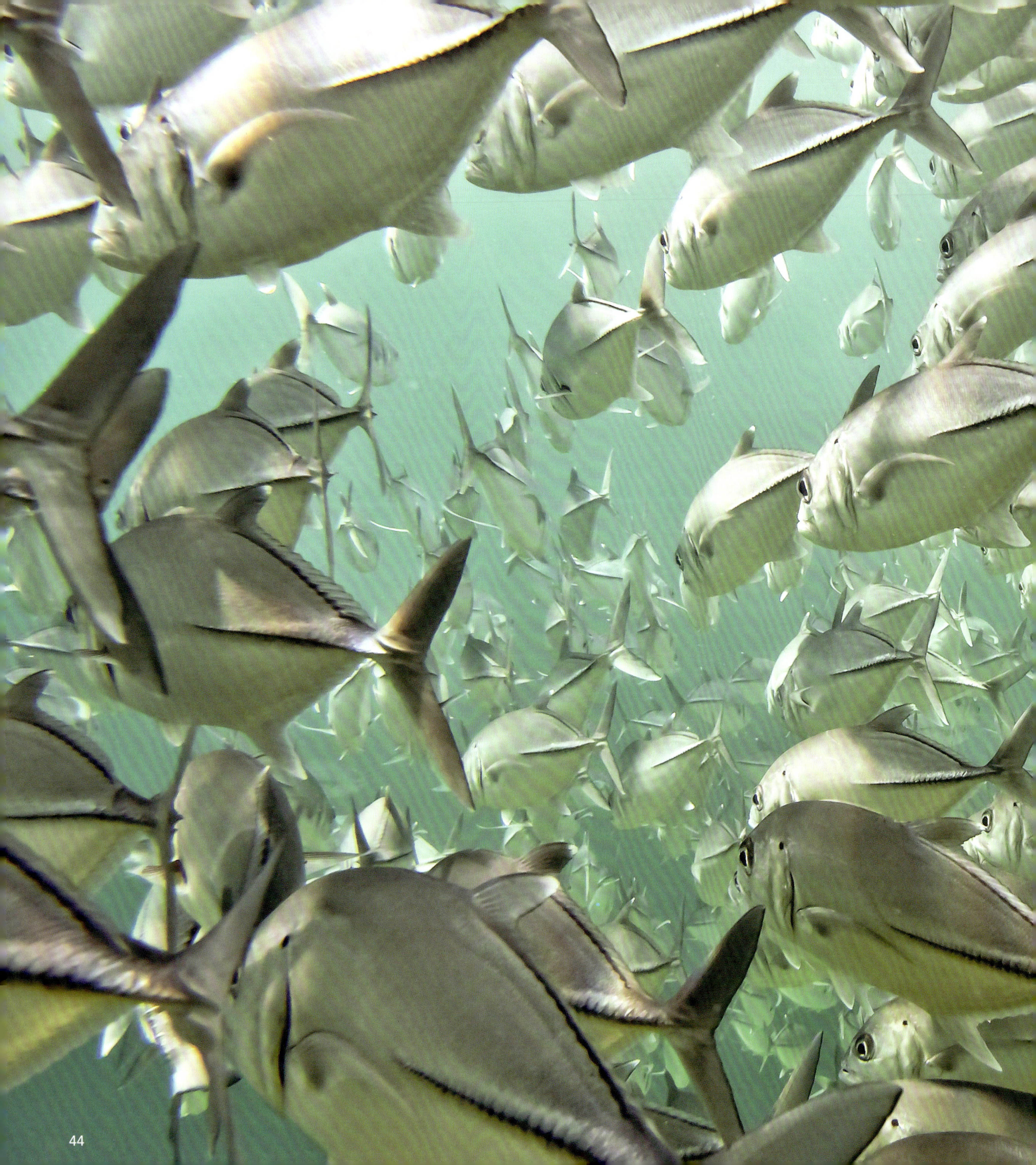

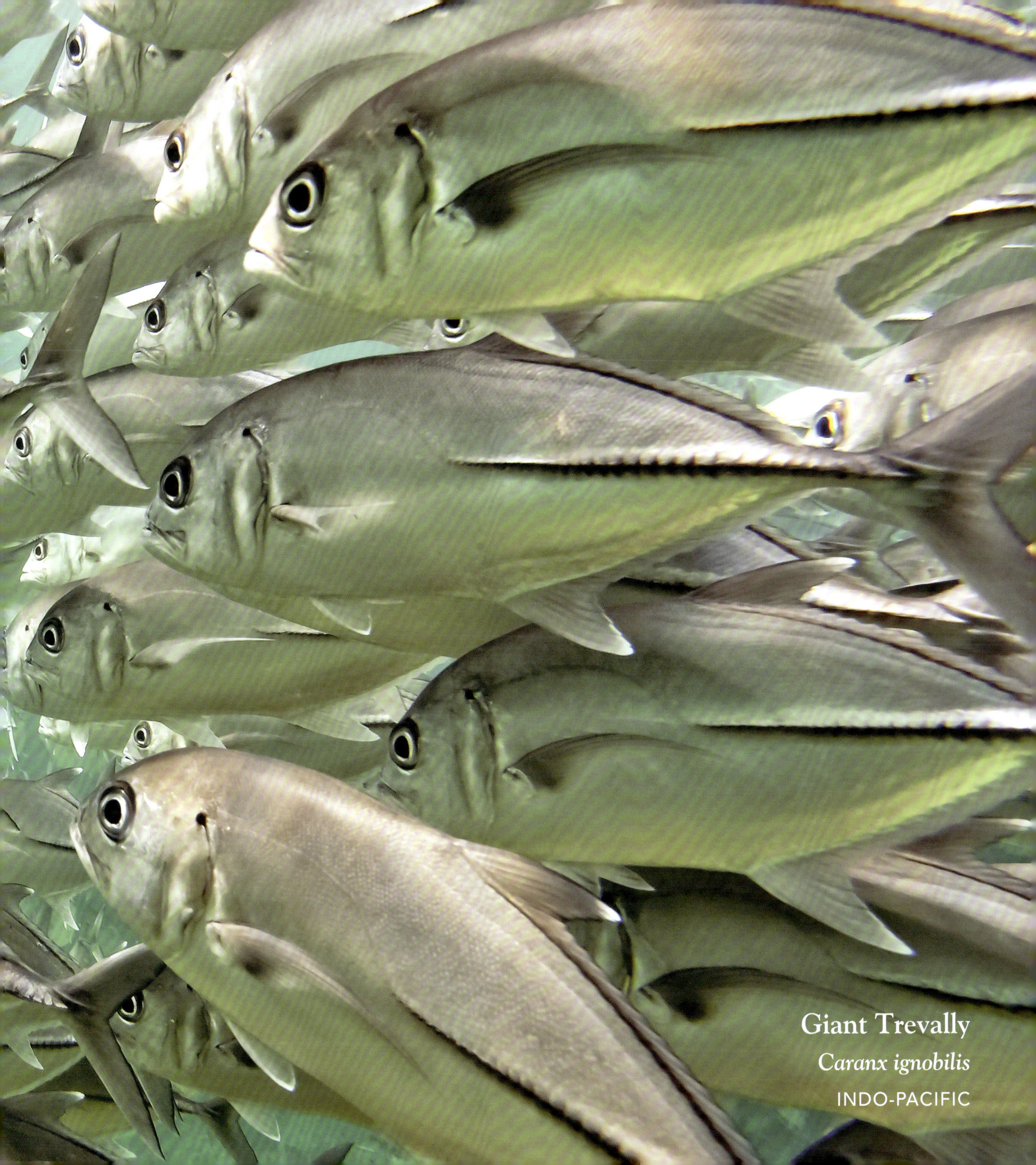

Giant Trevally

Caranx ignobilis

INDO-PACIFIC

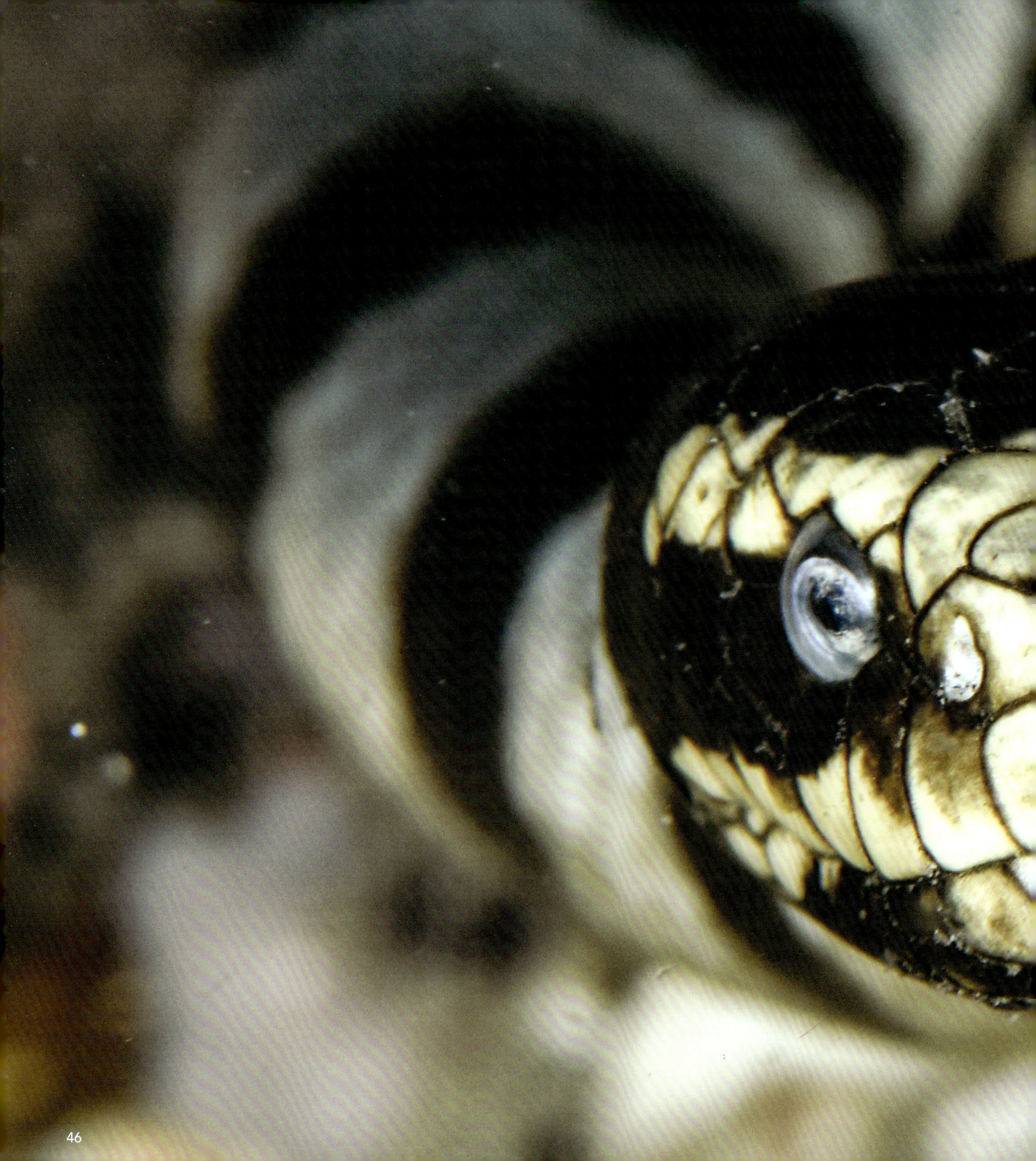

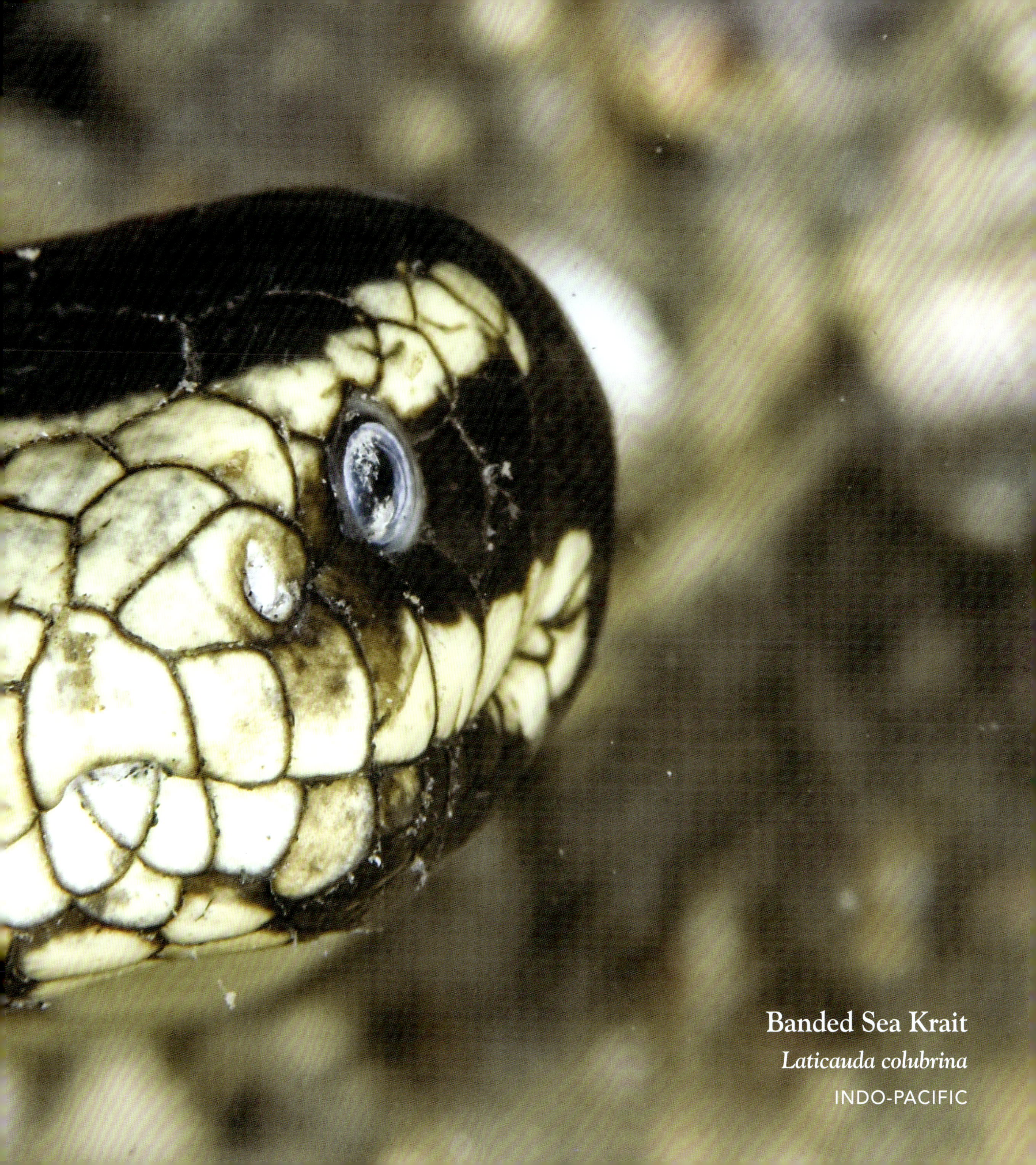

Banded Sea Krait

Laticauda colubrina

INDO-PACIFIC

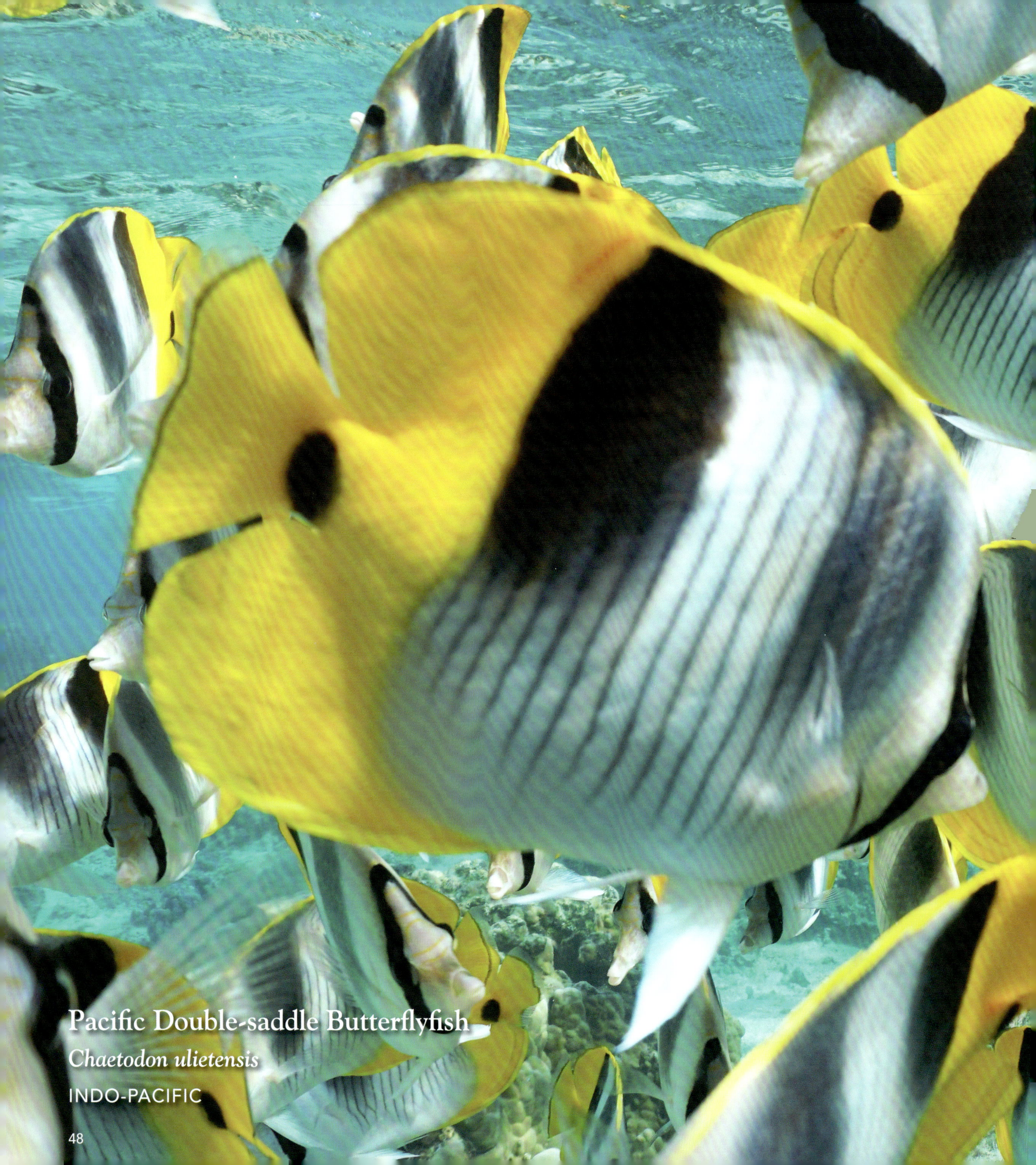

Pacific Double-saddle Butterflyfish

Chaetodon ulietensis

INDO-PACIFIC

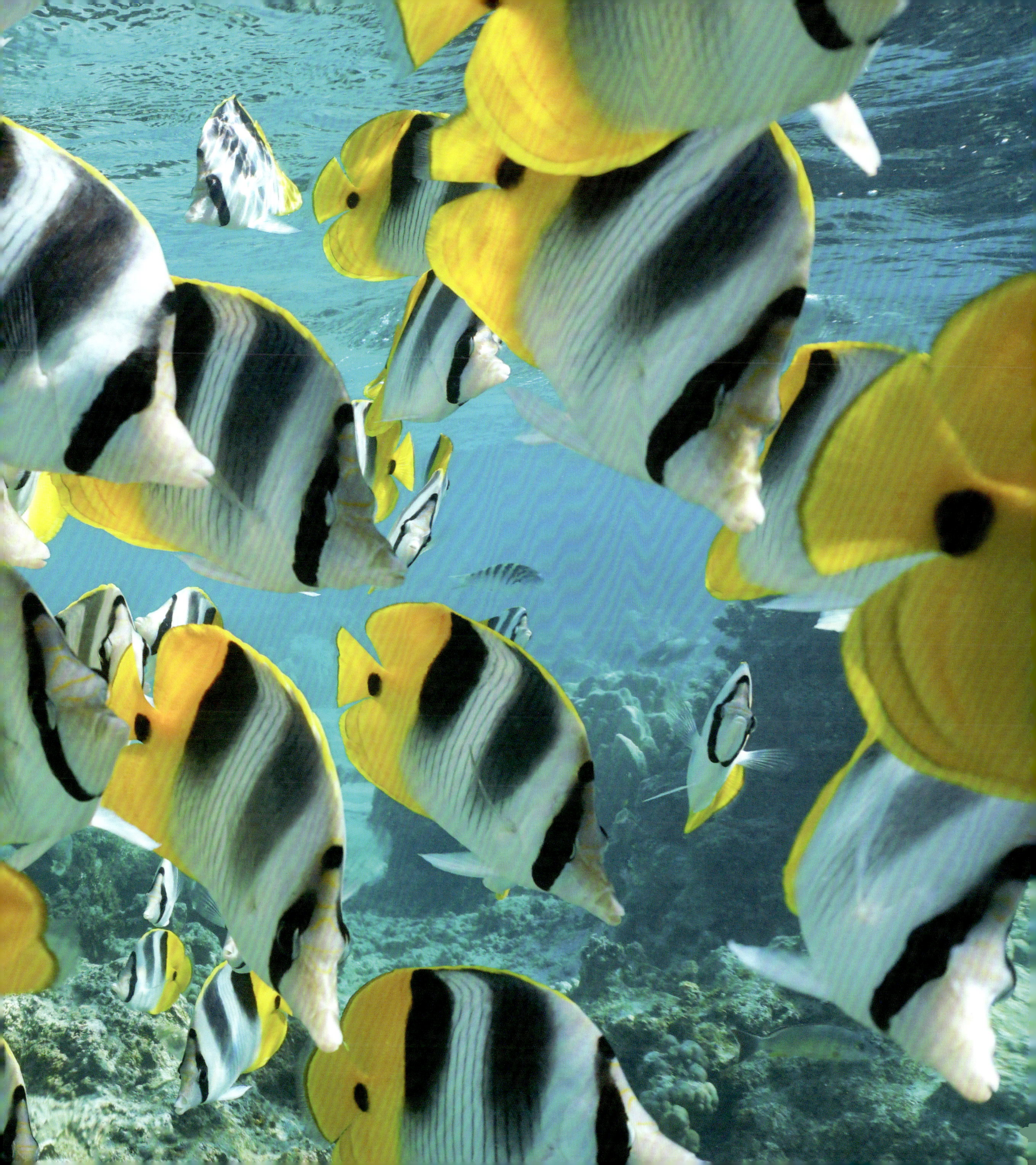

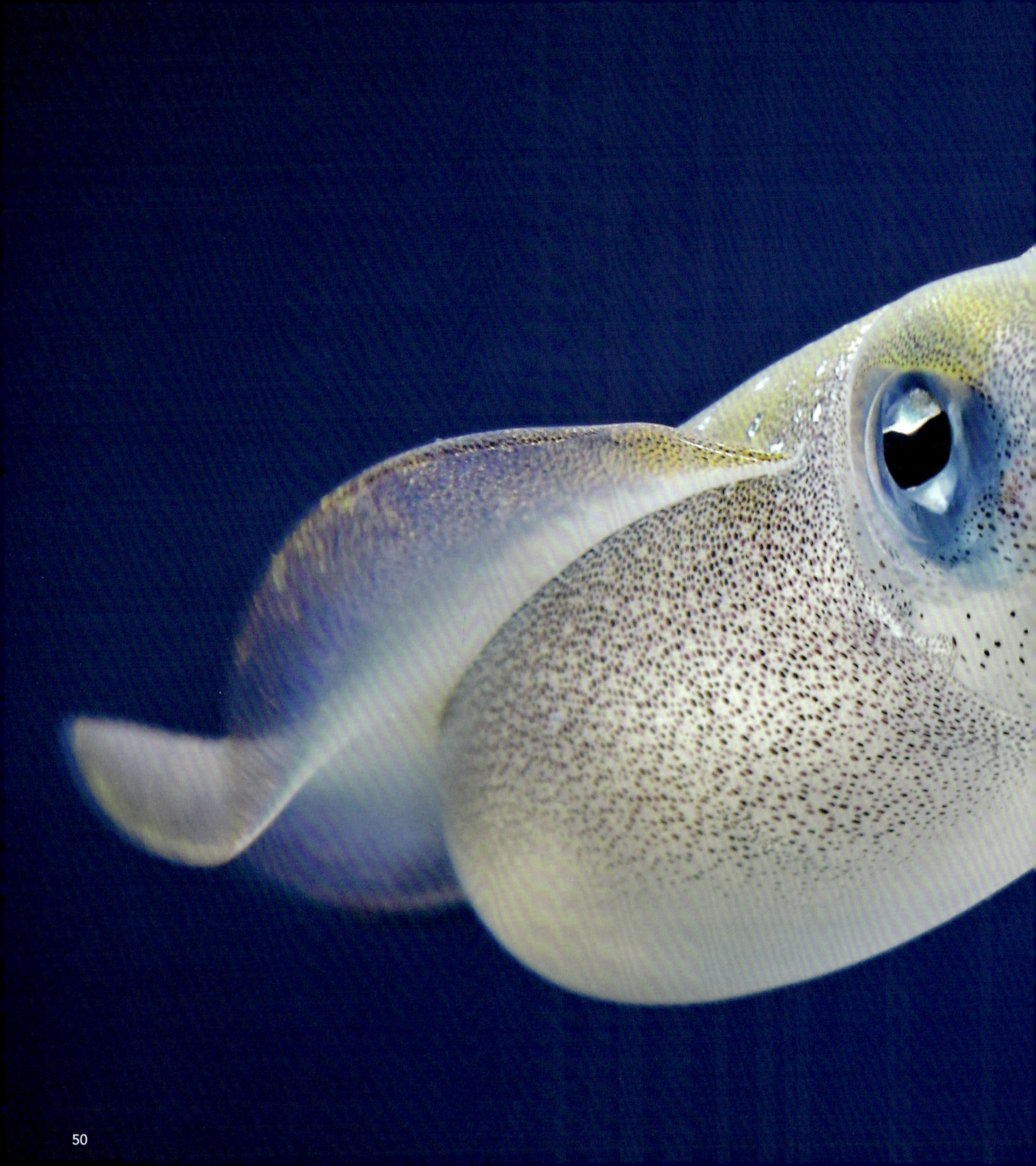

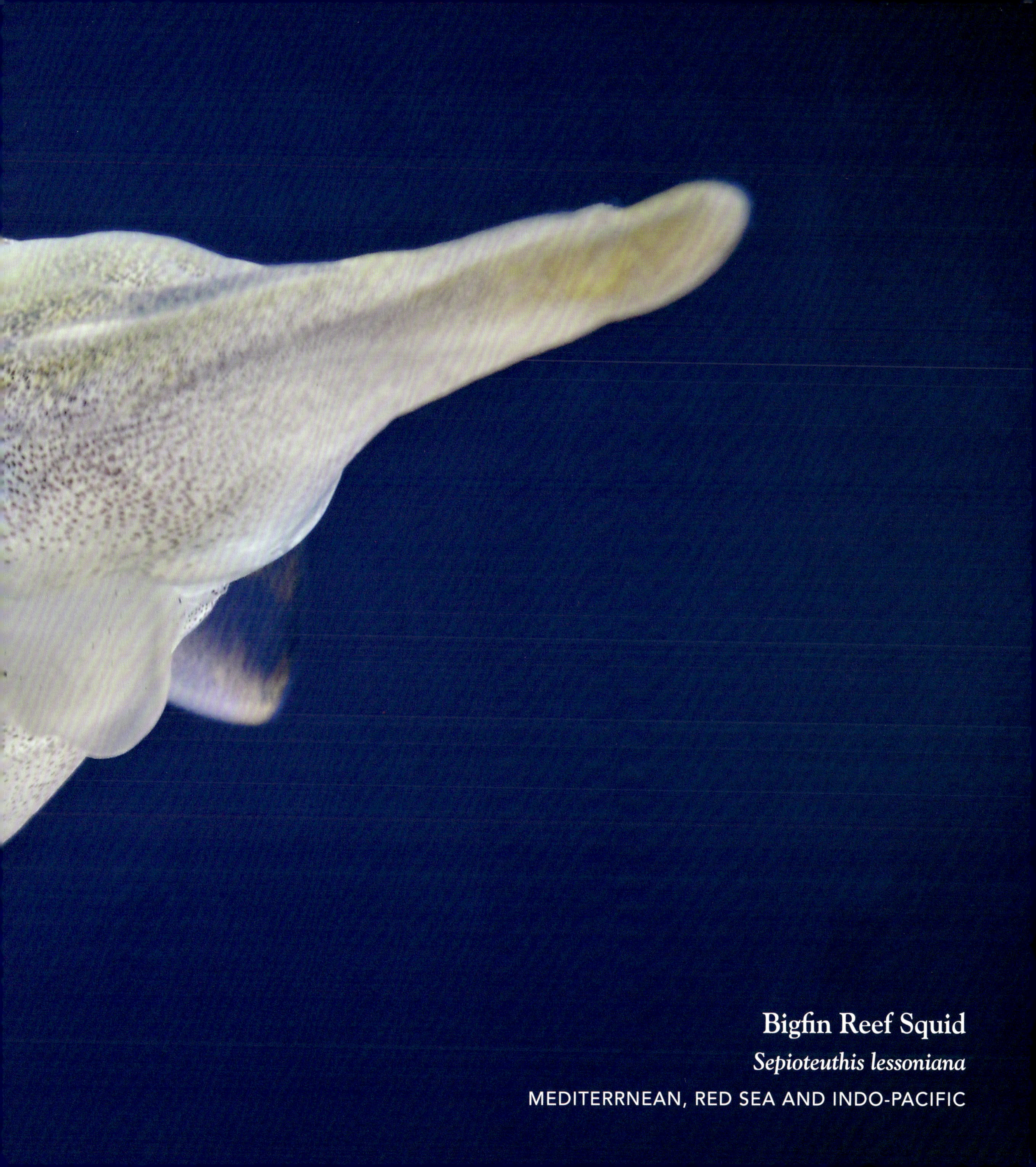

Bigfin Reef Squid

Sepioteuthis lessoniana

MEDITERRNEAN, RED SEA AND INDO-PACIFIC

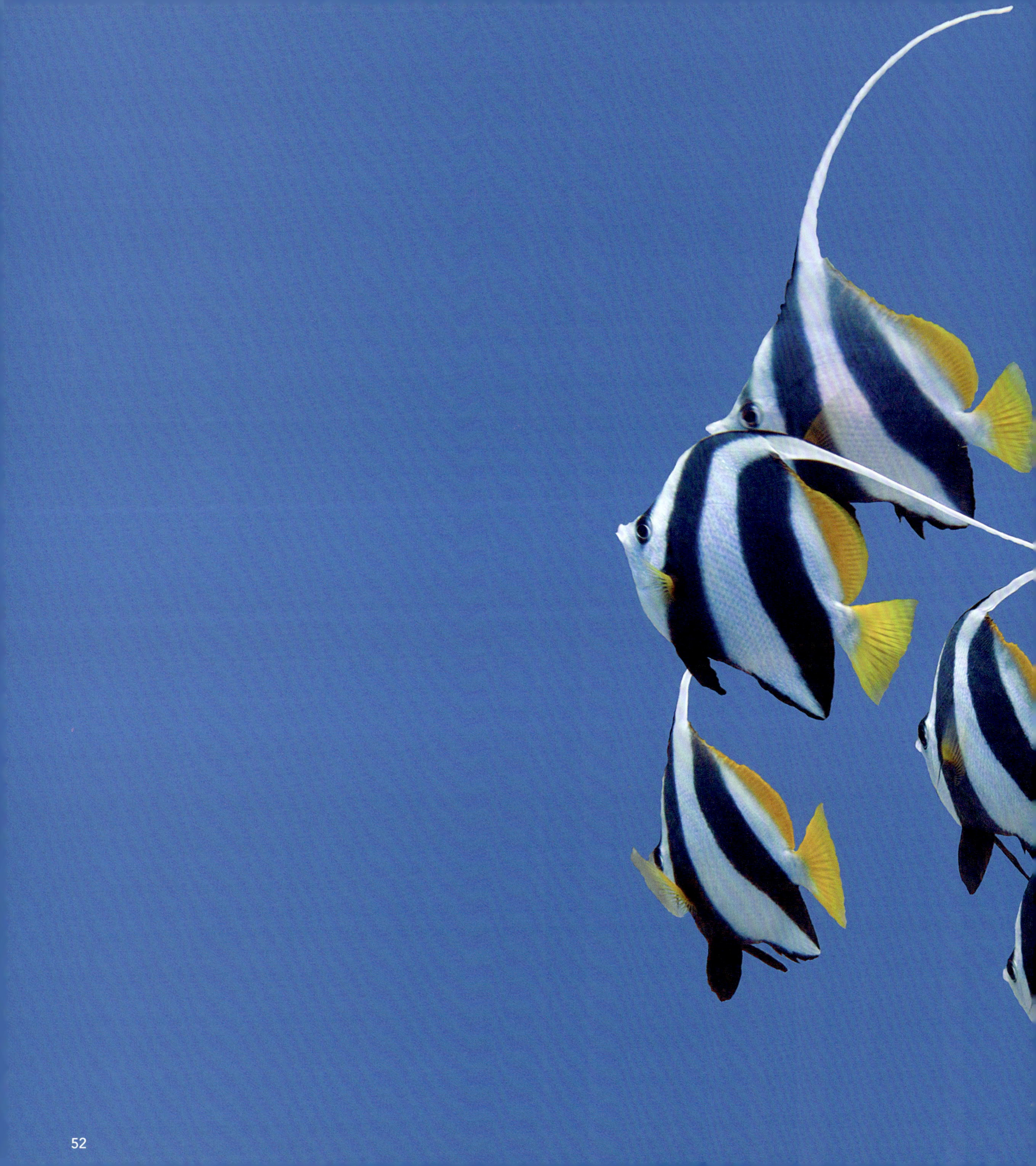

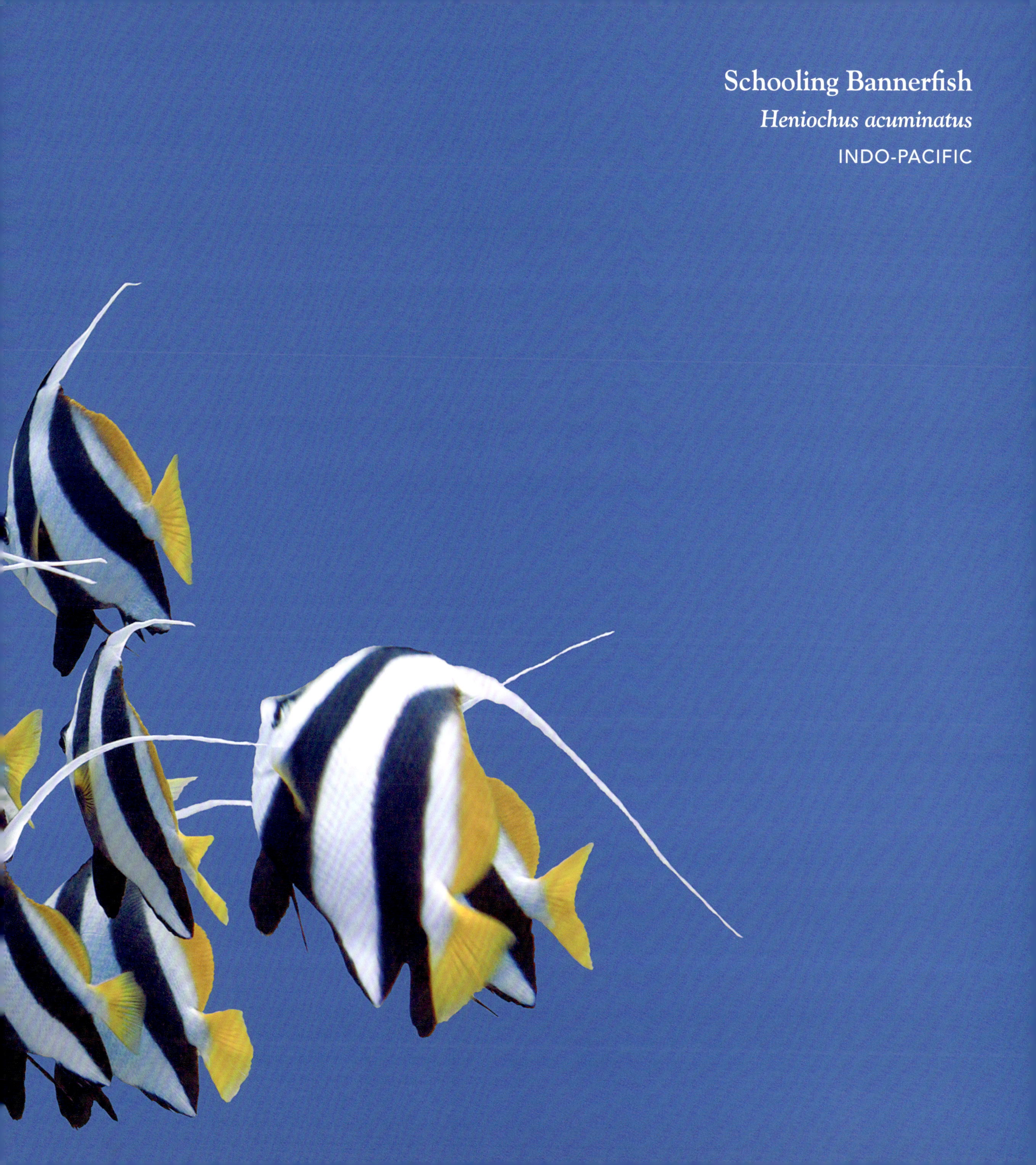

Schooling Bannerfish

Heniochus acuminatus

INDO-PACIFIC

Nudibranch species

Nudibranchia

TROPICAL OCEANS

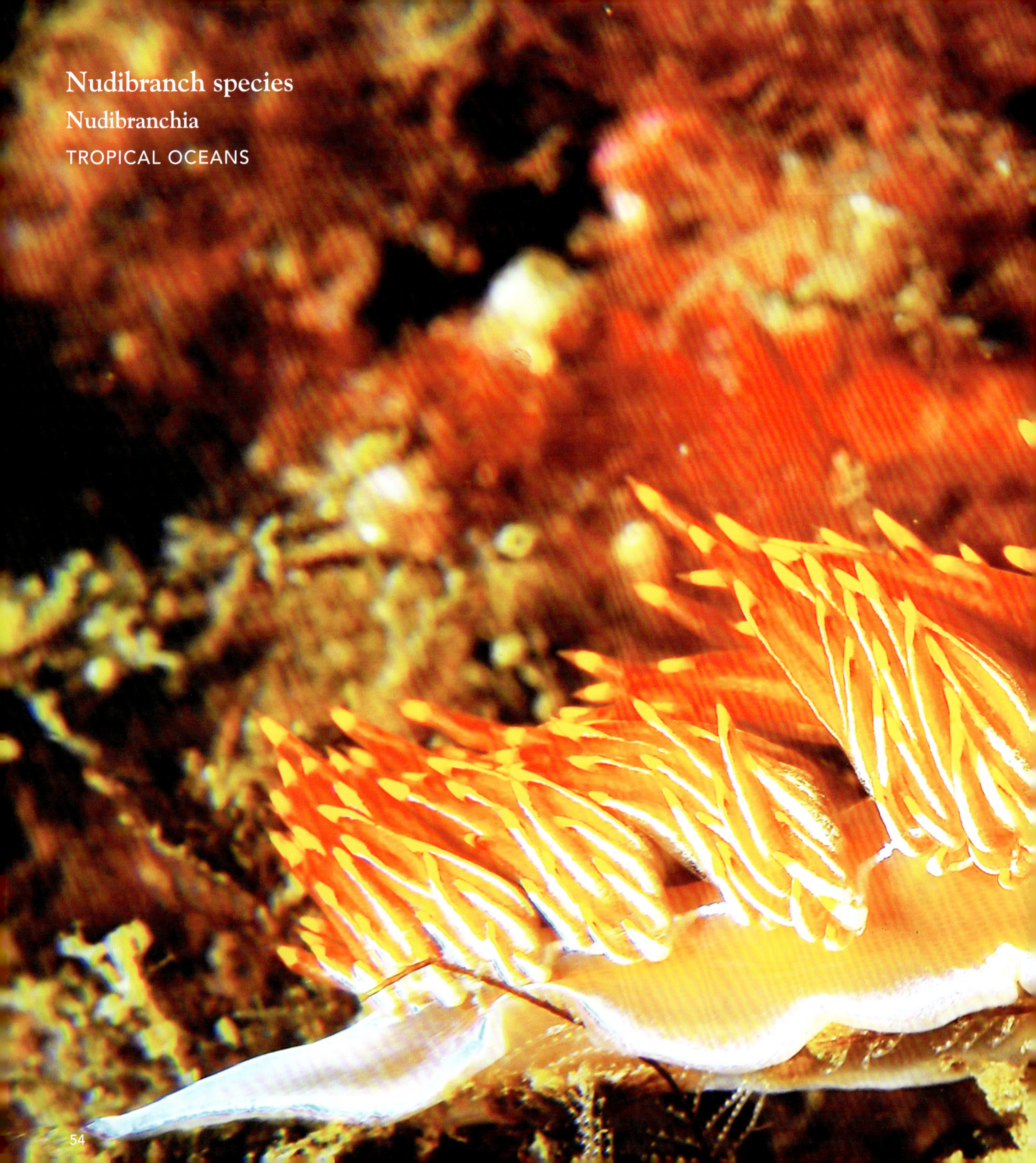

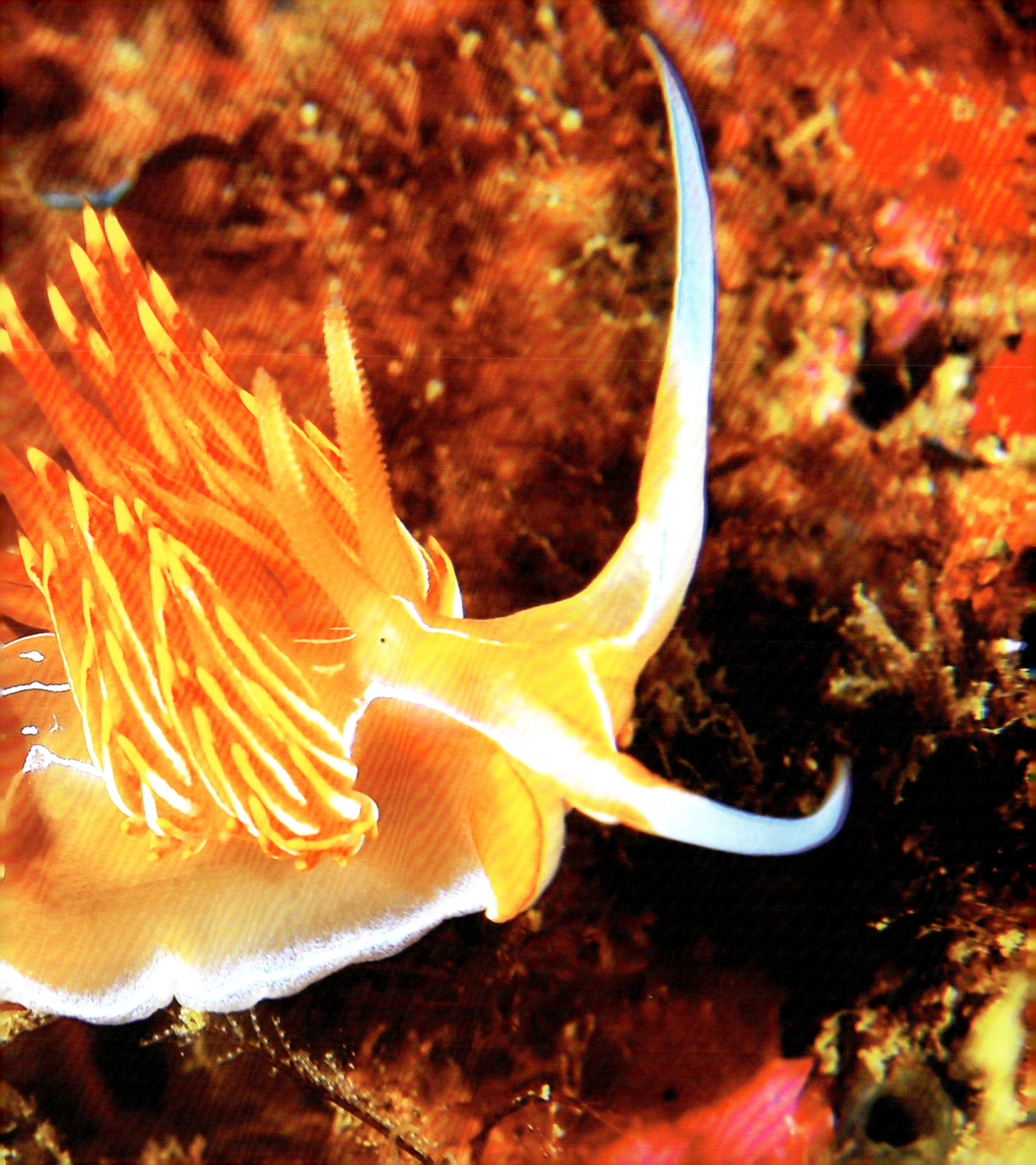

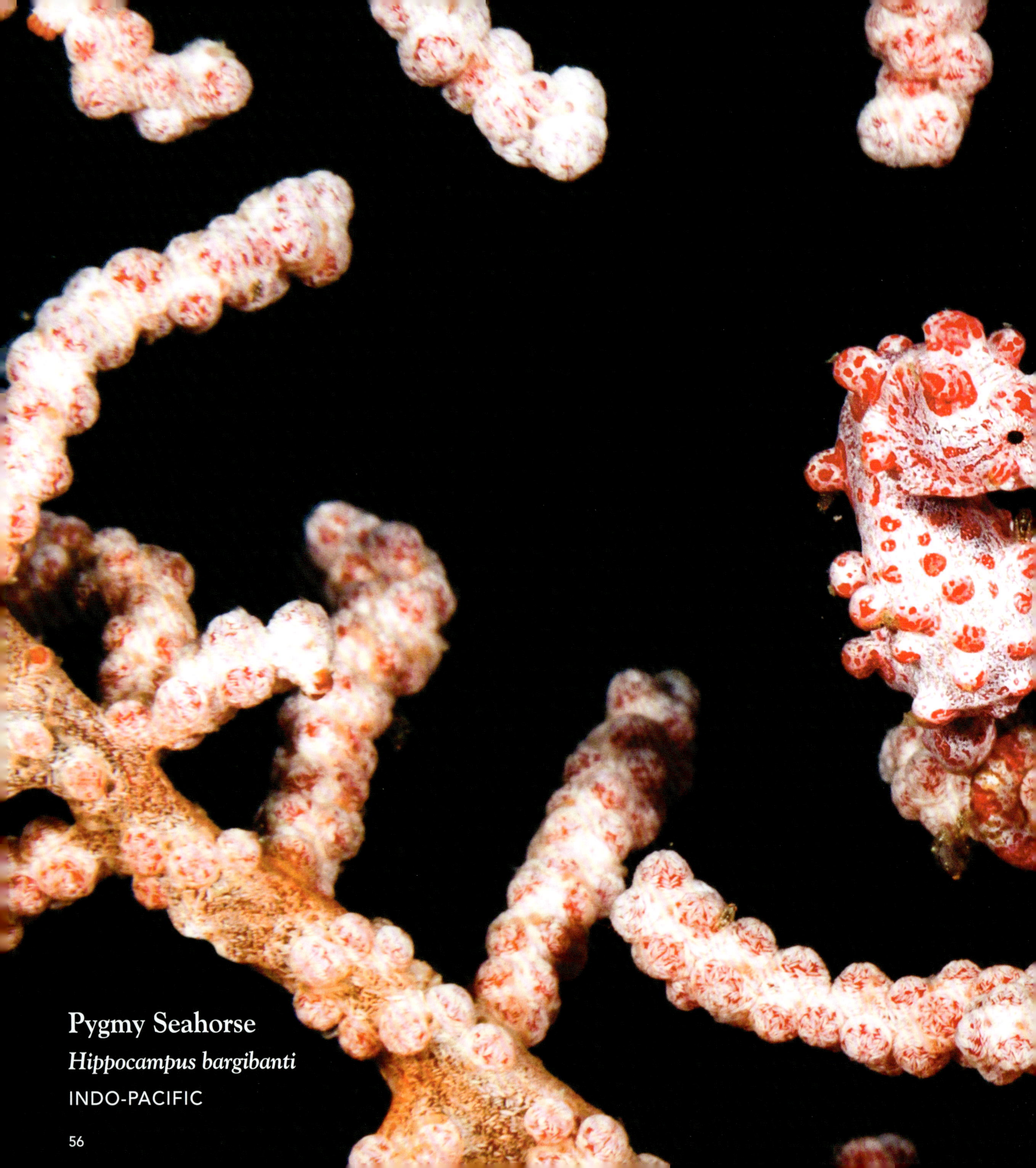

Pygmy Seahorse

Hippocampus bargibanti

INDO-PACIFIC

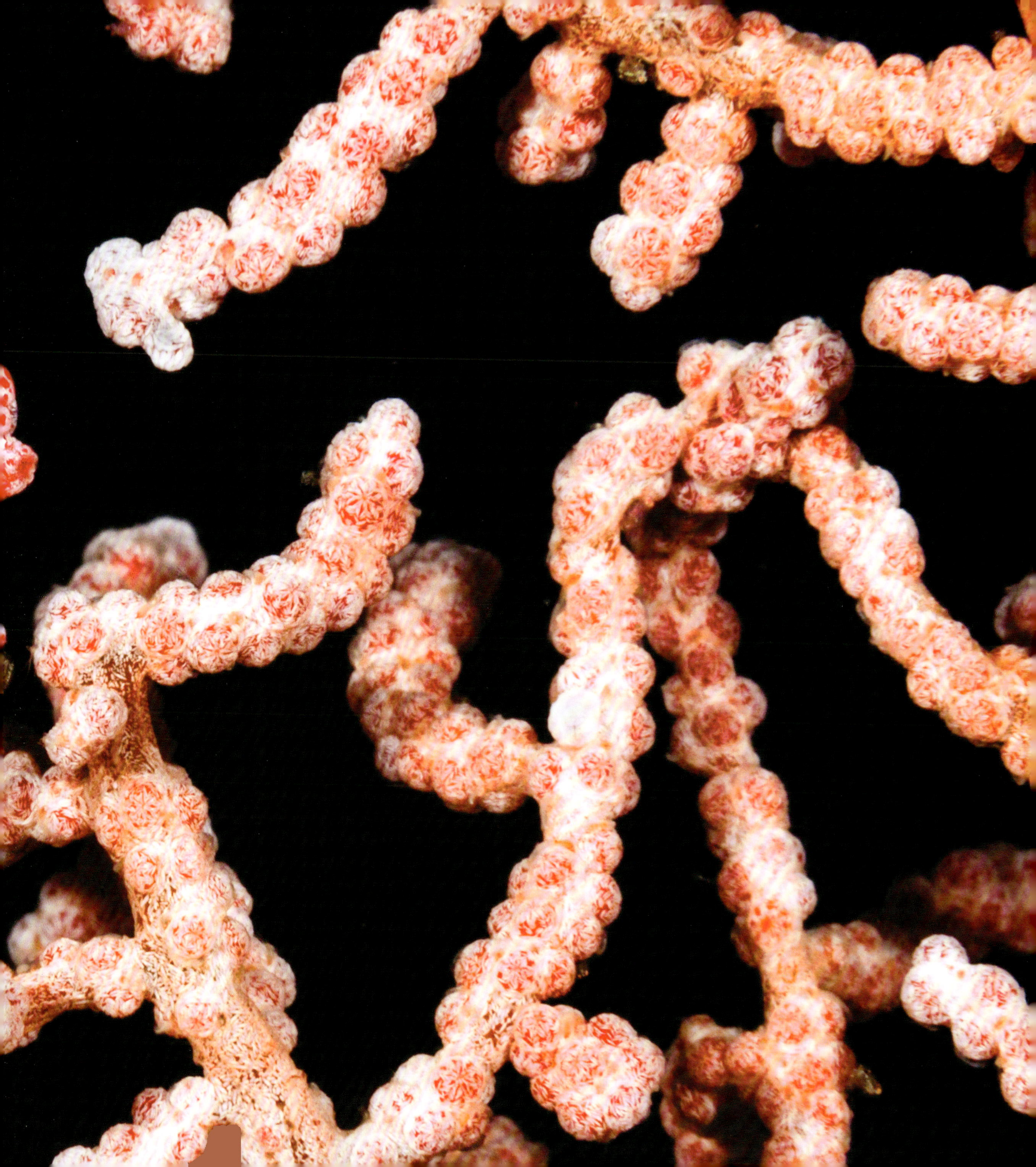

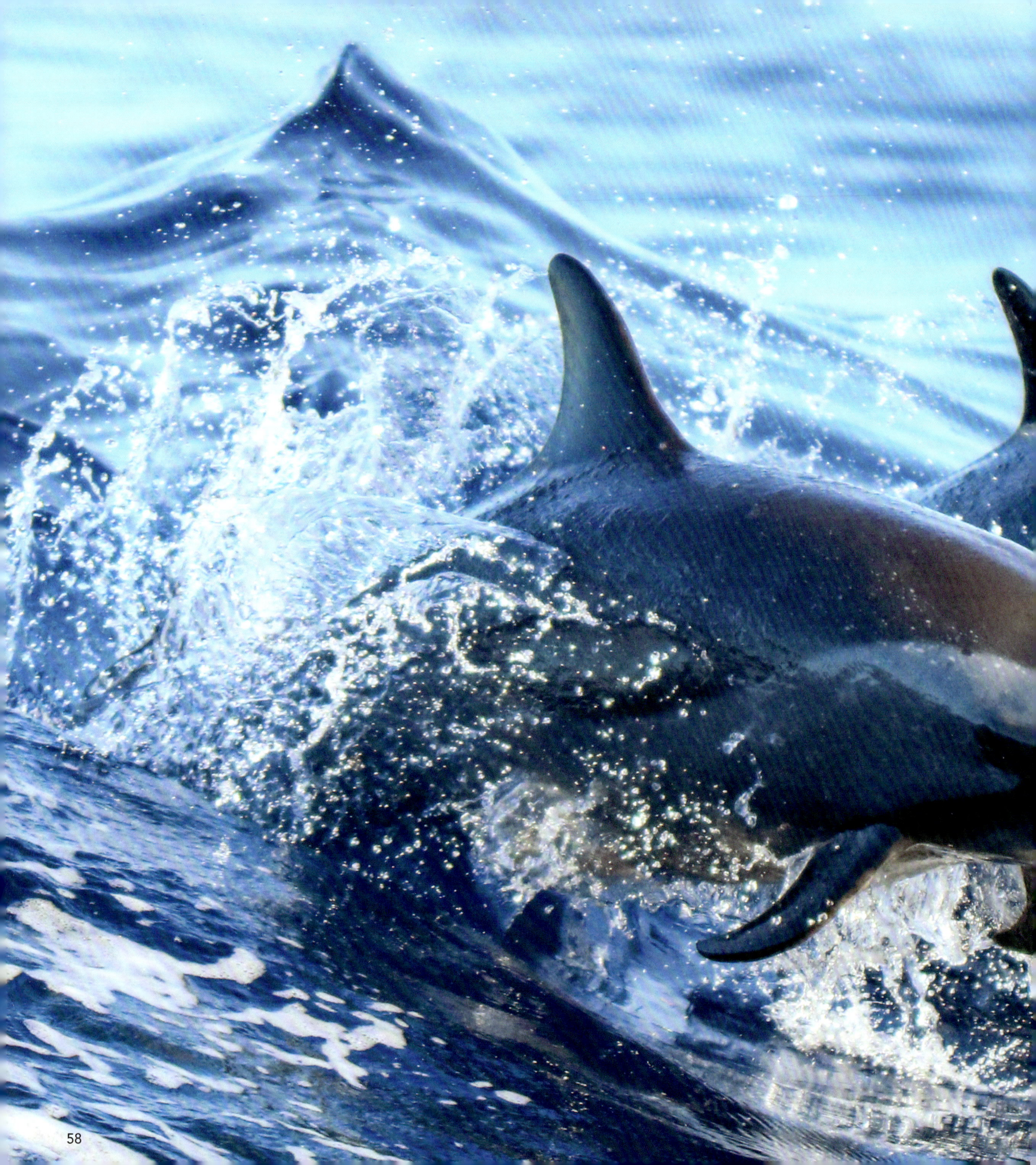

Pantropical Spotted Dolphin

Stenella attenuata

TROPICAL AND TEMPERATE OCEANS WORLDWIDE

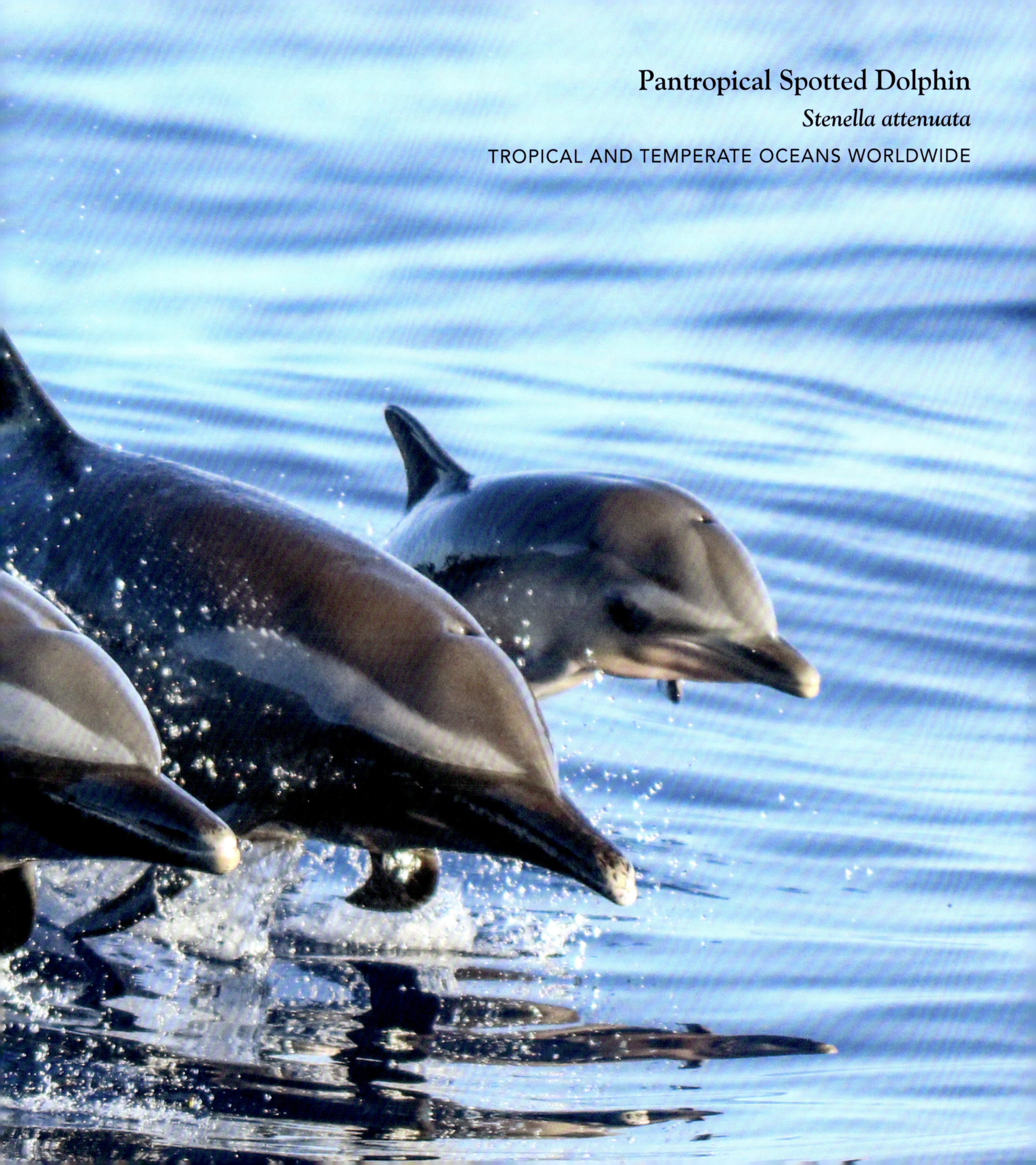

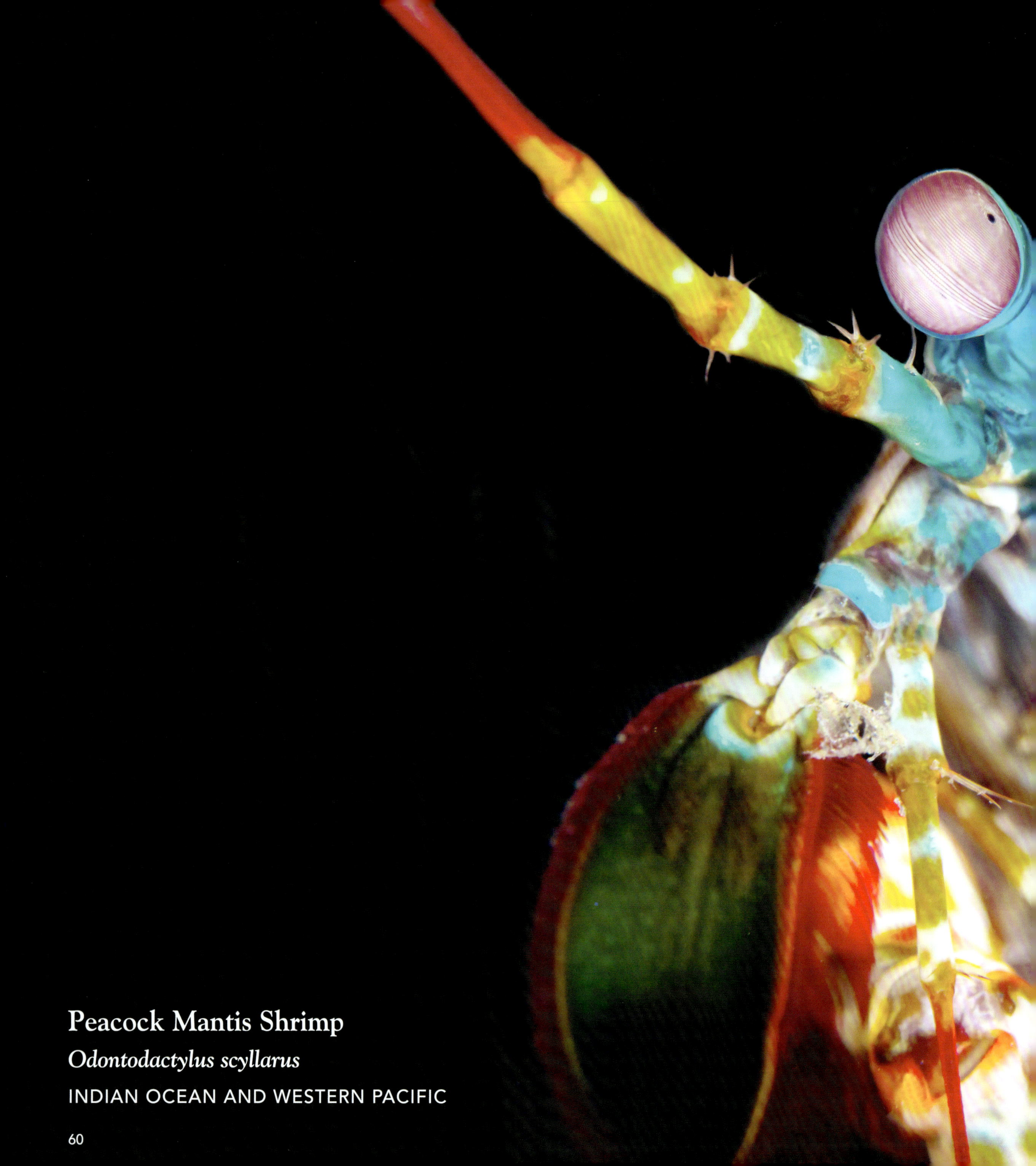

Peacock Mantis Shrimp

Odontodactylus scyllarus

INDIAN OCEAN AND WESTERN PACIFIC

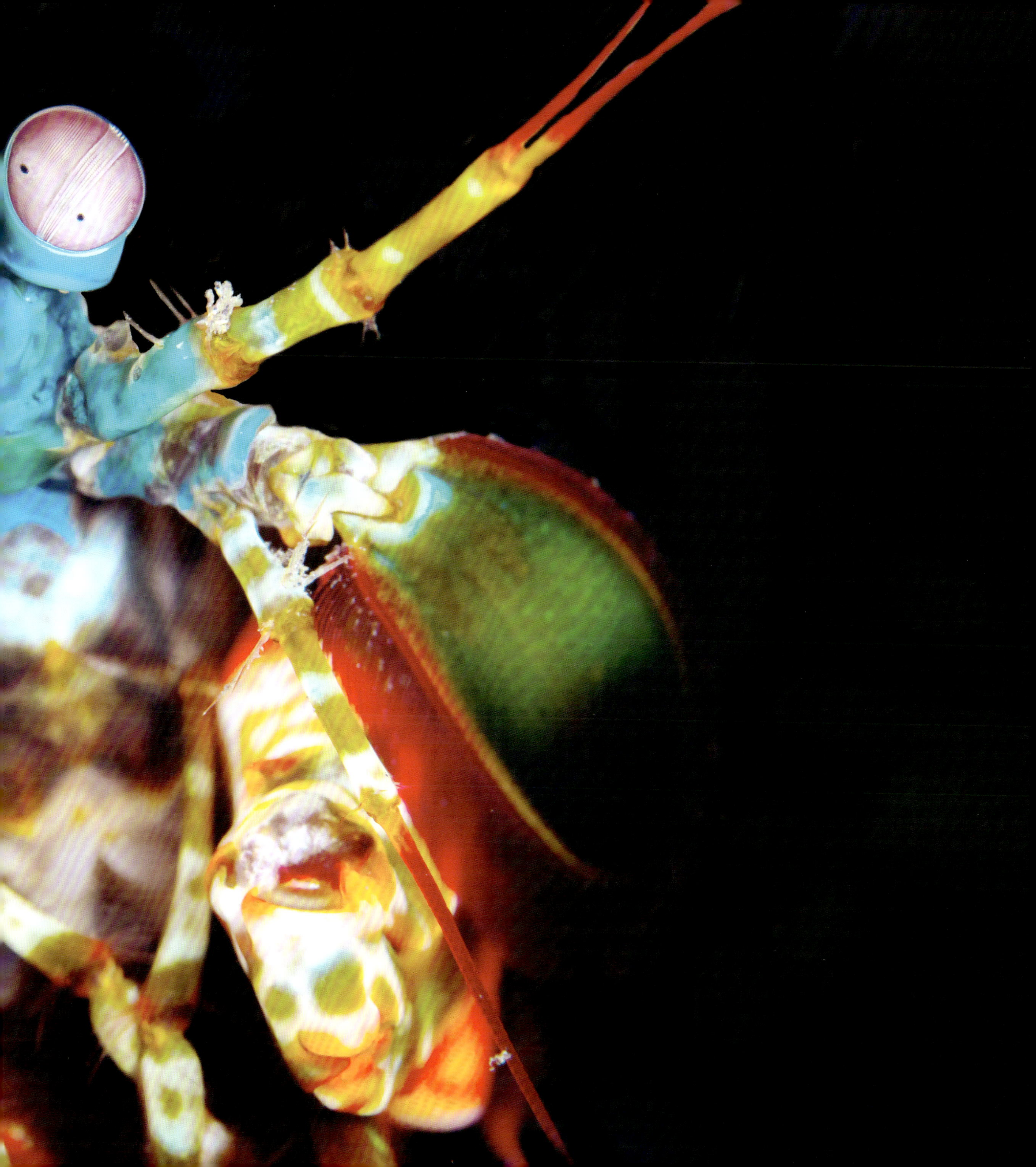

Bluefin Tuna

Thunnus thynnus

OCEANS WORLDWIDE

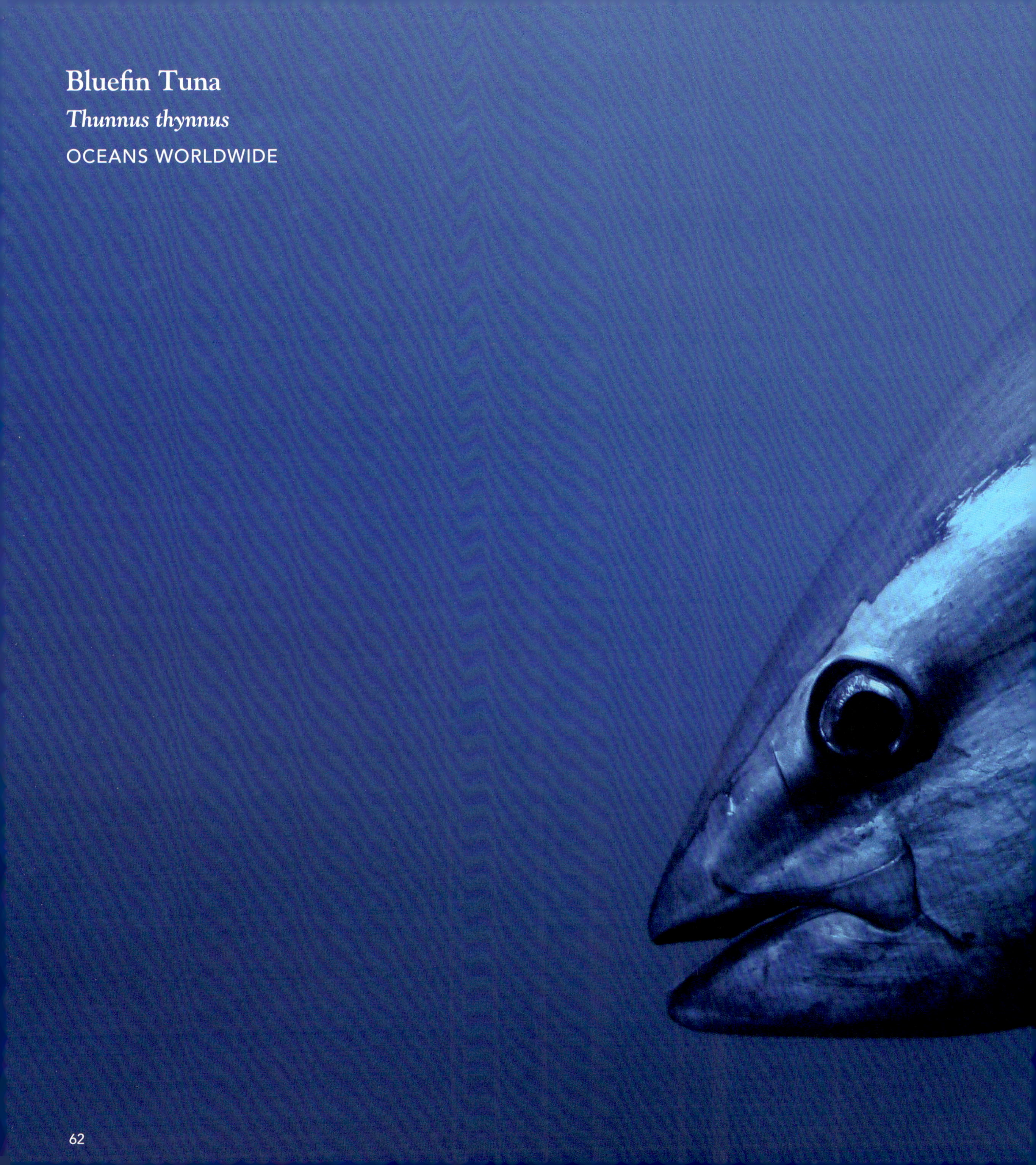

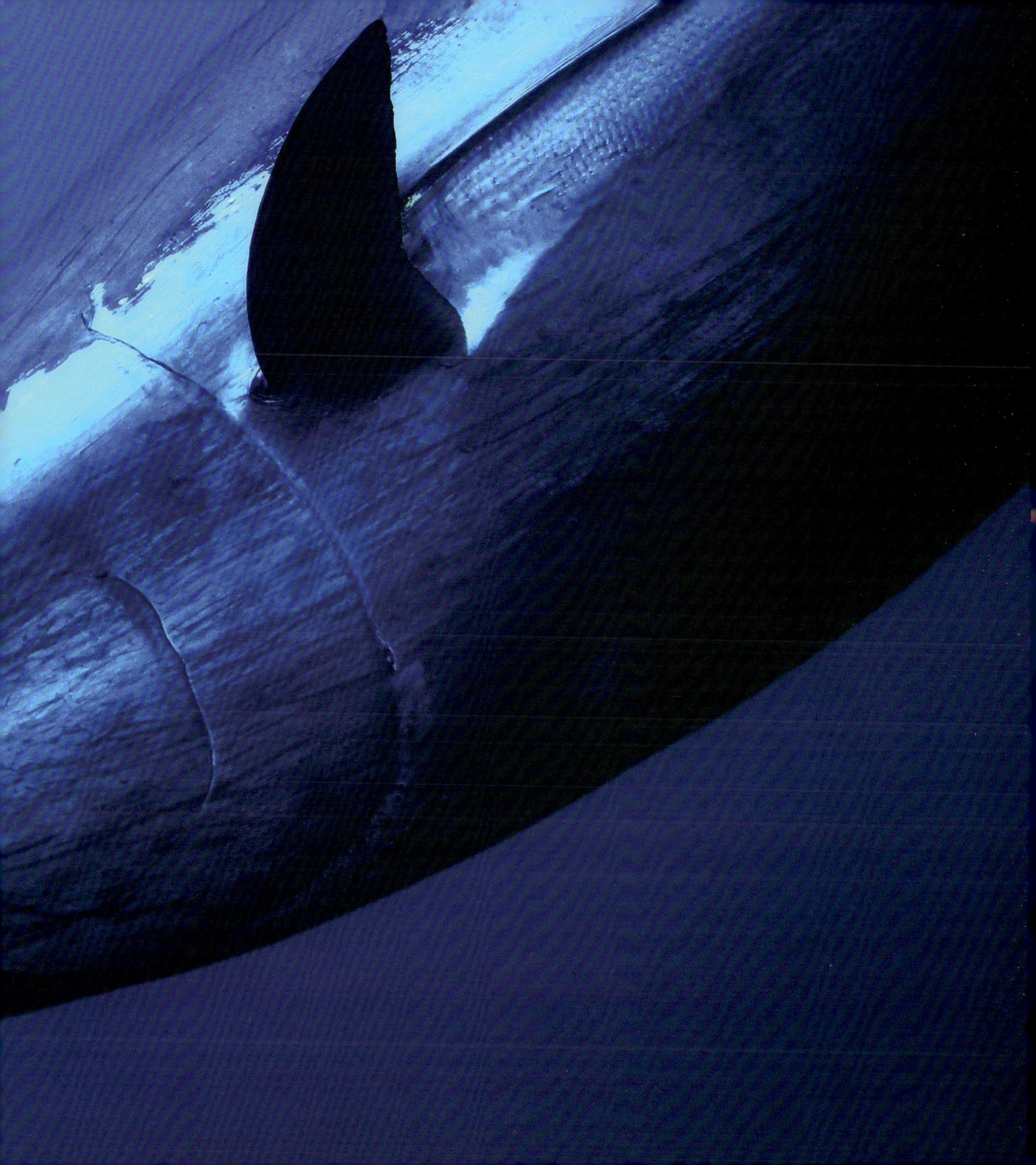

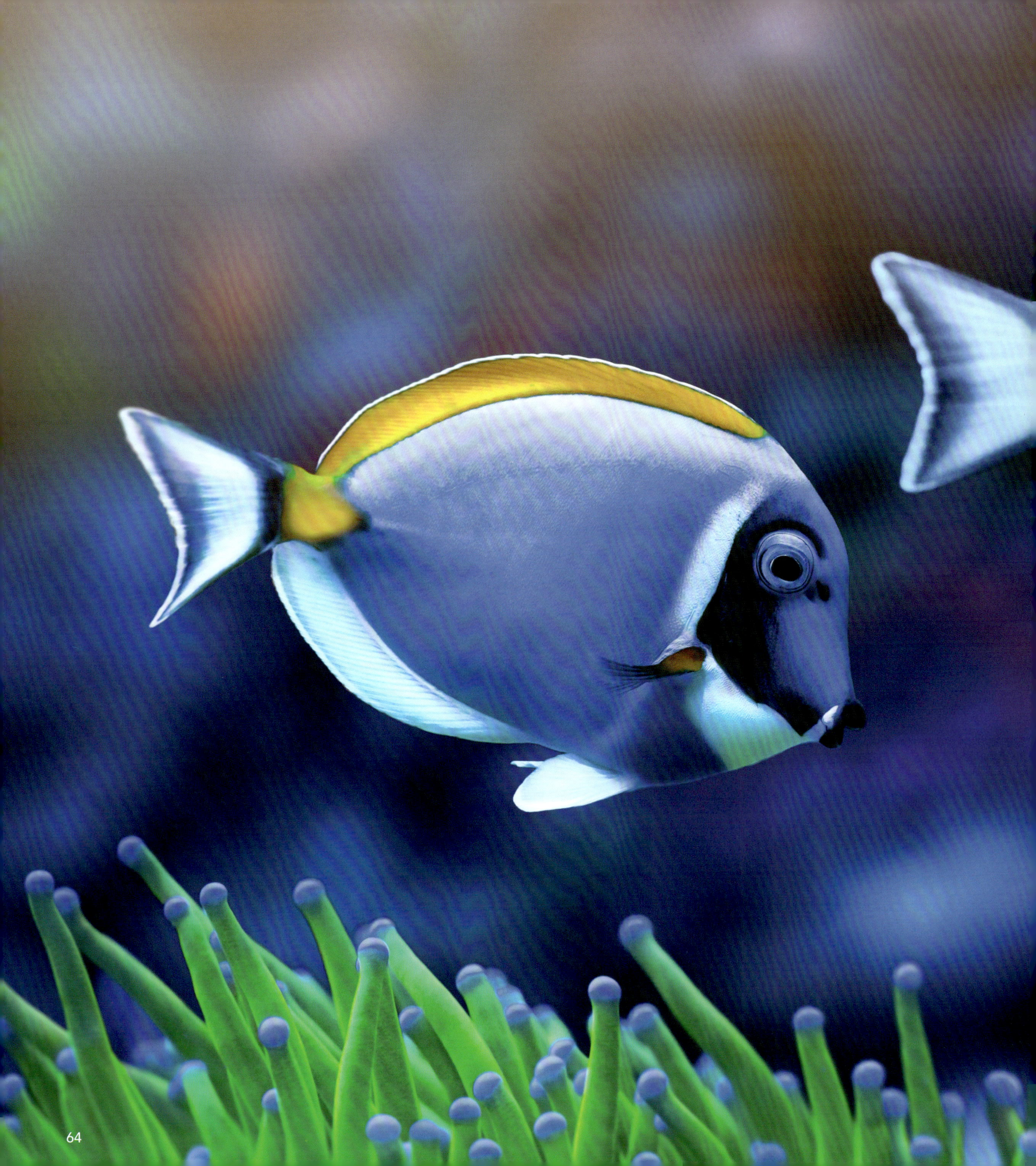

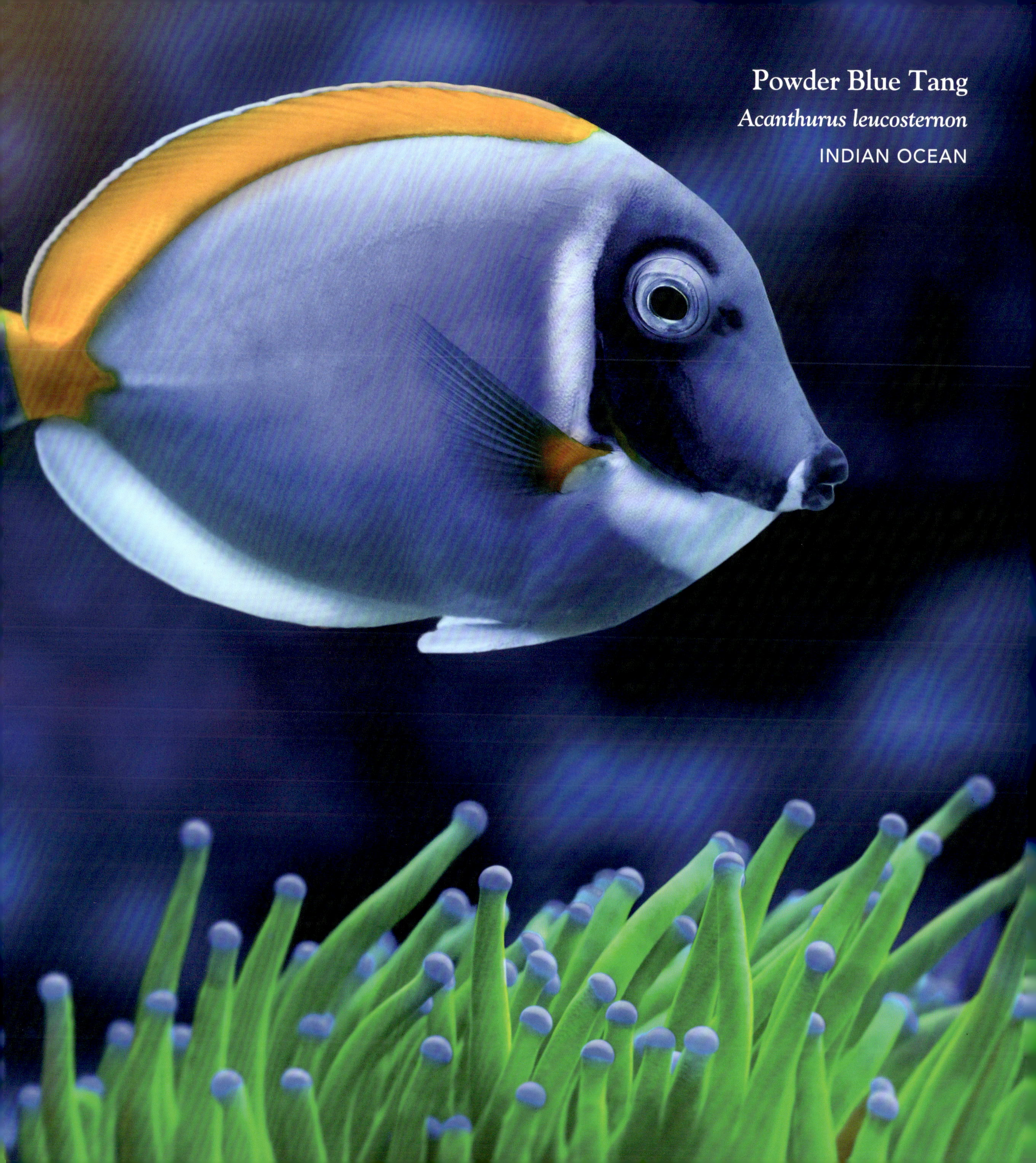

Powder Blue Tang

Acanthurus leucosternon

INDIAN OCEAN

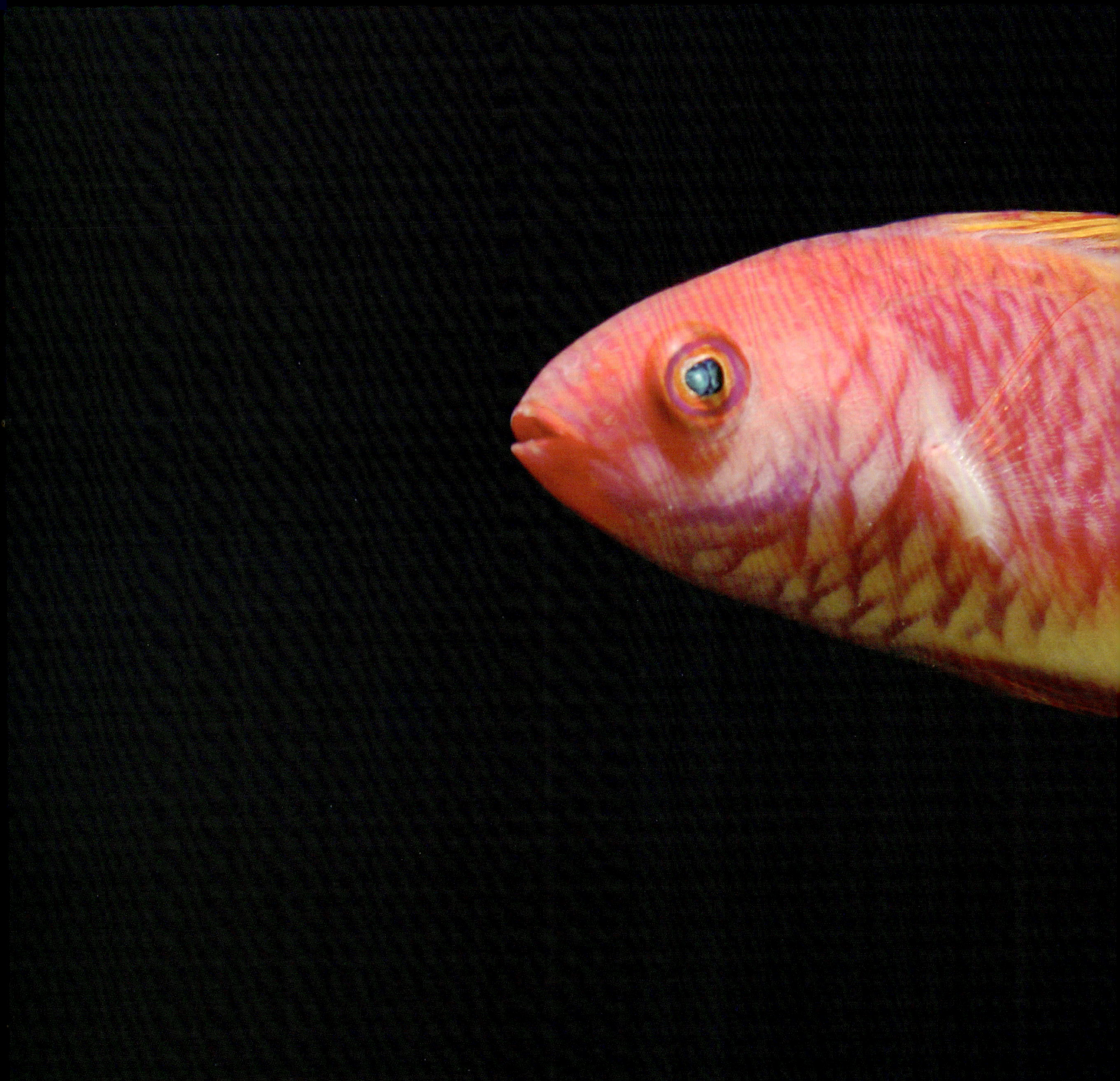

Rosy-scaled Fairy Wrasse

Cirrhilabrus rubrisquamis

INDIAN OCEAN

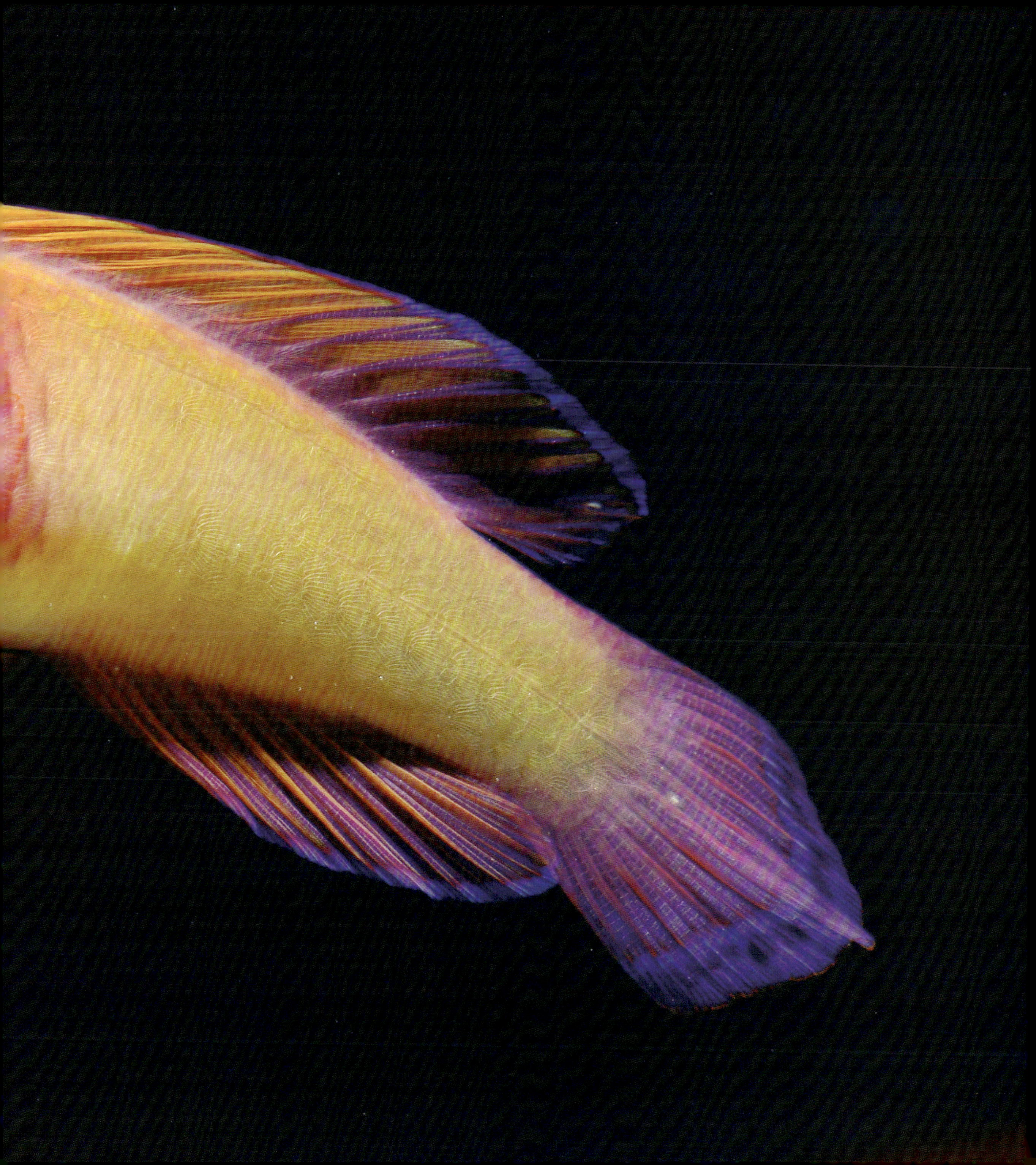

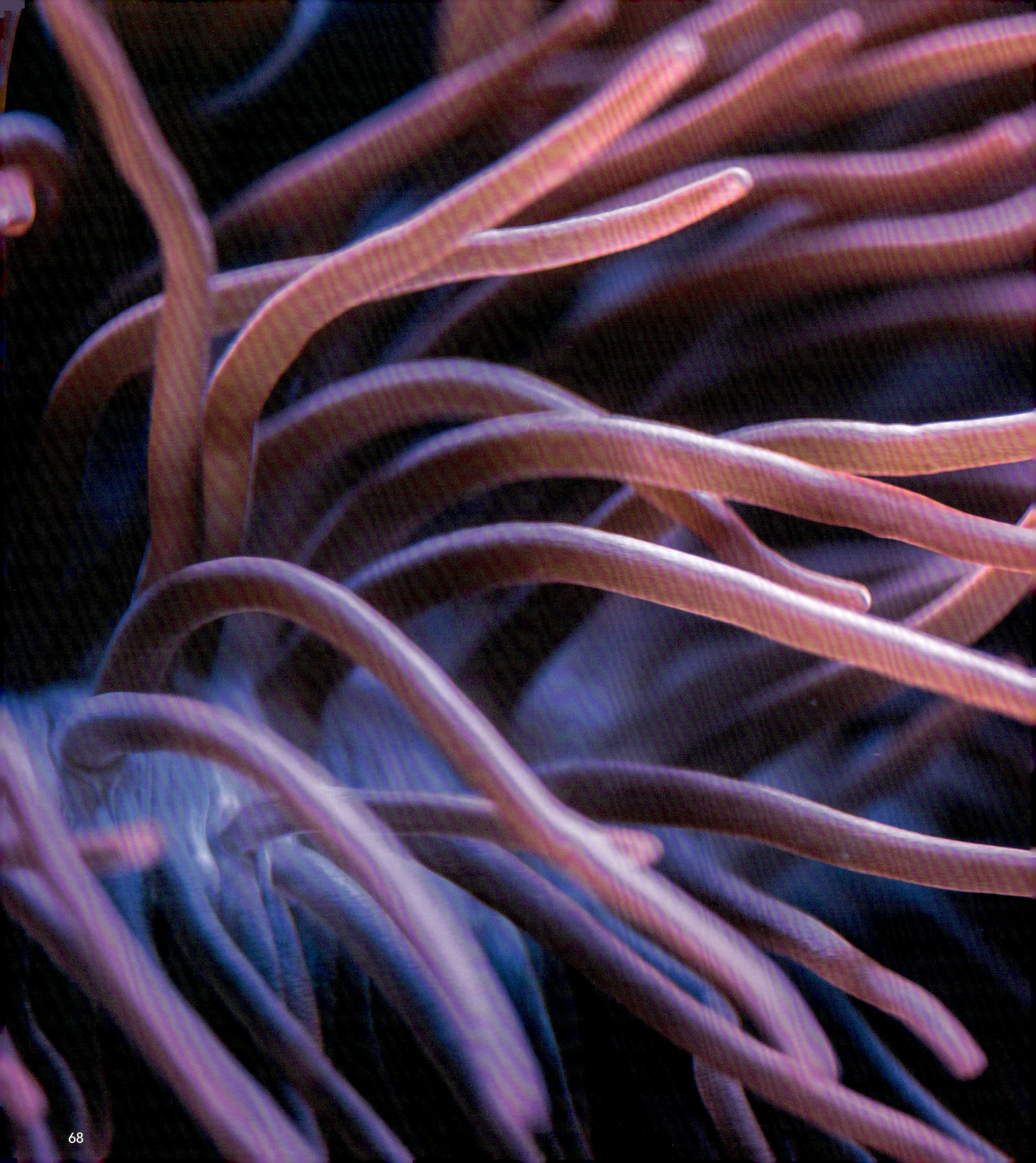

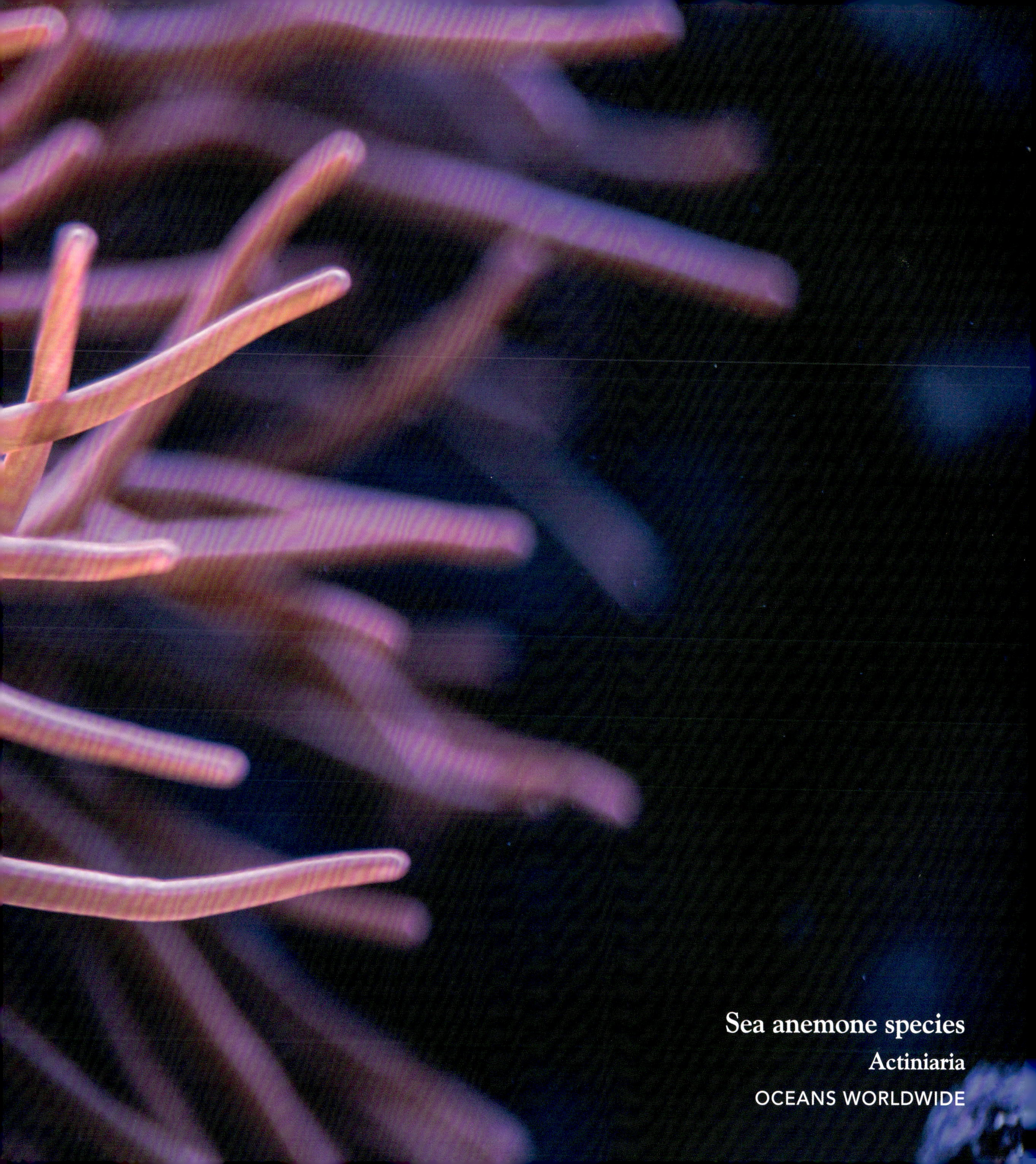

Sea anemone species

Actiniaria

OCEANS WORLDWIDE

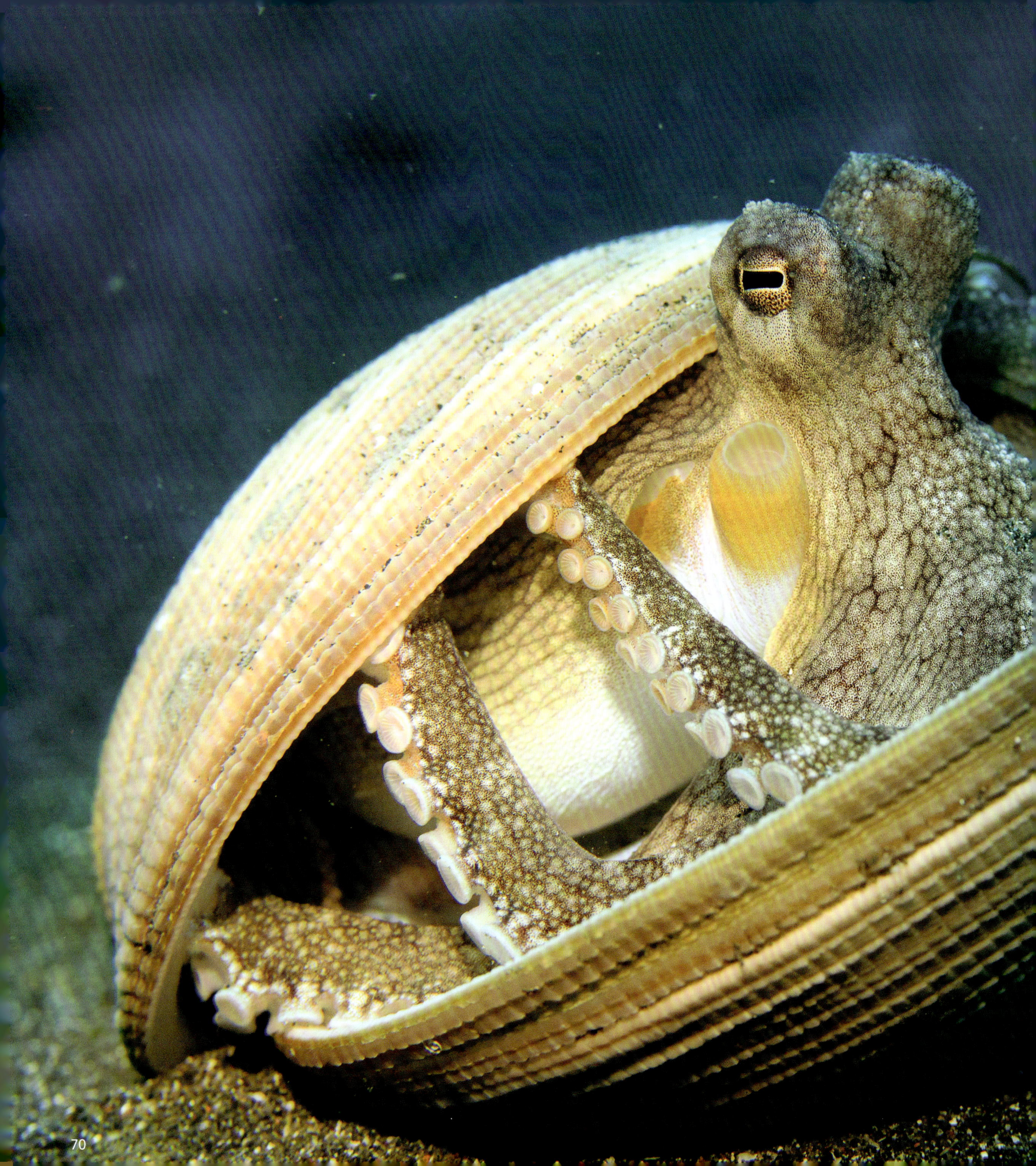

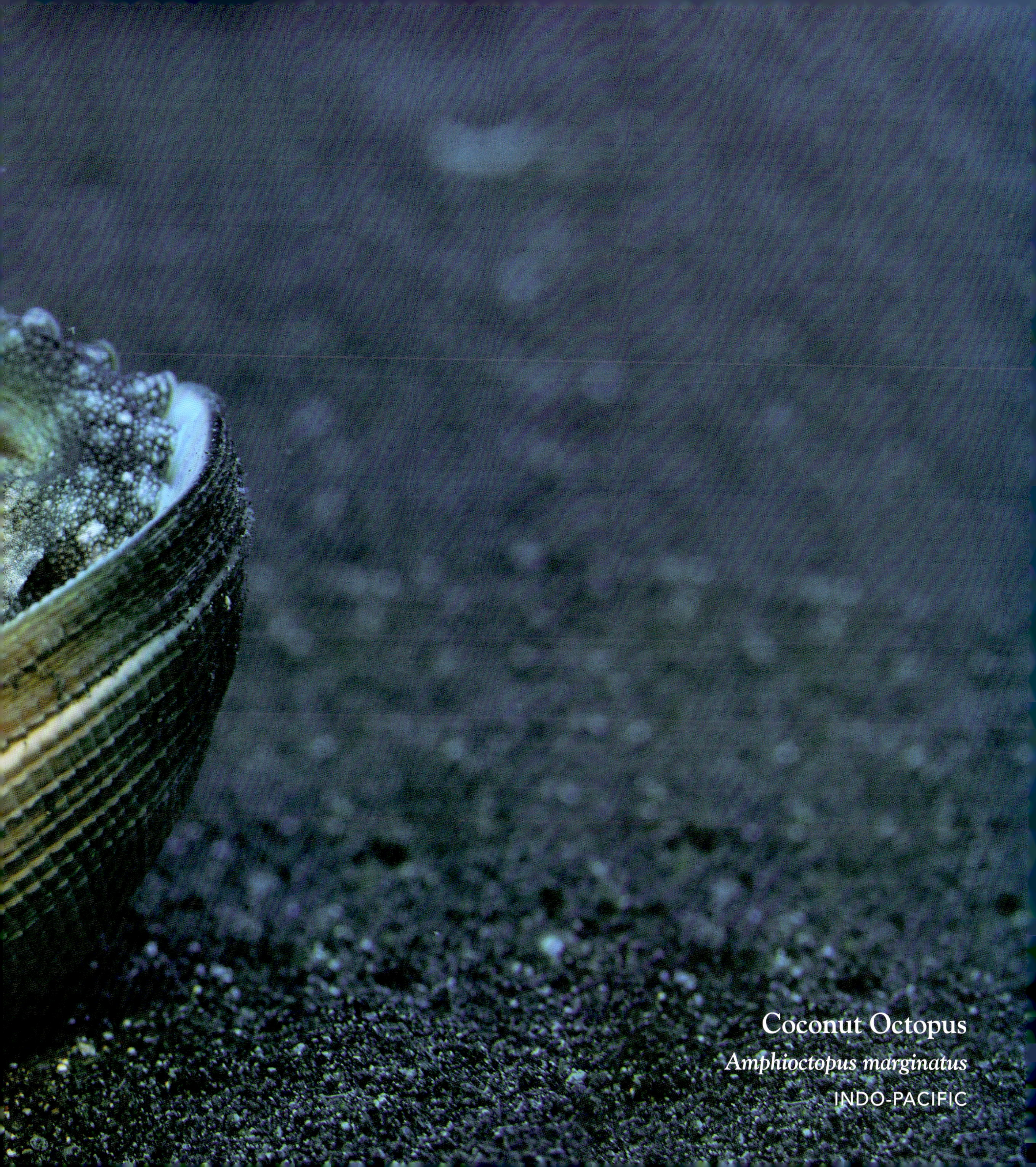

Coconut Octopus

Amphioctopus marginatus

INDO-PACIFIC

White-faced Storm Petrel

Pelagodroma marina

ATLANTIC, PACIFIC AND INDIAN OCEANS

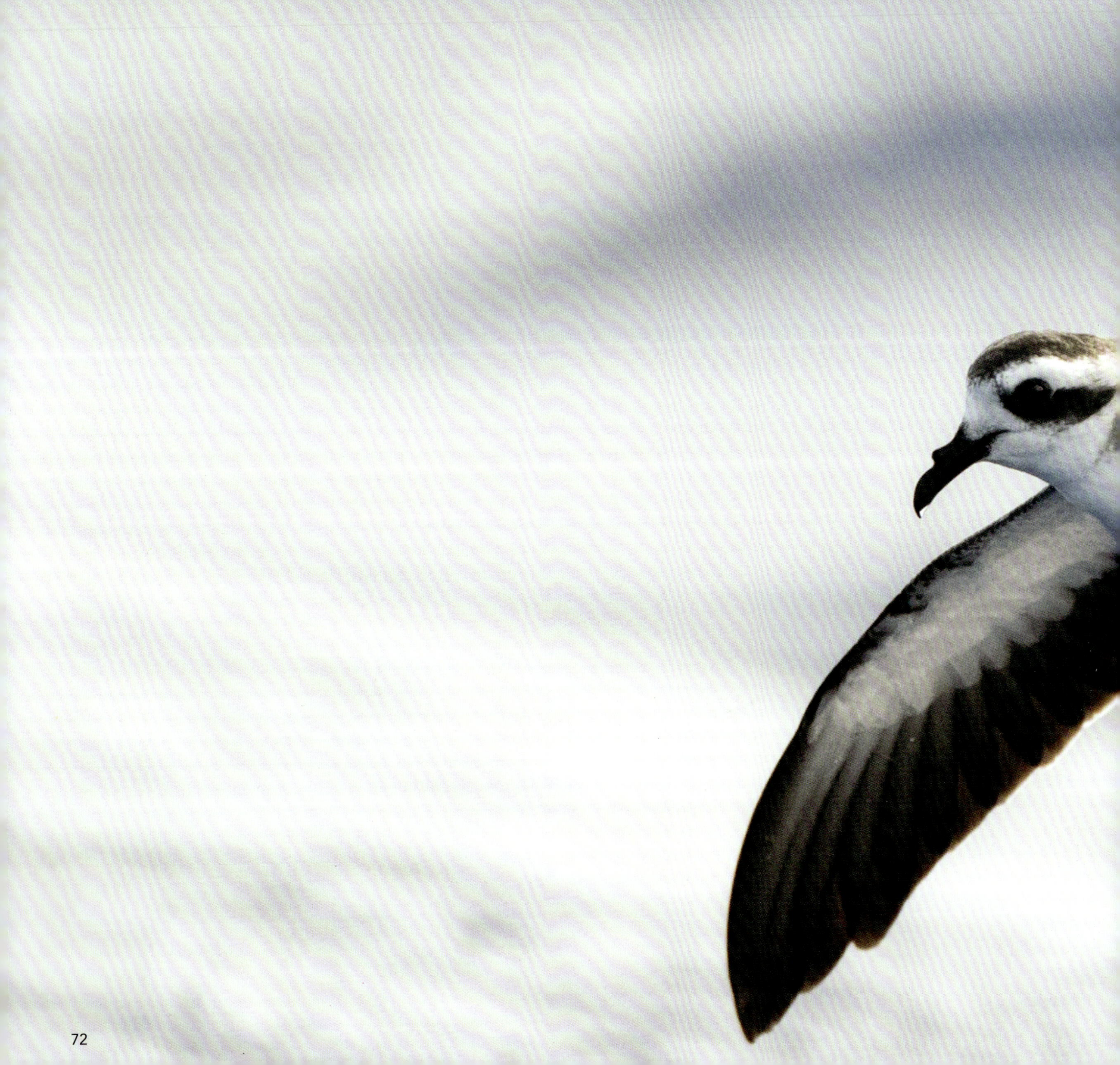

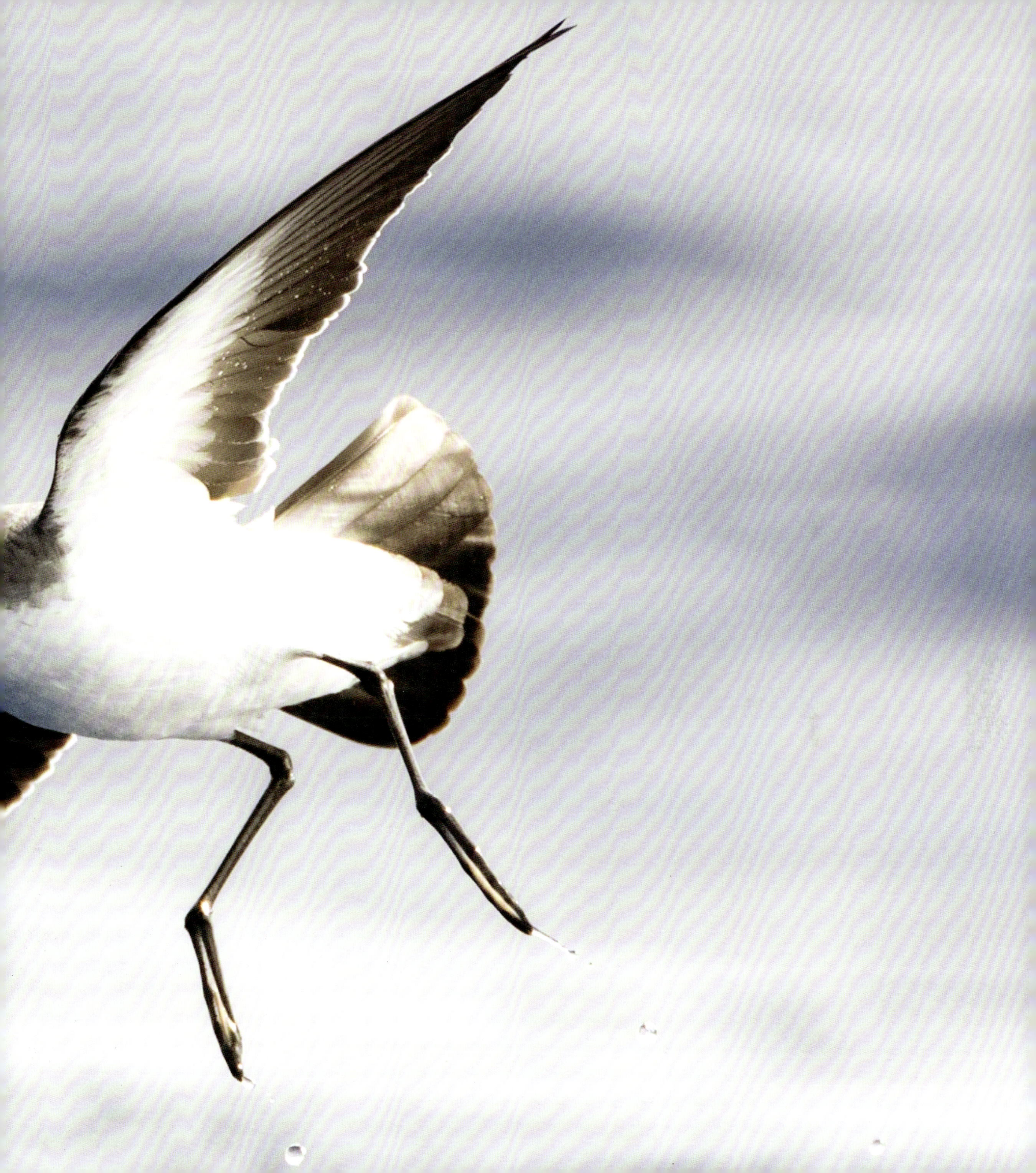

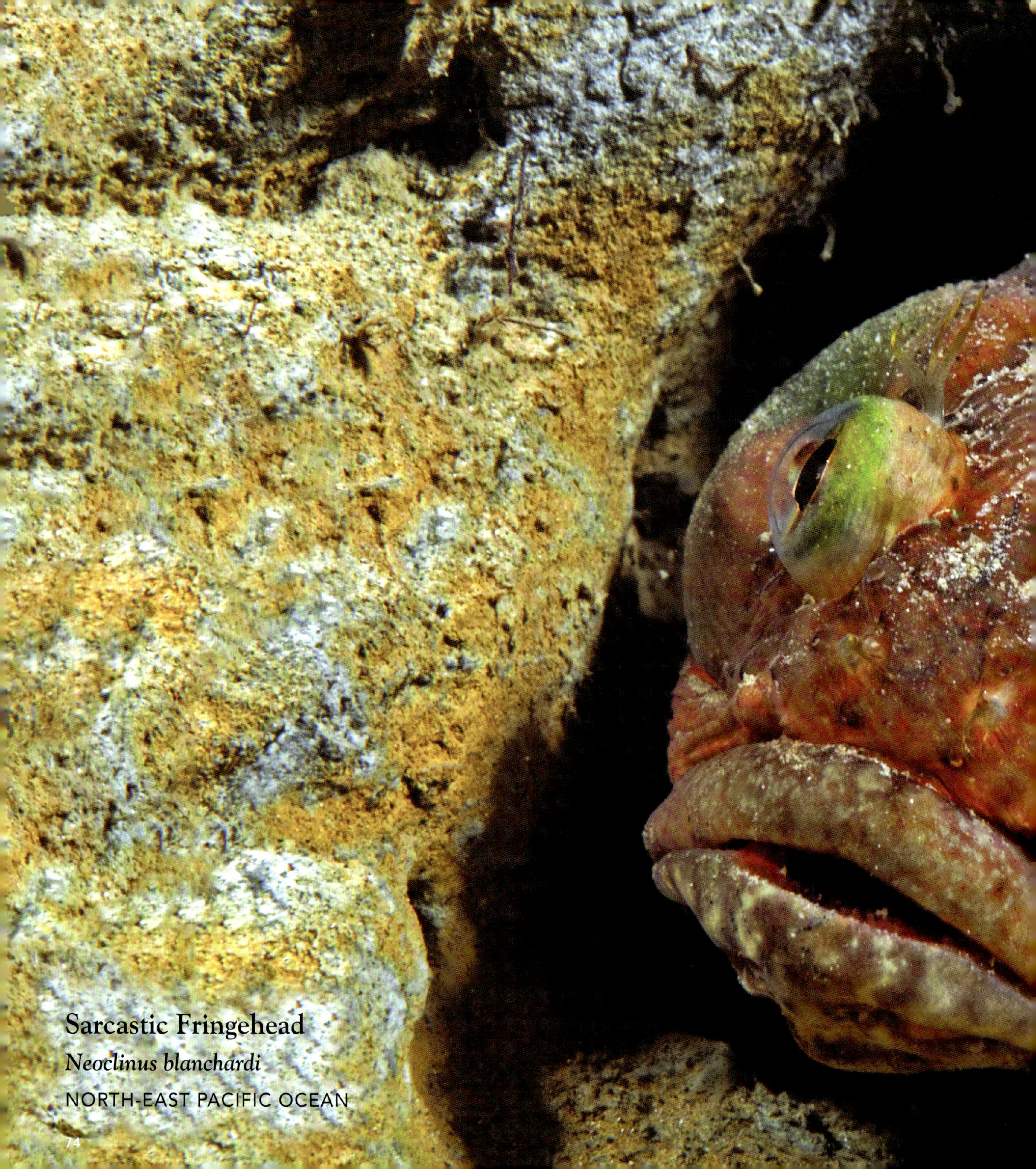

Sarcastic Fringehead

Neoclinus blanchardi

NORTH-EAST PACIFIC OCEAN

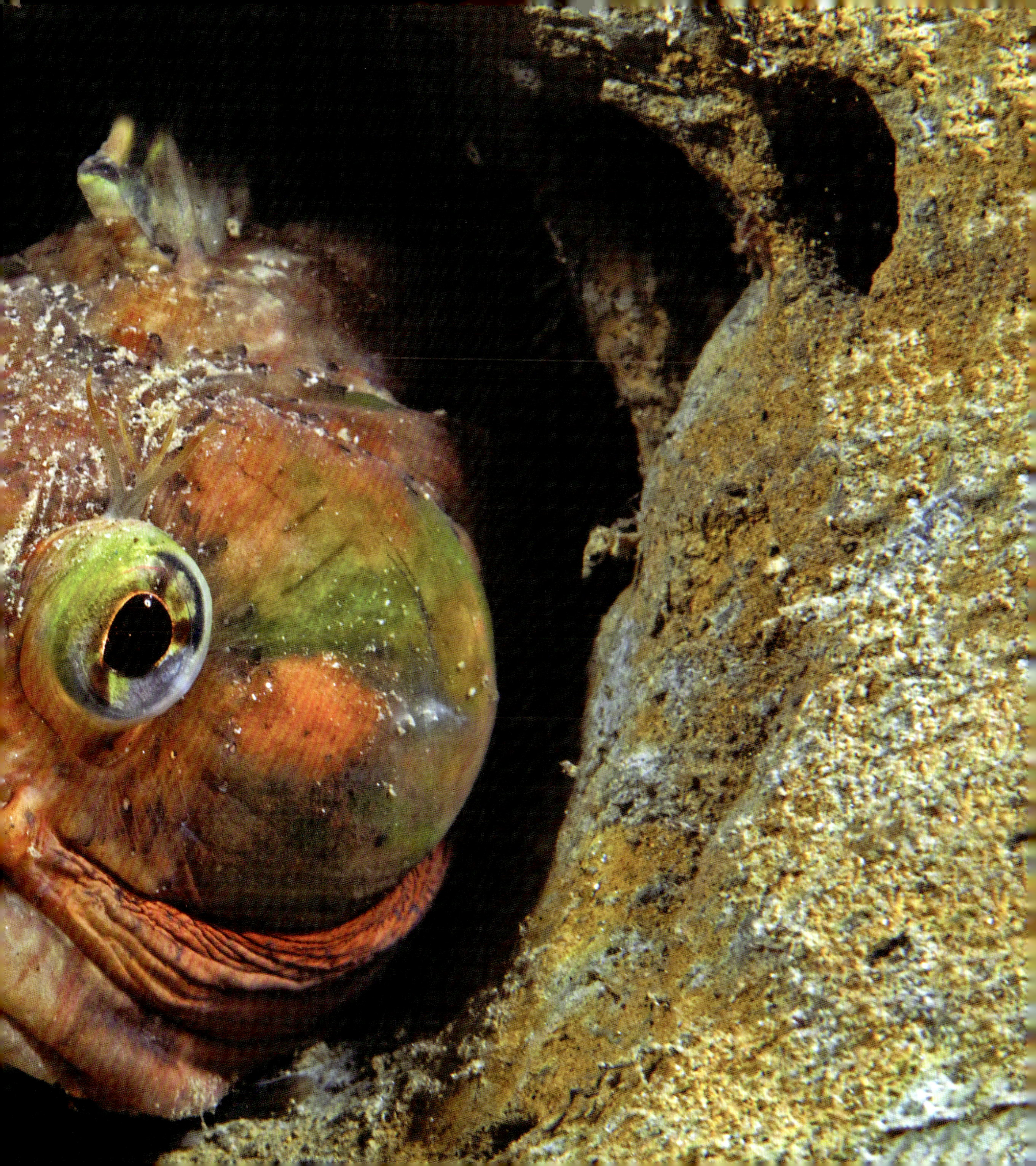

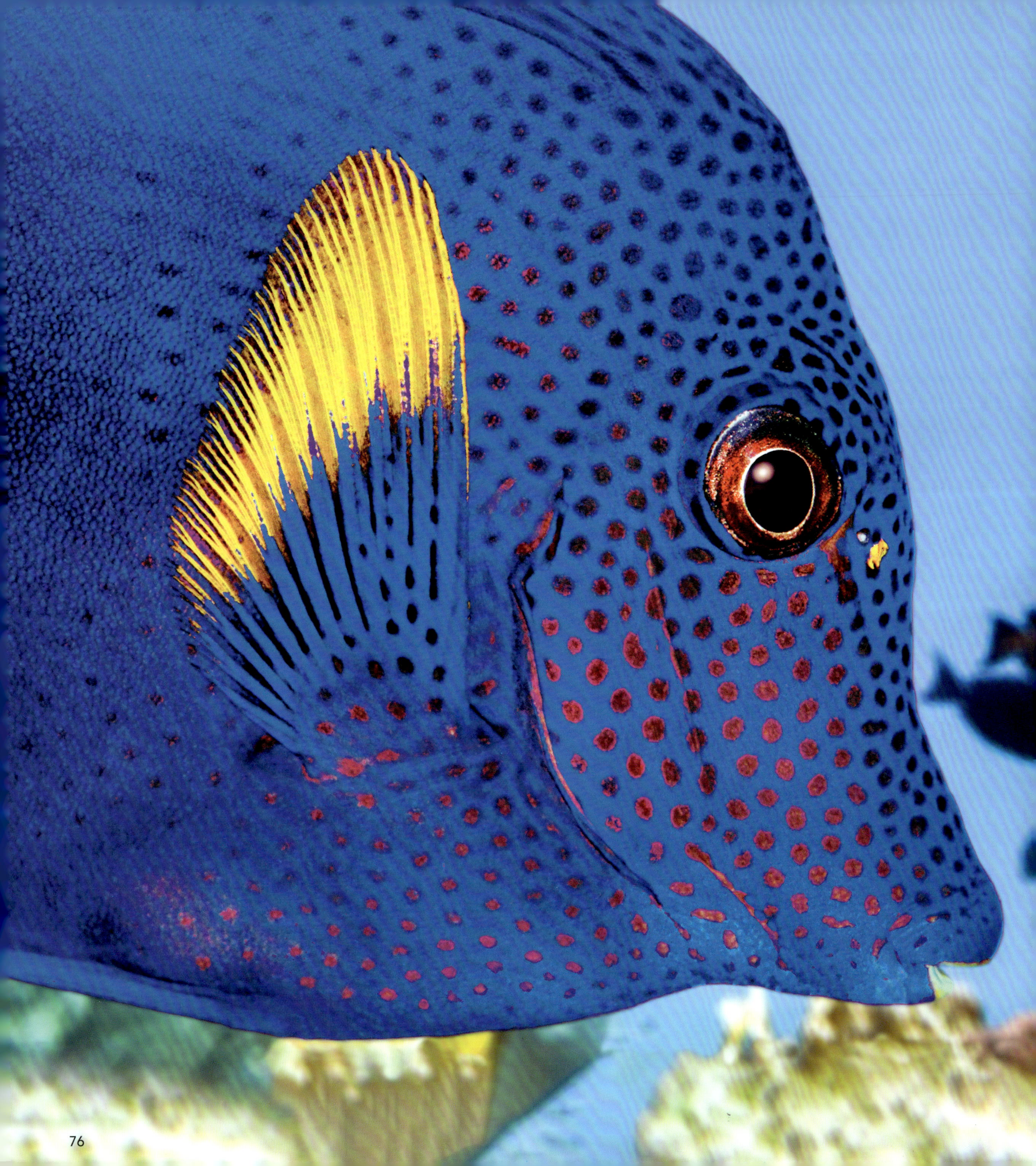

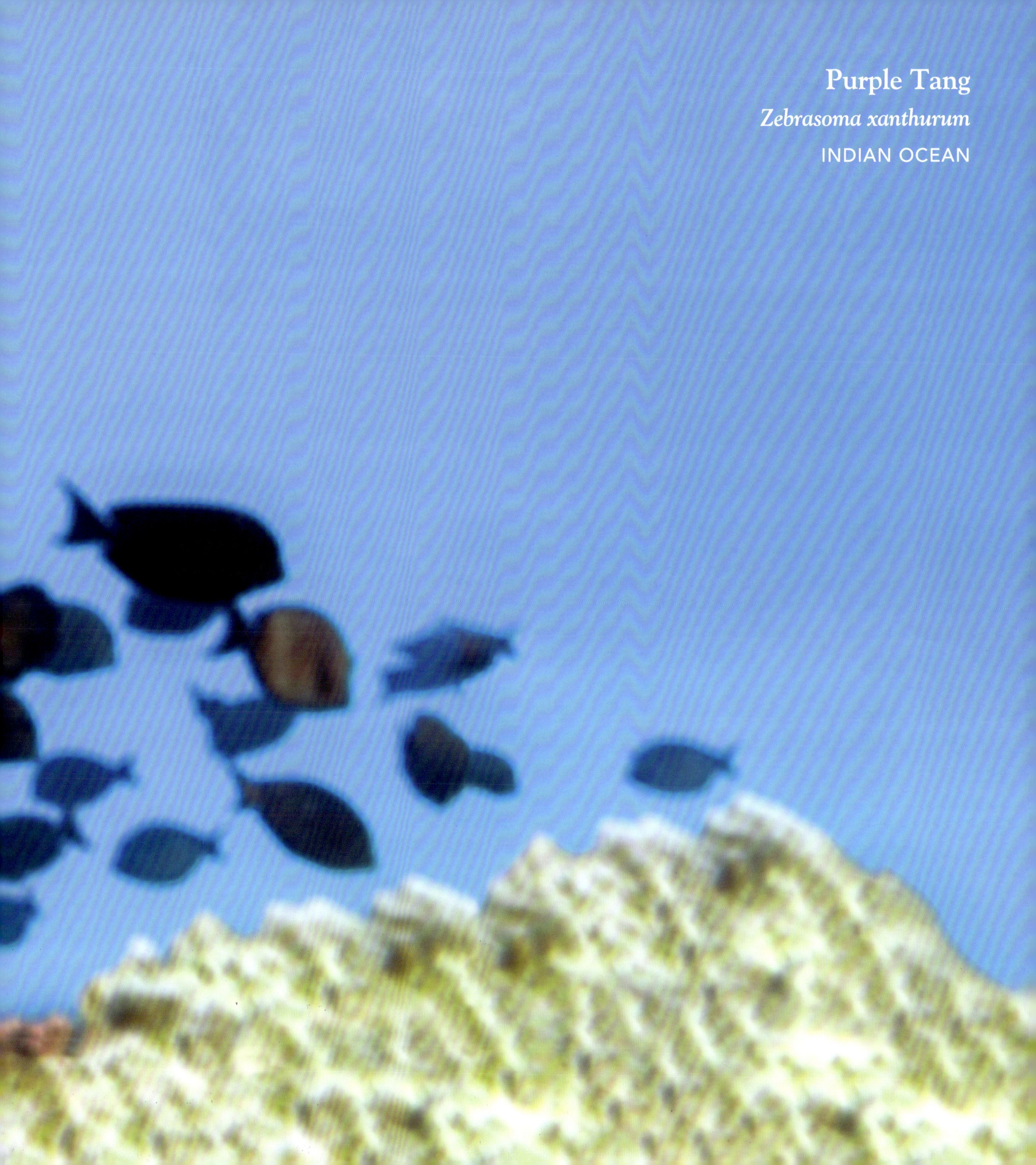

Purple Tang

Zebrasoma xanthurum

INDIAN OCEAN

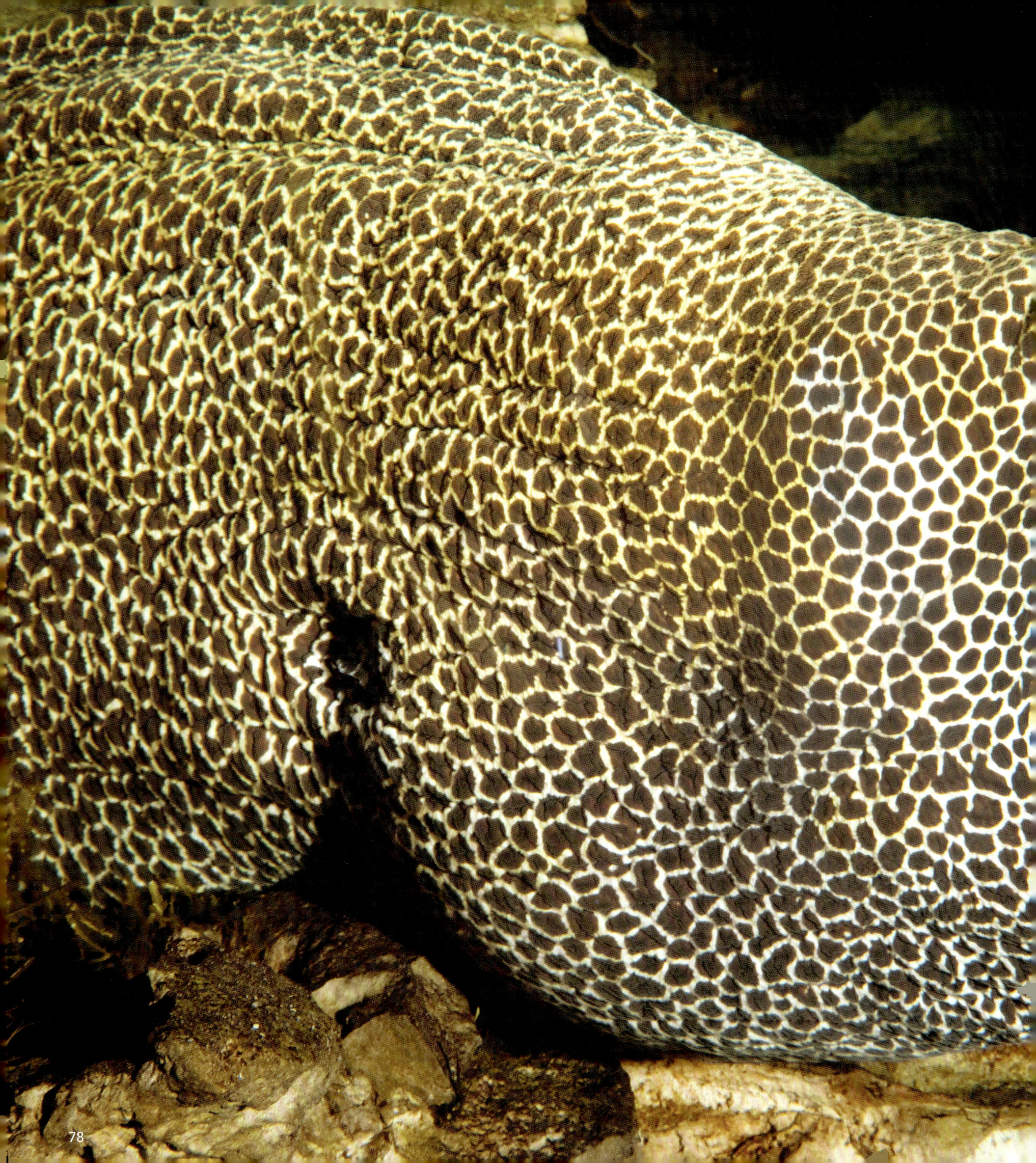

Honeycomb Moray and Bluestreak Cleaner Wrasse

Gymnothorax favagineus and *Labroides dimidiatus*

INDO-PACIFIC

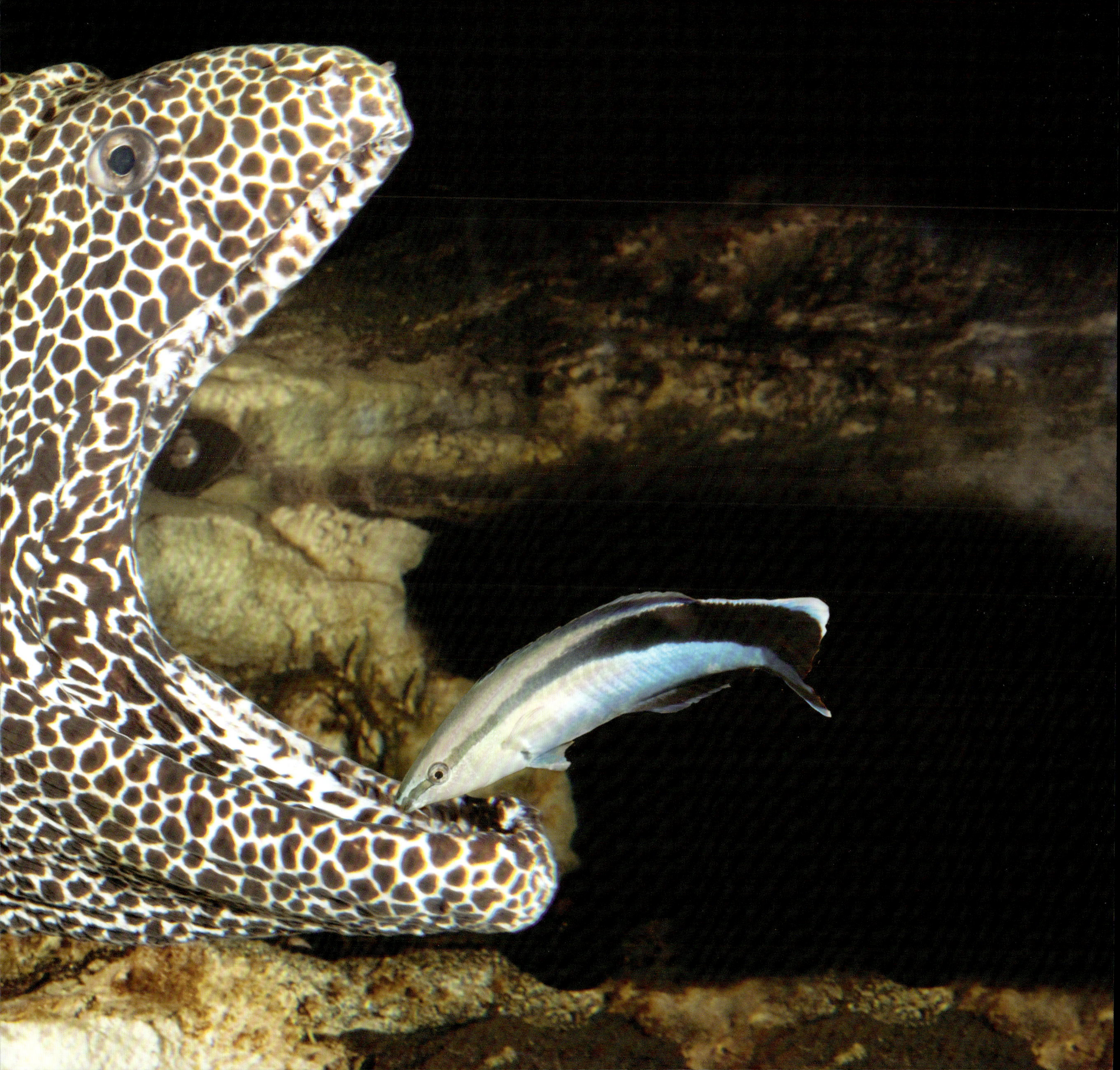

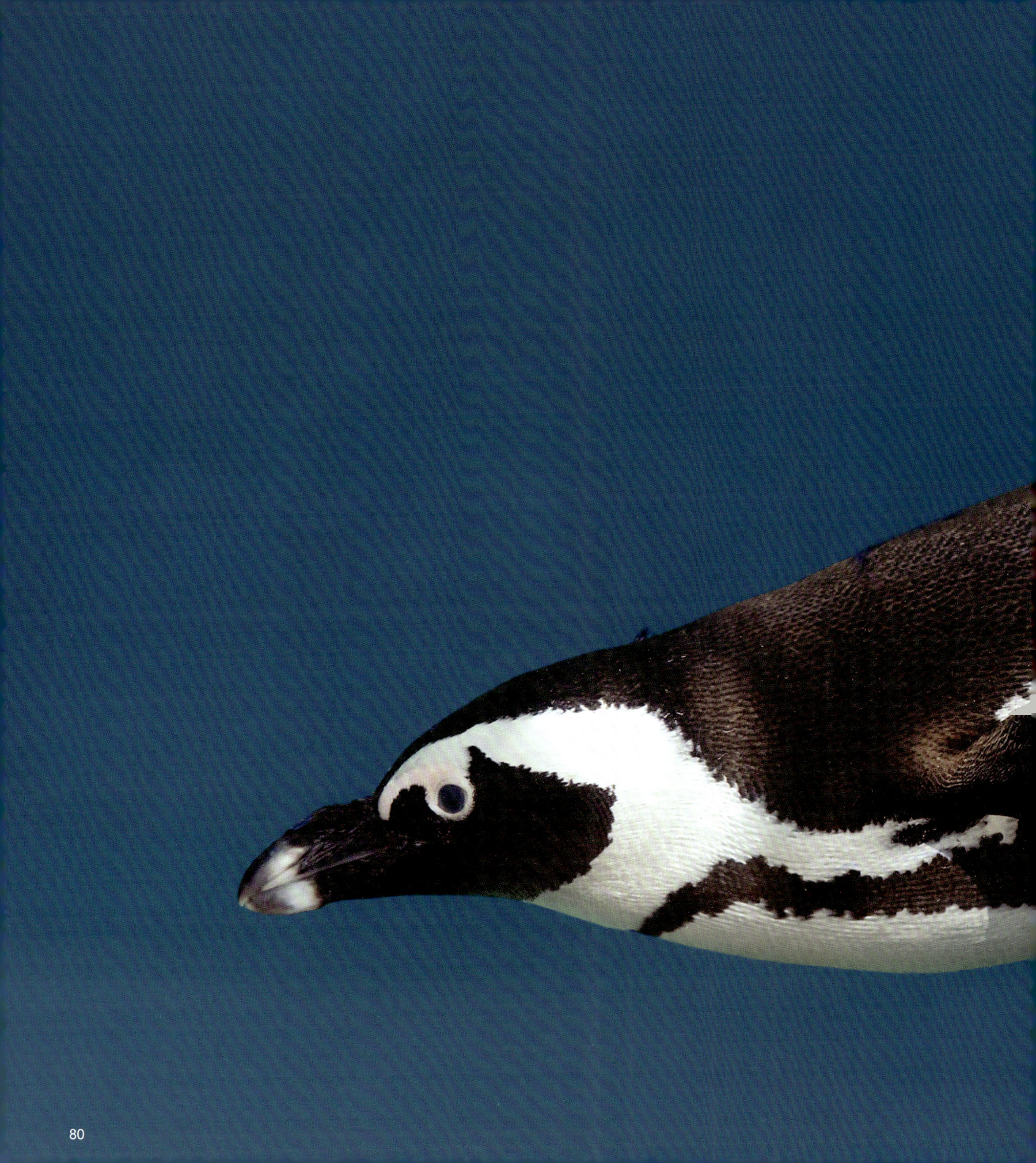

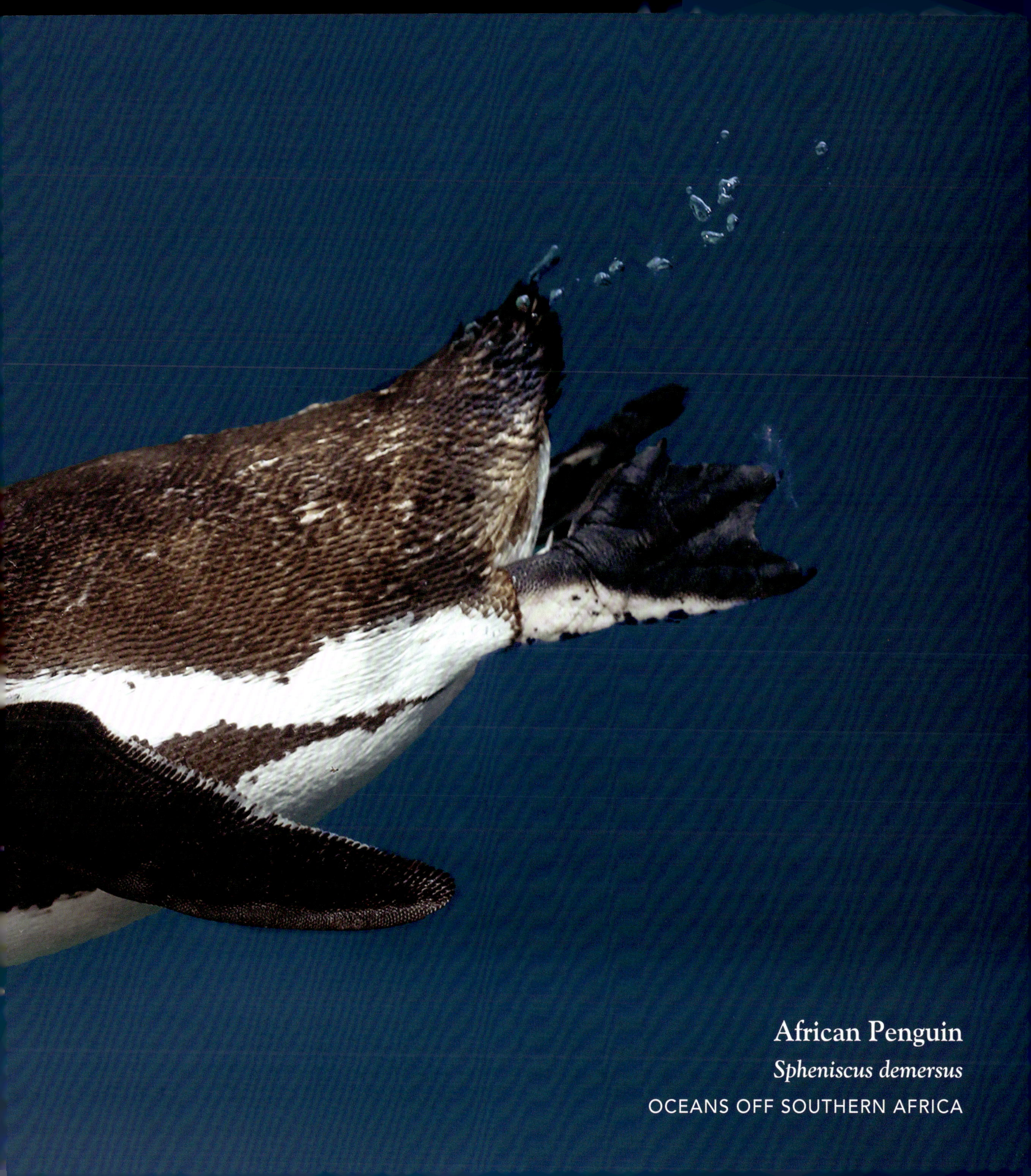

African Penguin

Spheniscus demersus

OCEANS OFF SOUTHERN AFRICA

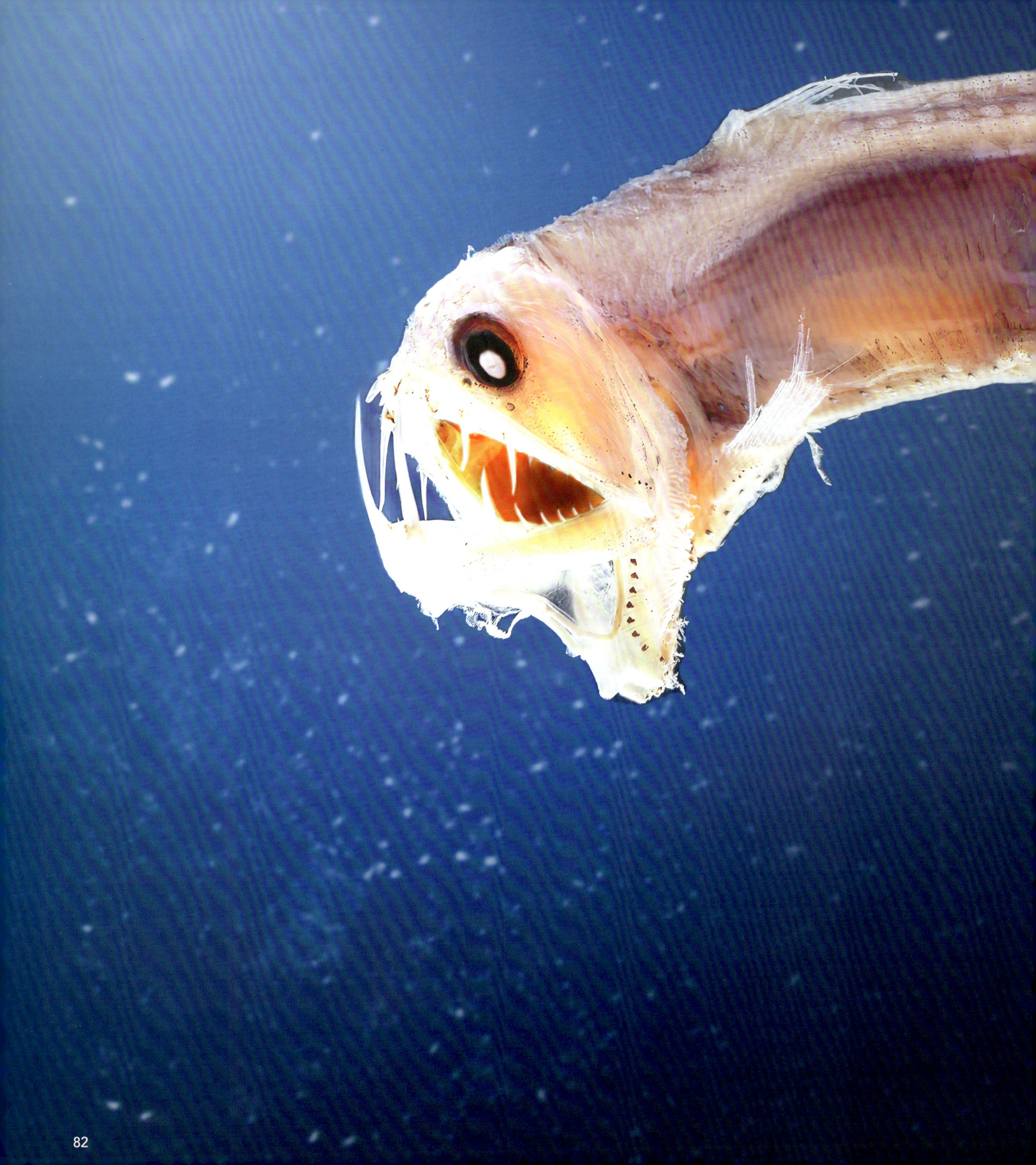

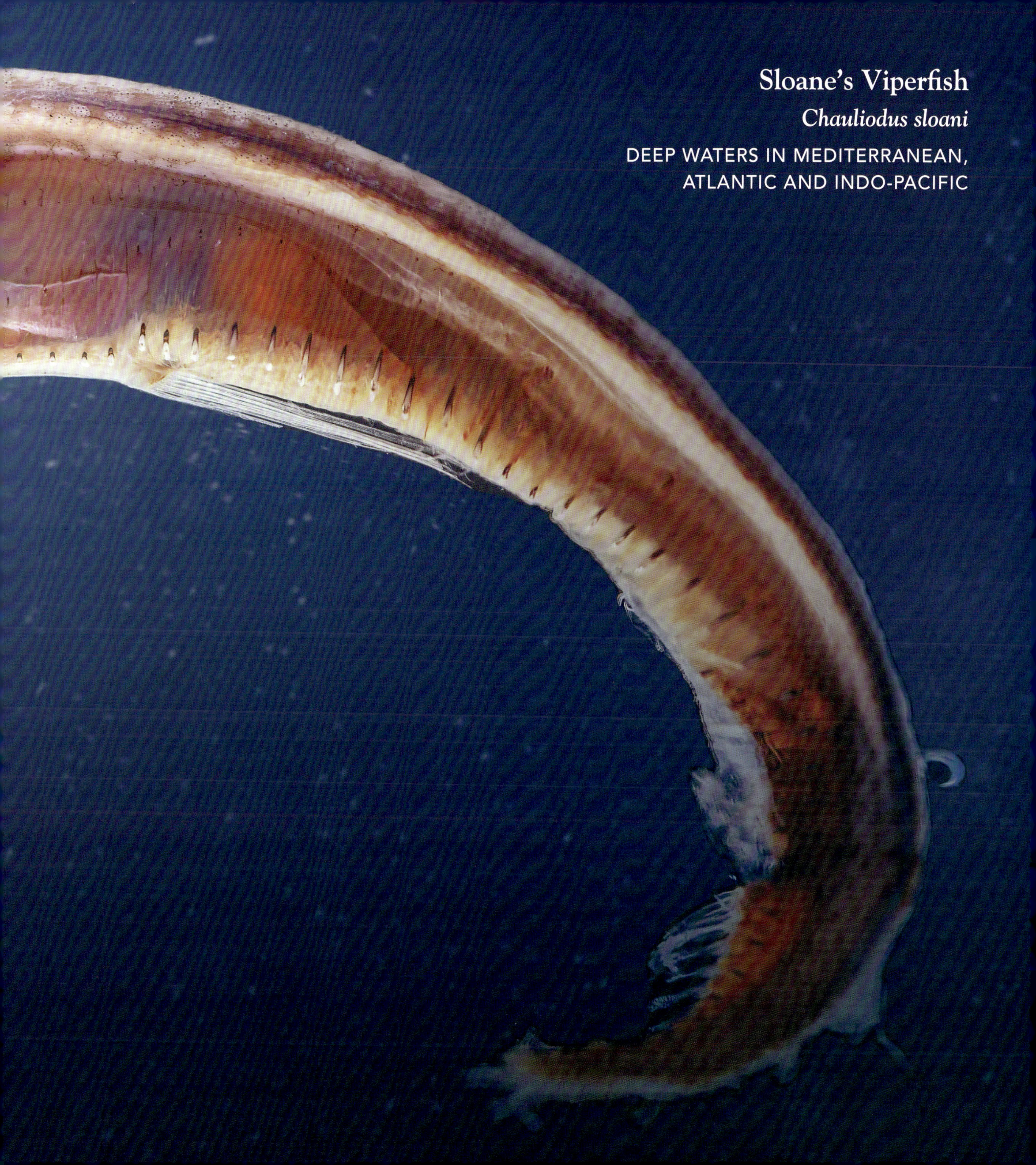

Sloane's Viperfish

Chauliodus sloani

DEEP WATERS IN MEDITERRANEAN,
ATLANTIC AND INDO-PACIFIC

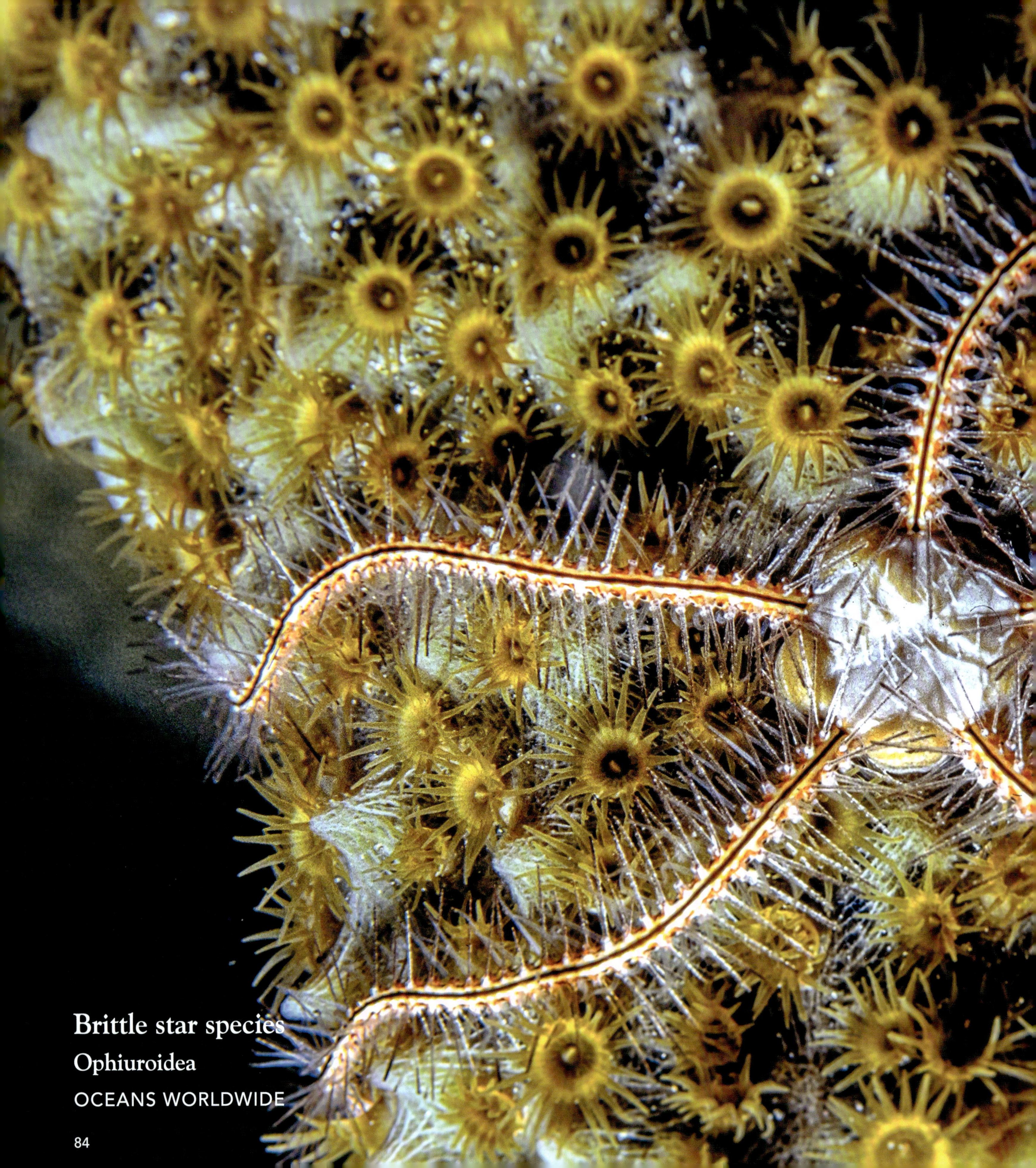

Brittle star species

Ophiuroidea

OCEANS WORLDWIDE

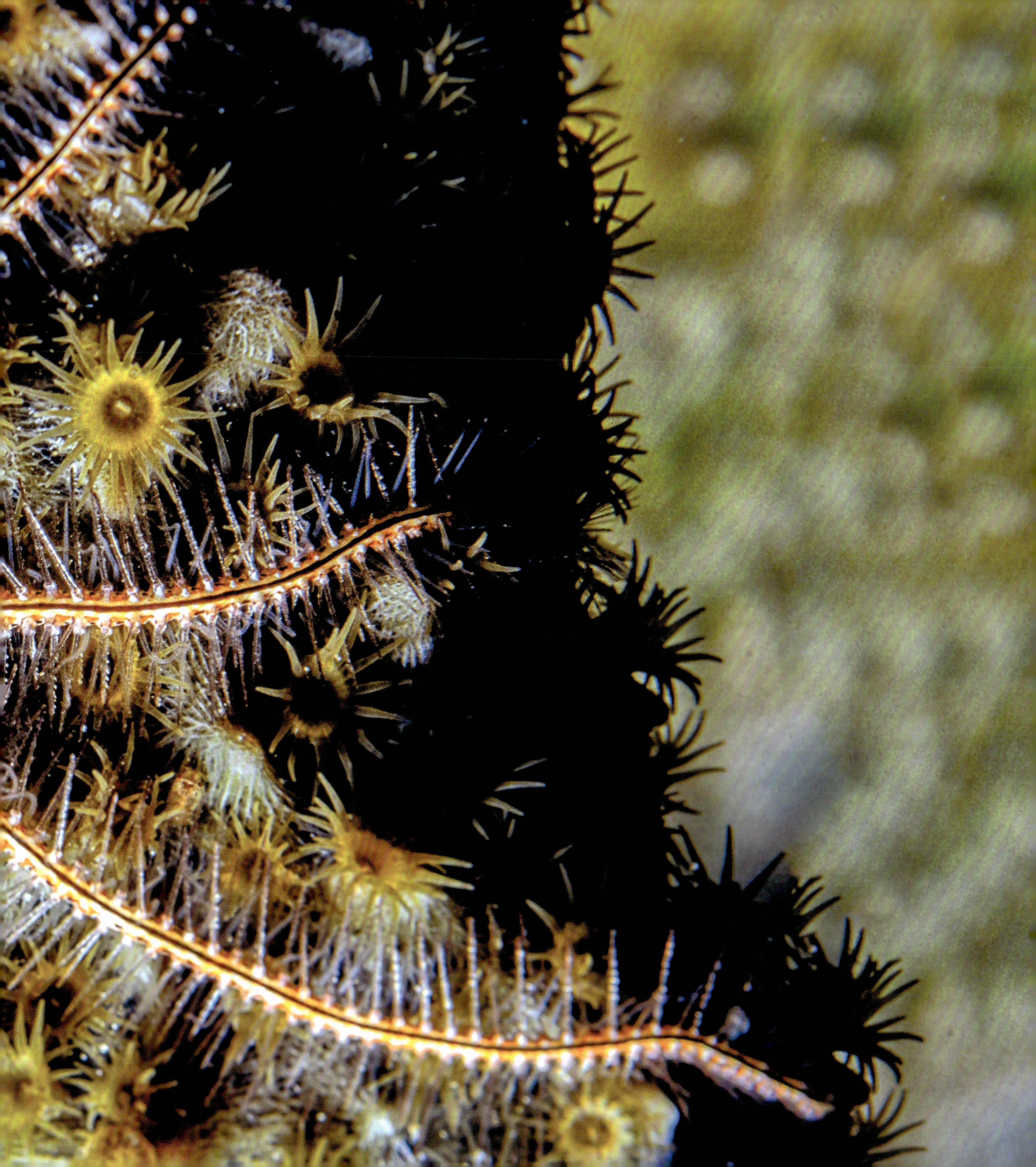

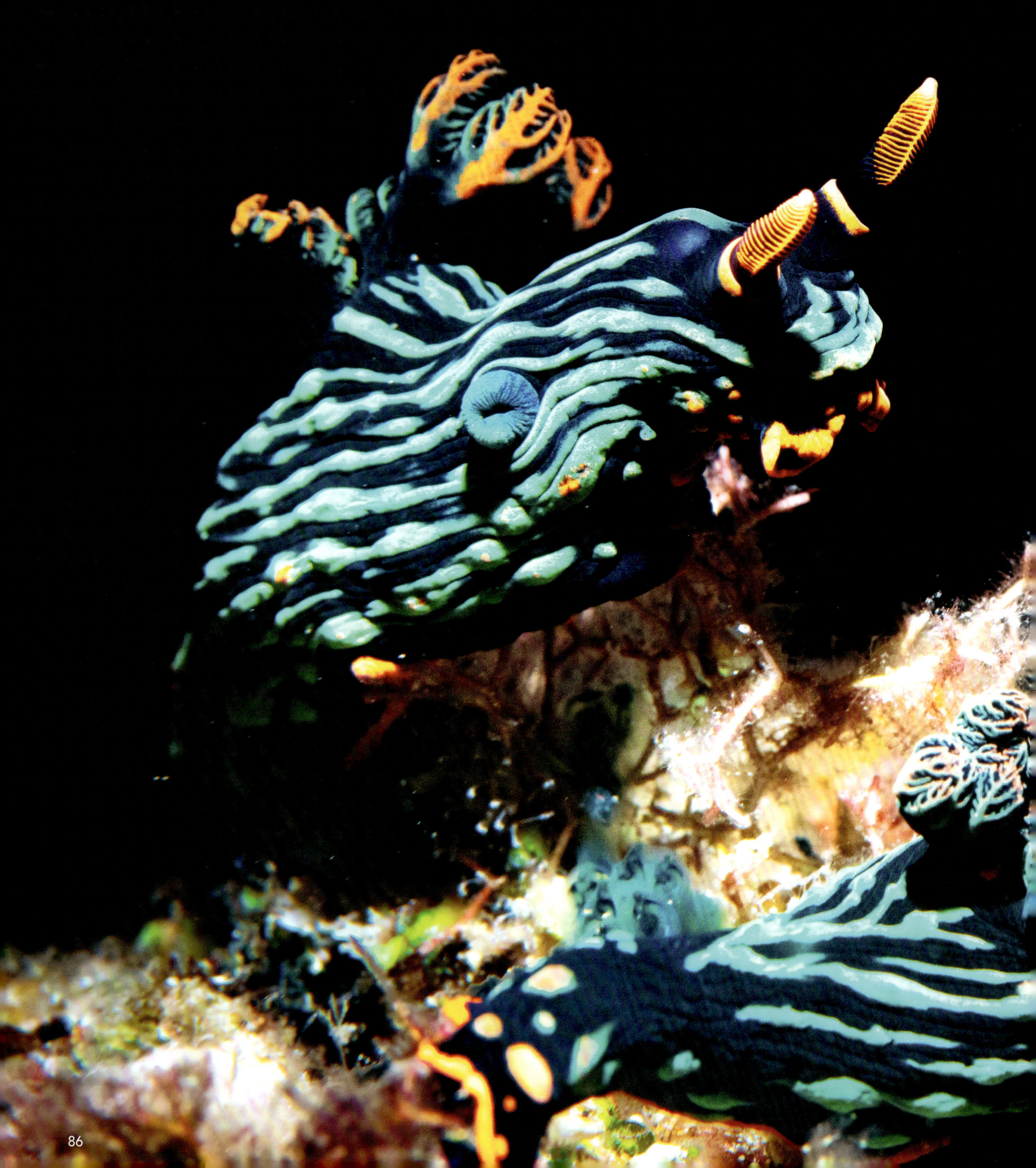

Nudibranch species

Nudibranchia

TROPICAL OCEANS

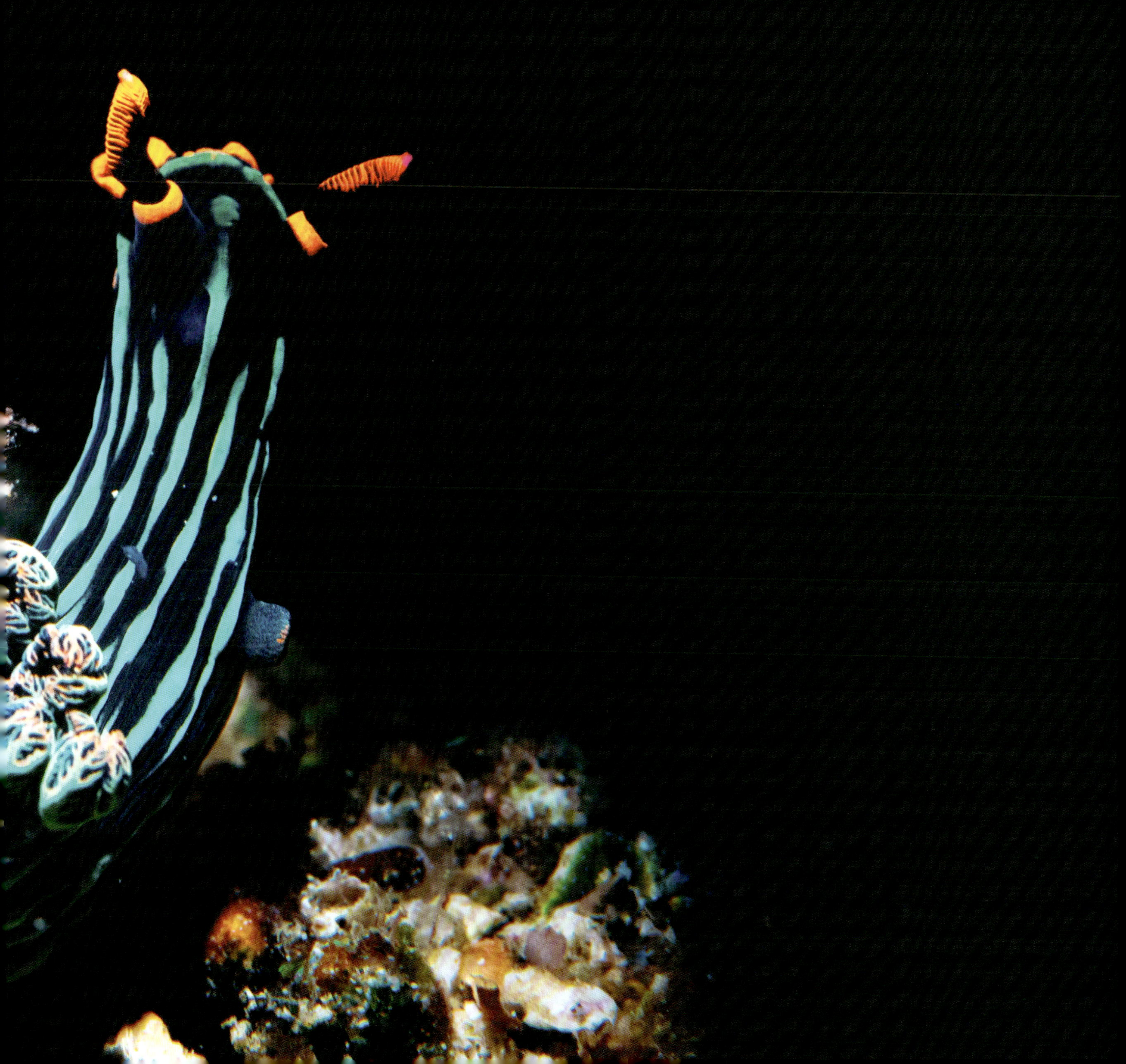

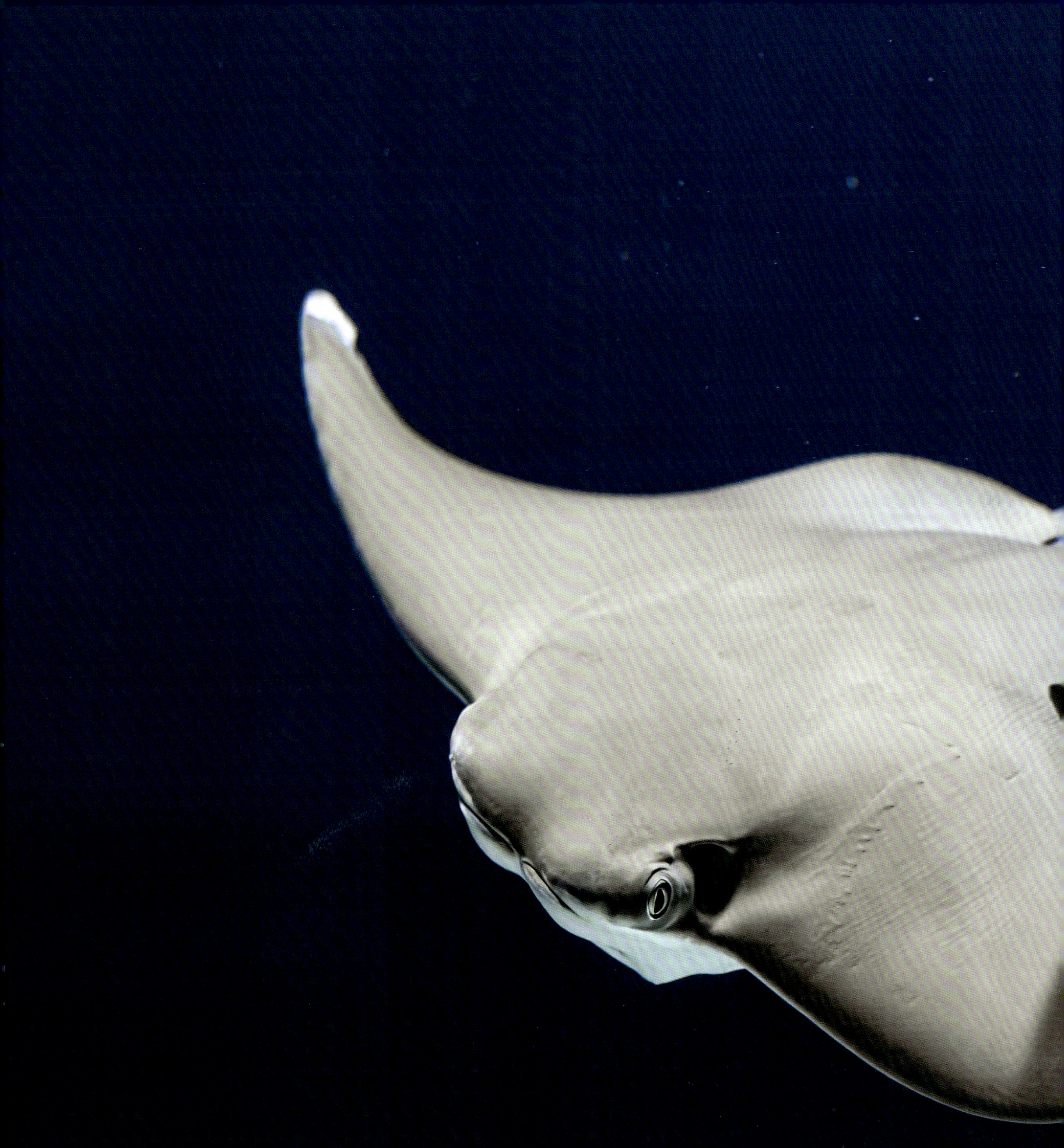

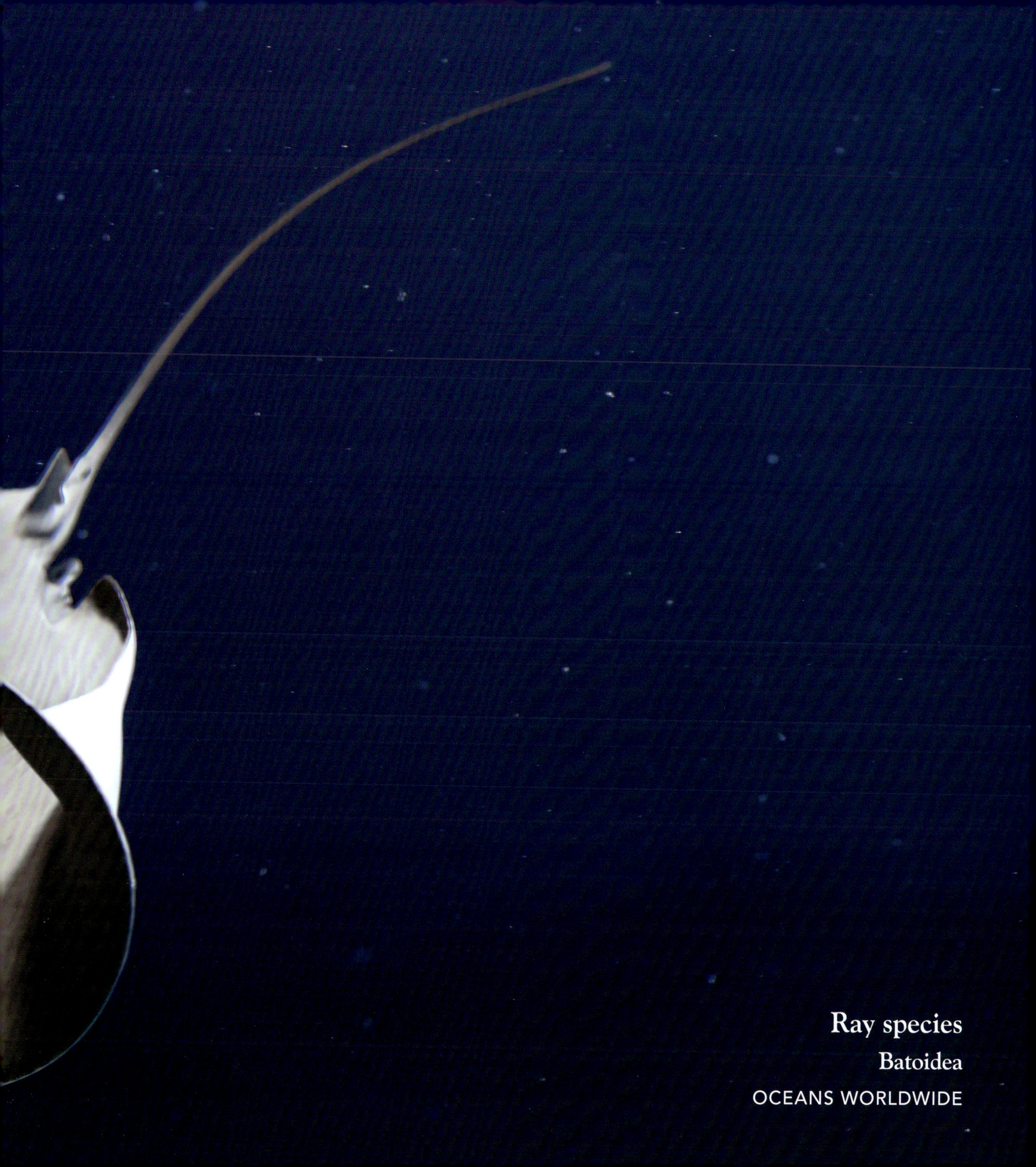

Ray species

Batoidea

OCEANS WORLDWIDE

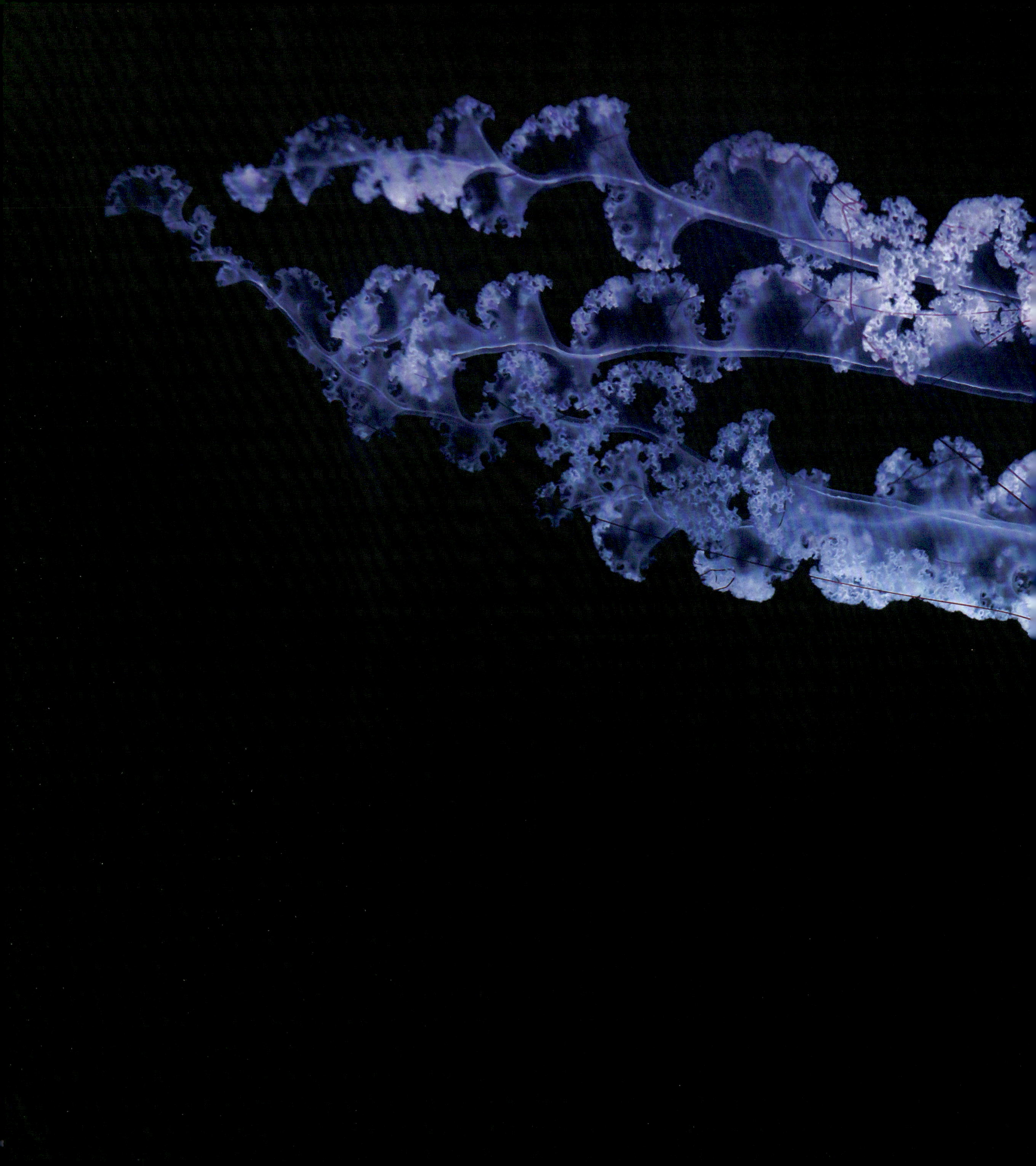

Purple-striped Jellyfish

Chrysaora colorata

NORTH-EAST ATLANTIC OCEAN

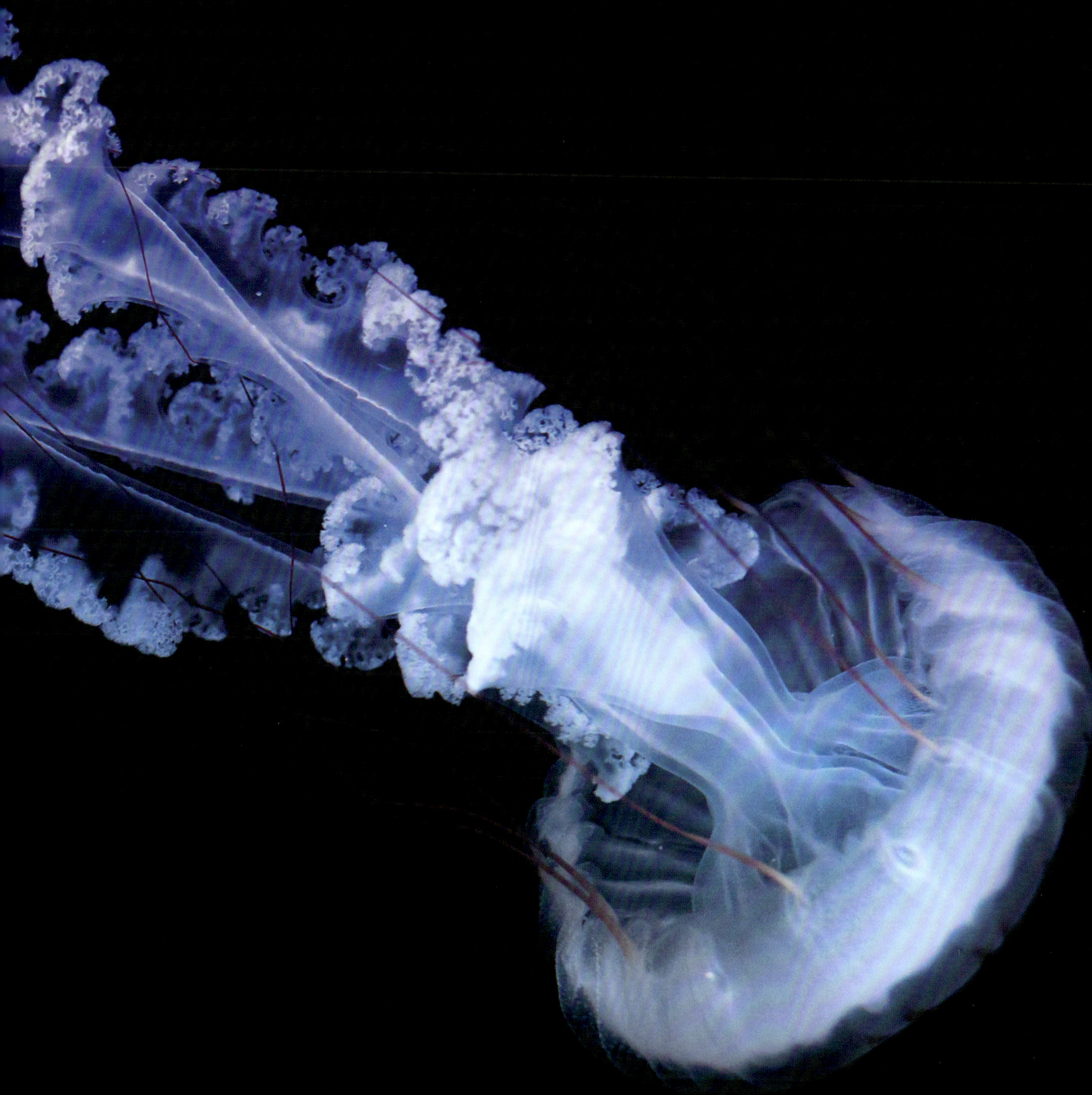

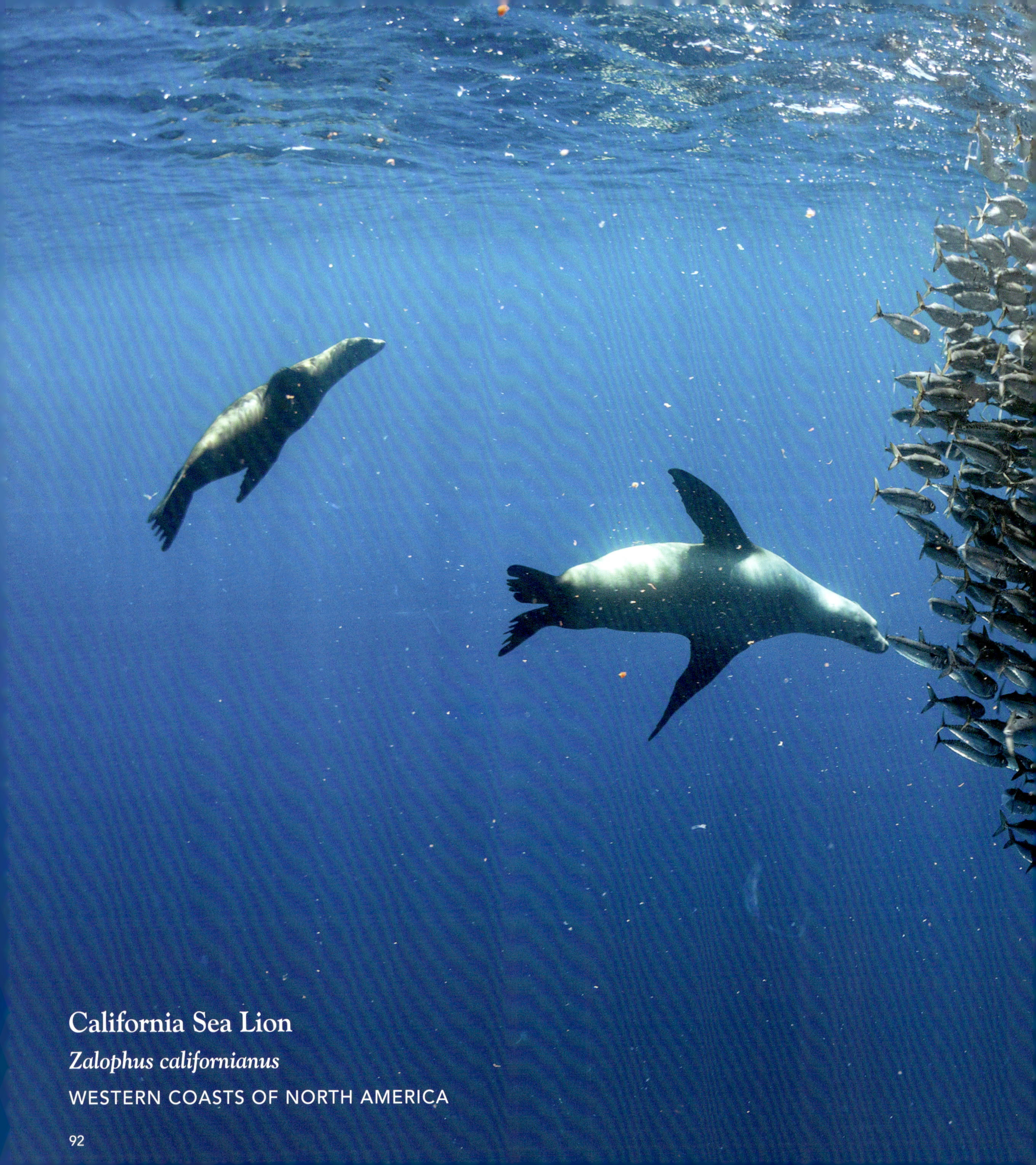

California Sea Lion

Zalophus californianus

WESTERN COASTS OF NORTH AMERICA

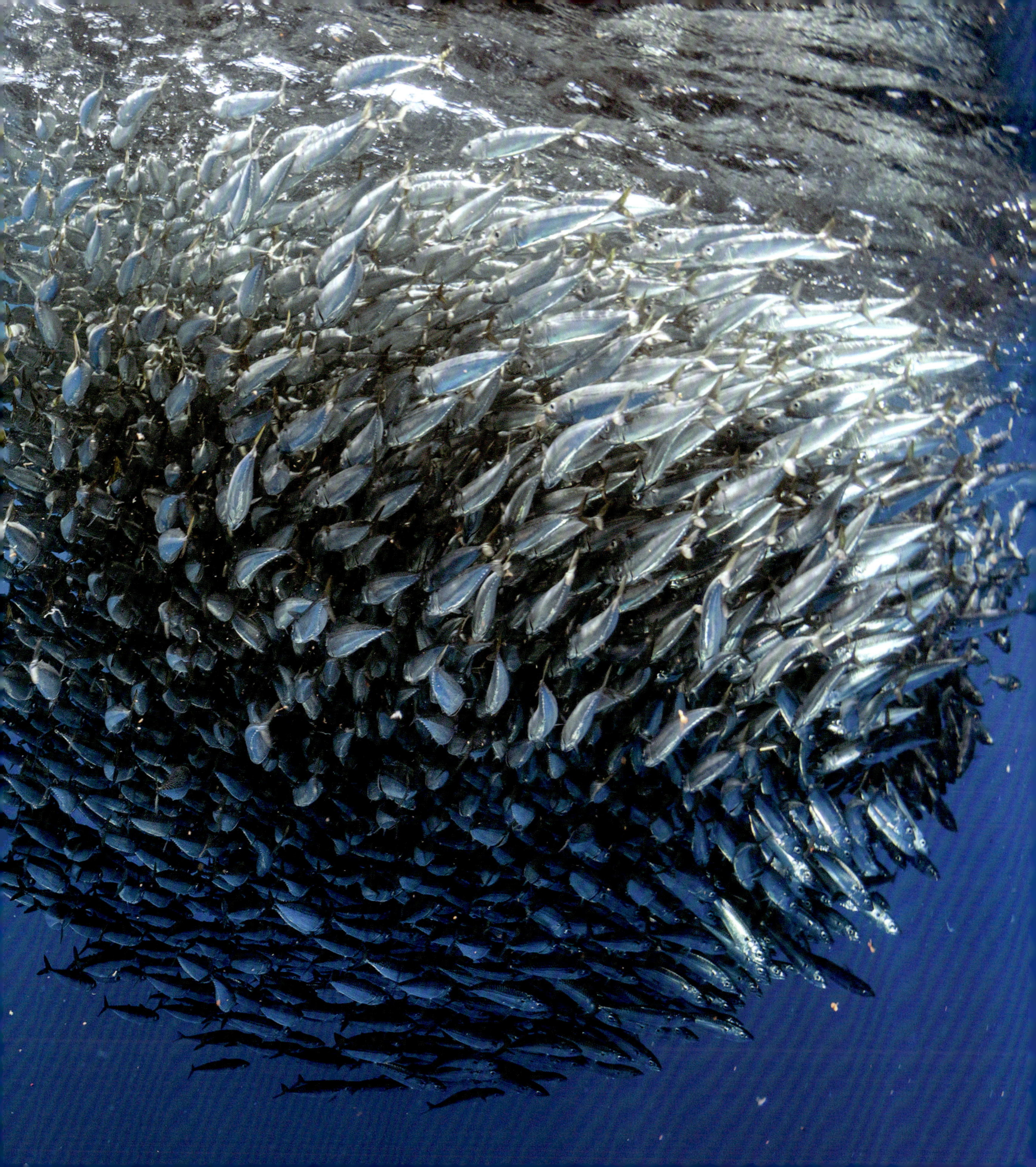

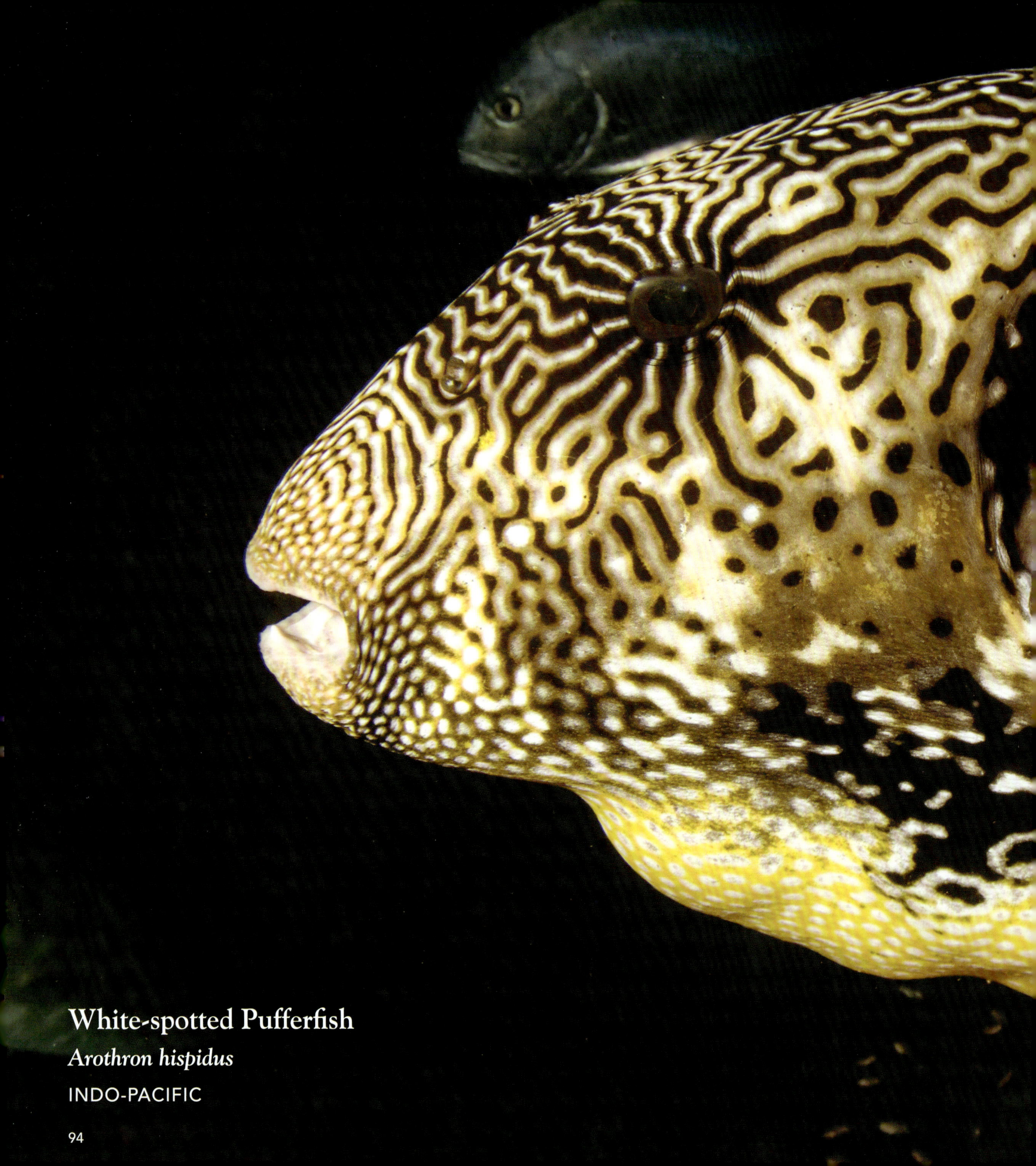

White-spotted Pufferfish

Arothron hispidus

INDO-PACIFIC

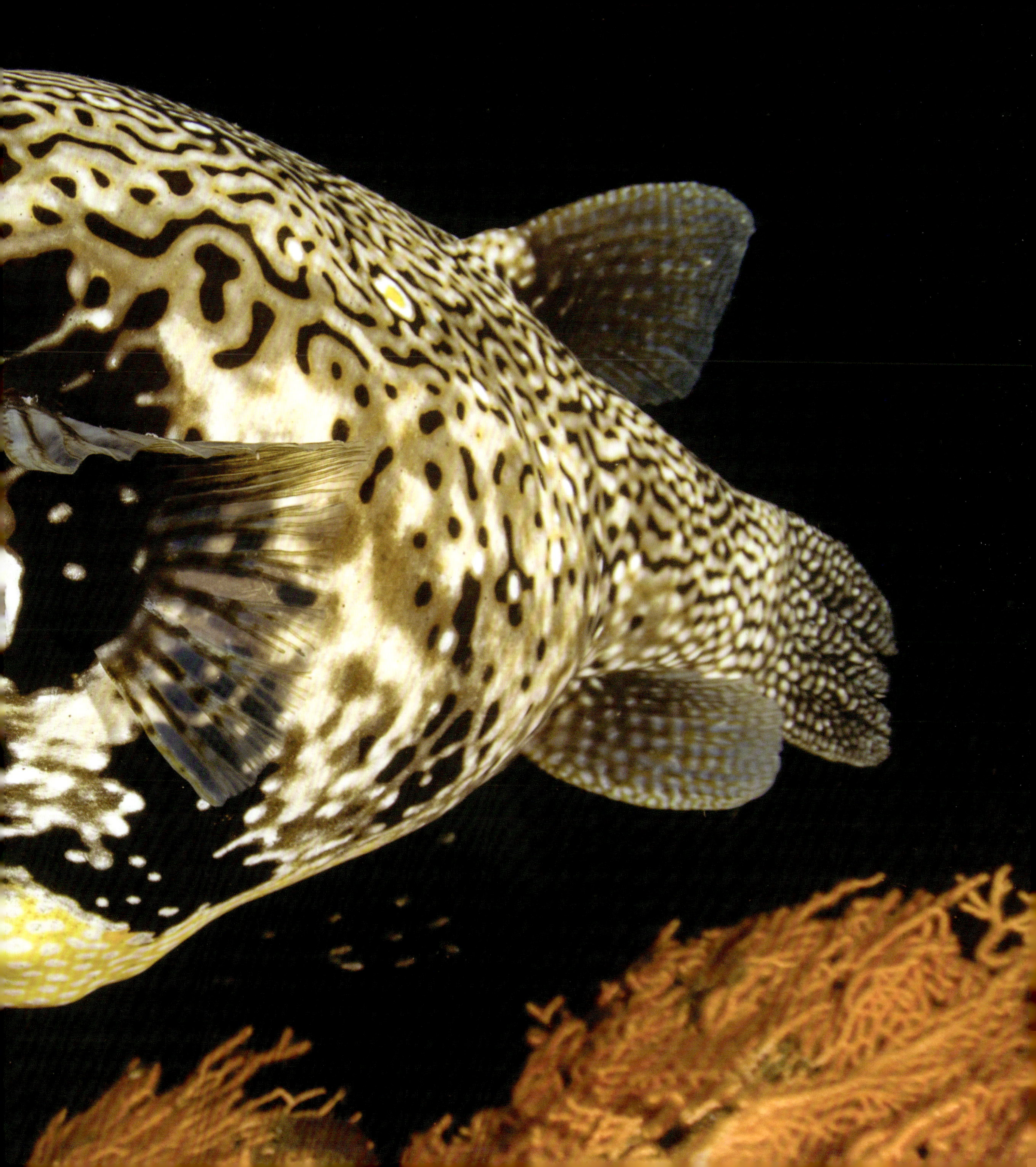

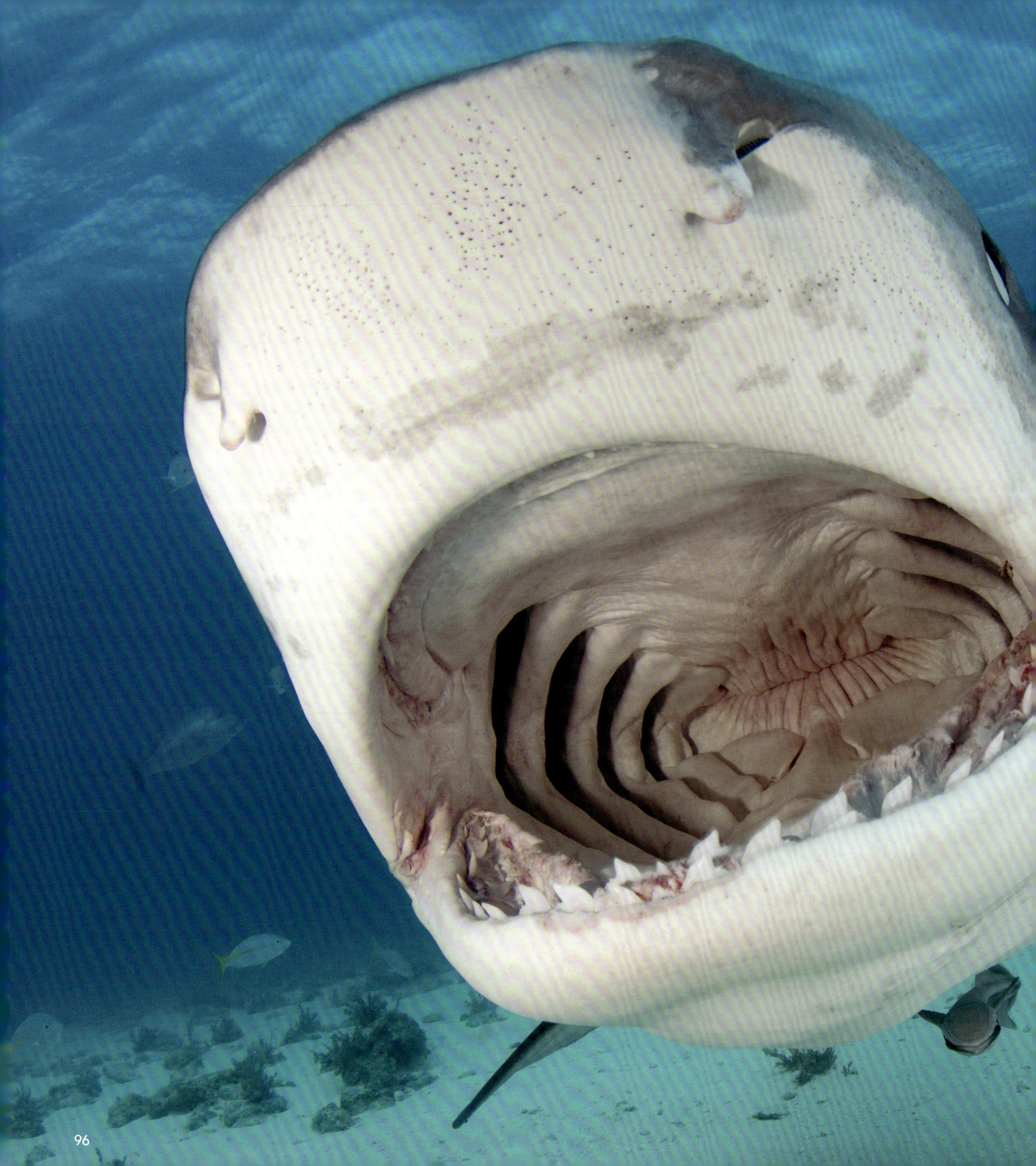

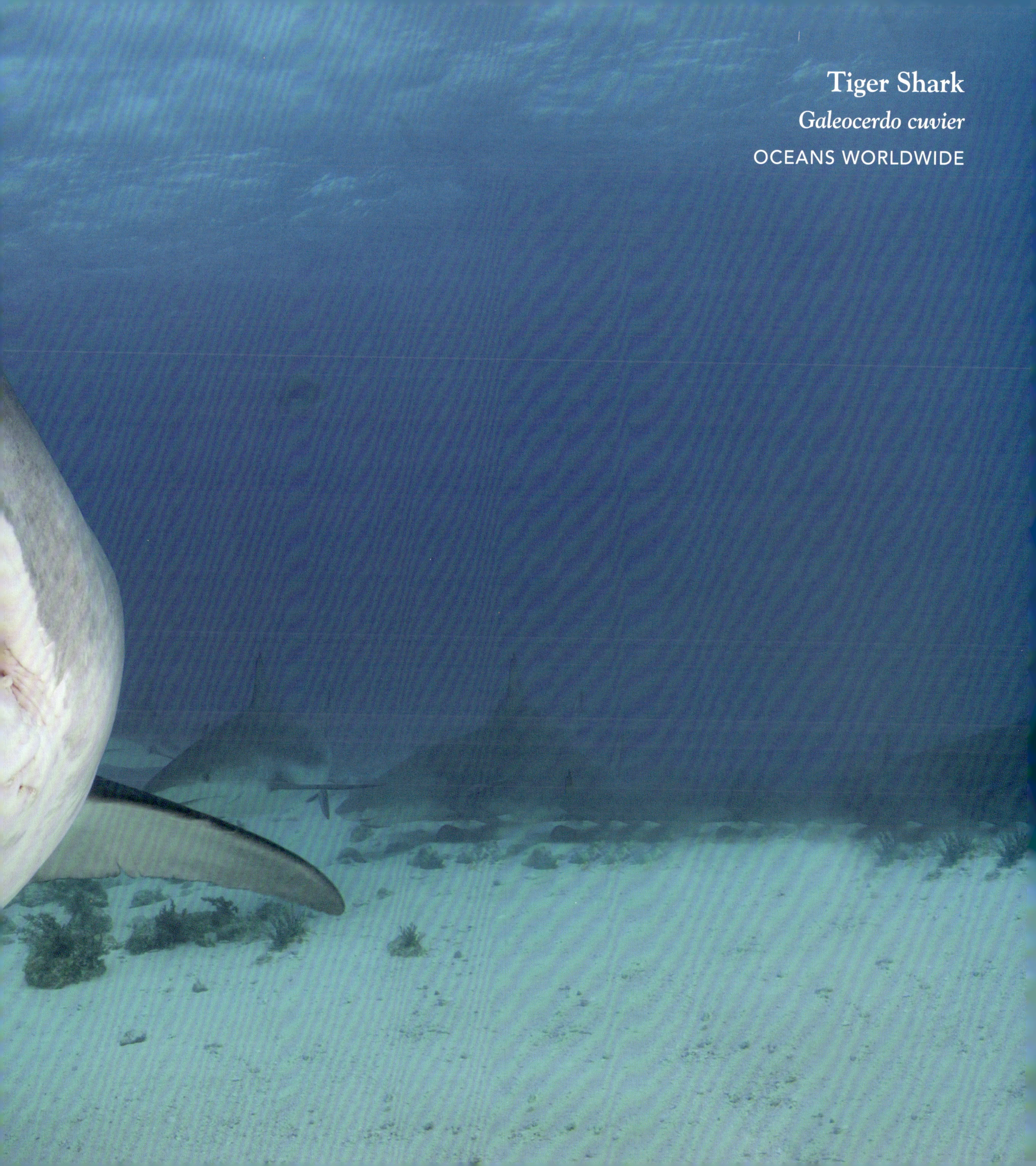

Tiger Shark

Galeocerdo cuvier

OCEANS WORLDWIDE

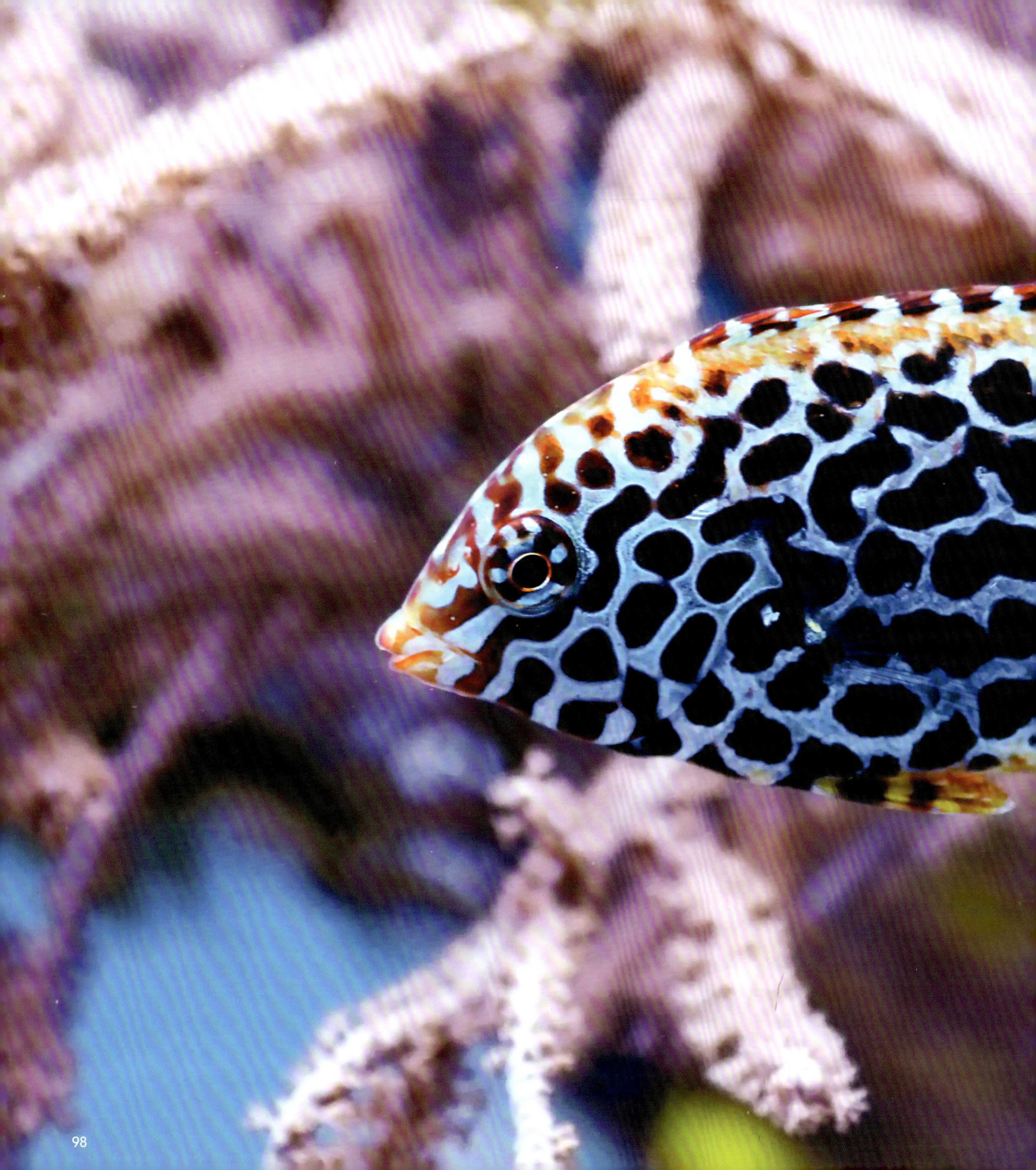

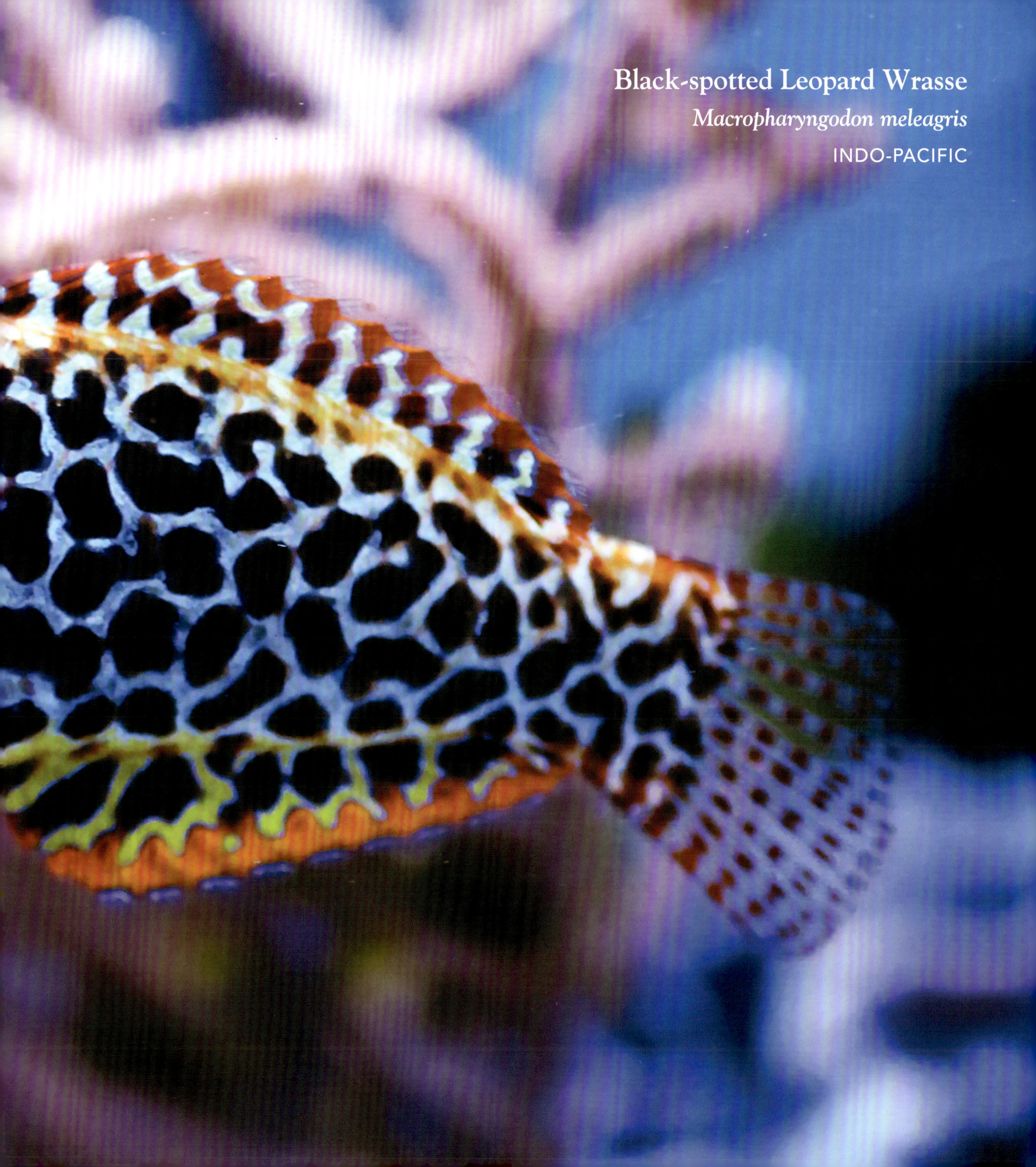
Black-spotted Leopard Wrasse
Macropharyngodon meleagris
INDO-PACIFIC

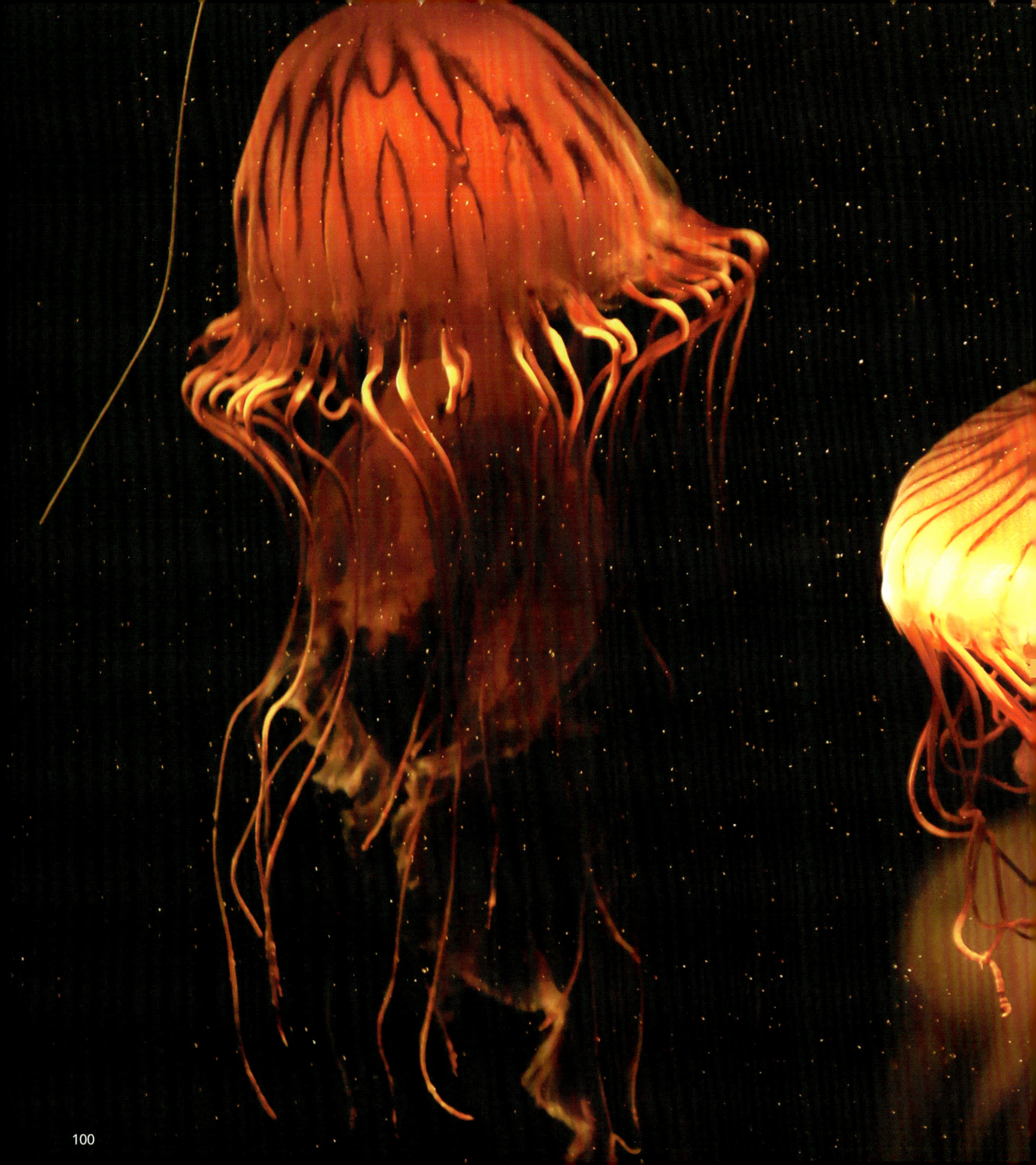

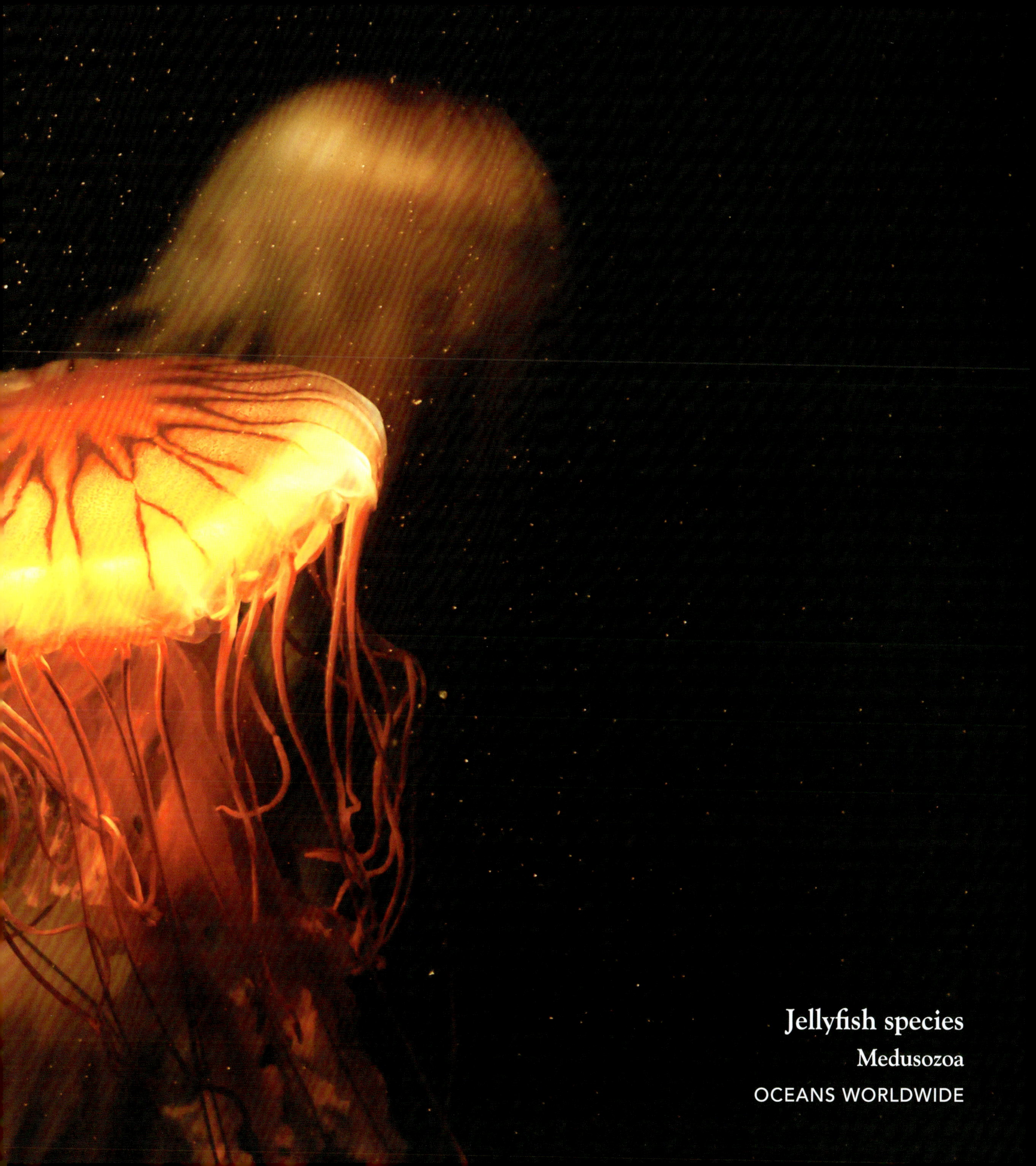

Jellyfish species

Medusozoa

OCEANS WORLDWIDE

Pipefish species

Syngnathinae

OCEANS WORLDWIDE

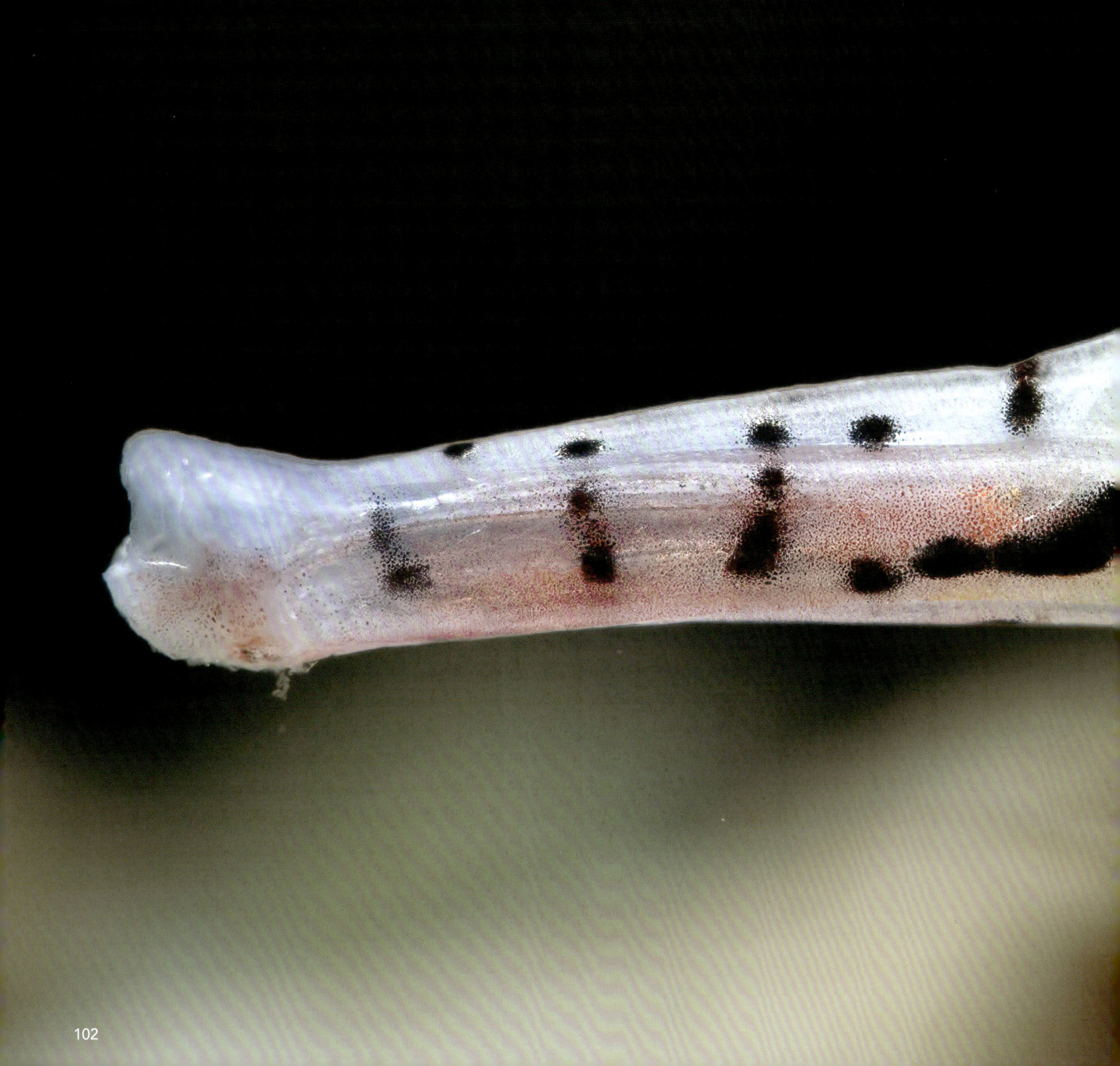

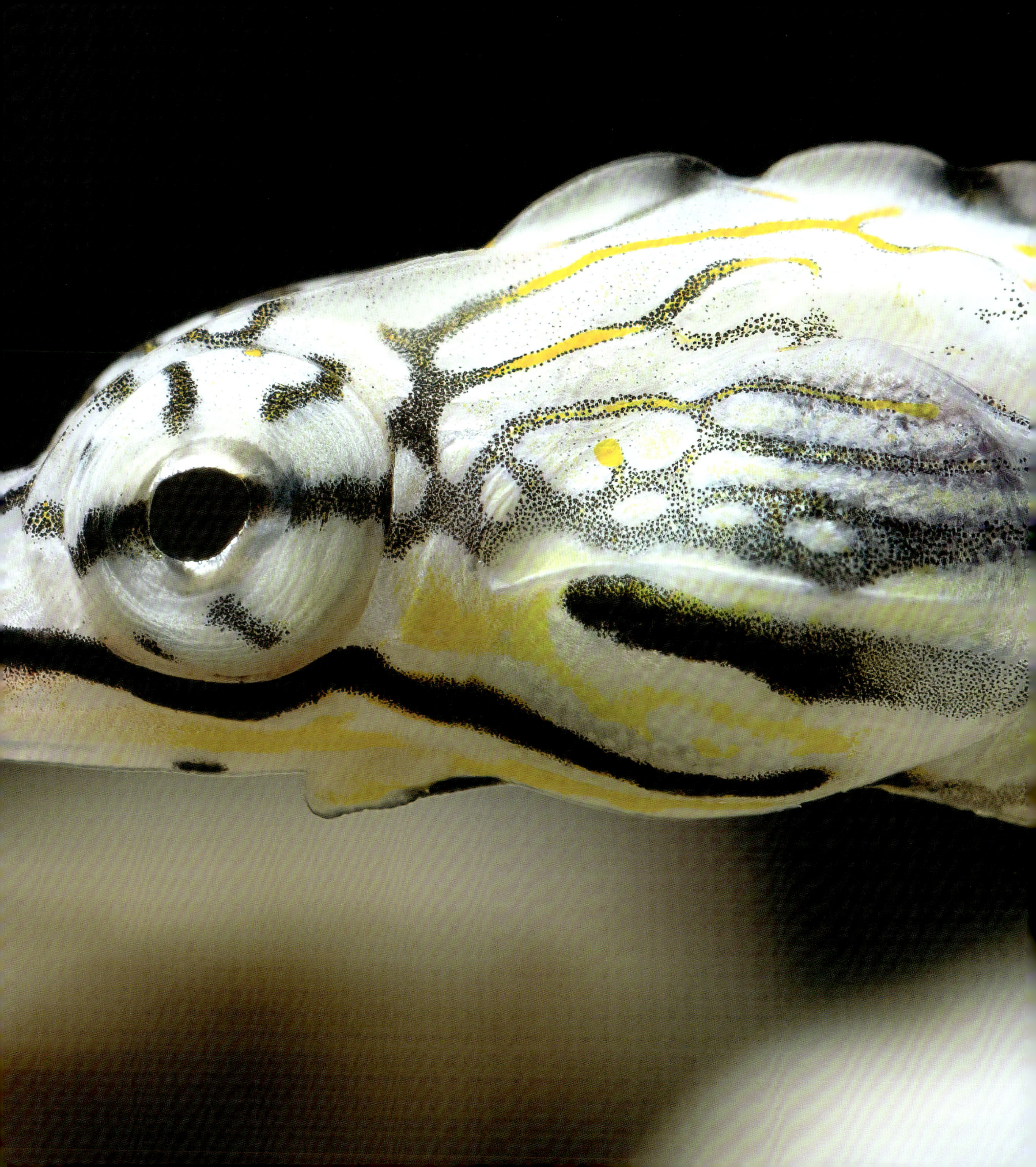

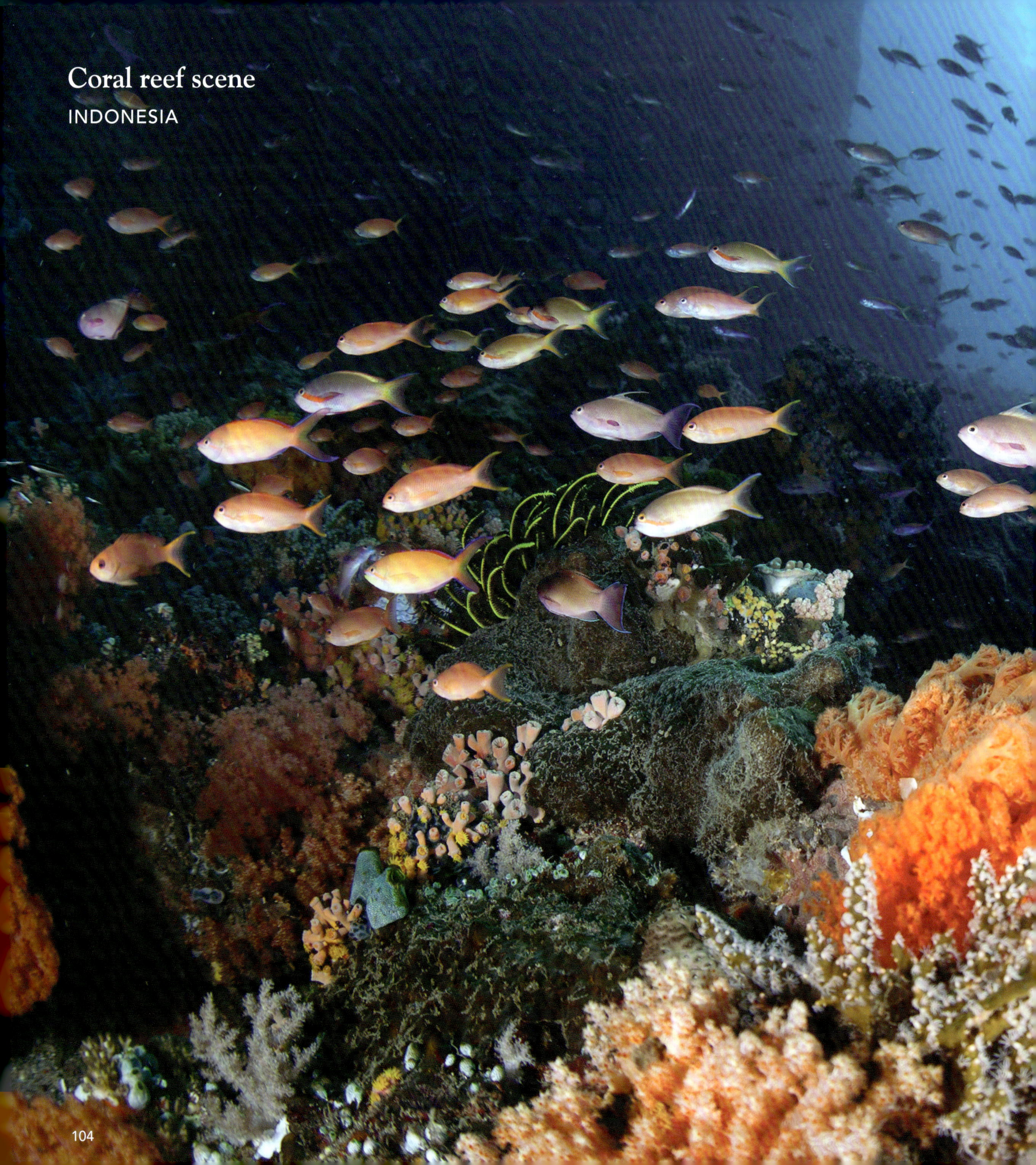

Coral reef scene

INDONESIA

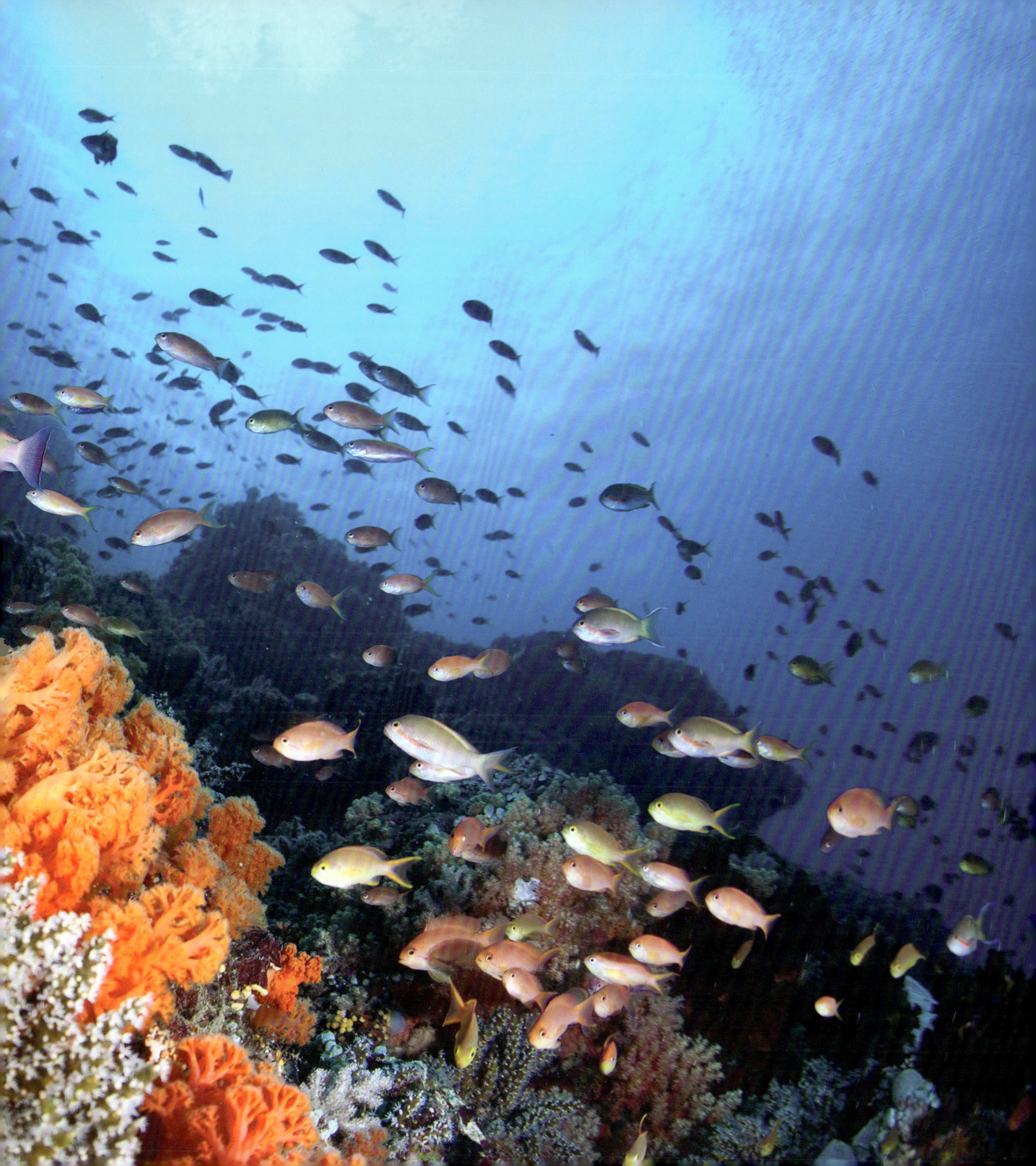

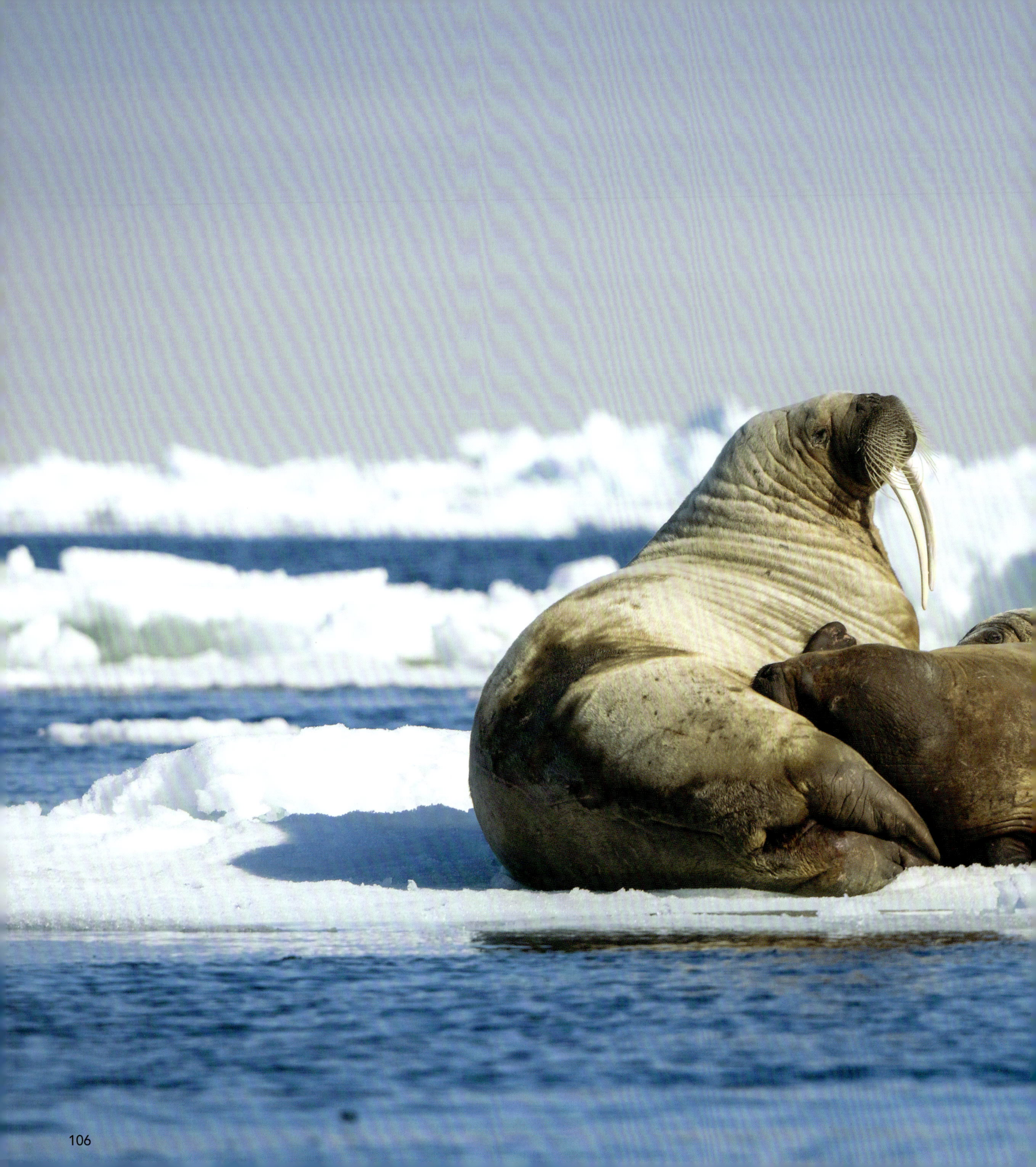

Walrus

Odobenus rosmarus

ARCTIC AND SUBARCTIC OCEANS

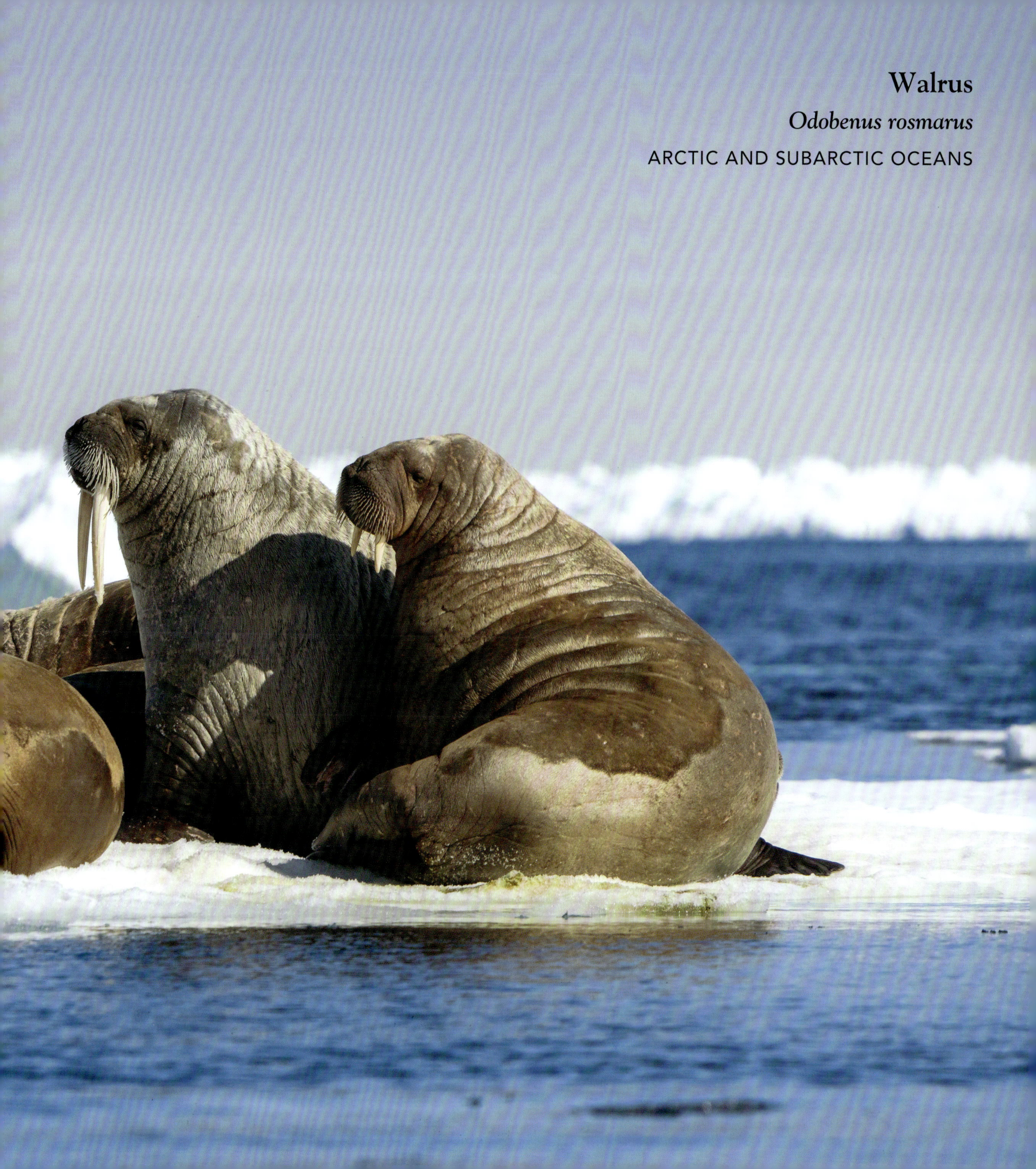

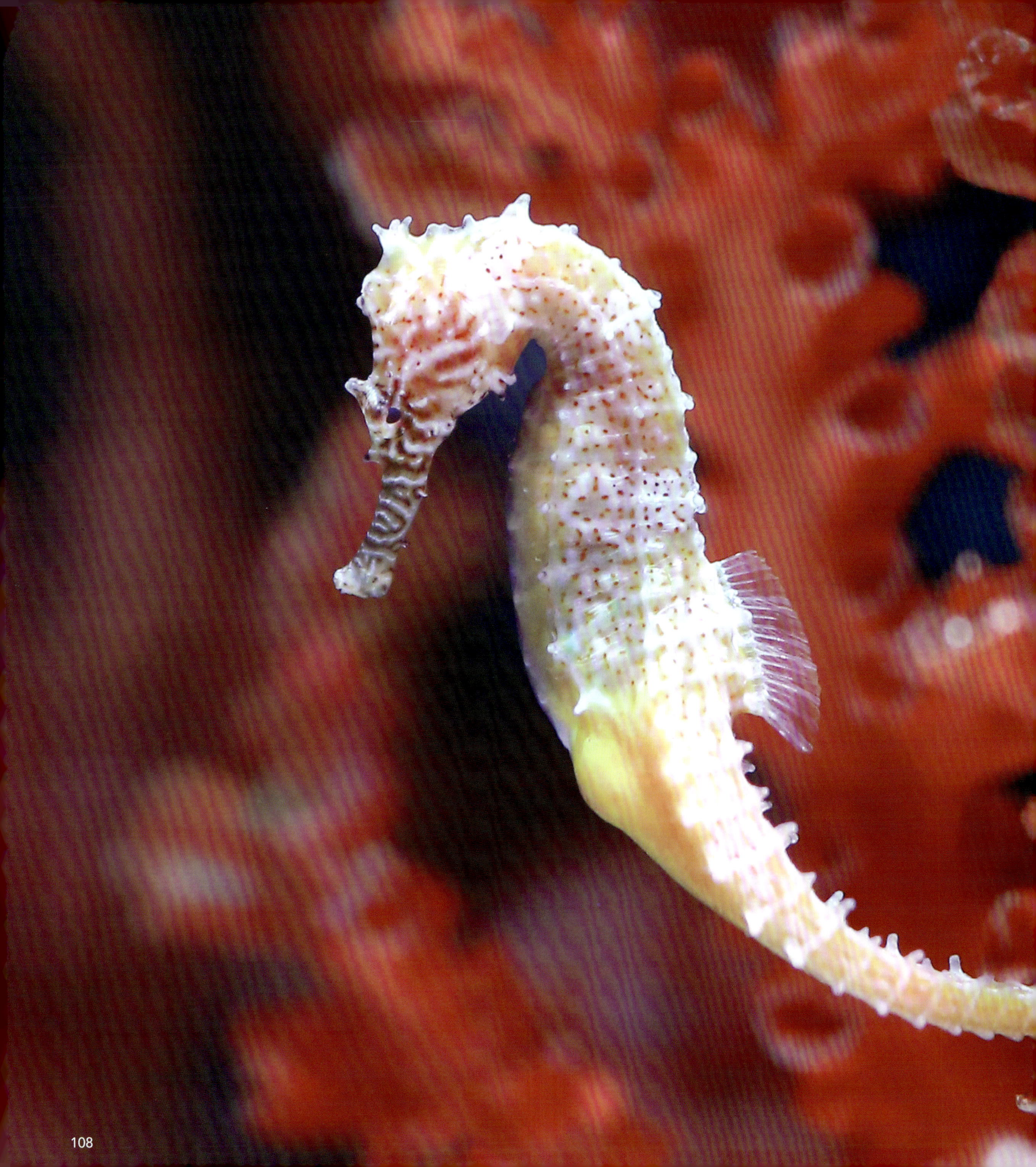

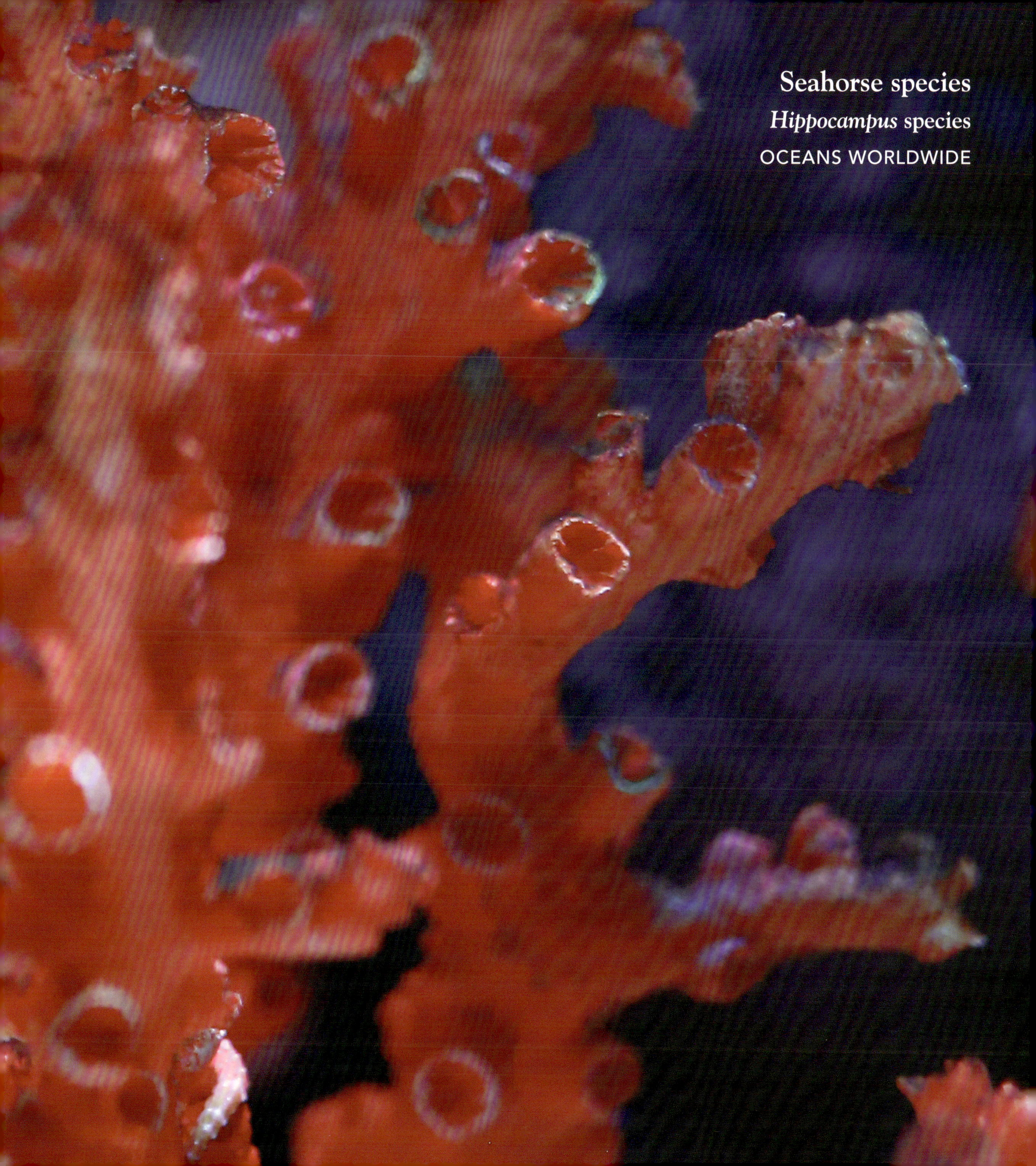
Seahorse species
Hippocampus species
OCEANS WORLDWIDE

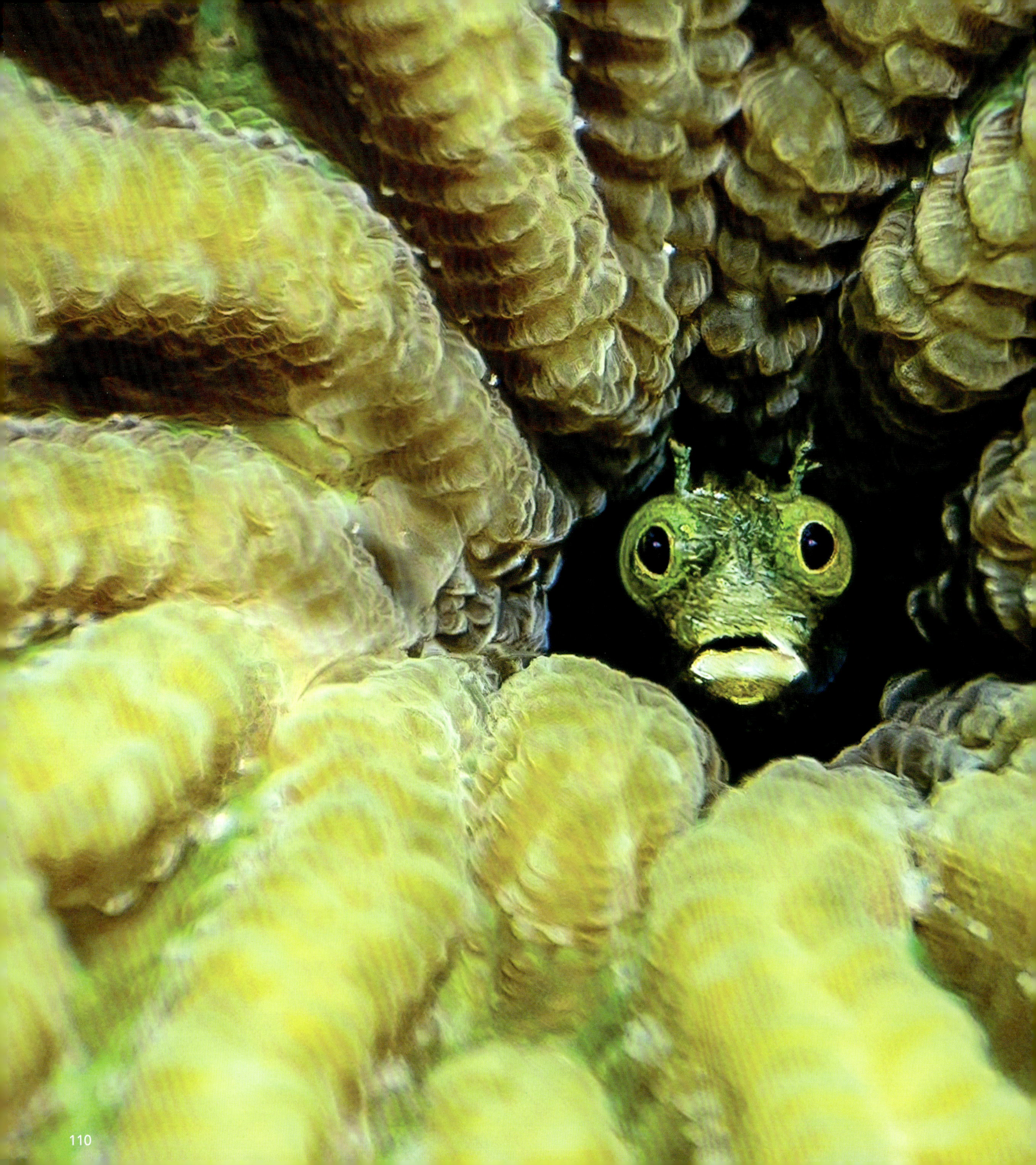

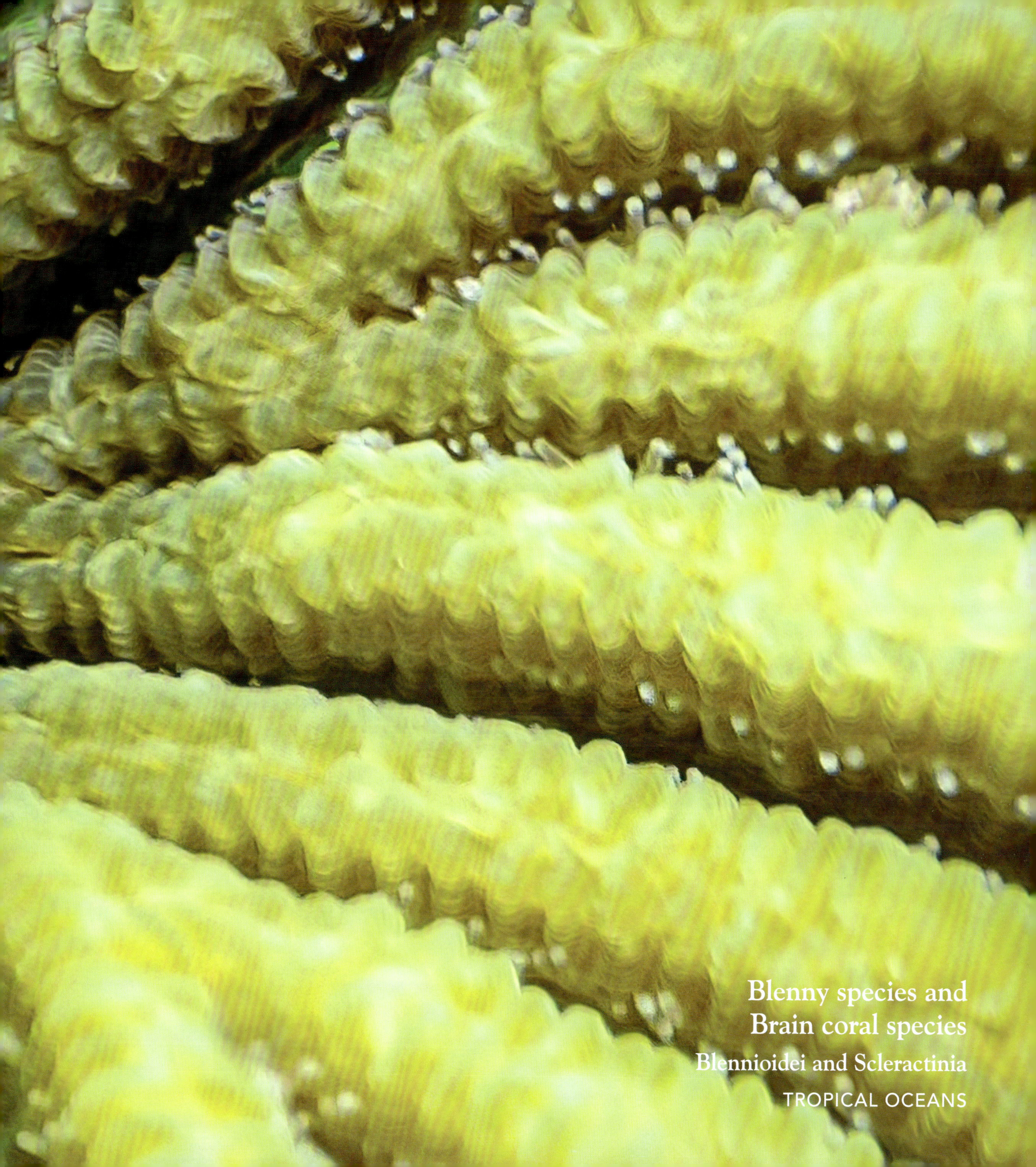

Blenny species and
Brain coral species
Blennioidei and Scleractinia
TROPICAL OCEANS

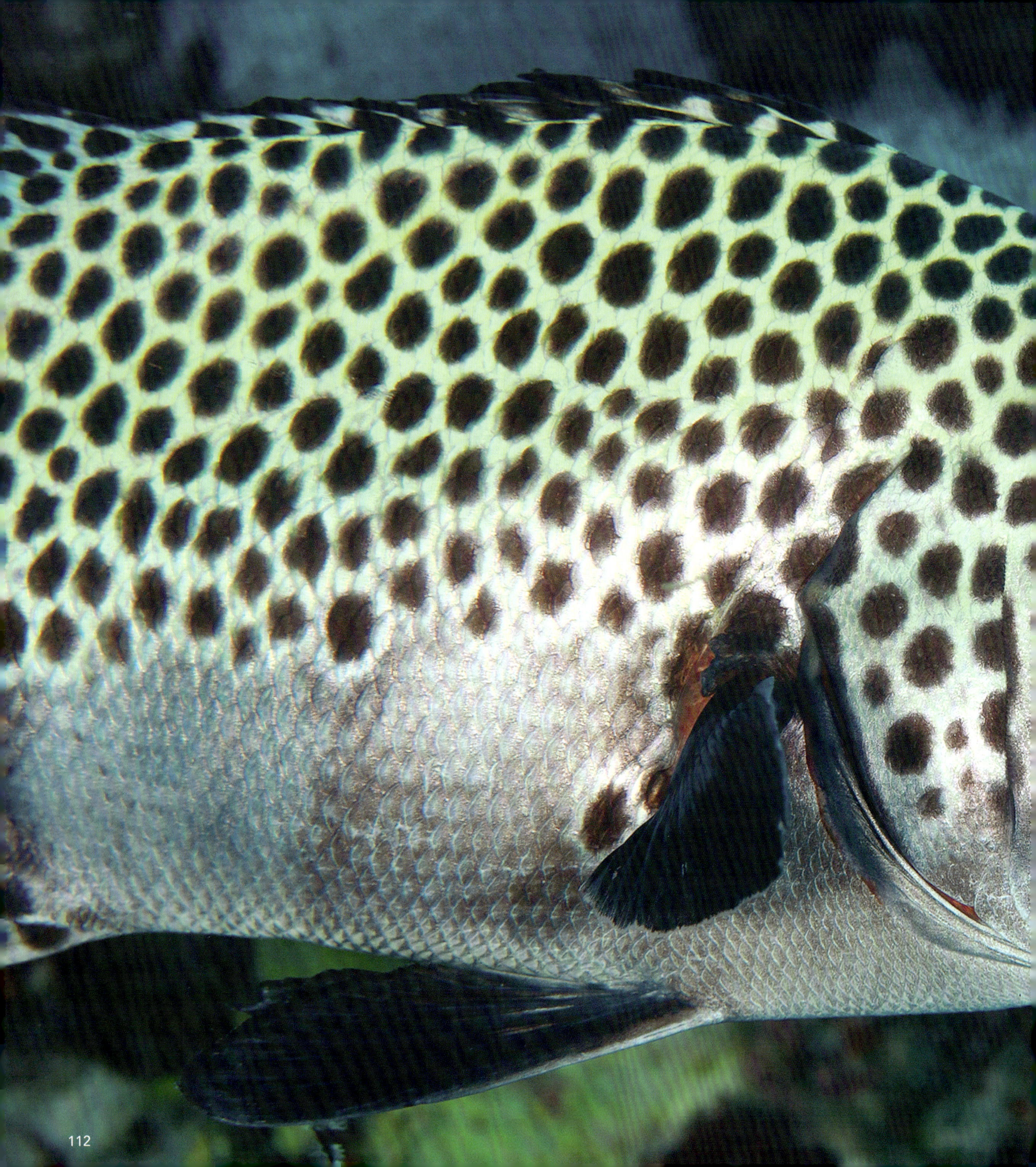

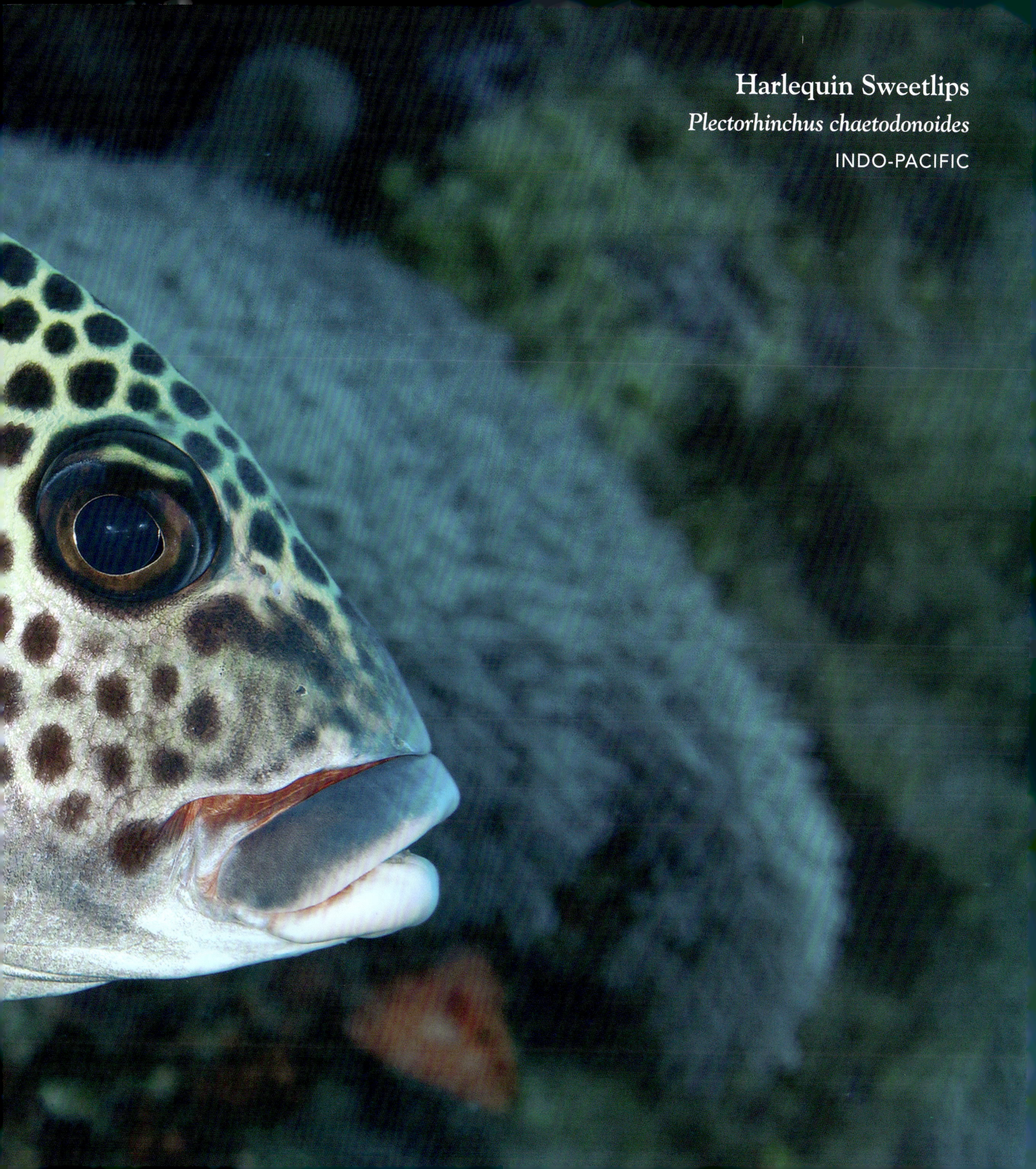

Harlequin Sweetlips

Plectorhinchus chaetodonoides

INDO-PACIFIC

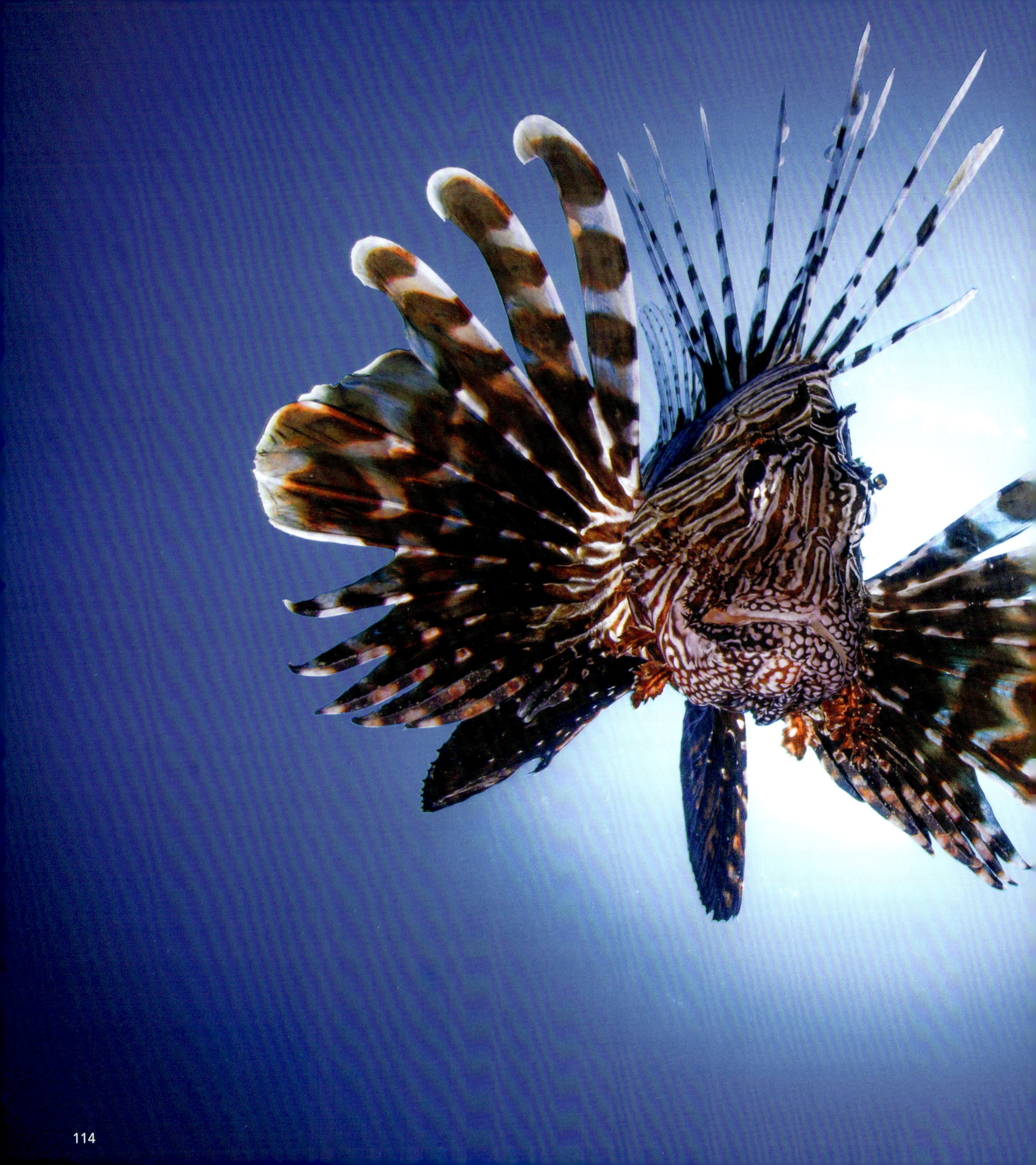

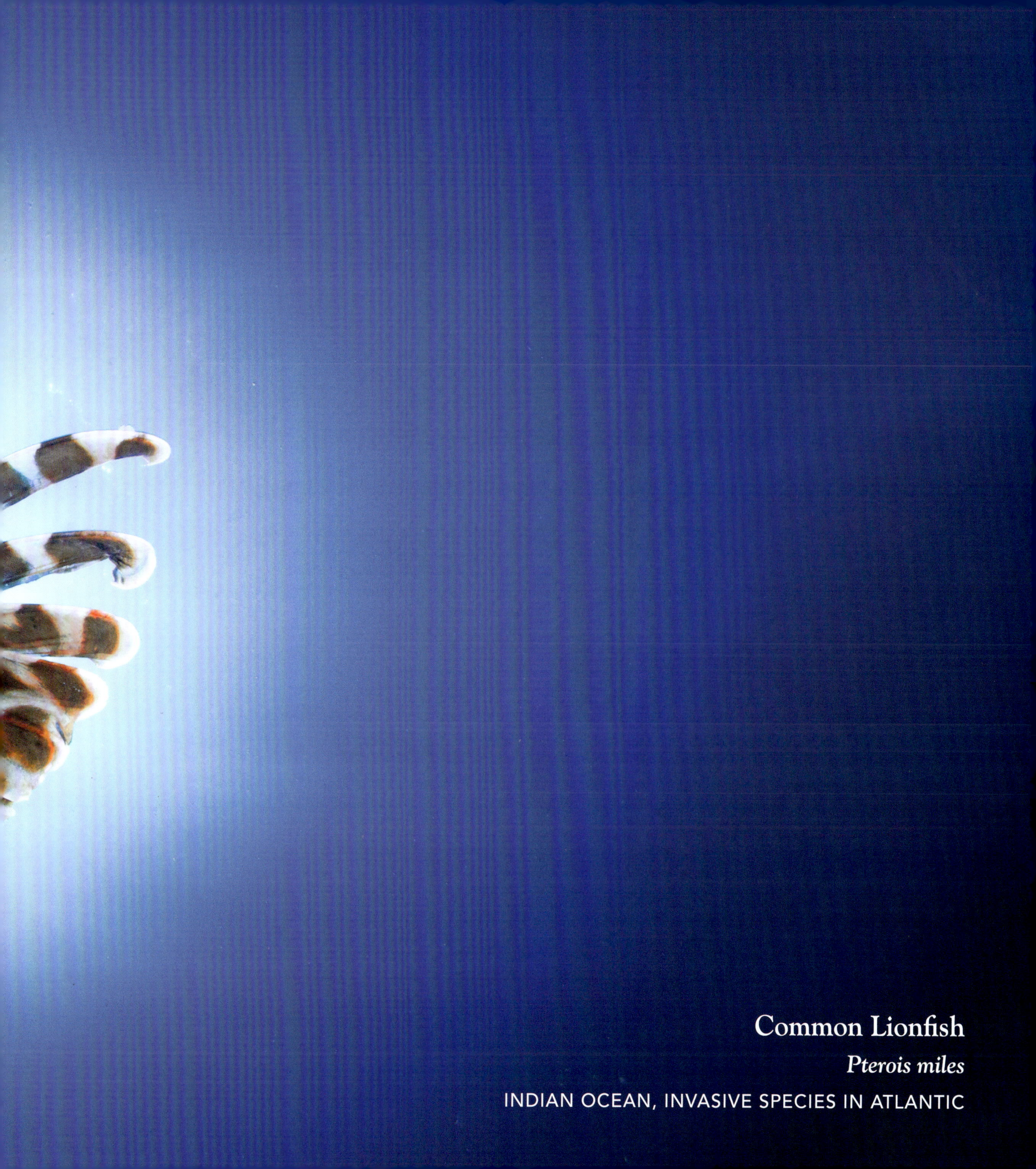

Common Lionfish

Pterois miles

INDIAN OCEAN, INVASIVE SPECIES IN ATLANTIC

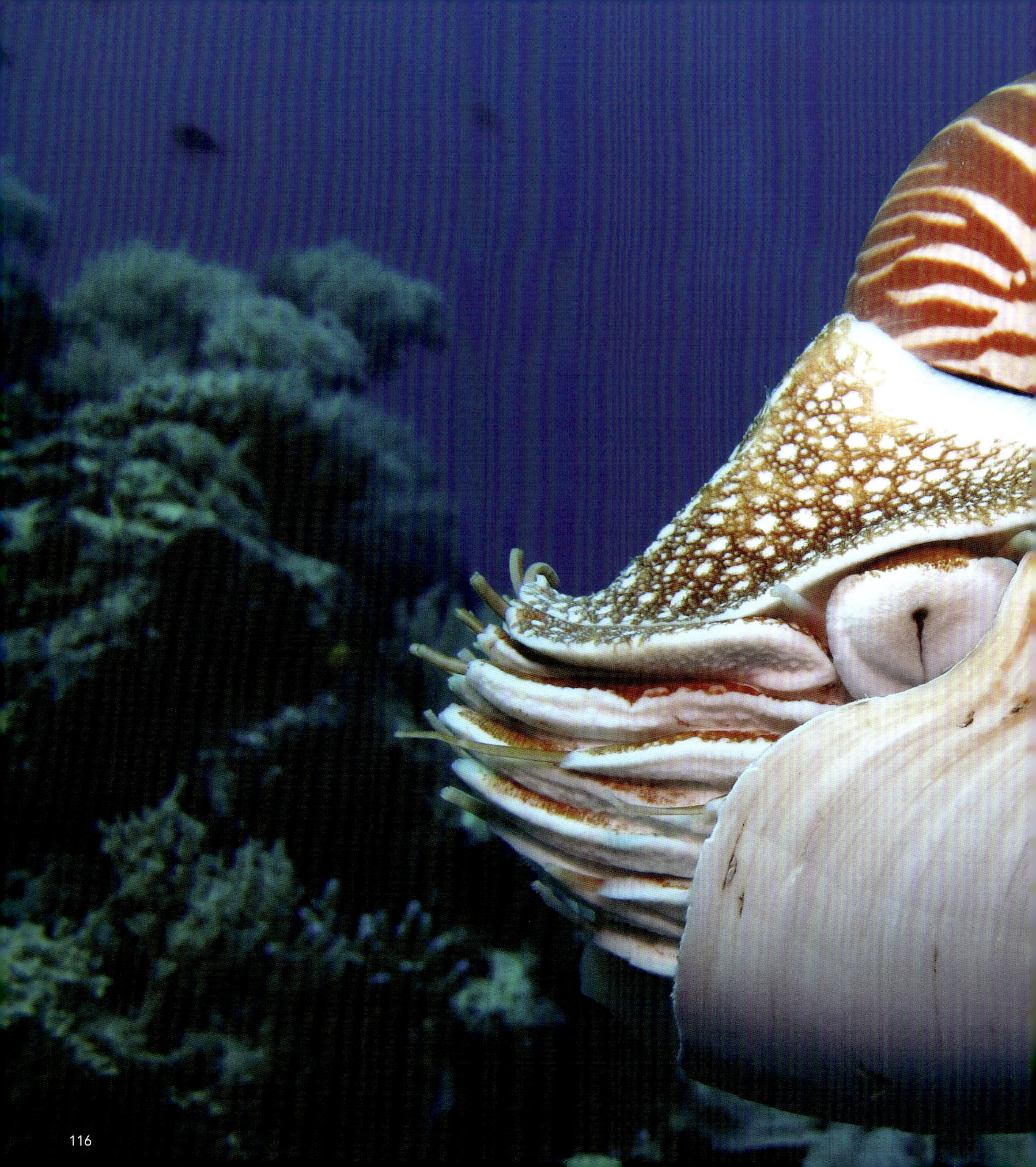

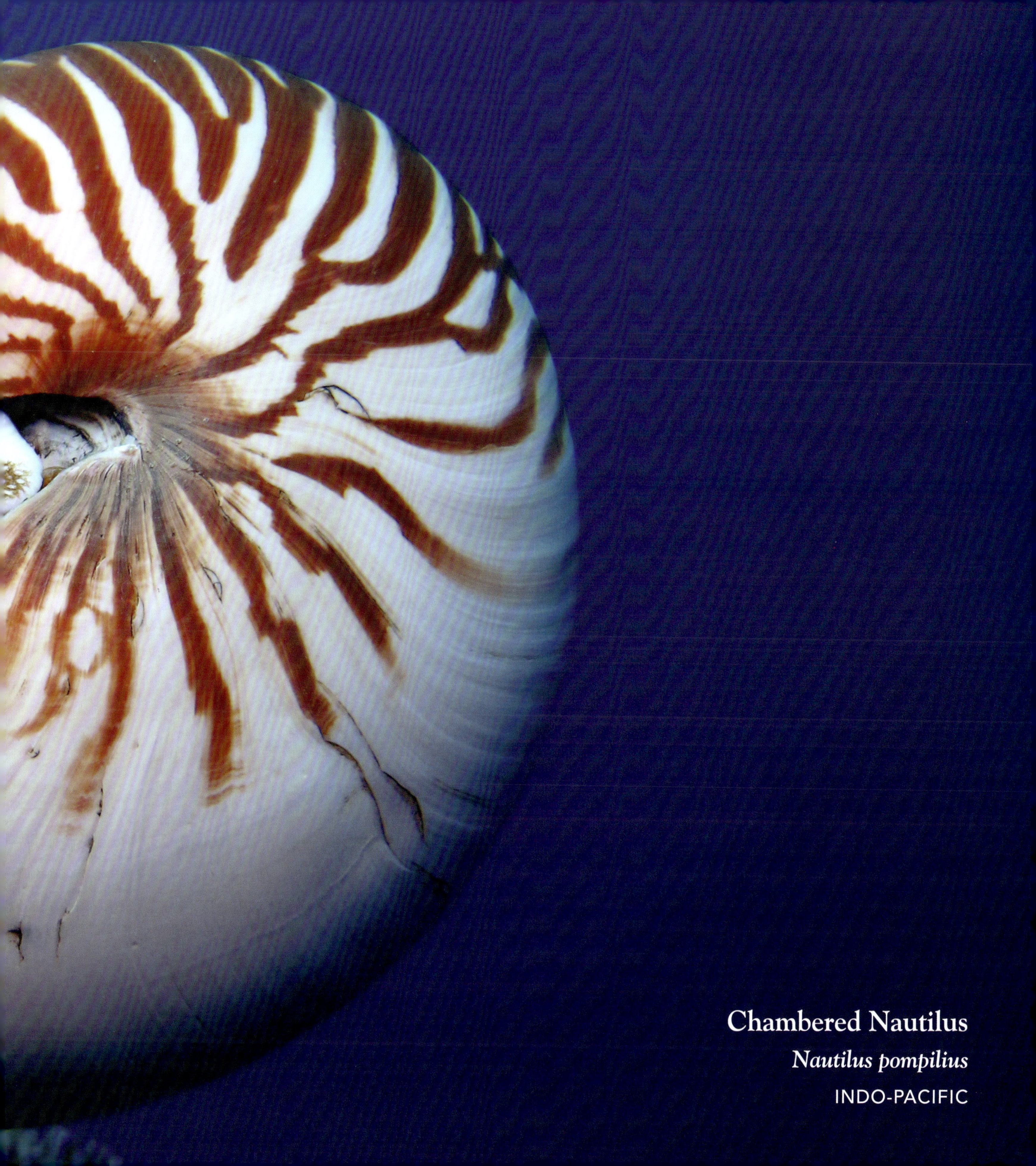

Chambered Nautilus

Nautilus pompilius

INDO-PACIFIC

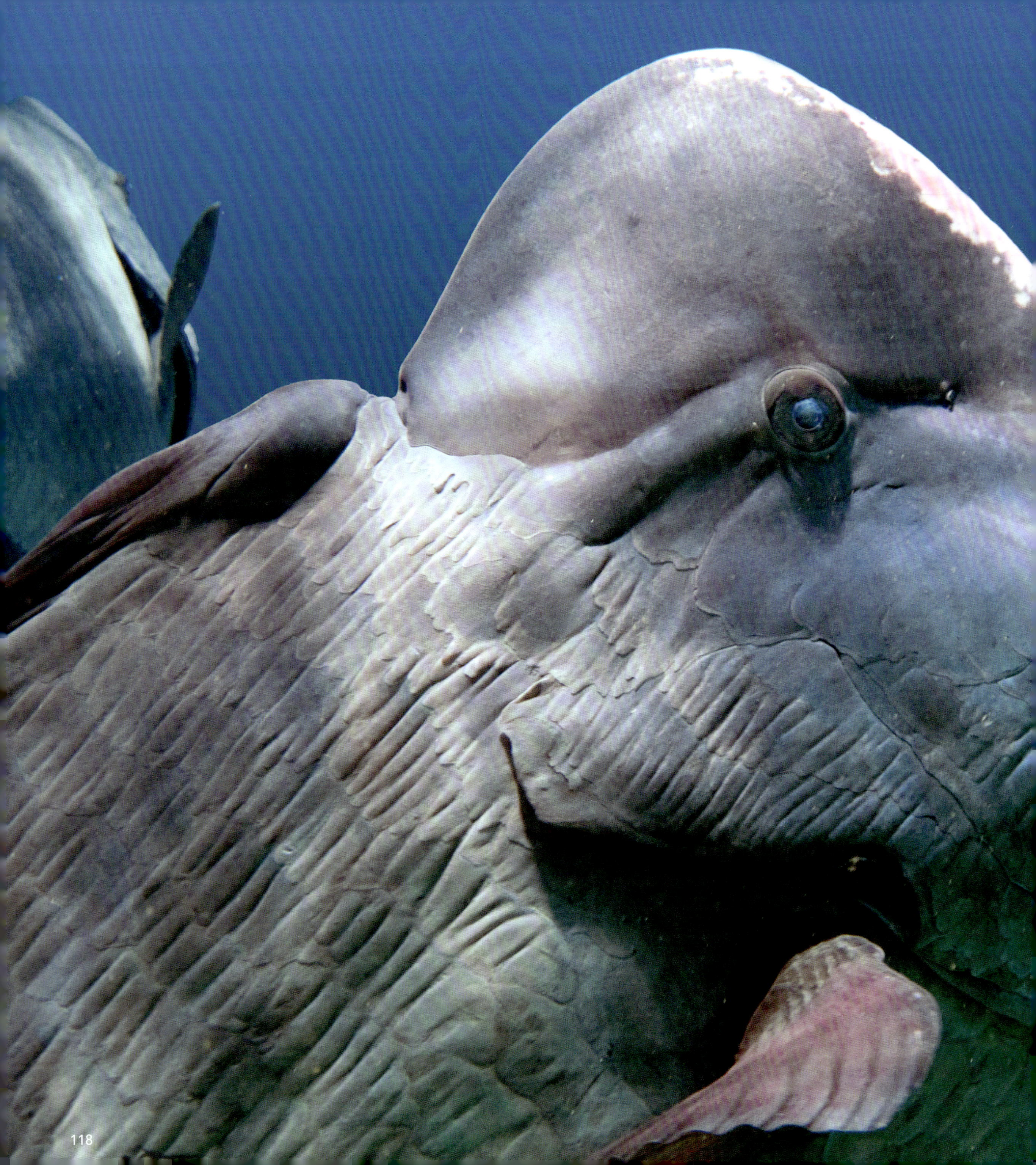

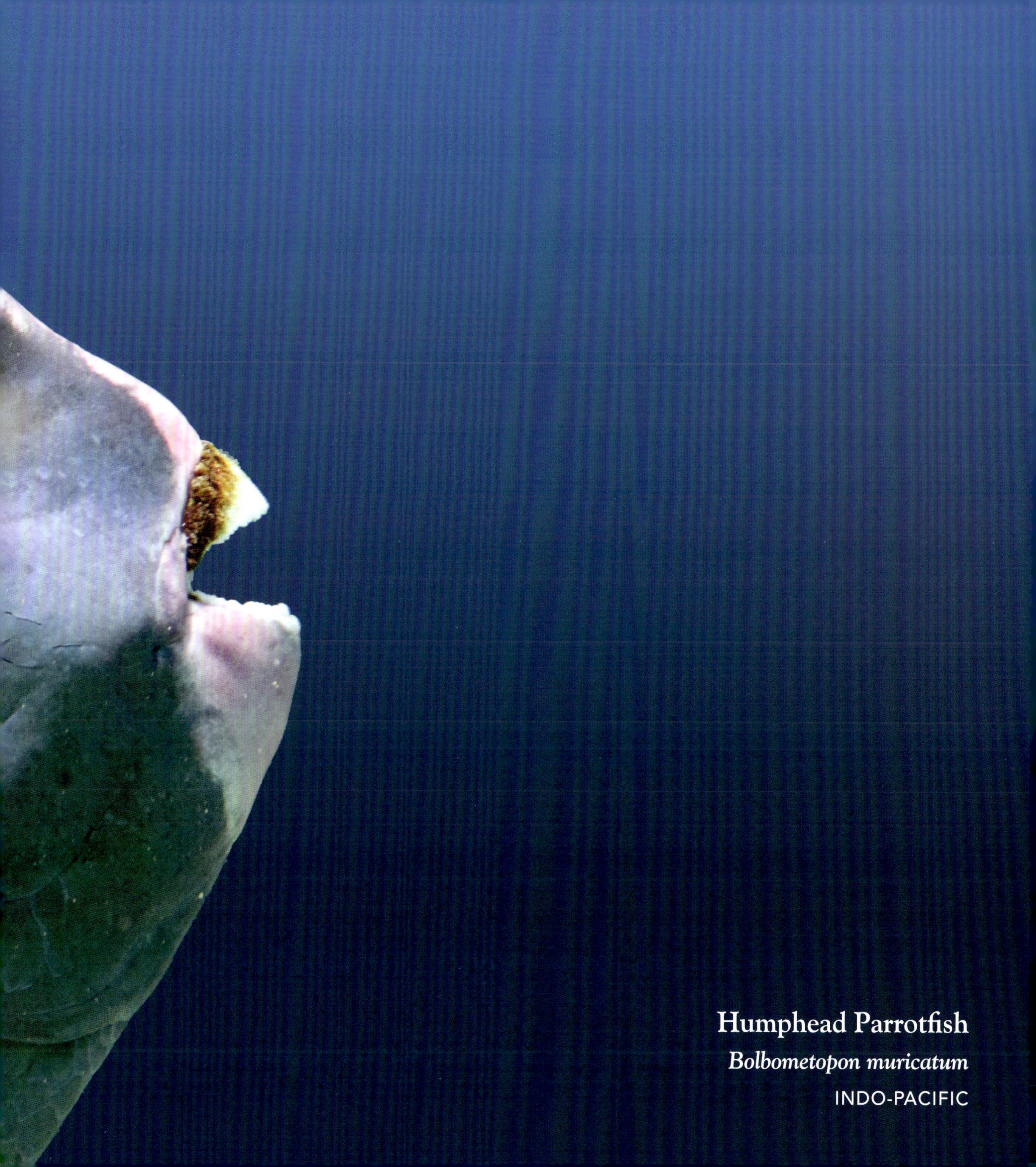

Humphead Parrotfish

Bolbometopon muricatum

INDO-PACIFIC

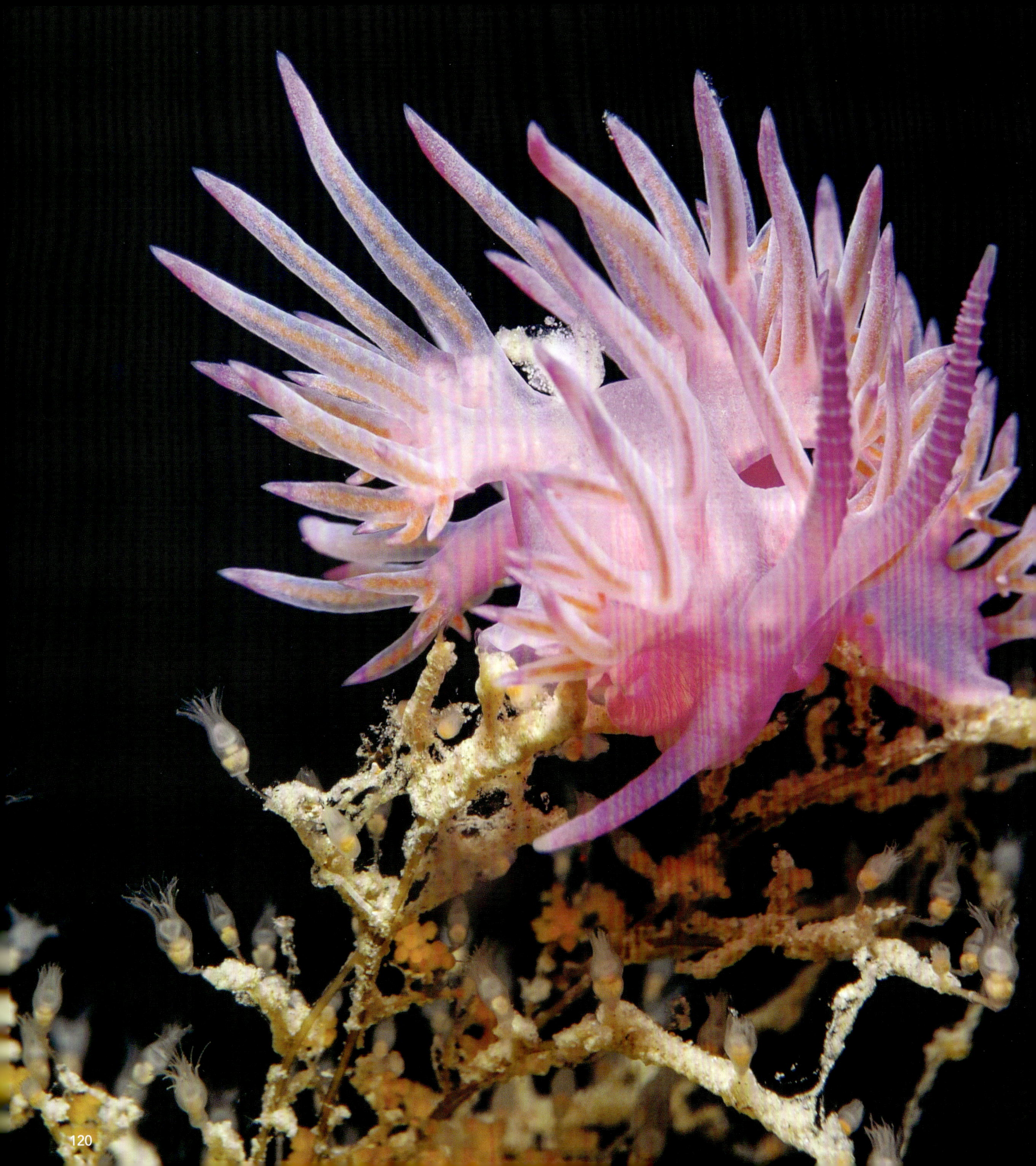

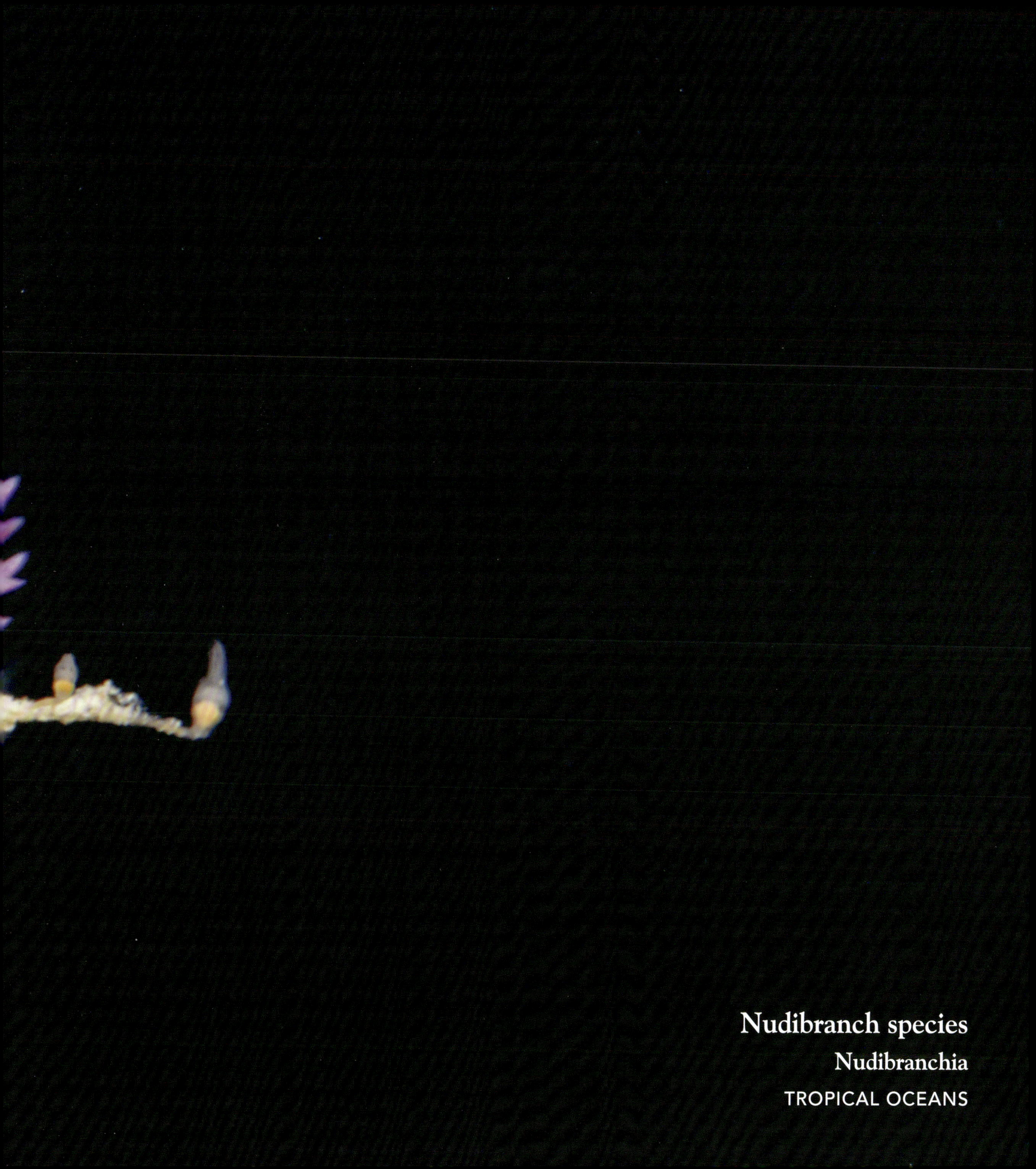

Nudibranch species

Nudibranchia

TROPICAL OCEANS

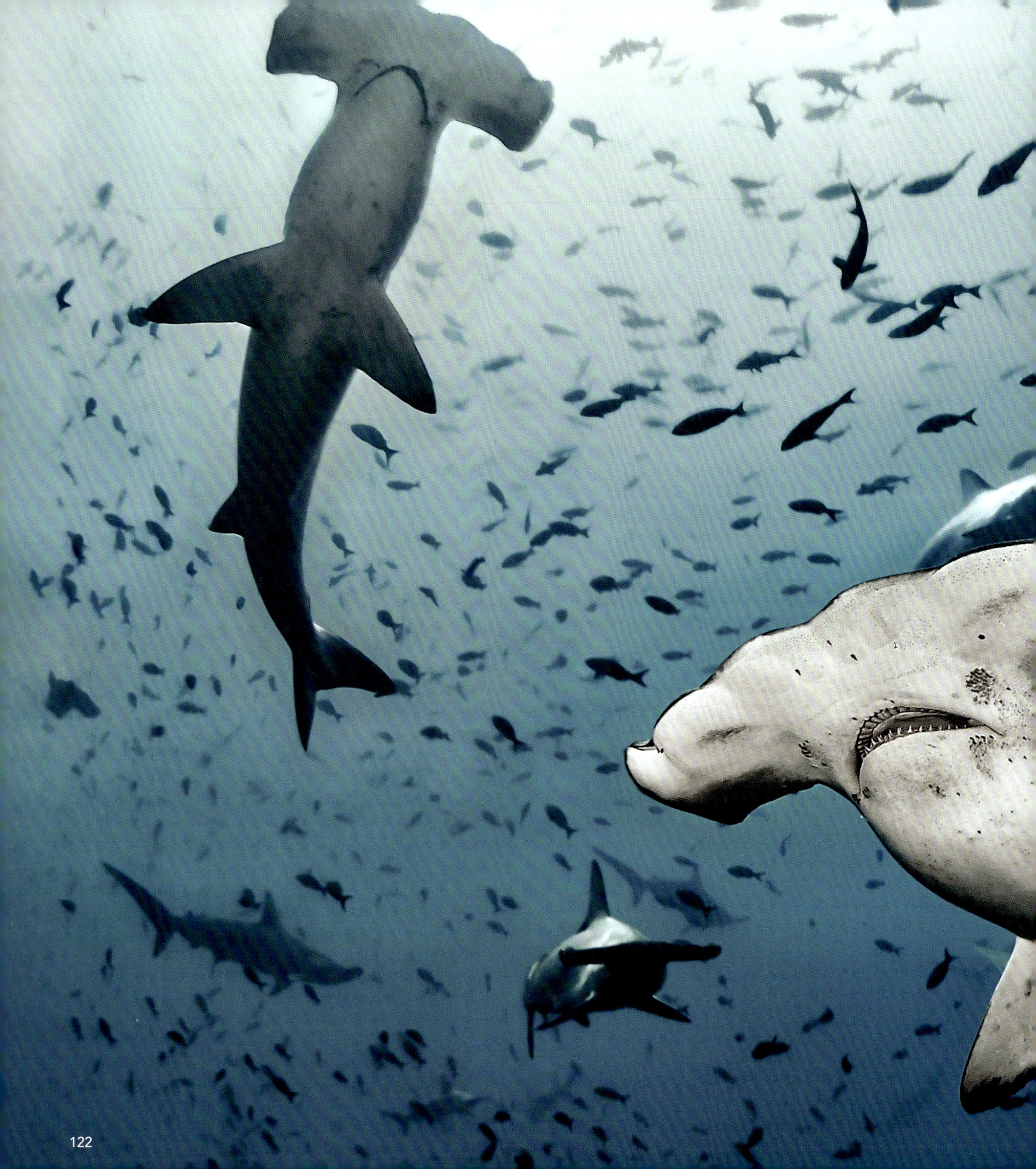

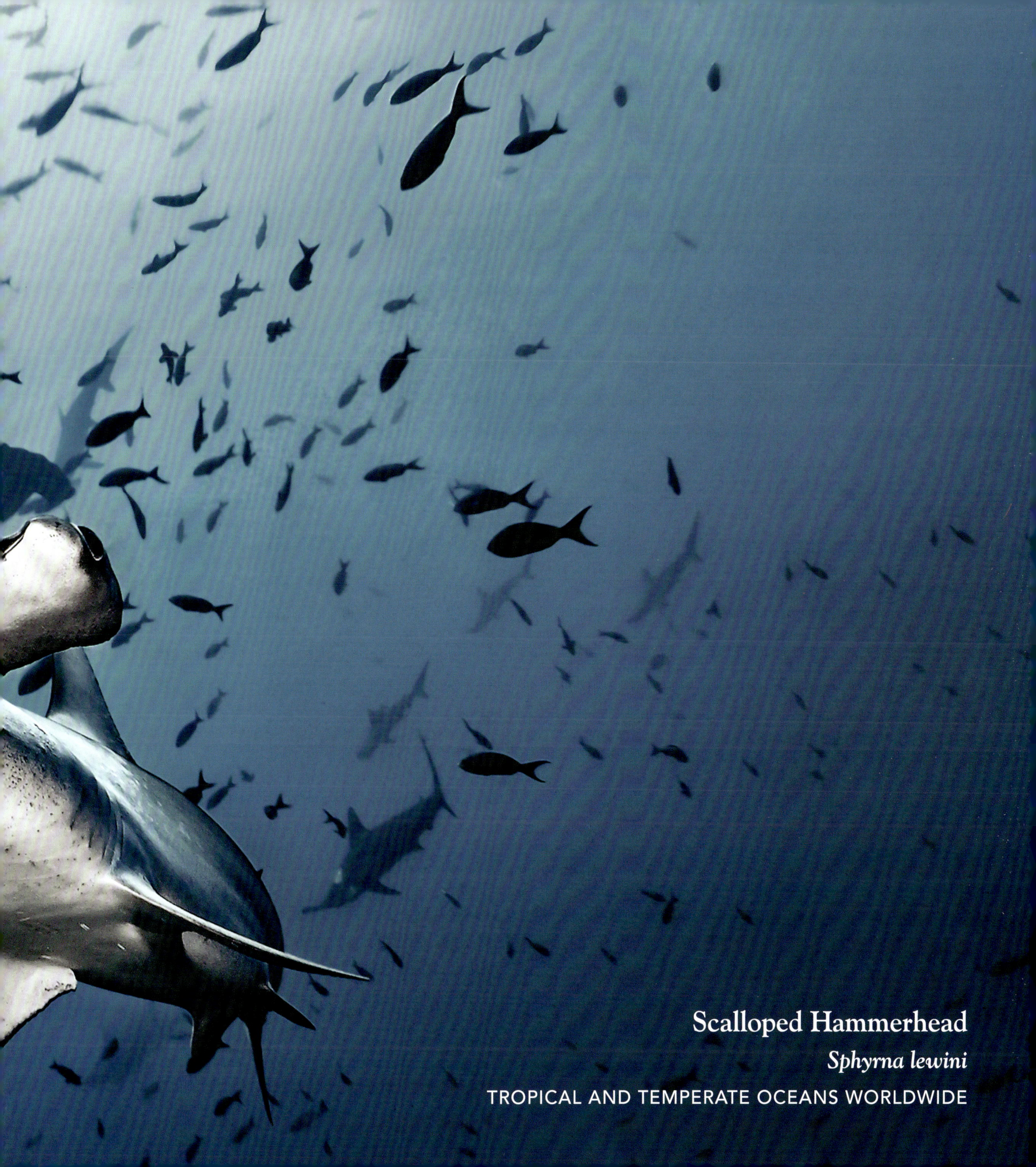

Scalloped Hammerhead

Sphyrna lewini

TROPICAL AND TEMPERATE OCEANS WORLDWIDE

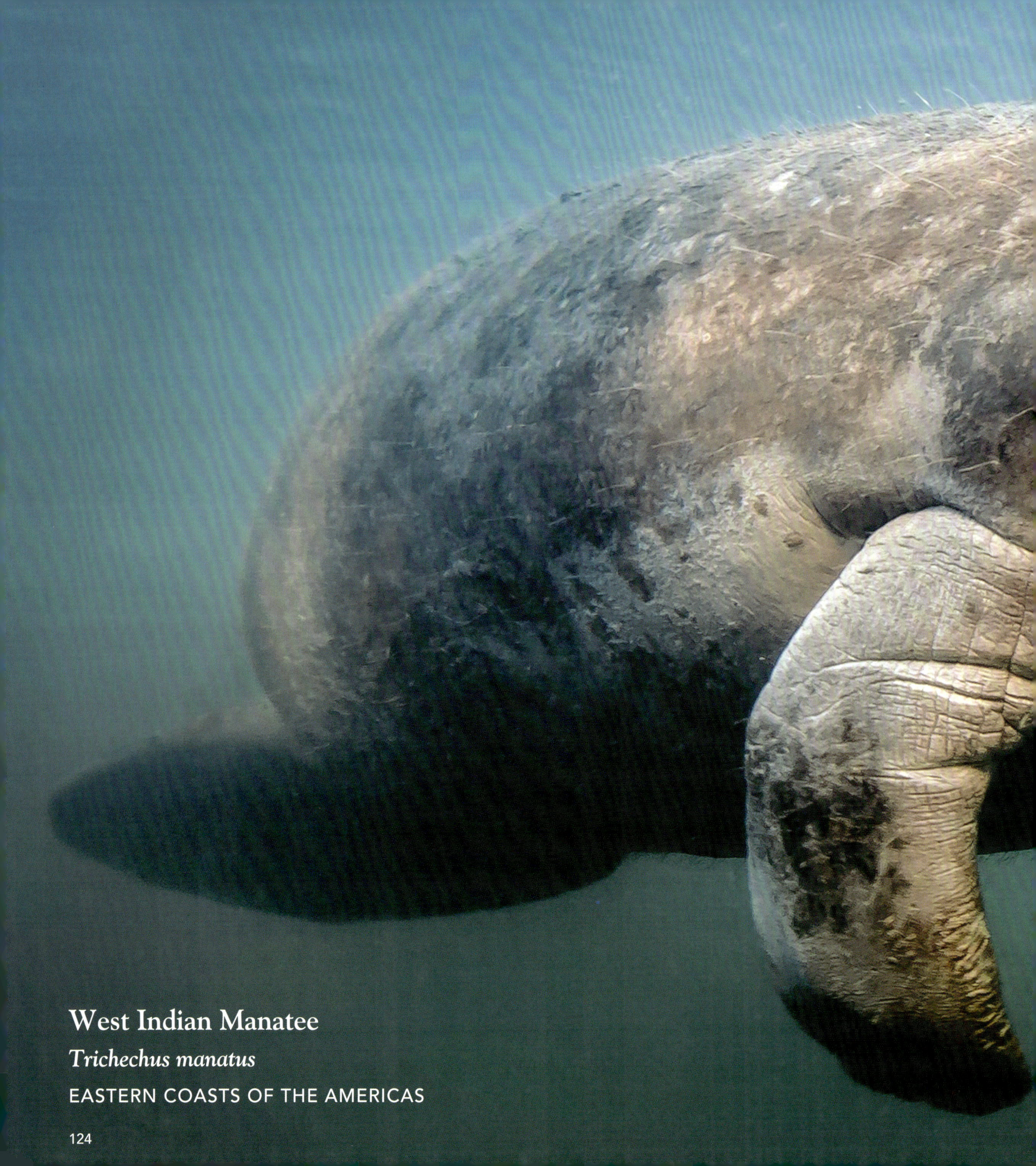

West Indian Manatee

Trichechus manatus

EASTERN COASTS OF THE AMERICAS

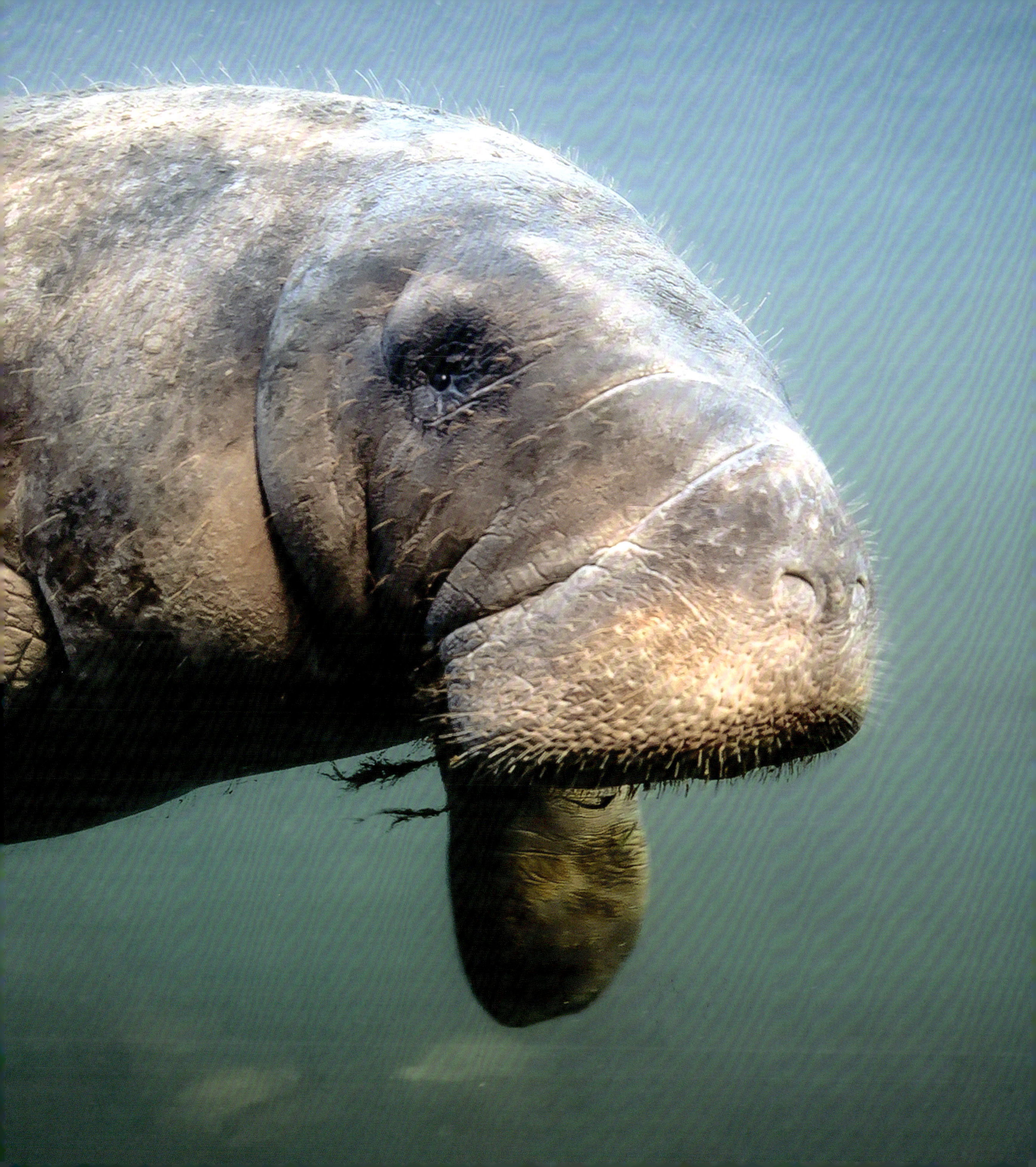

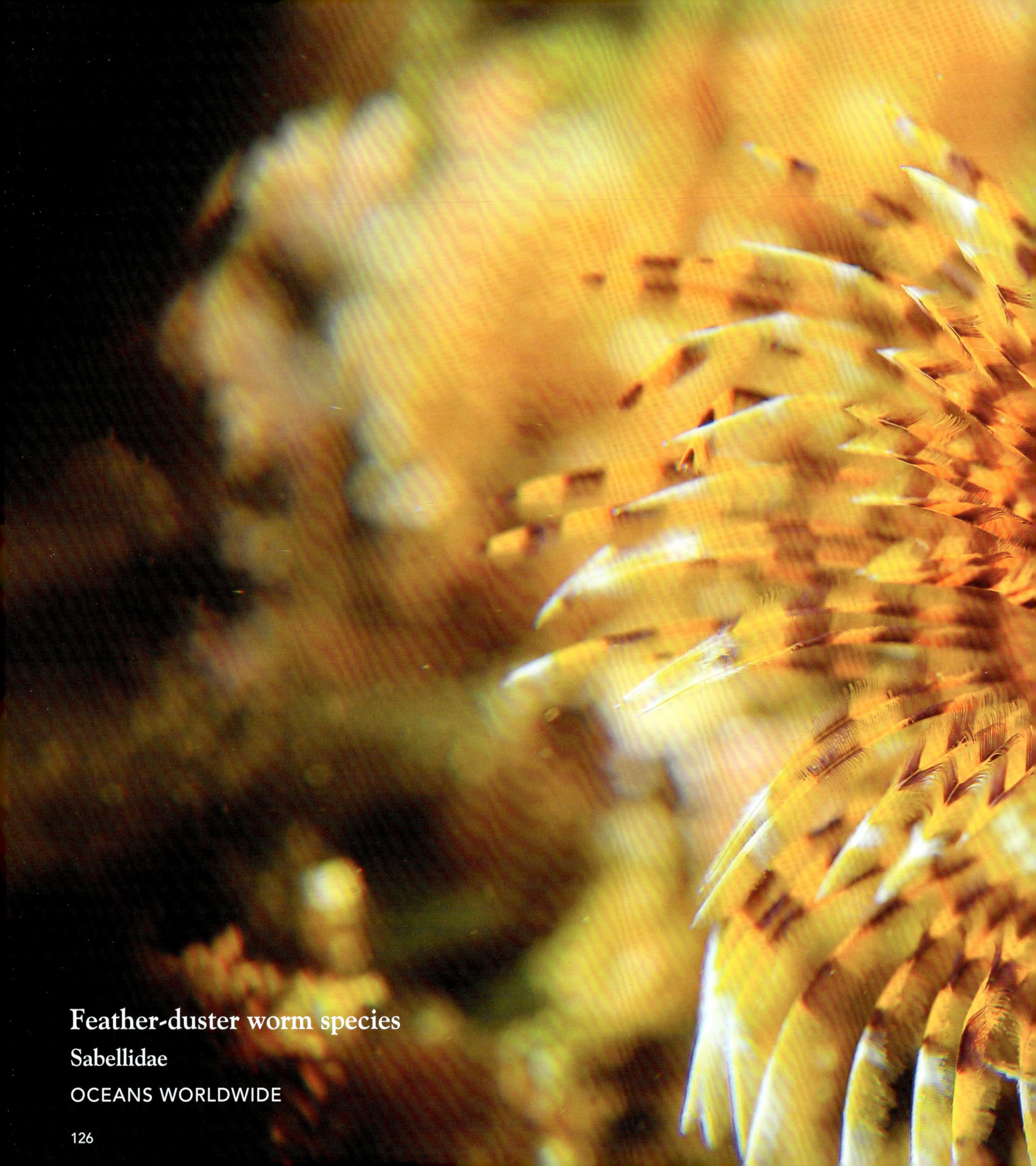

Feather-duster worm species

Sabellidae

OCEANS WORLDWIDE

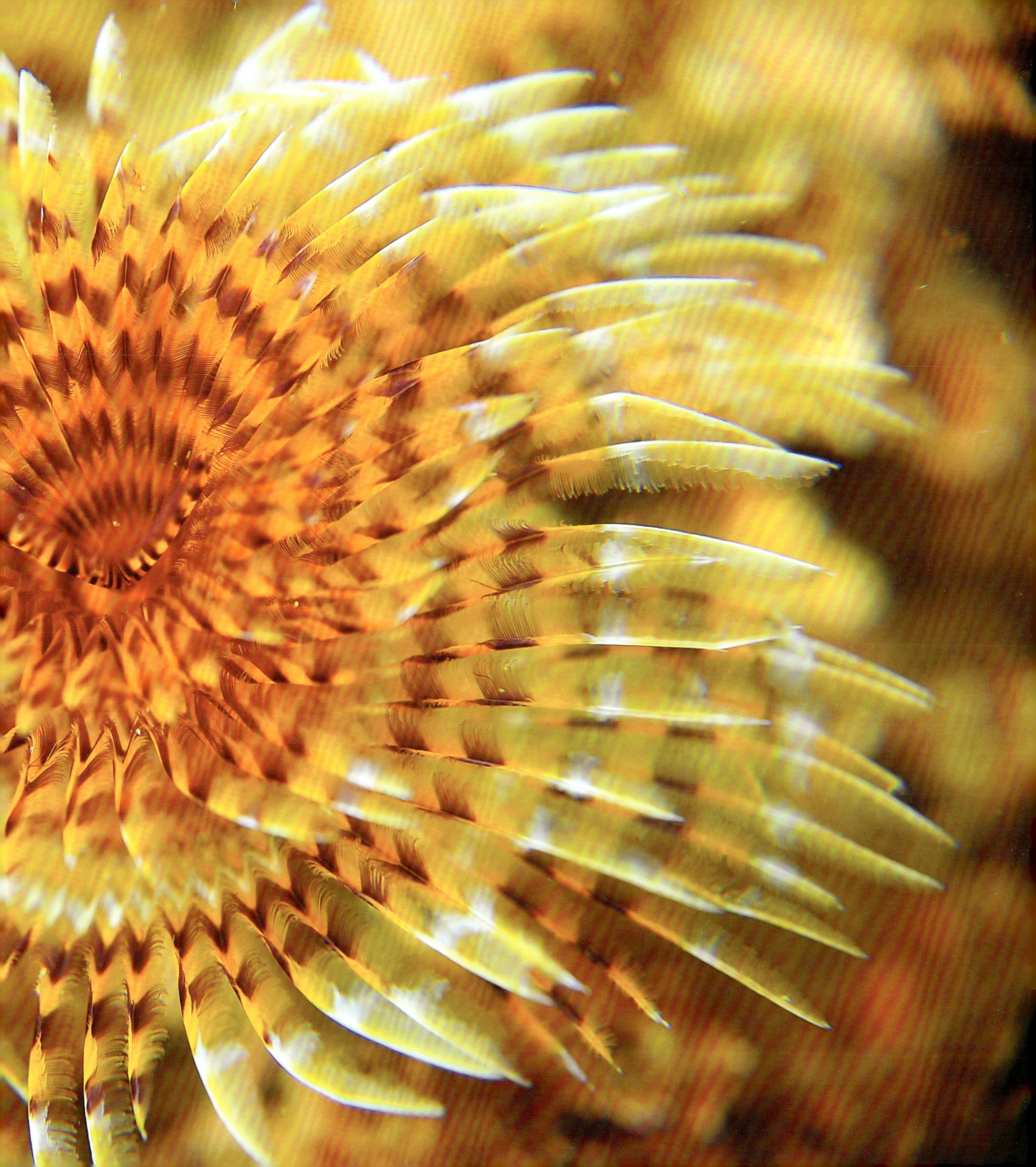

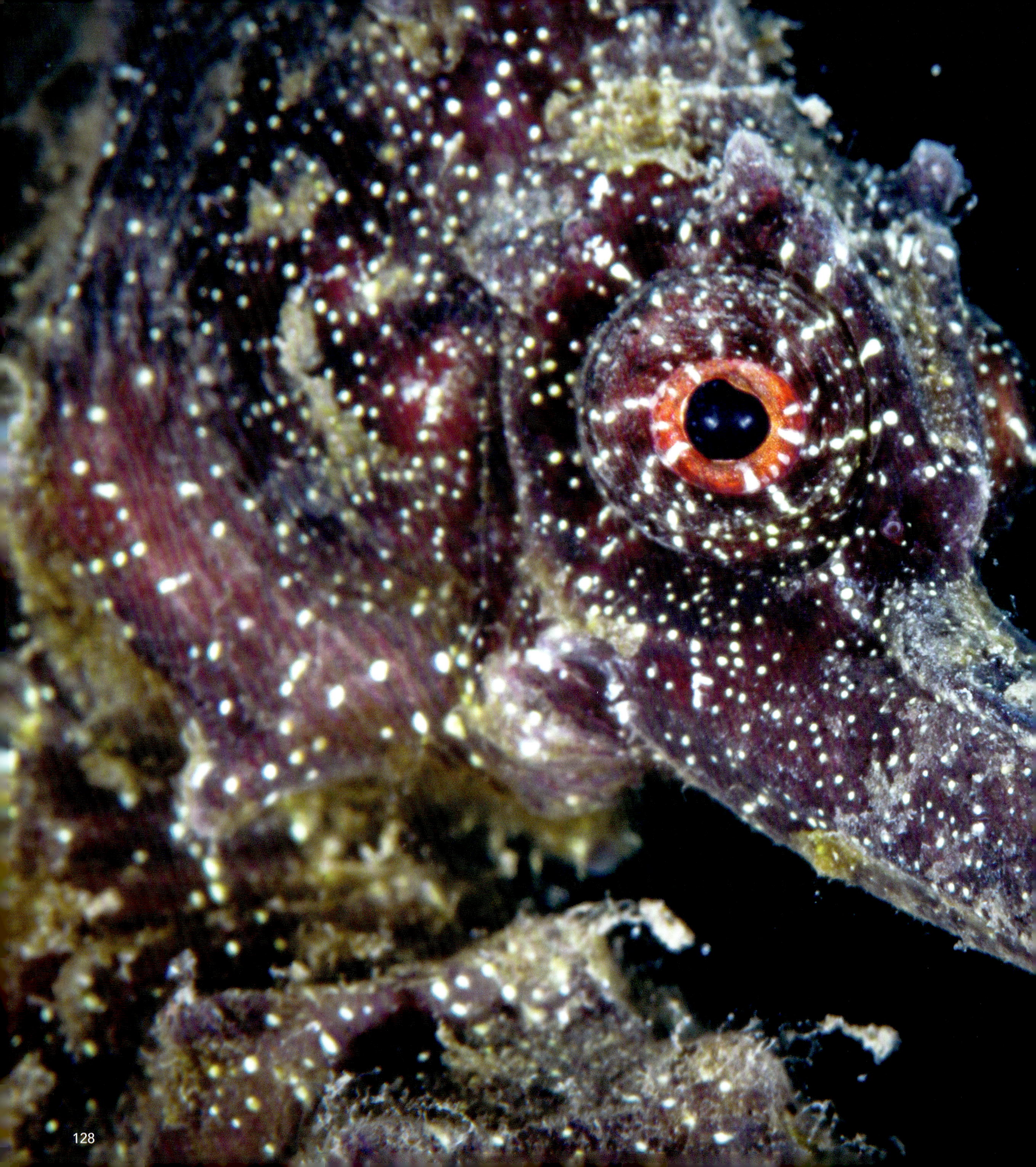

Seahorse species

Hippocampus species

OCEANS WORLDWIDE

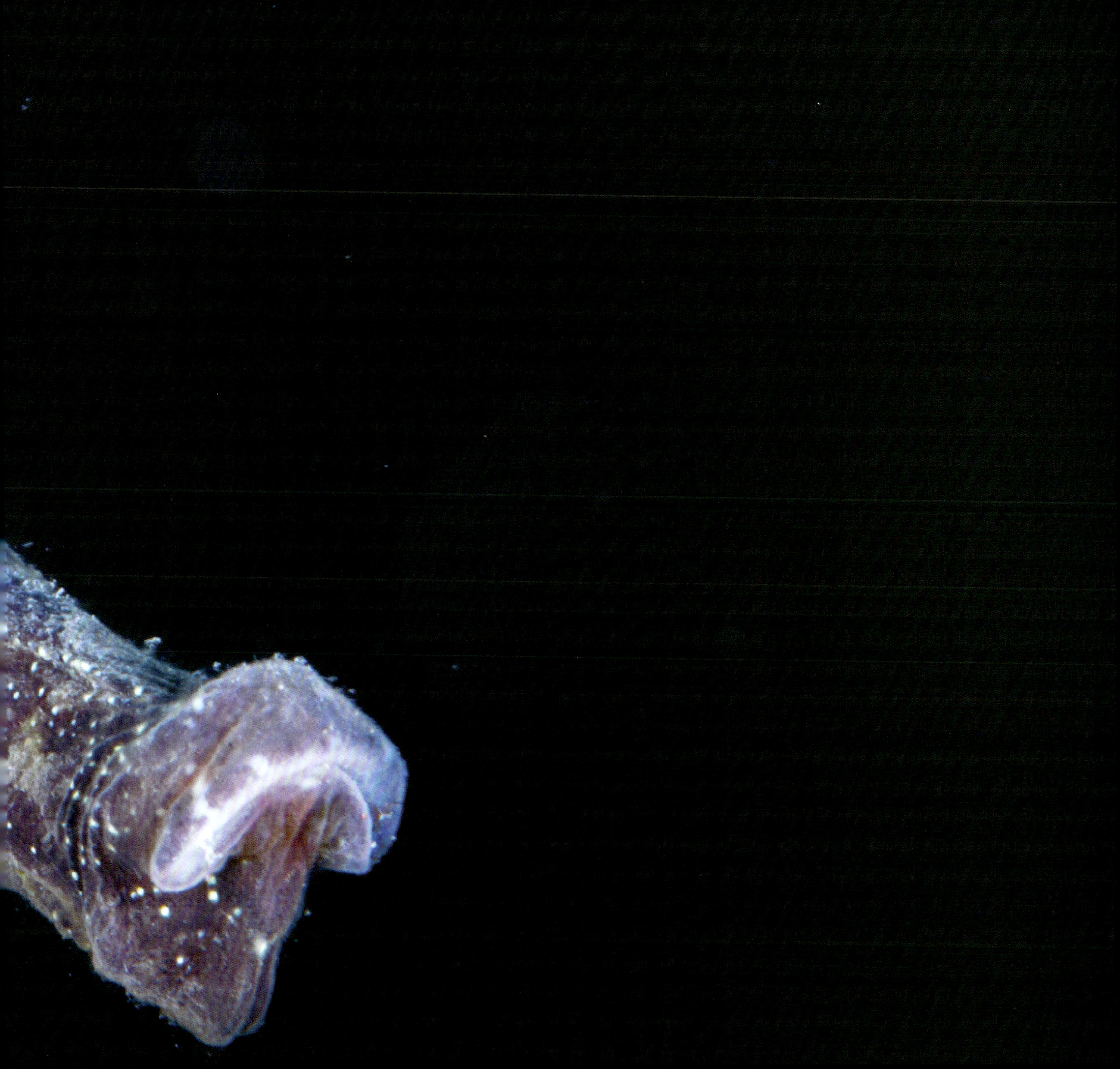

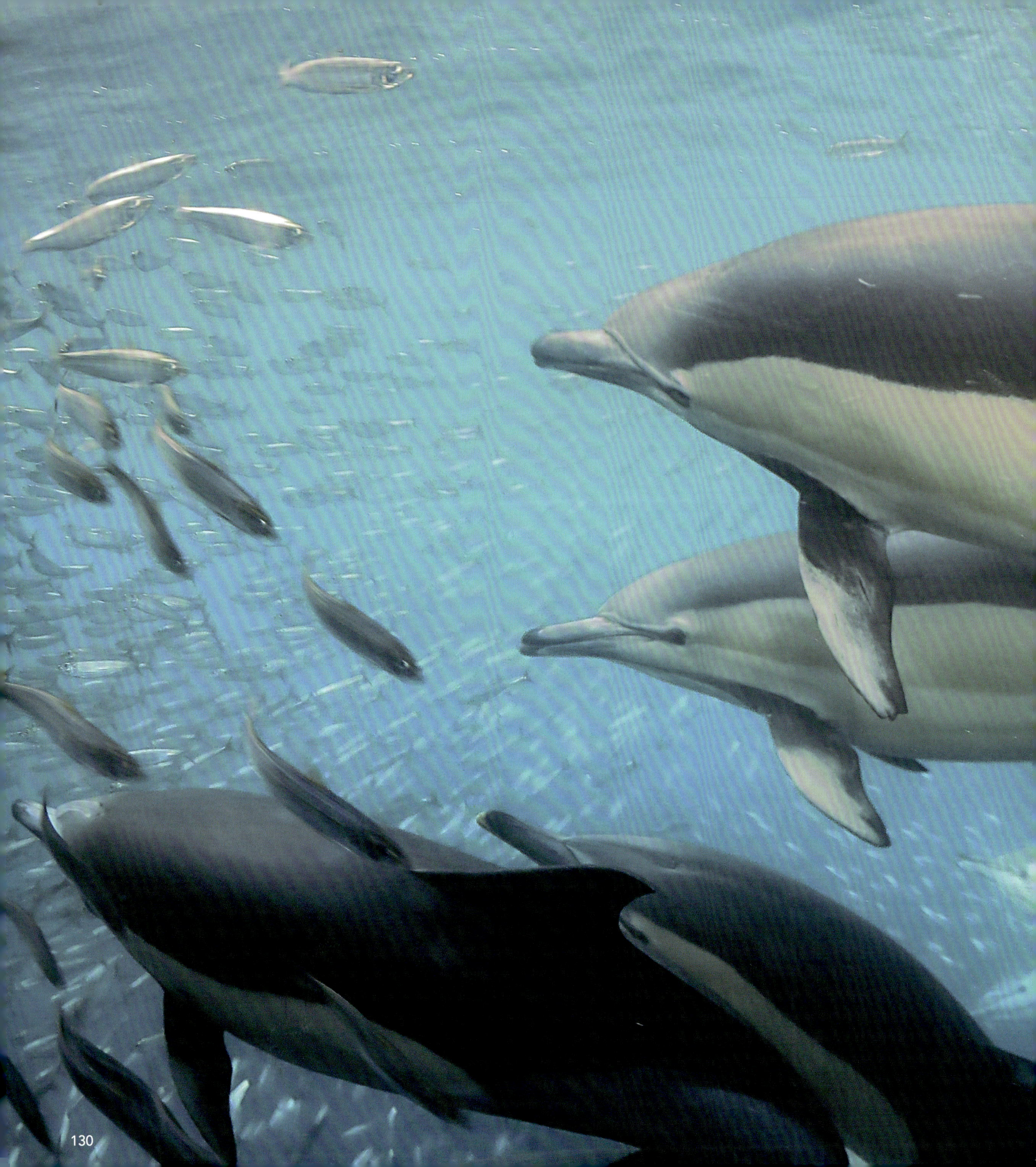

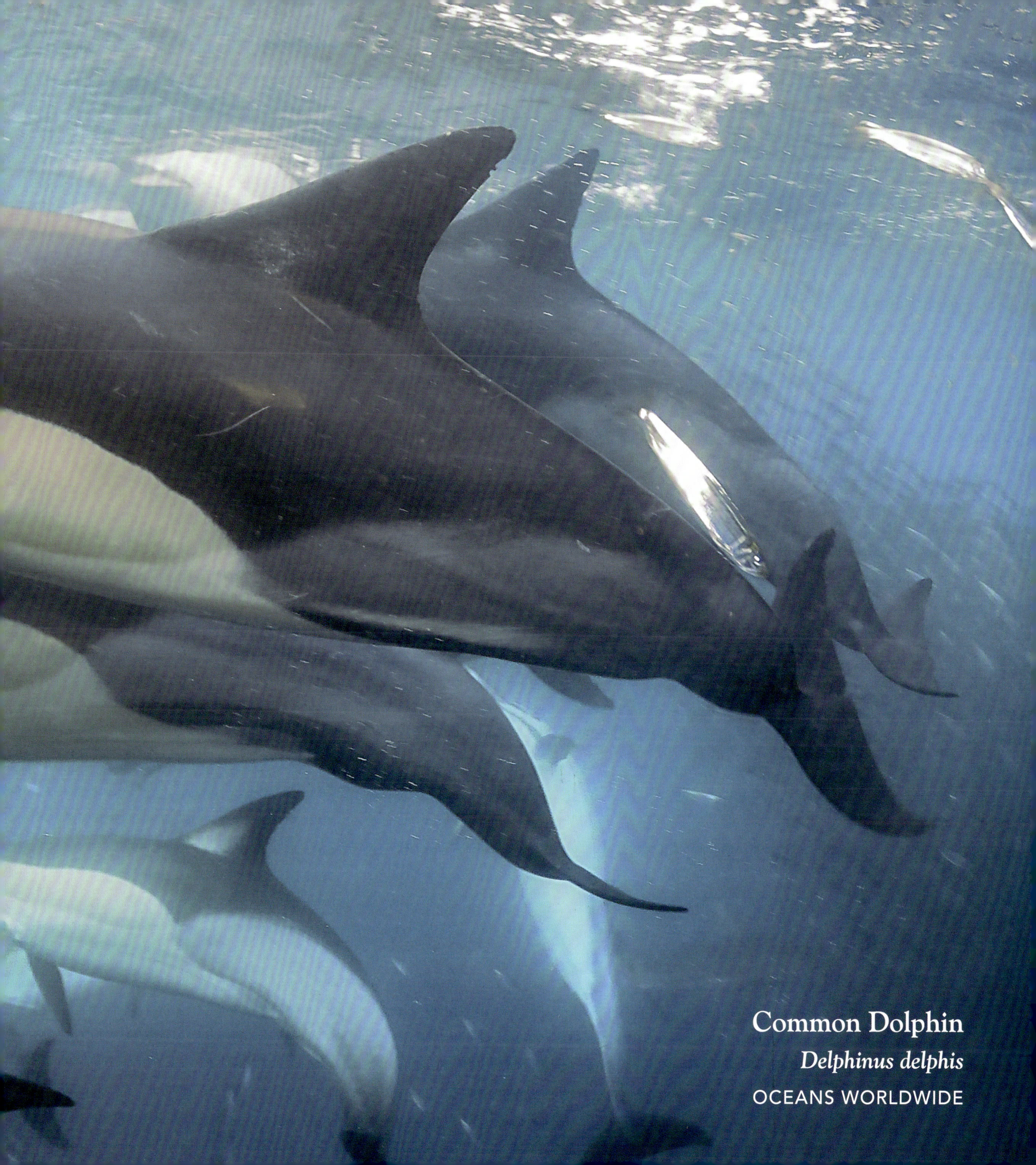

Common Dolphin
Delphinus delphis
OCEANS WORLDWIDE

Ruby Red Dragonet

Synchiropus sycorax

INDO-PACIFIC

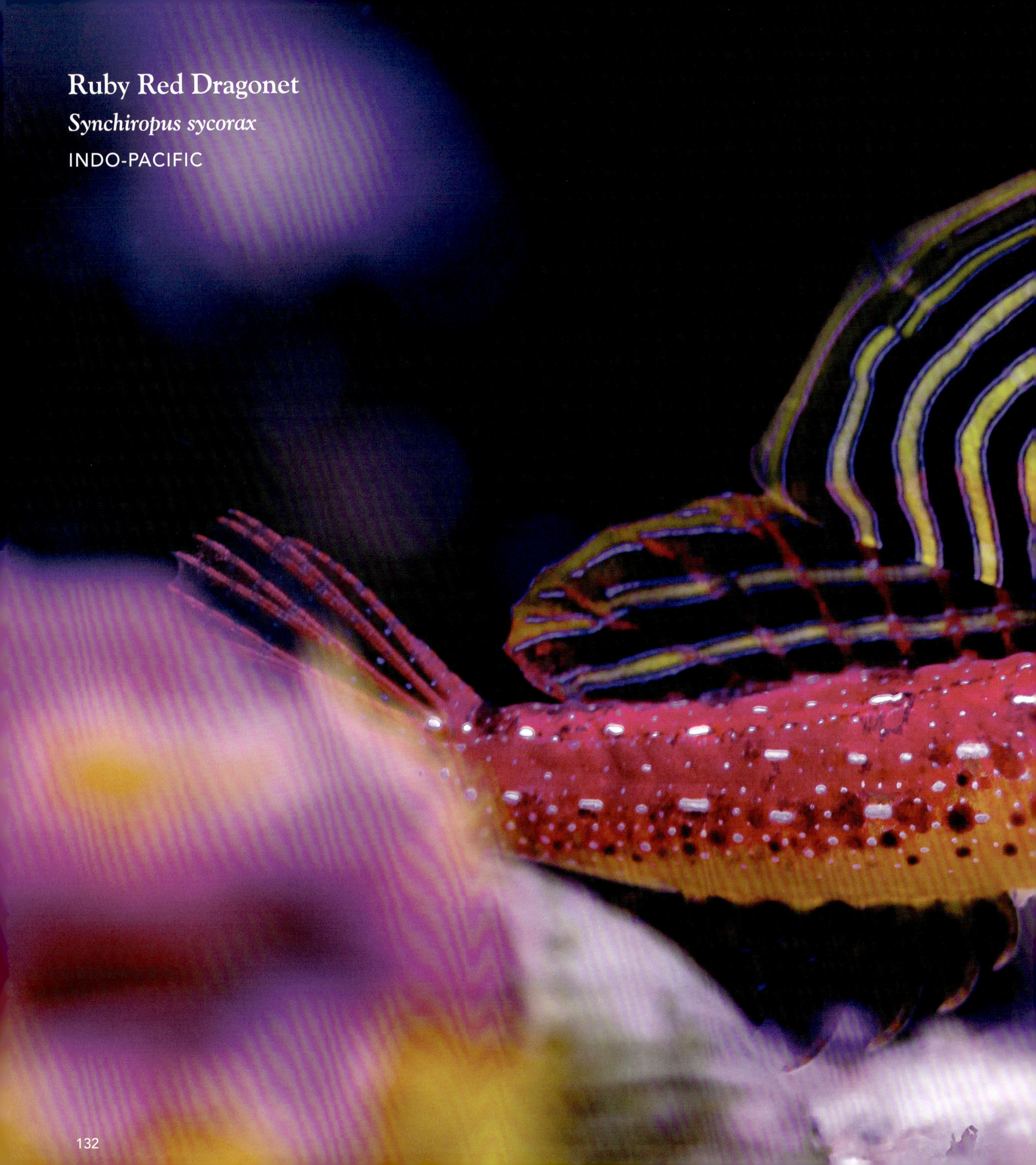

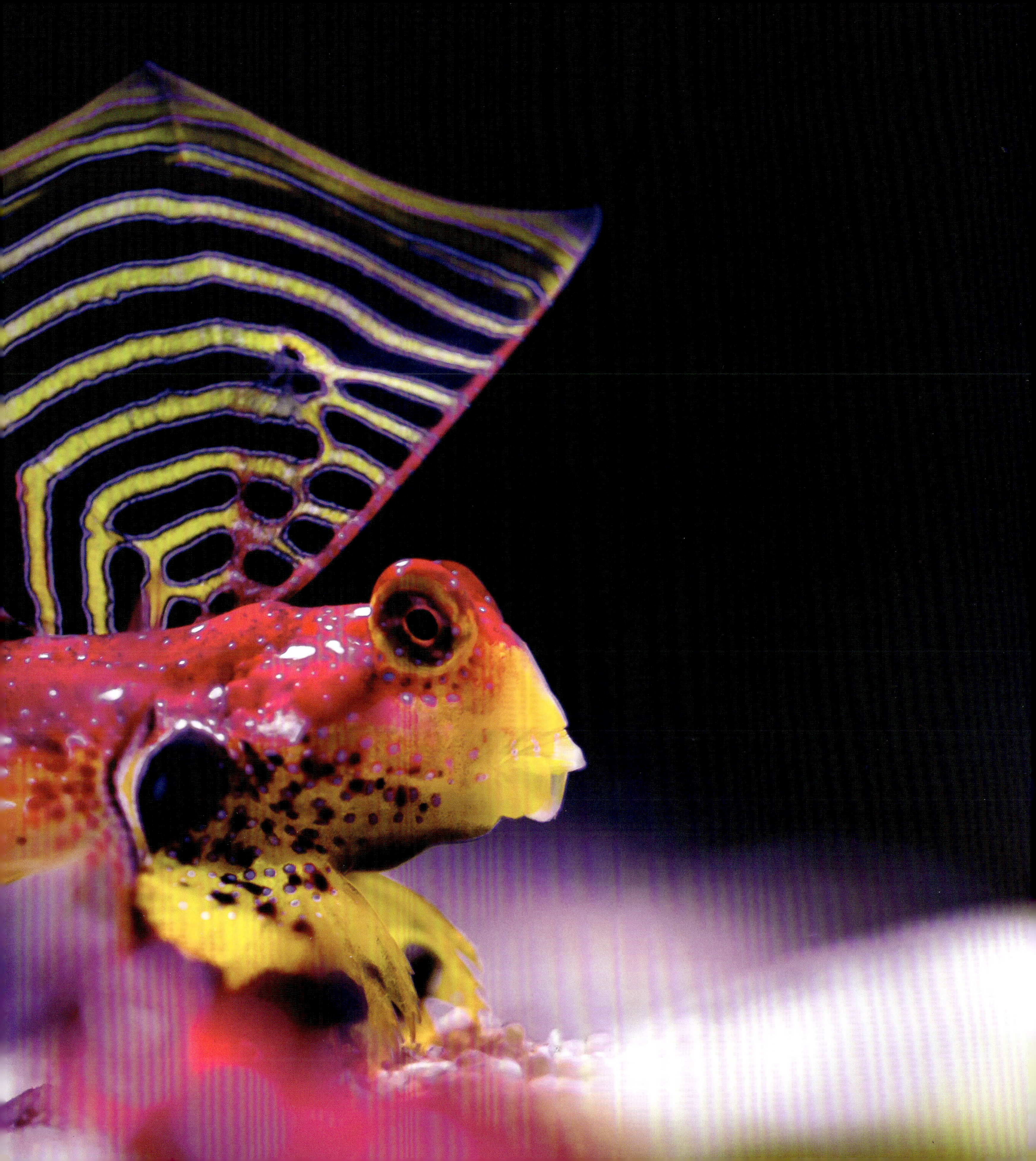

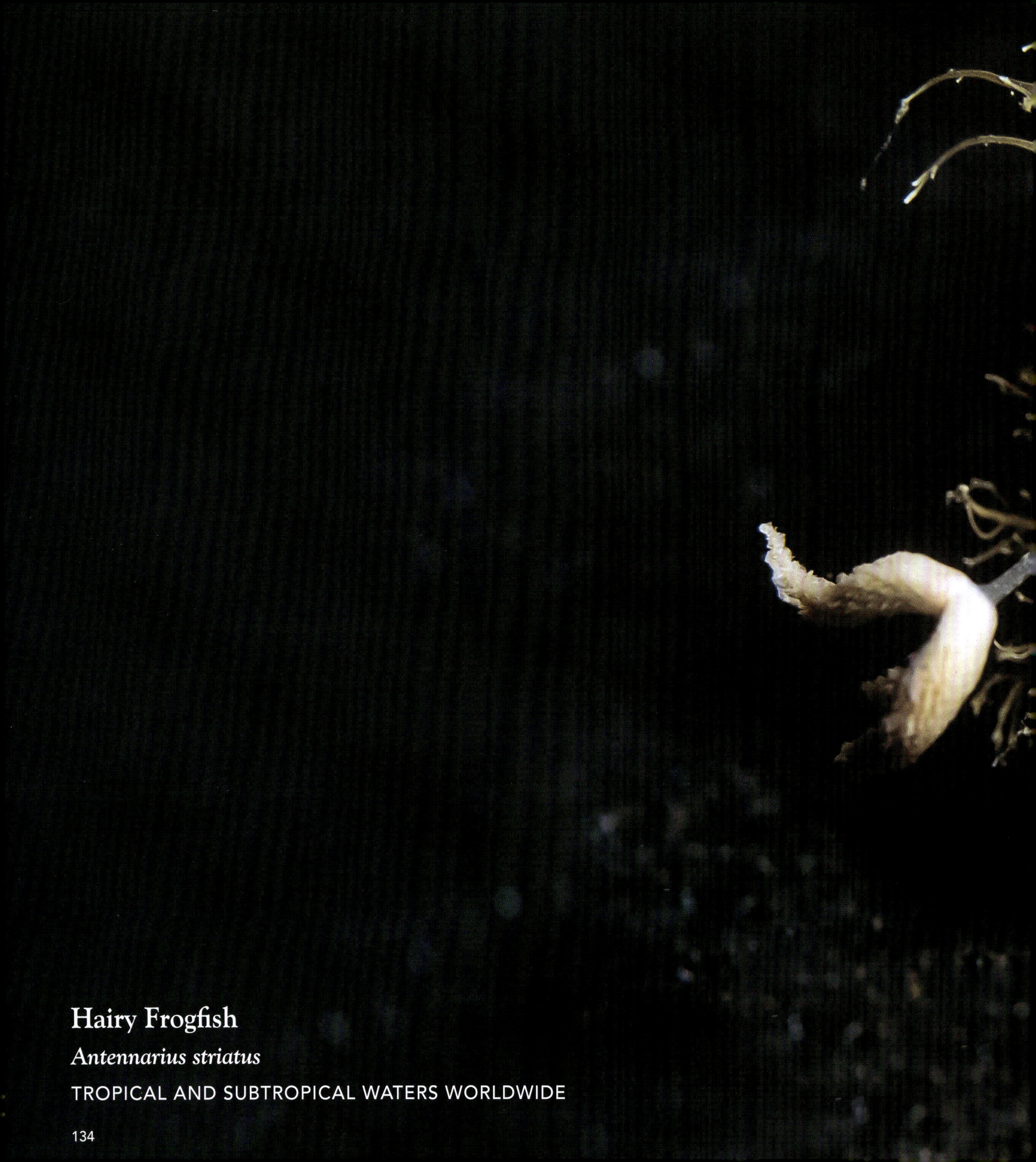

Hairy Frogfish

Antennarius striatus

TROPICAL AND SUBTROPICAL WATERS WORLDWIDE

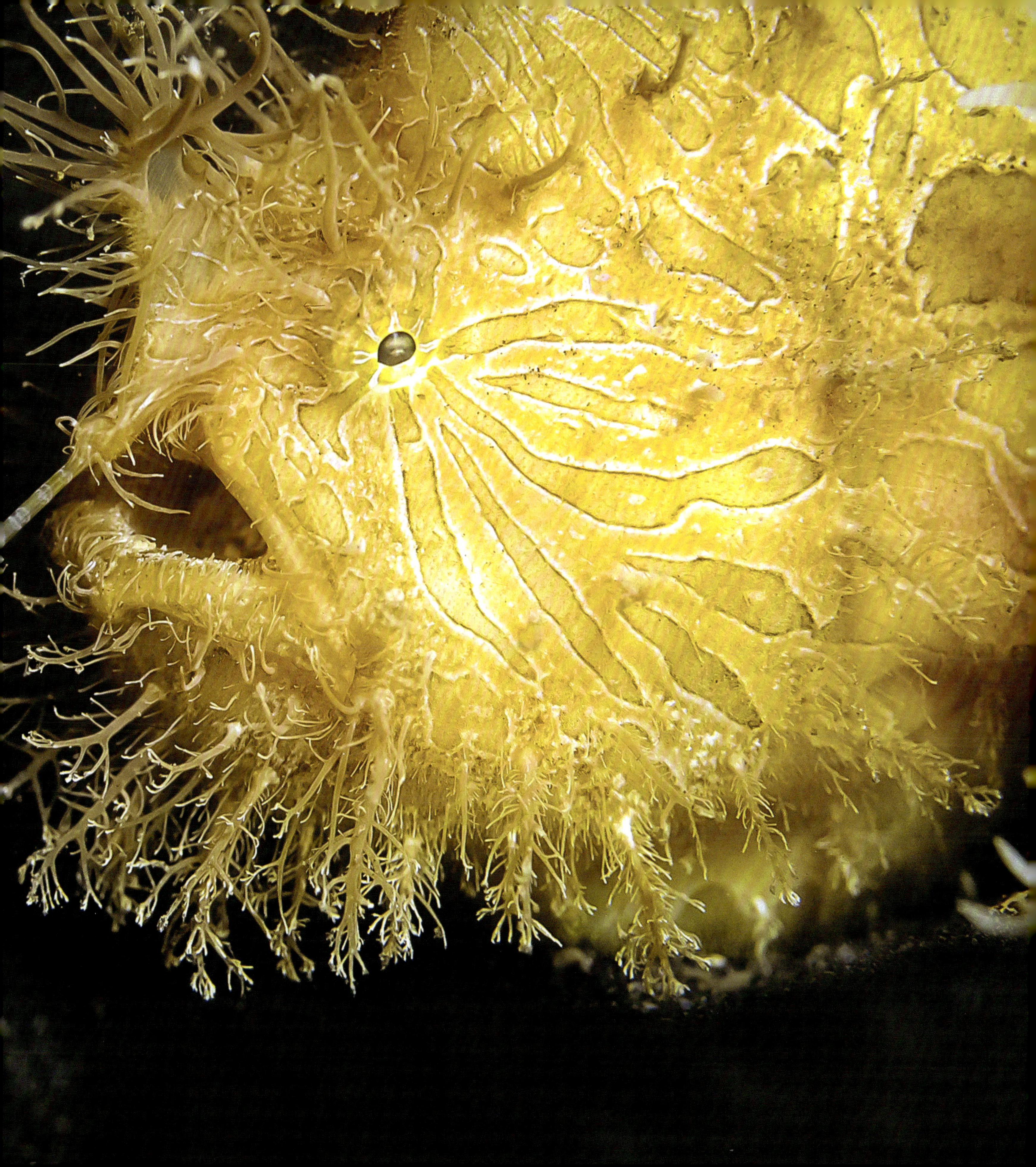

Tasselled Wobbegong

Eucrossorhinus dasypogon

REEFS OFF AUSTRALIA AND NEW GUINEA

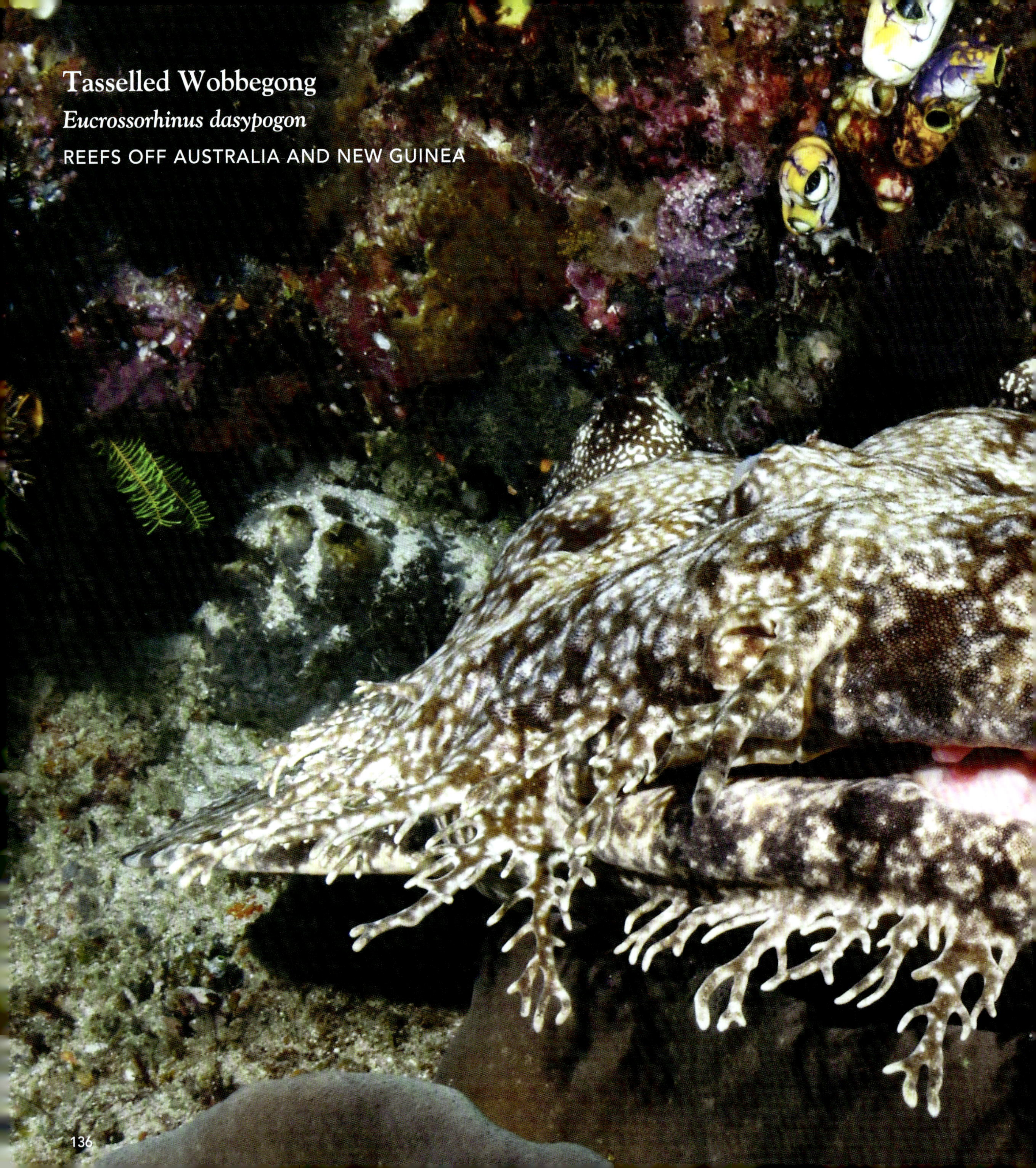

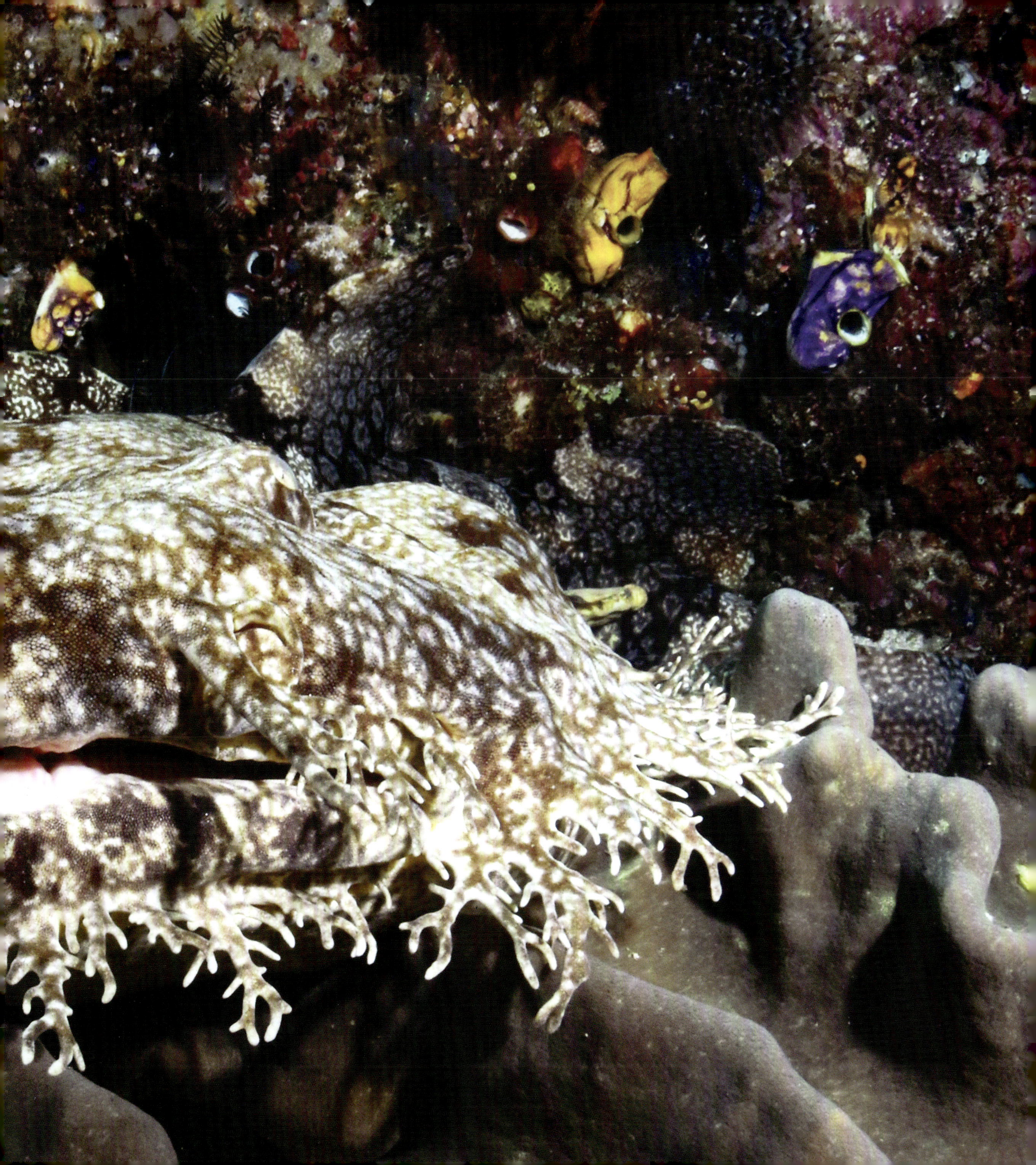

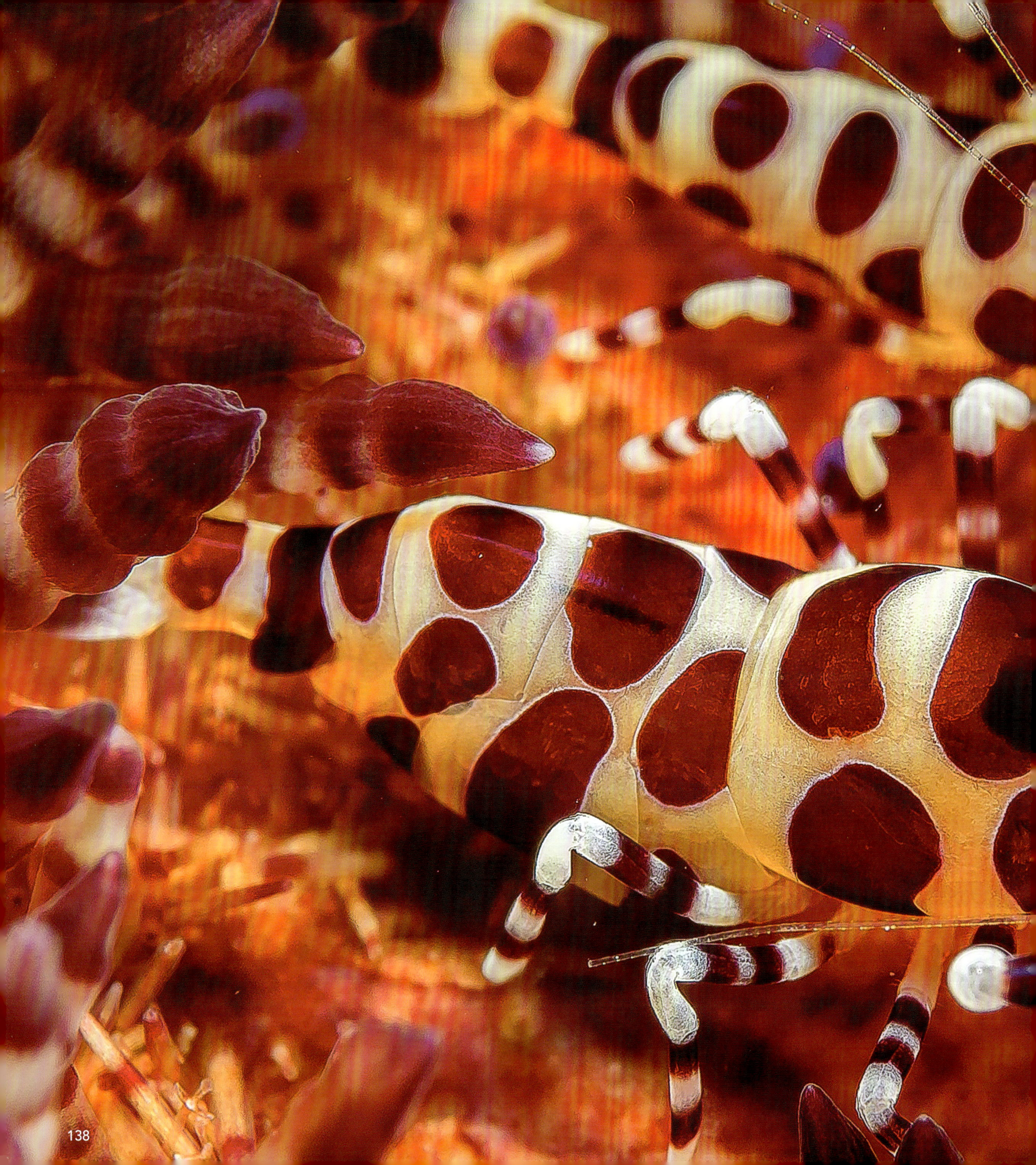

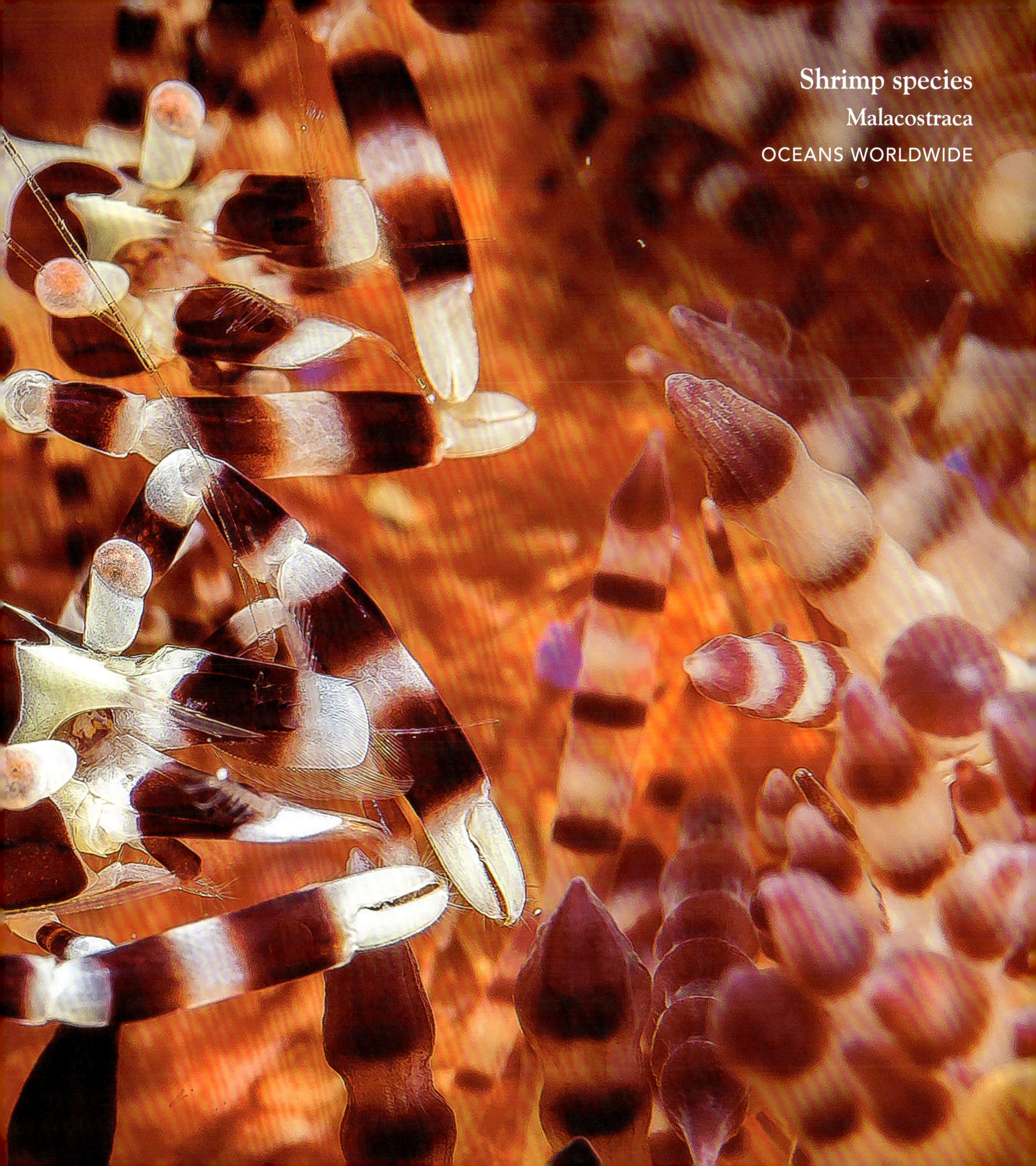
Shrimp species
Malacostraca
OCEANS WORLDWIDE

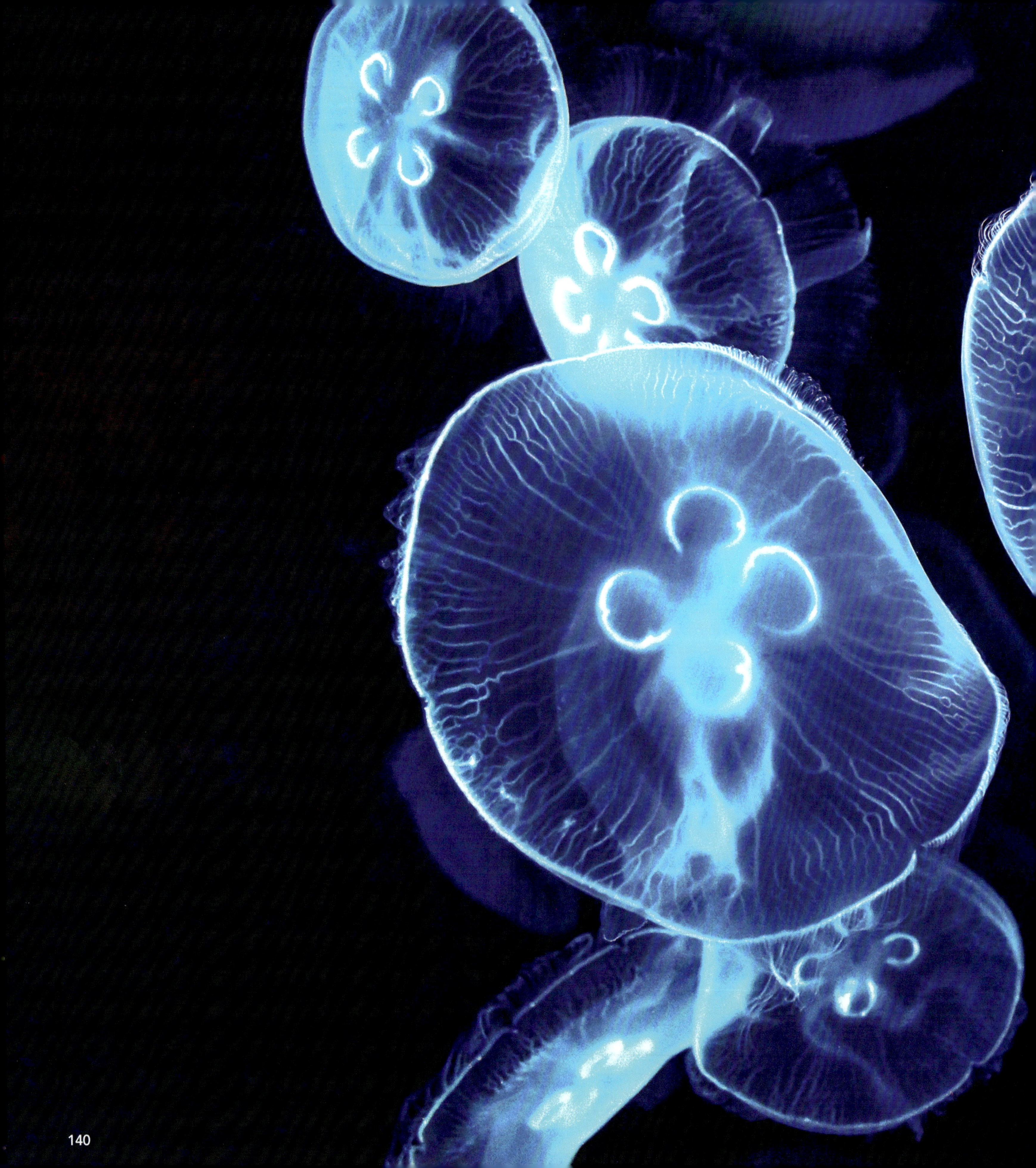

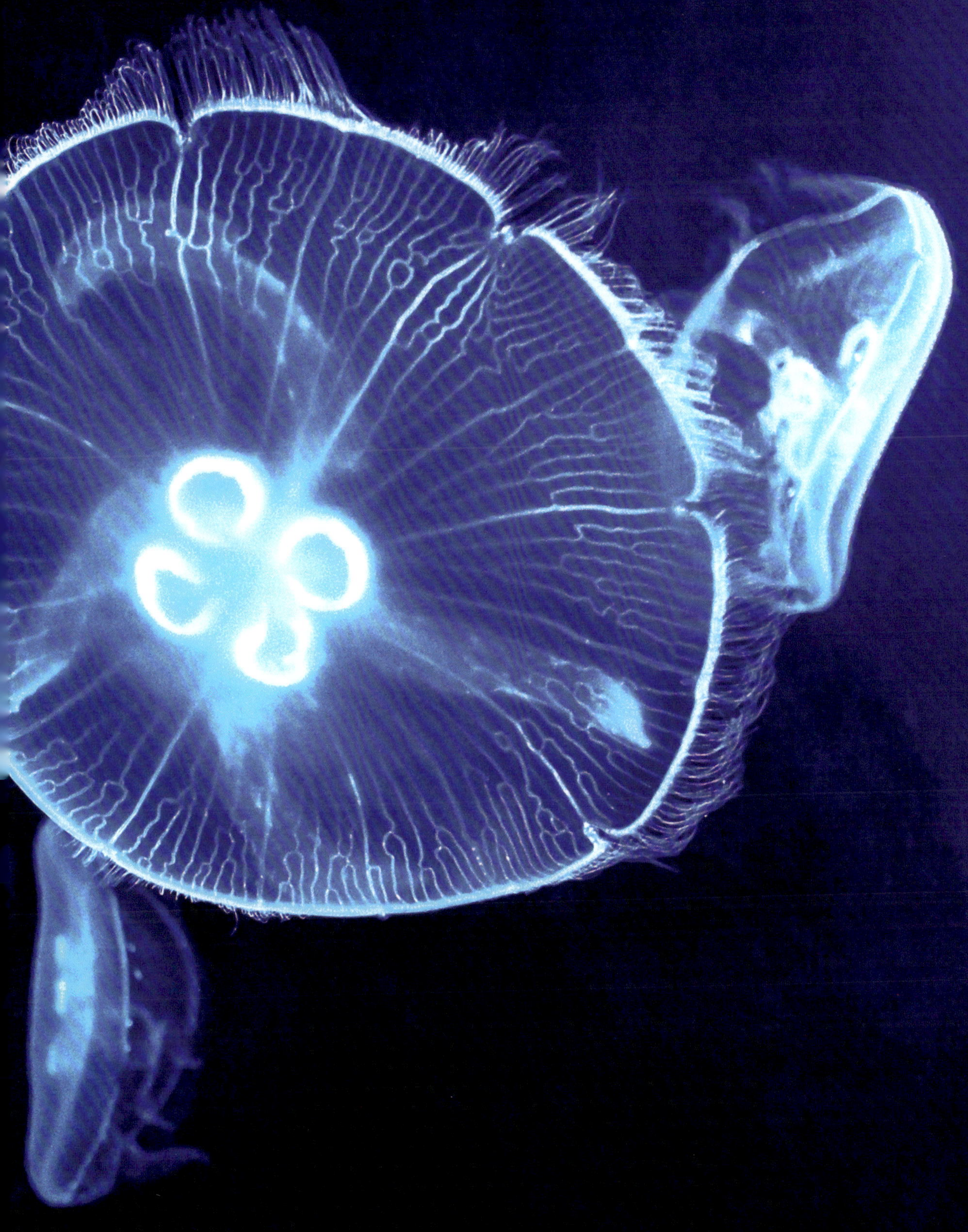

Jellyfish species

Medusozoa

OCEANS WORLDWIDE

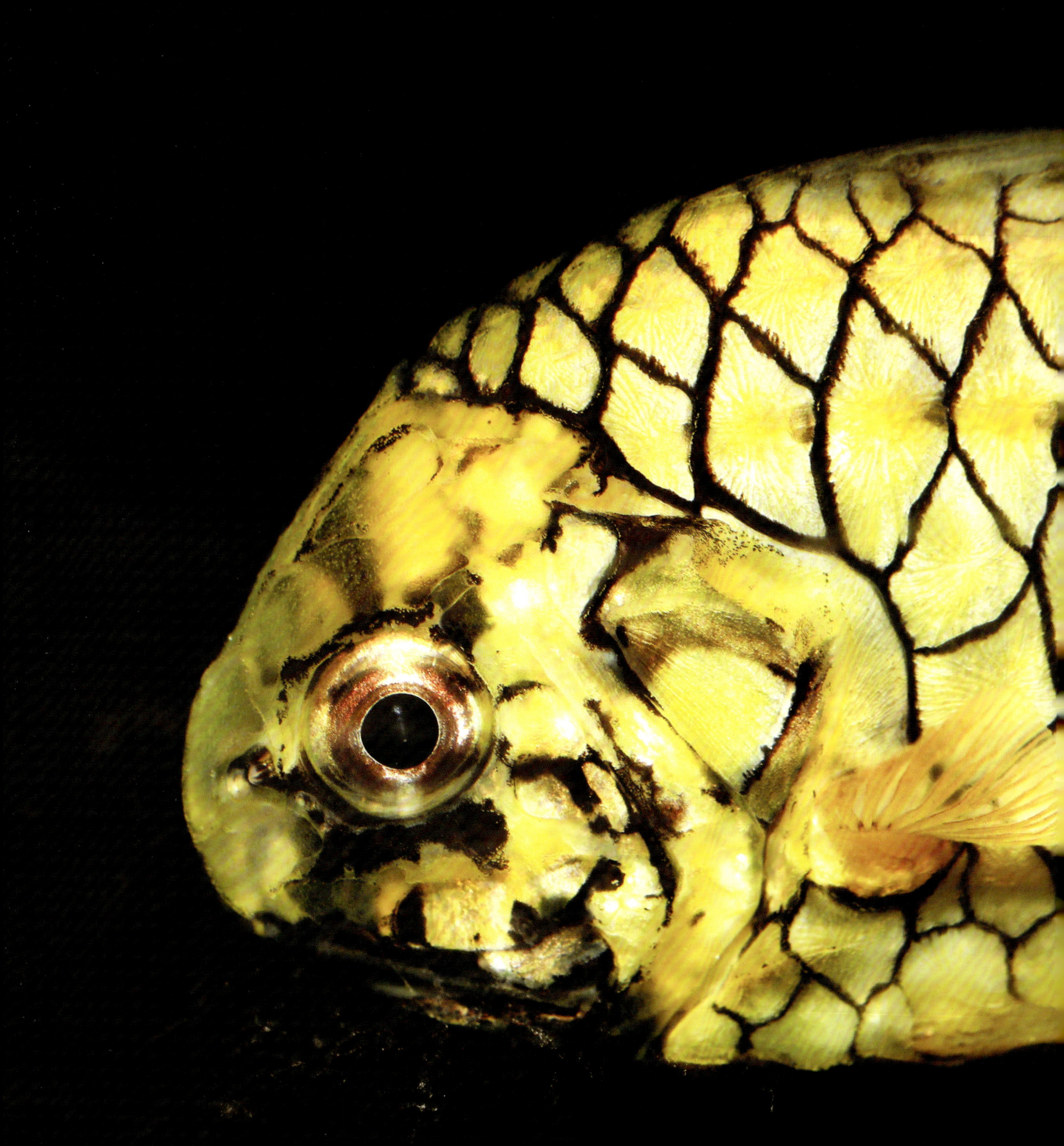

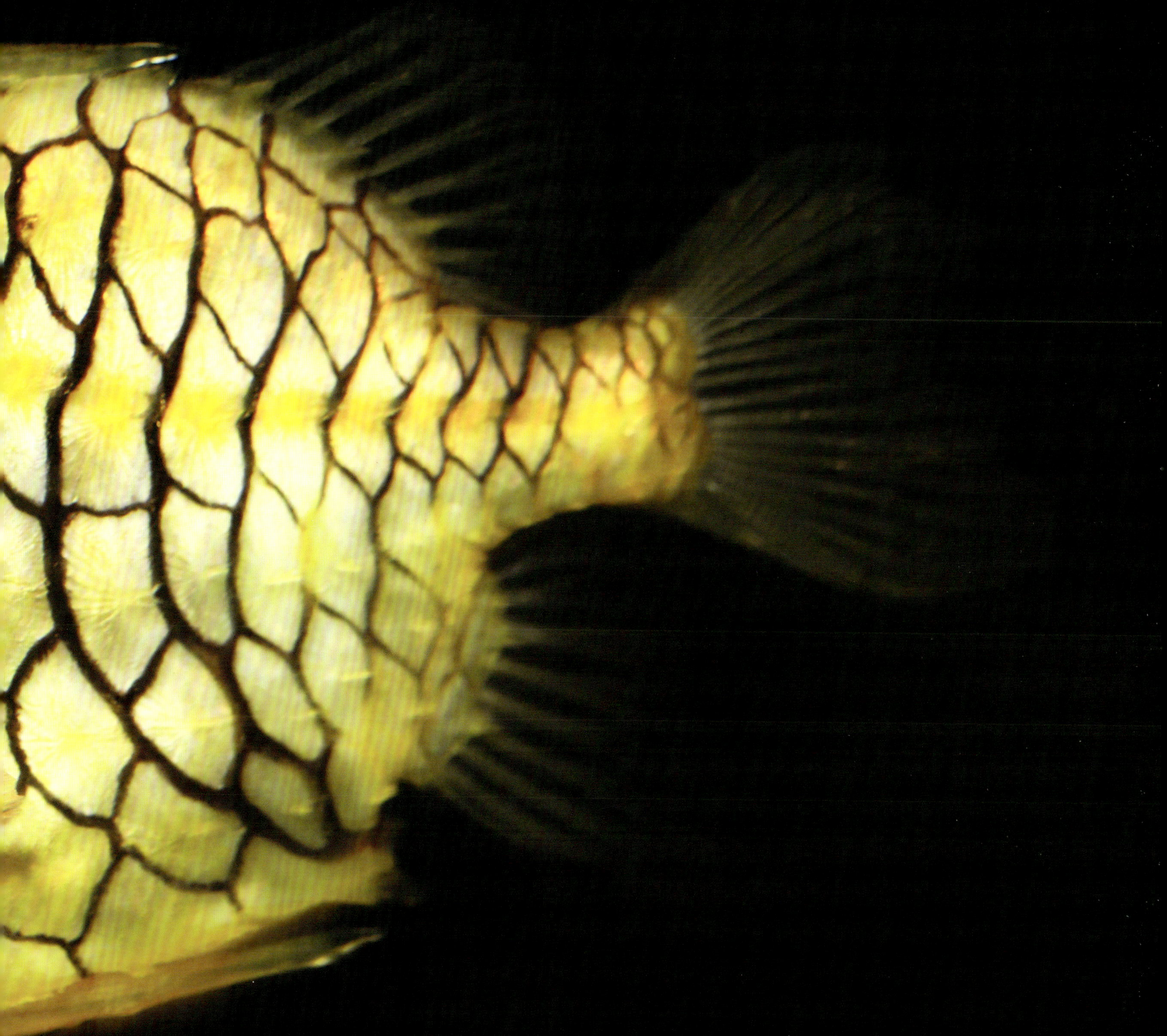

Pineapplefish

Monocentris japonica

INDO-PACIFIC

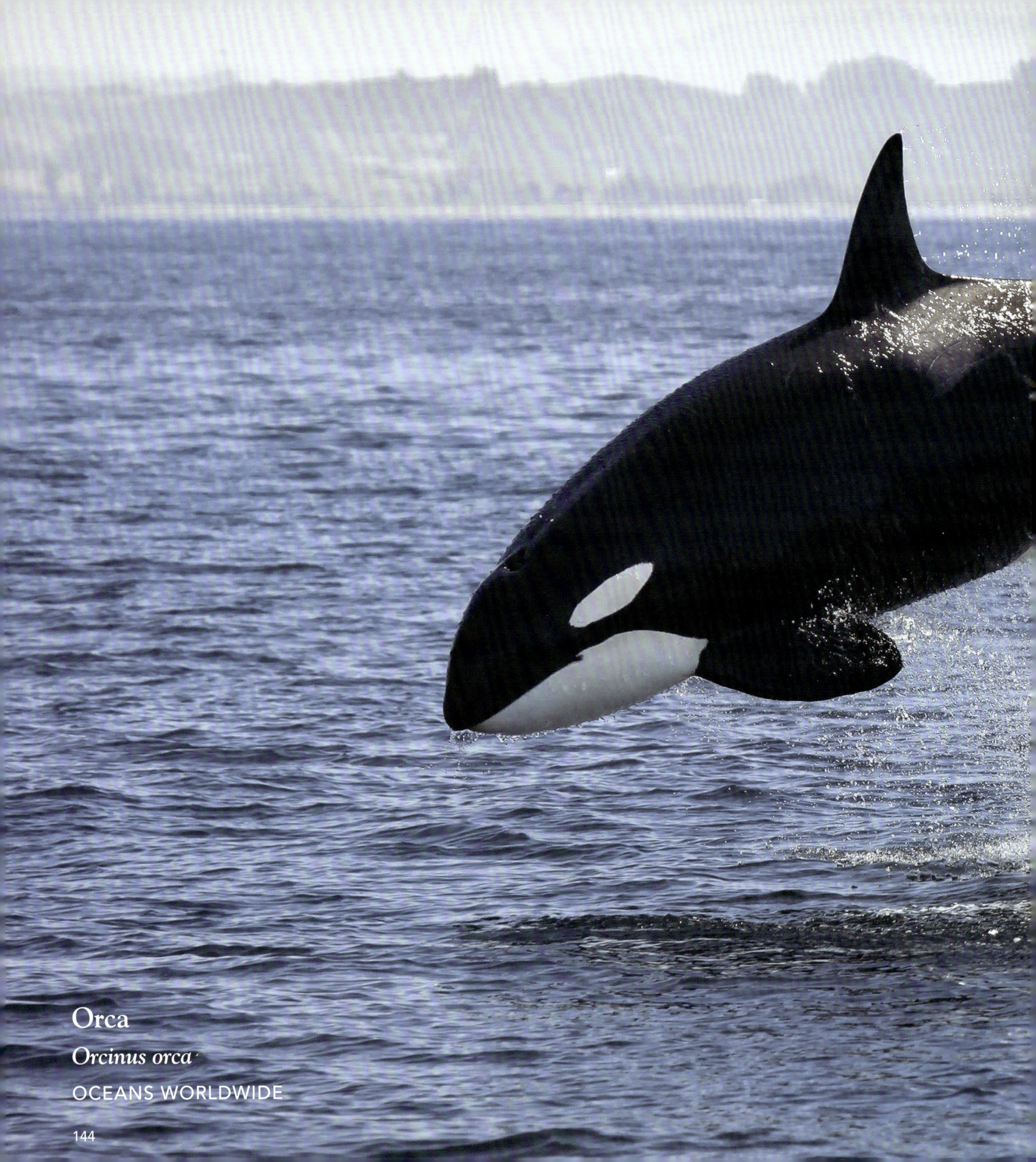

Orca

Orcinus orca

OCEANS WORLDWIDE

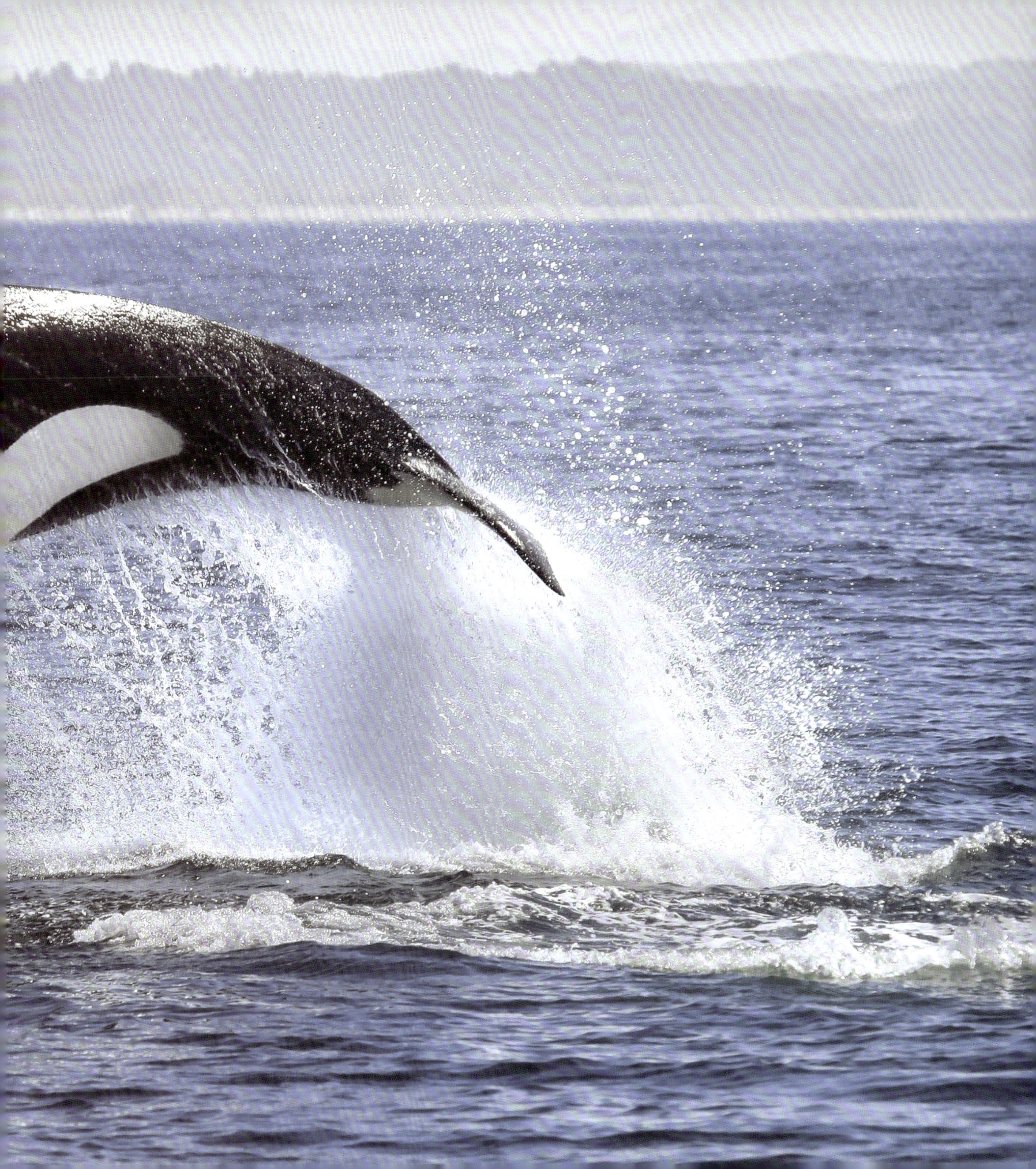

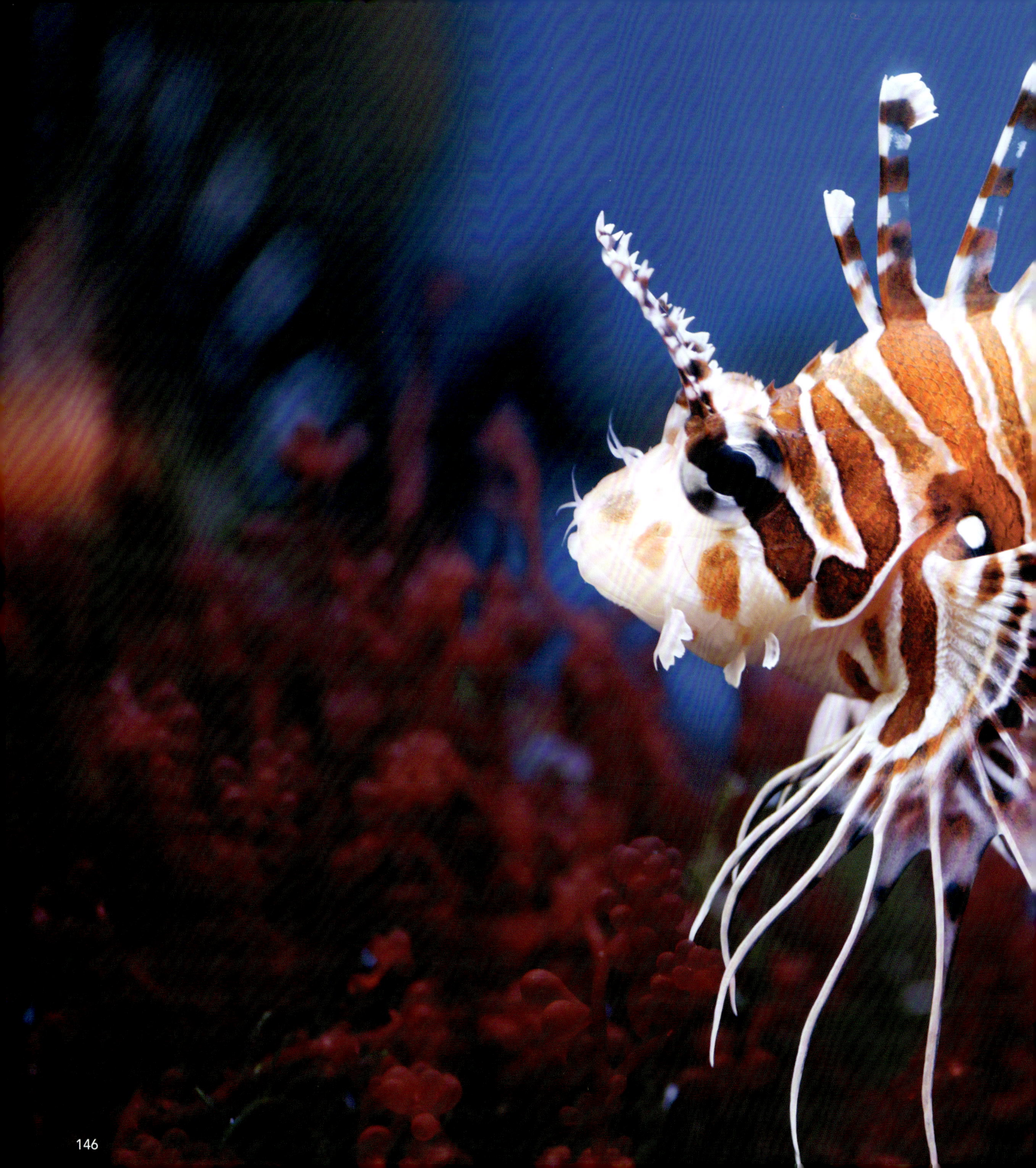

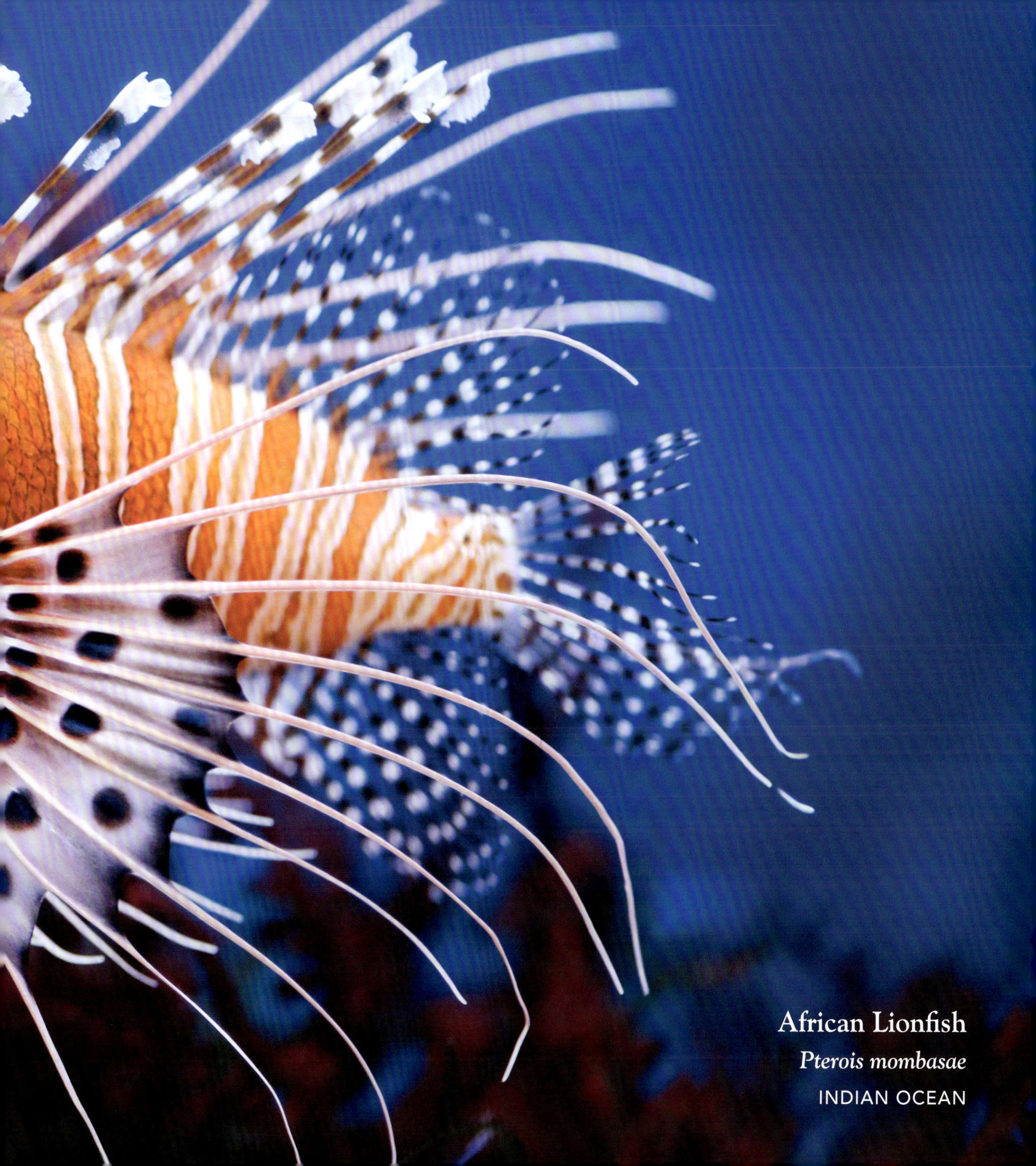

African Lionfish

Pterois mombasae

INDIAN OCEAN

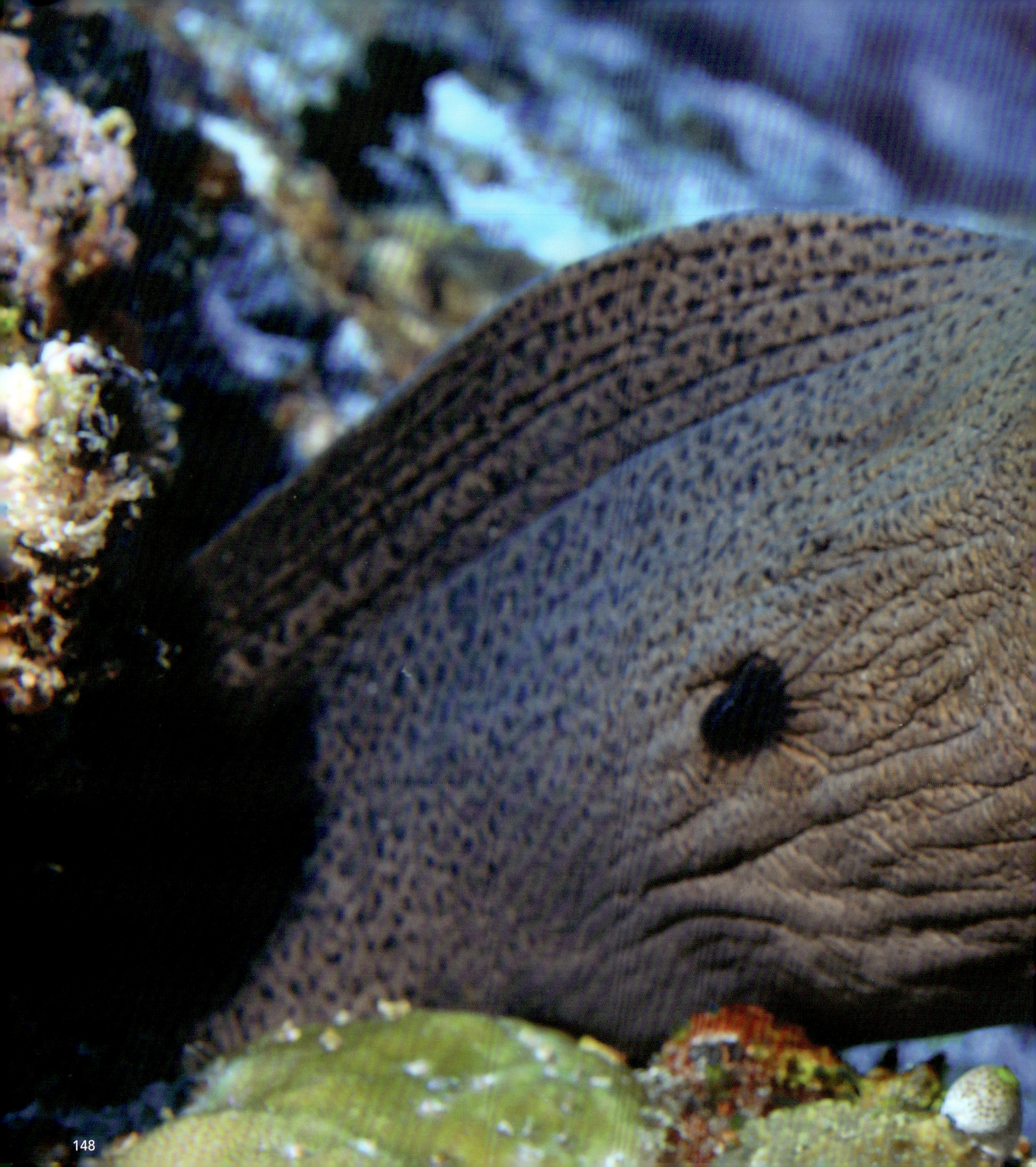

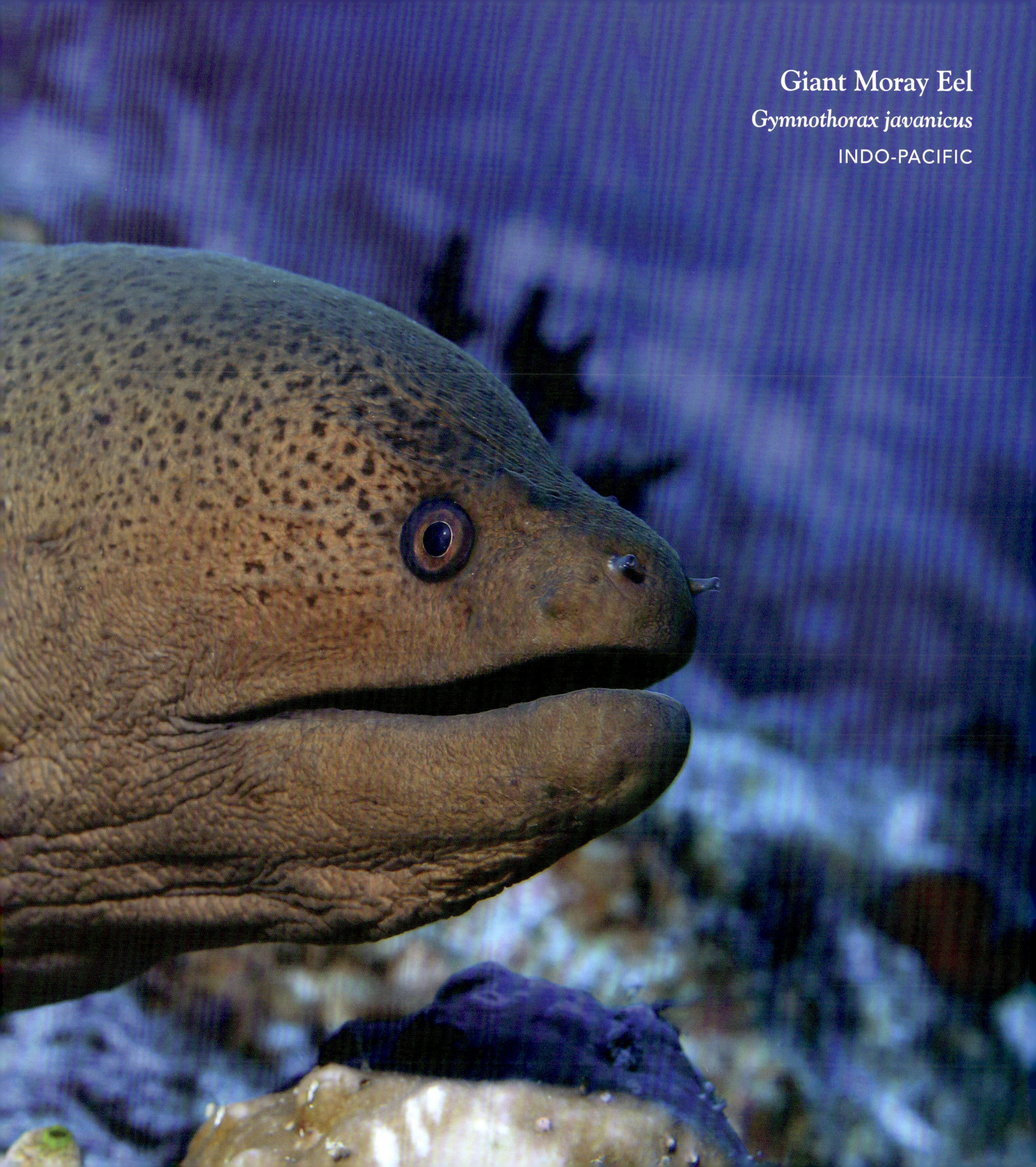

Giant Moray Eel

Gymnothorax javanicus

INDO-PACIFIC

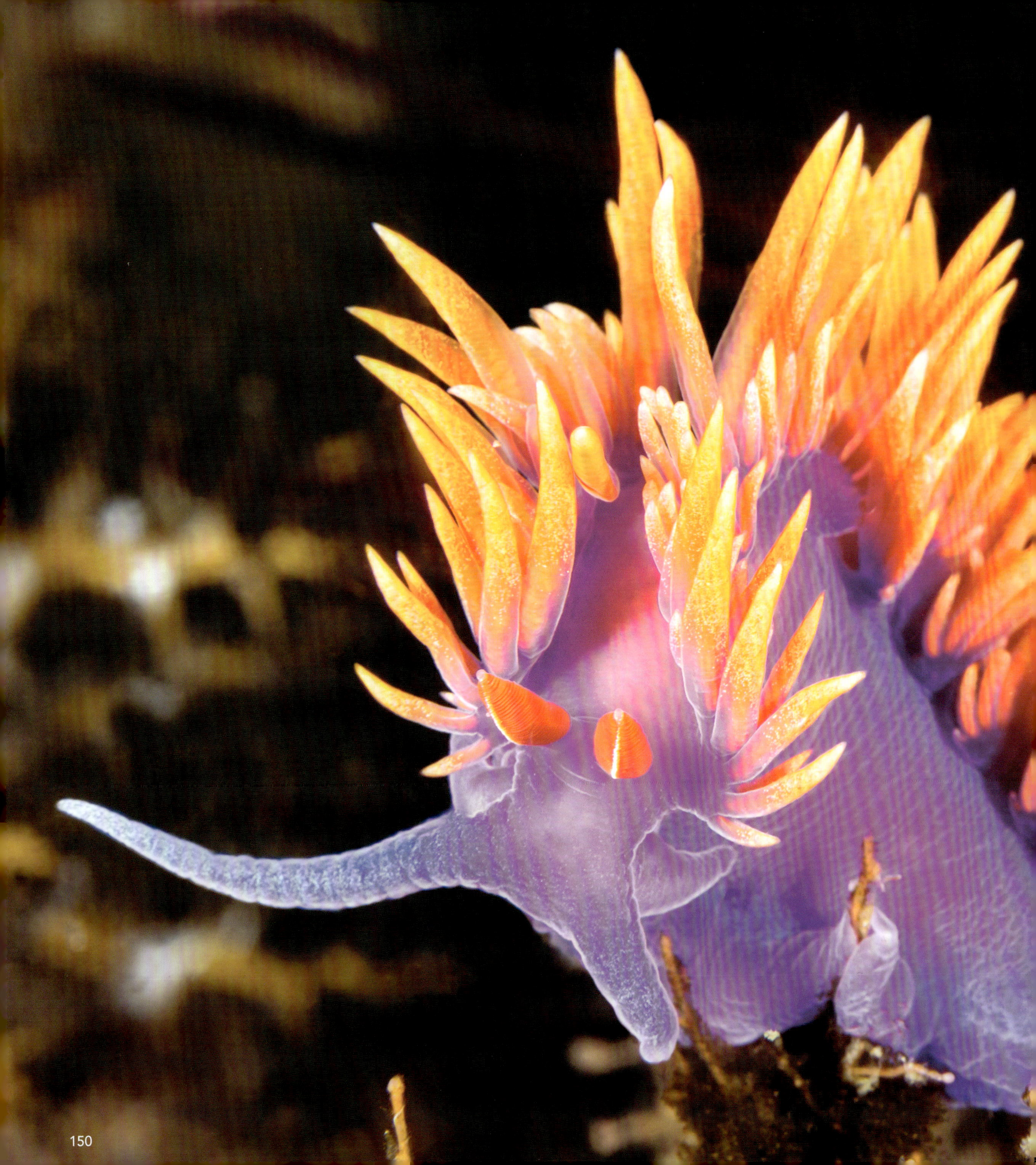

Nudibranch species

Nudibranchia

TROPICAL OCEANS

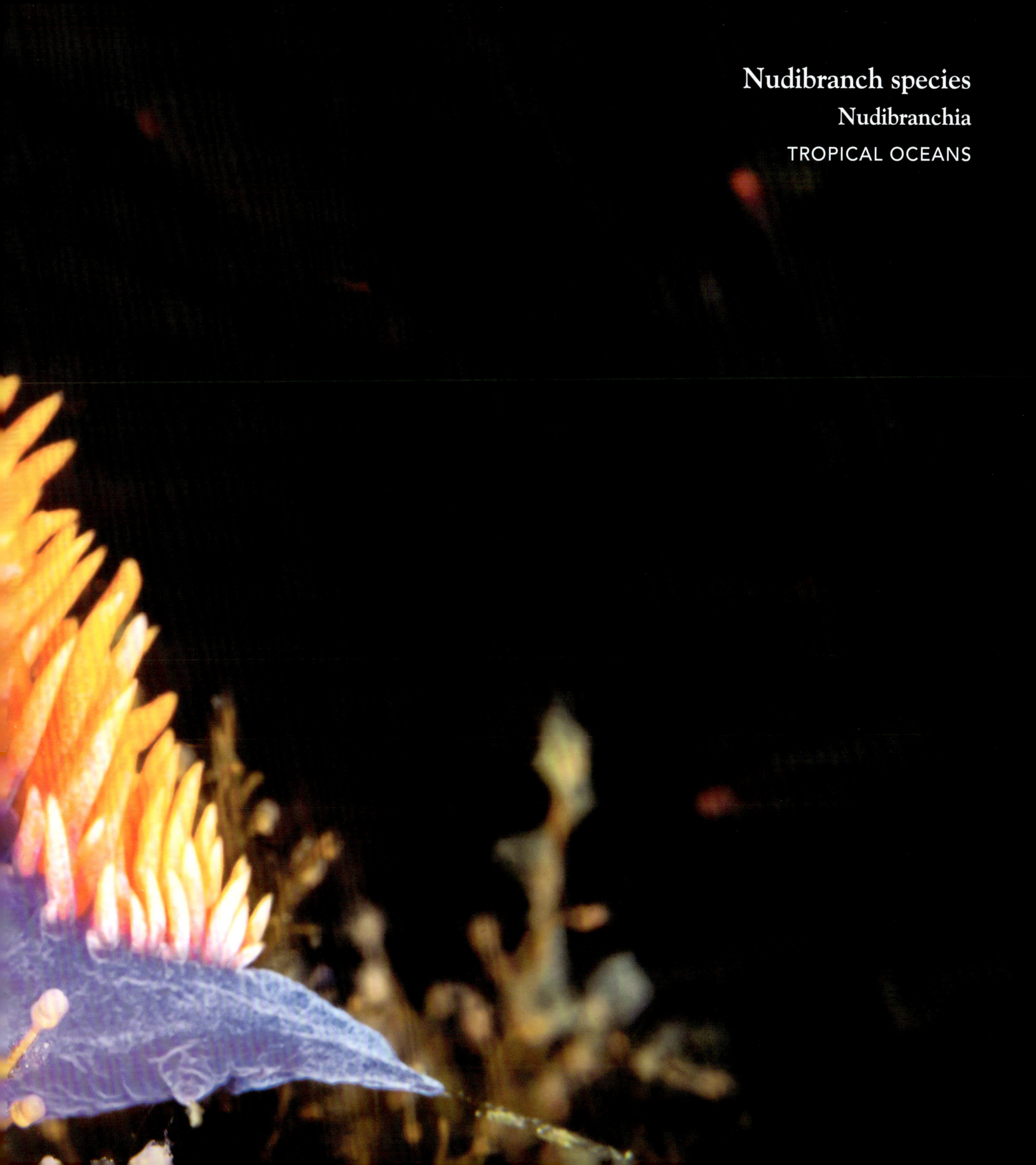

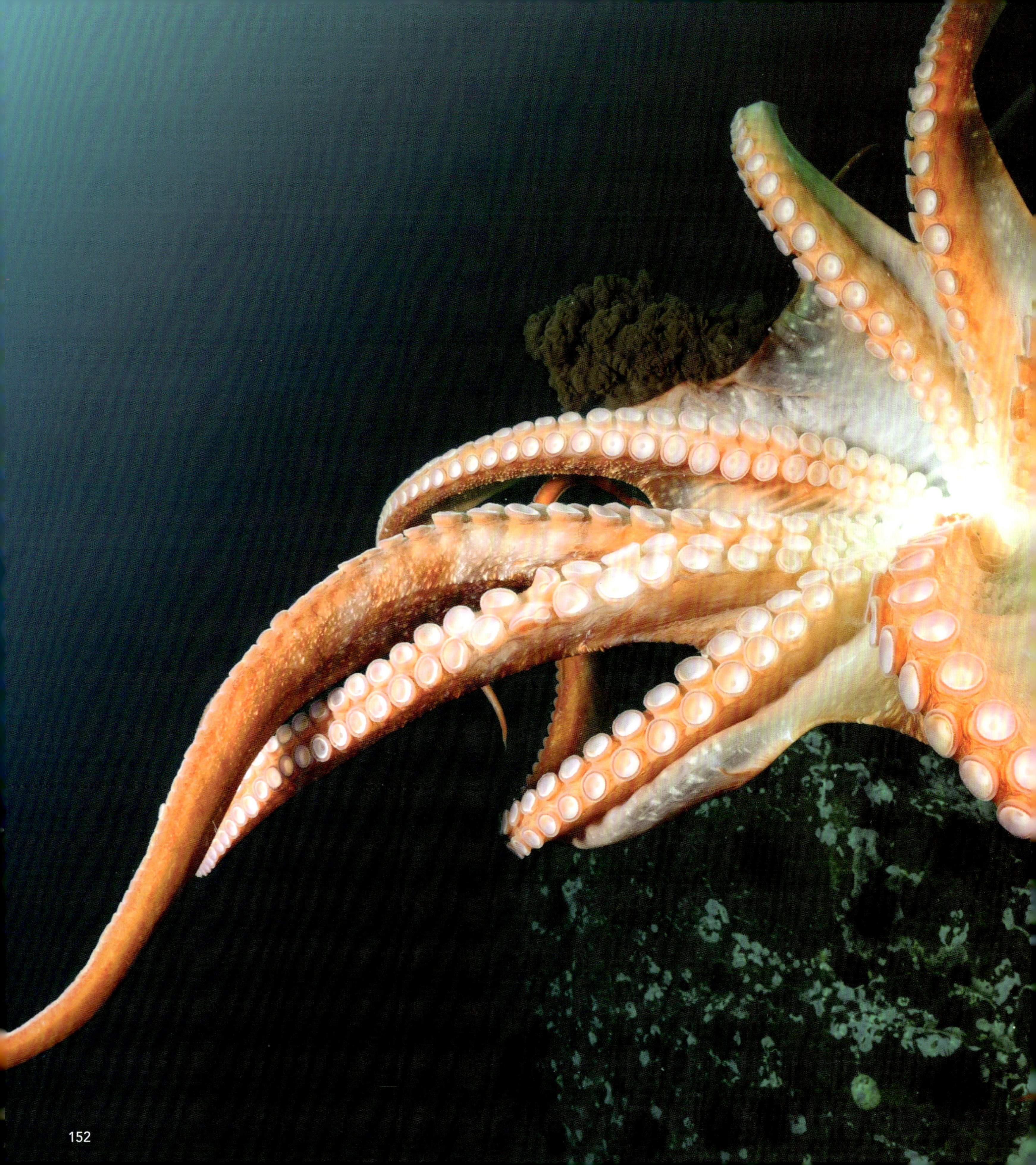

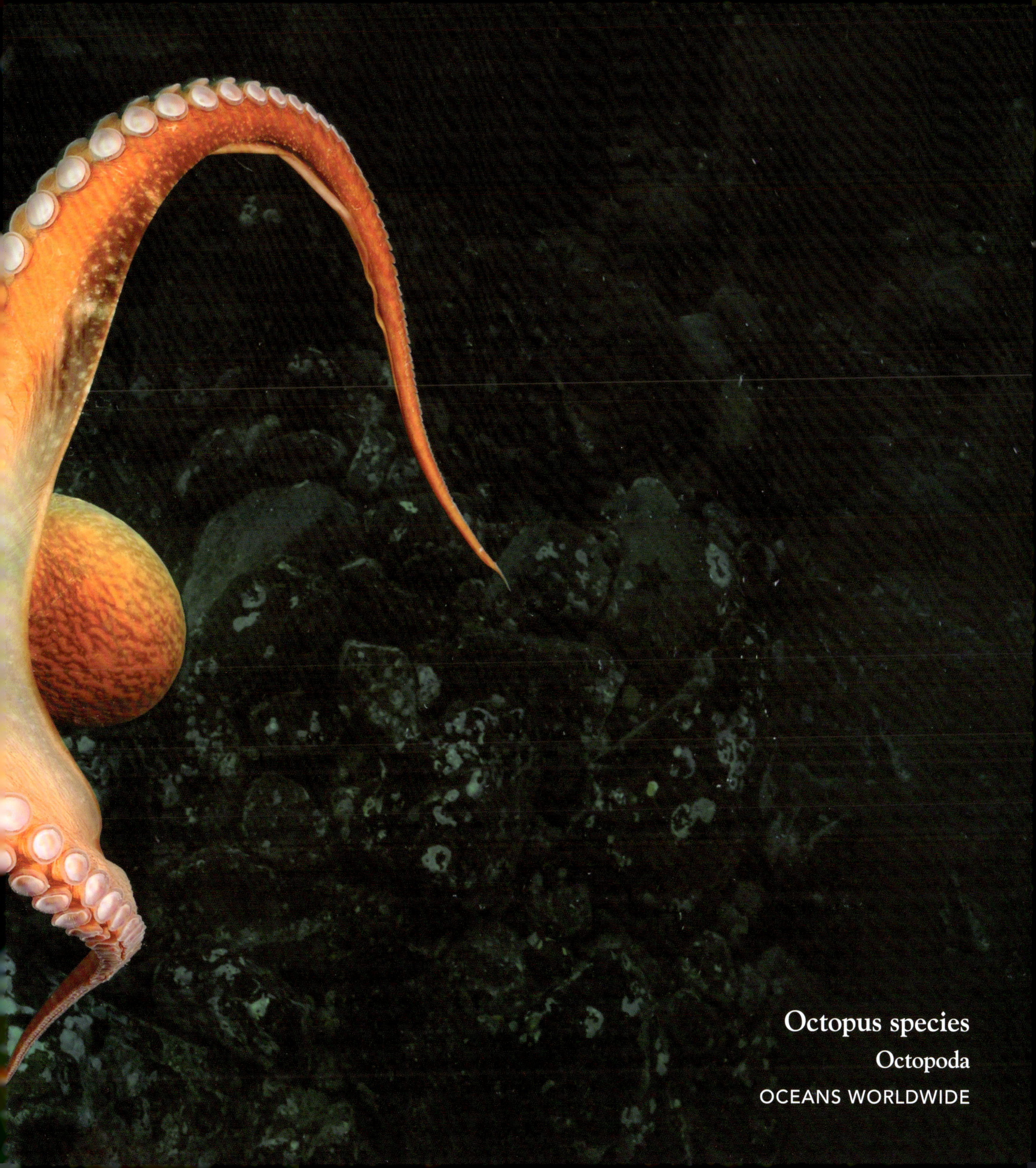

Octopus species

Octopoda

OCEANS WORLDWIDE

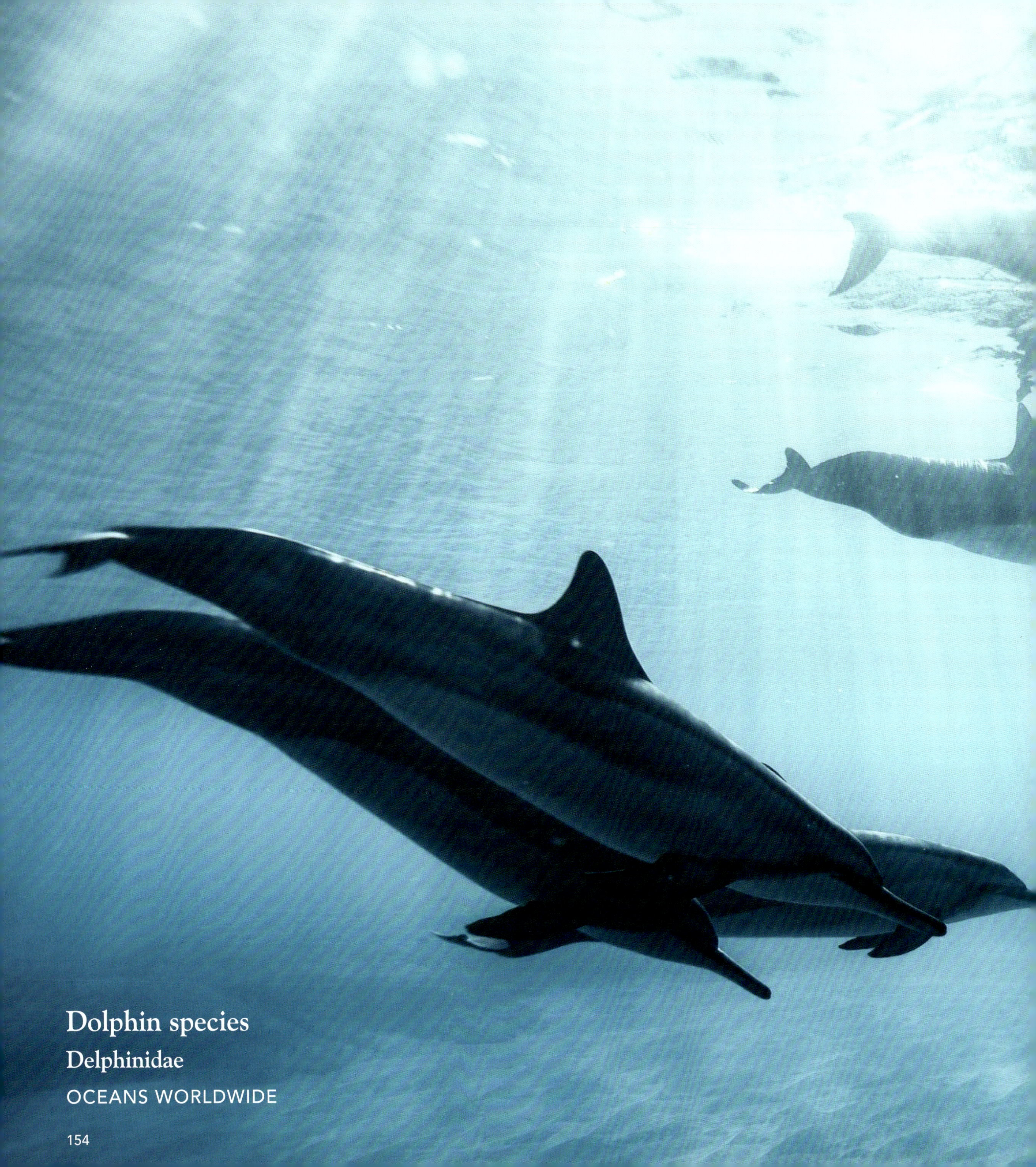

Dolphin species

Delphinidae

OCEANS WORLDWIDE

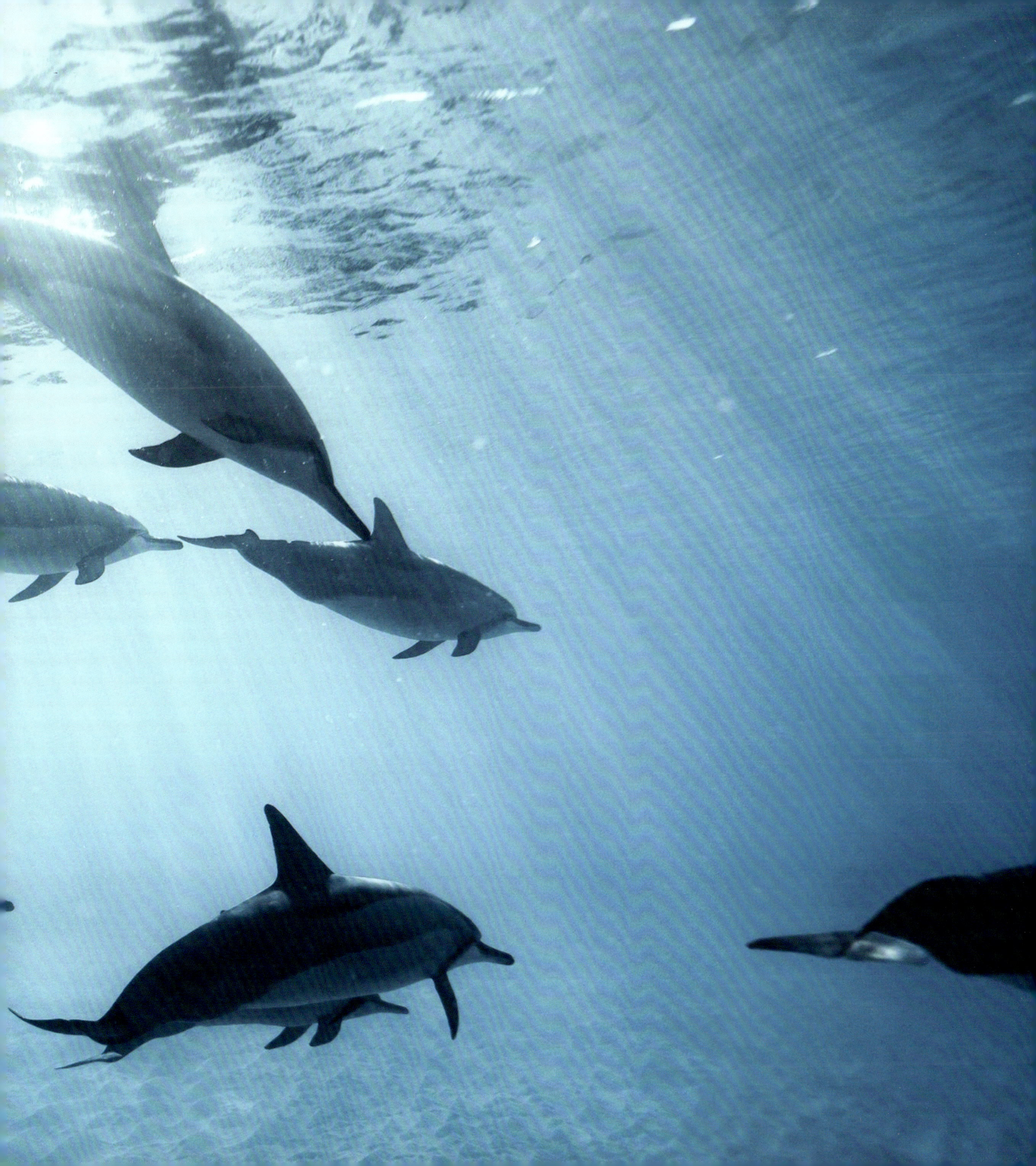

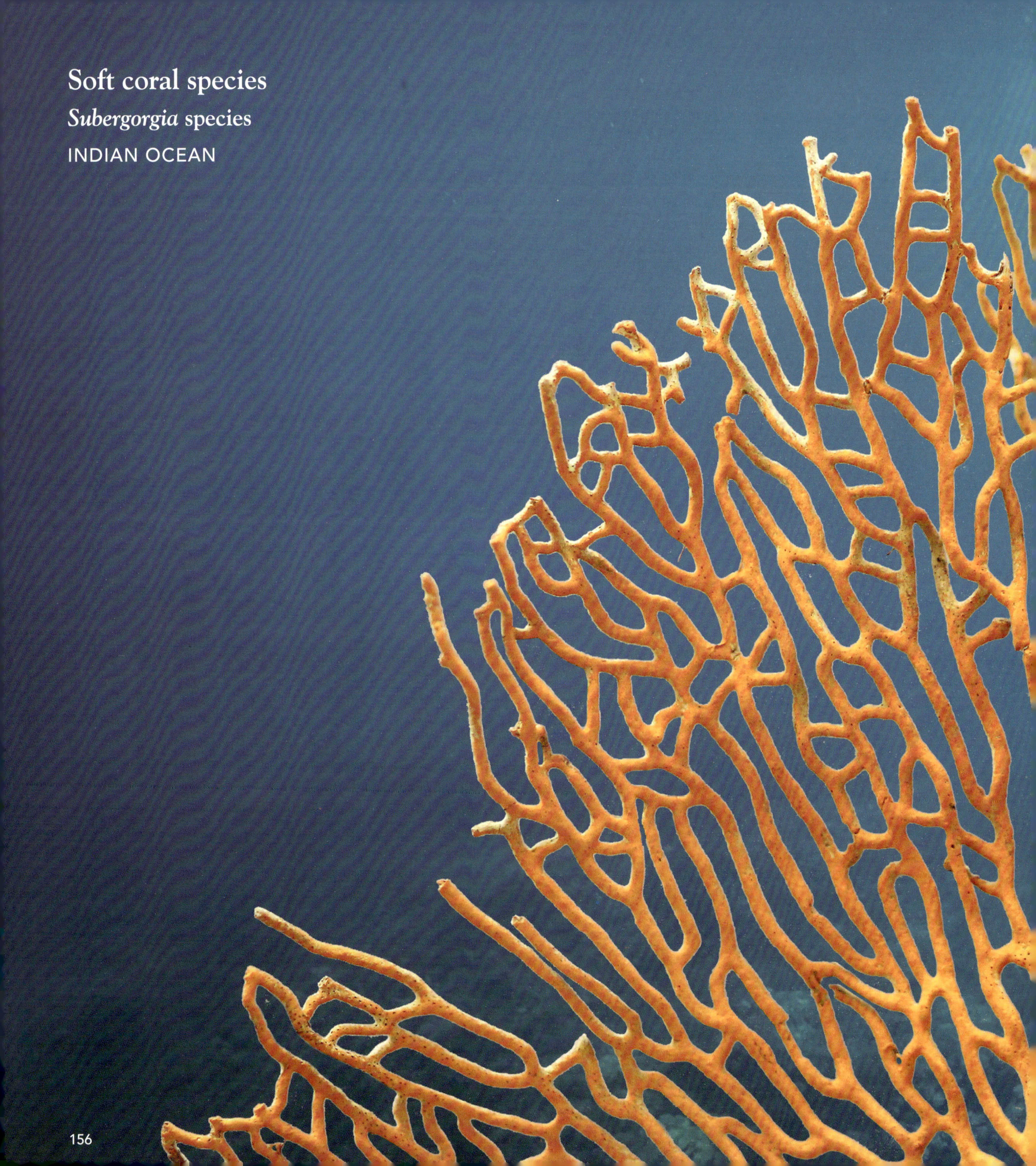

Soft coral species

Subergorgia species

INDIAN OCEAN

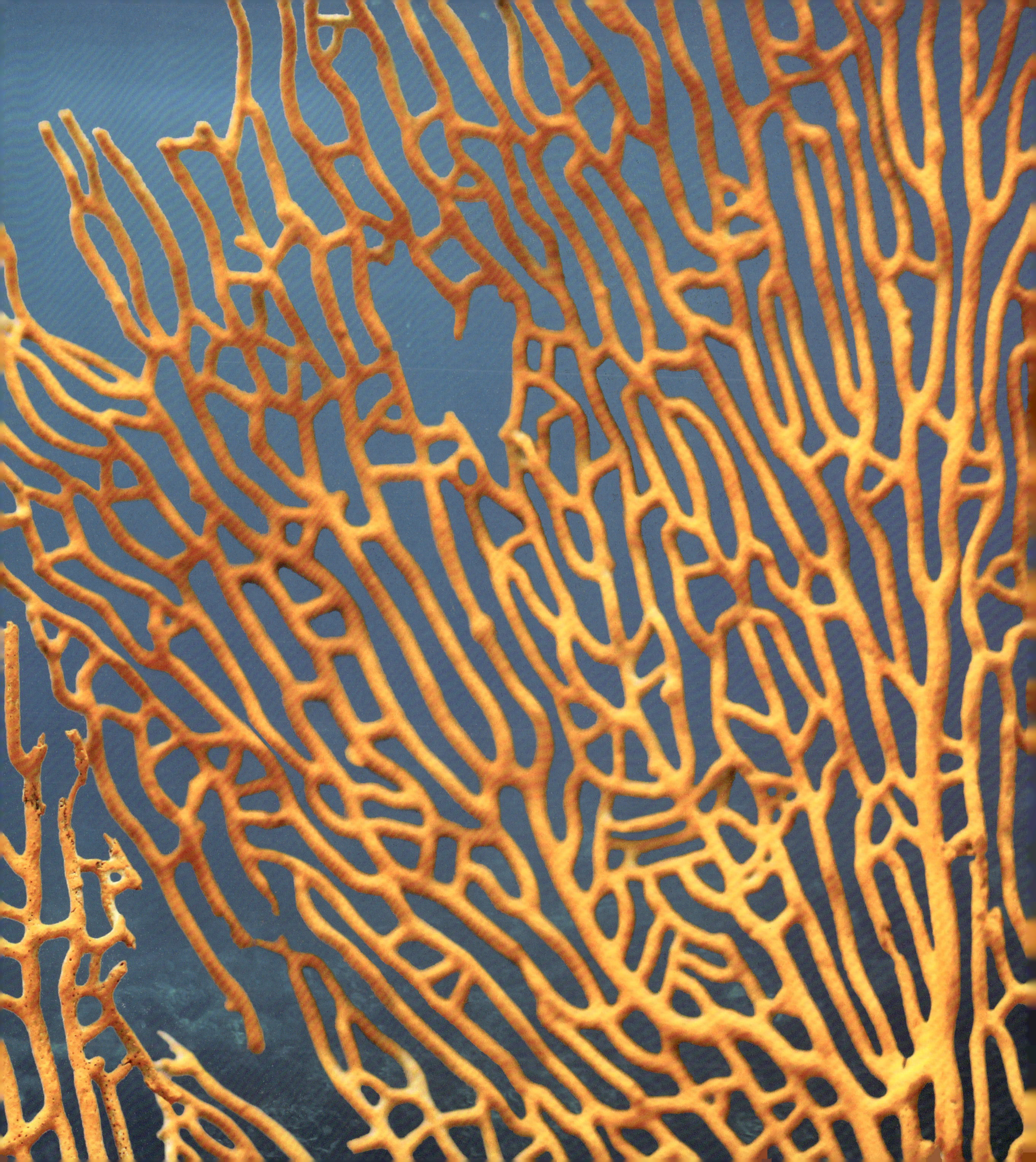

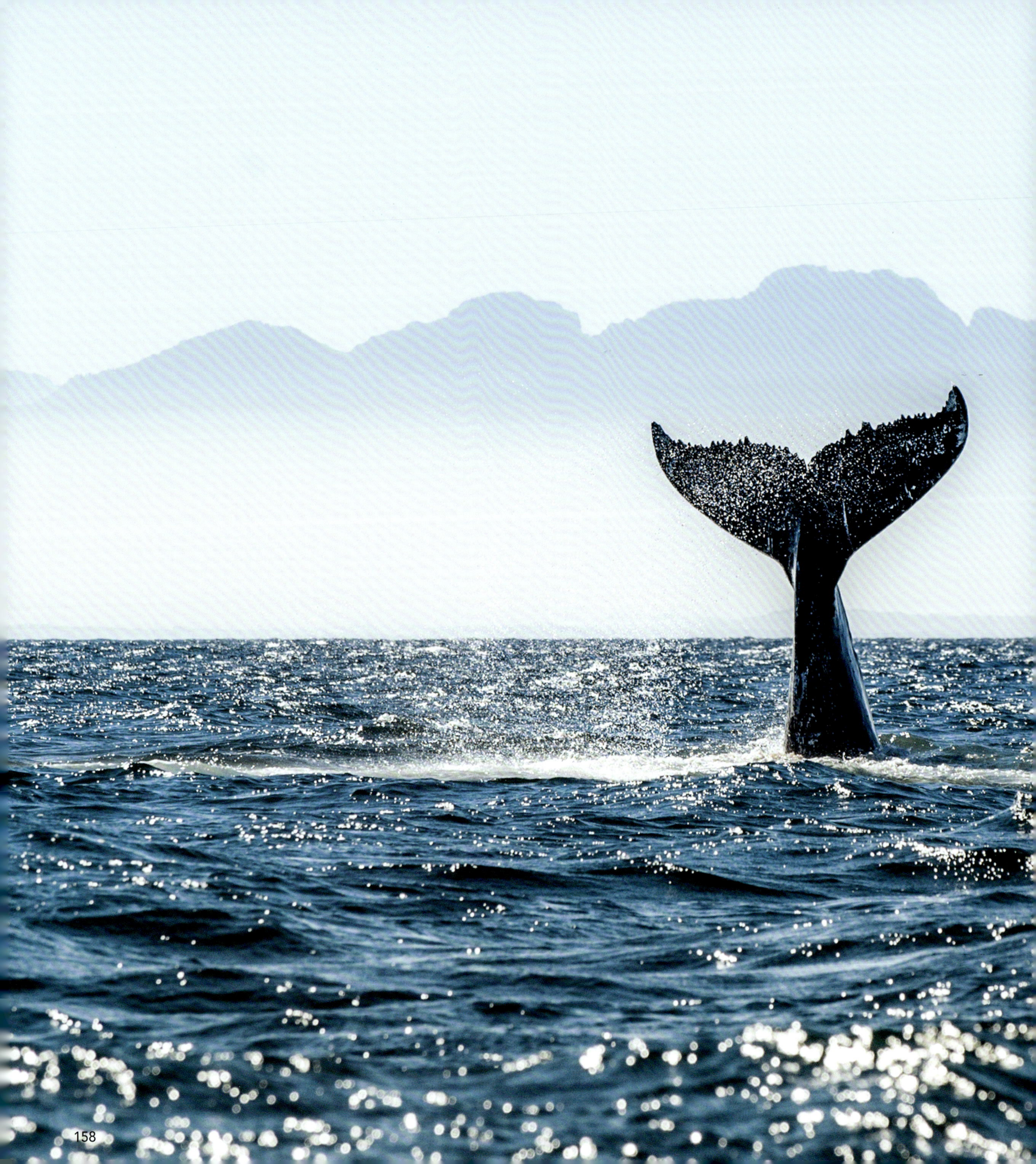

Humpback Whale

Megaptera novaeangliae

OCEANS WORLDWIDE

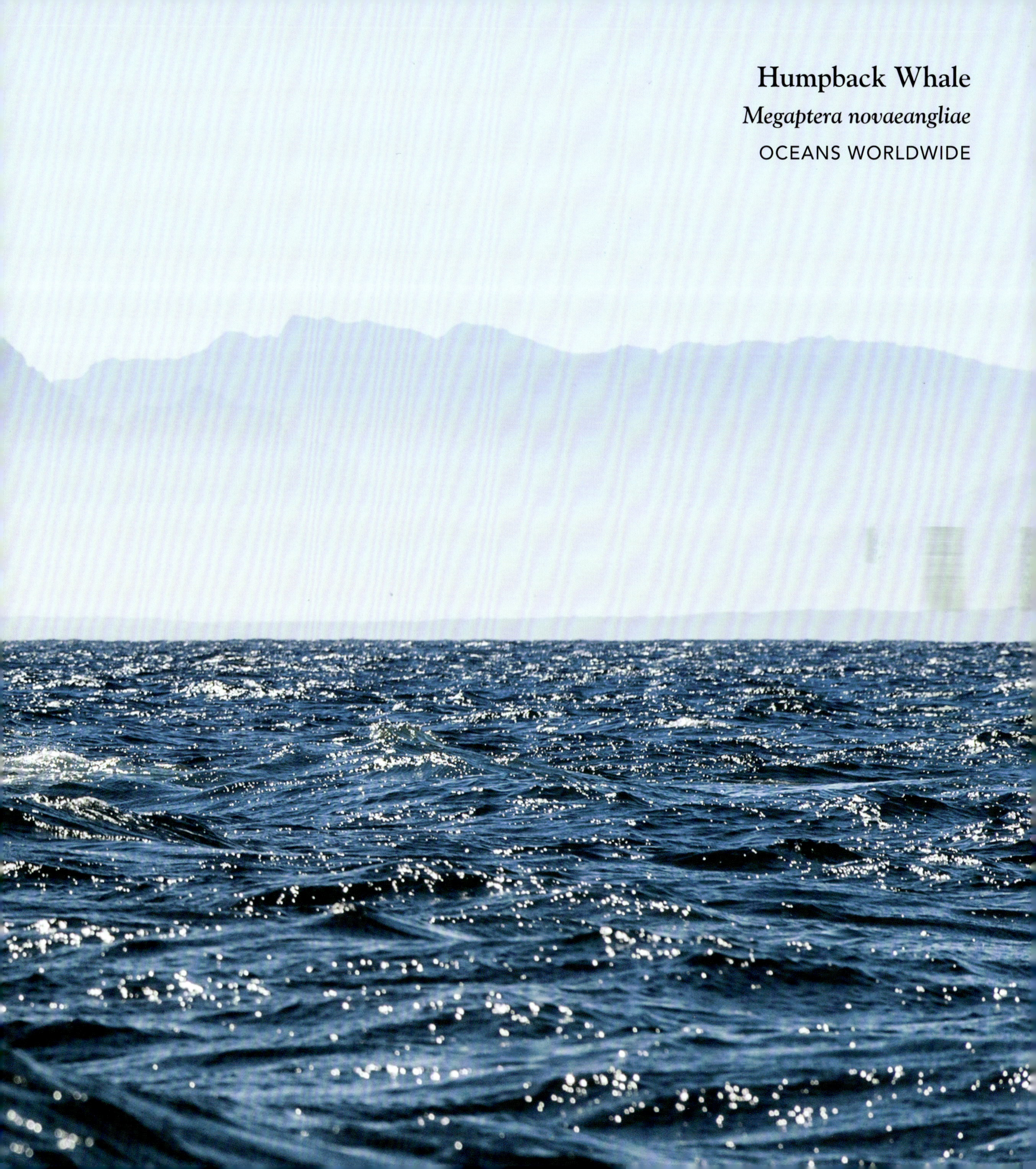

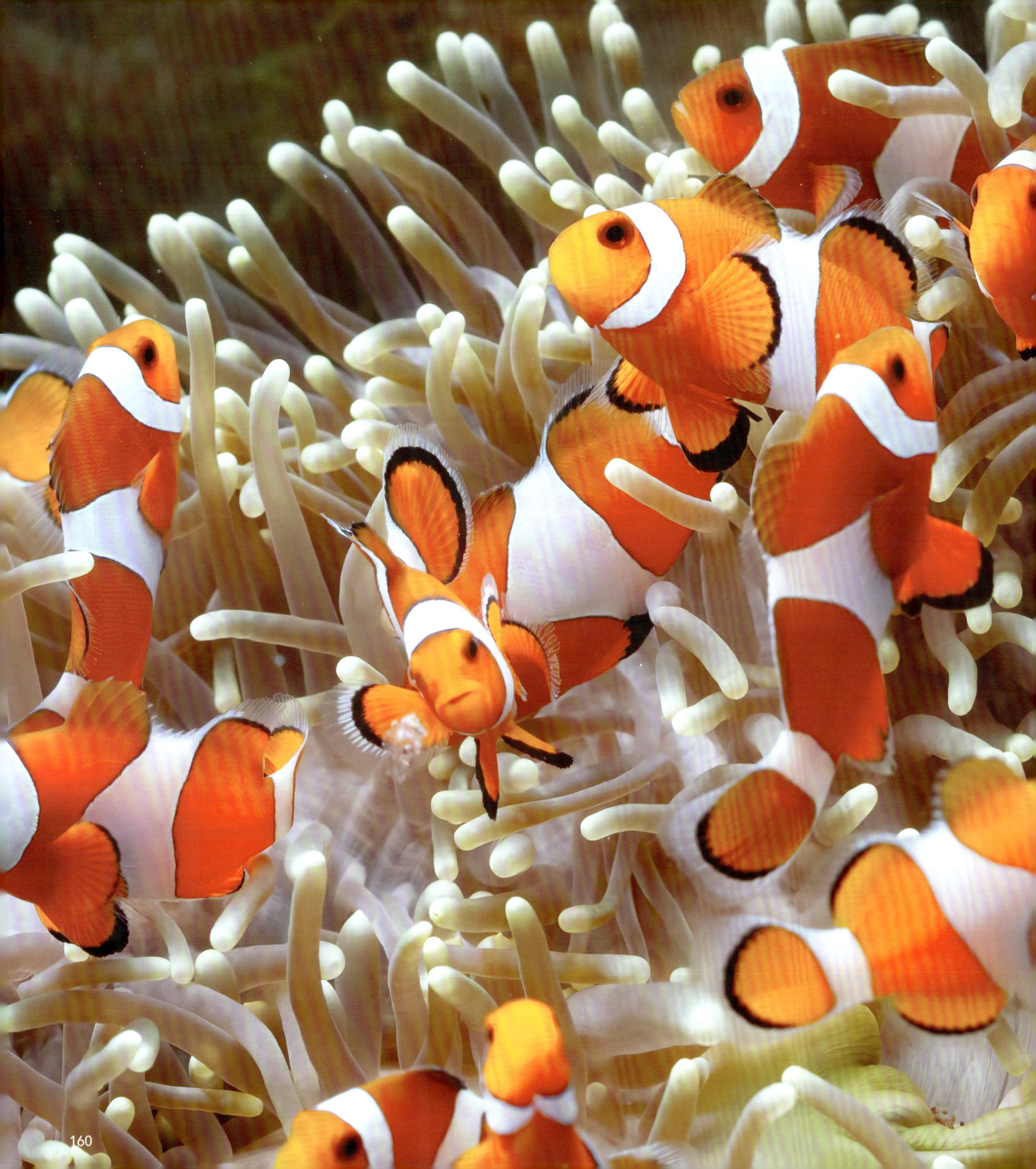

Ocellaris Anemonefish

Amphiprion ocellaris

INDO-PACIFIC

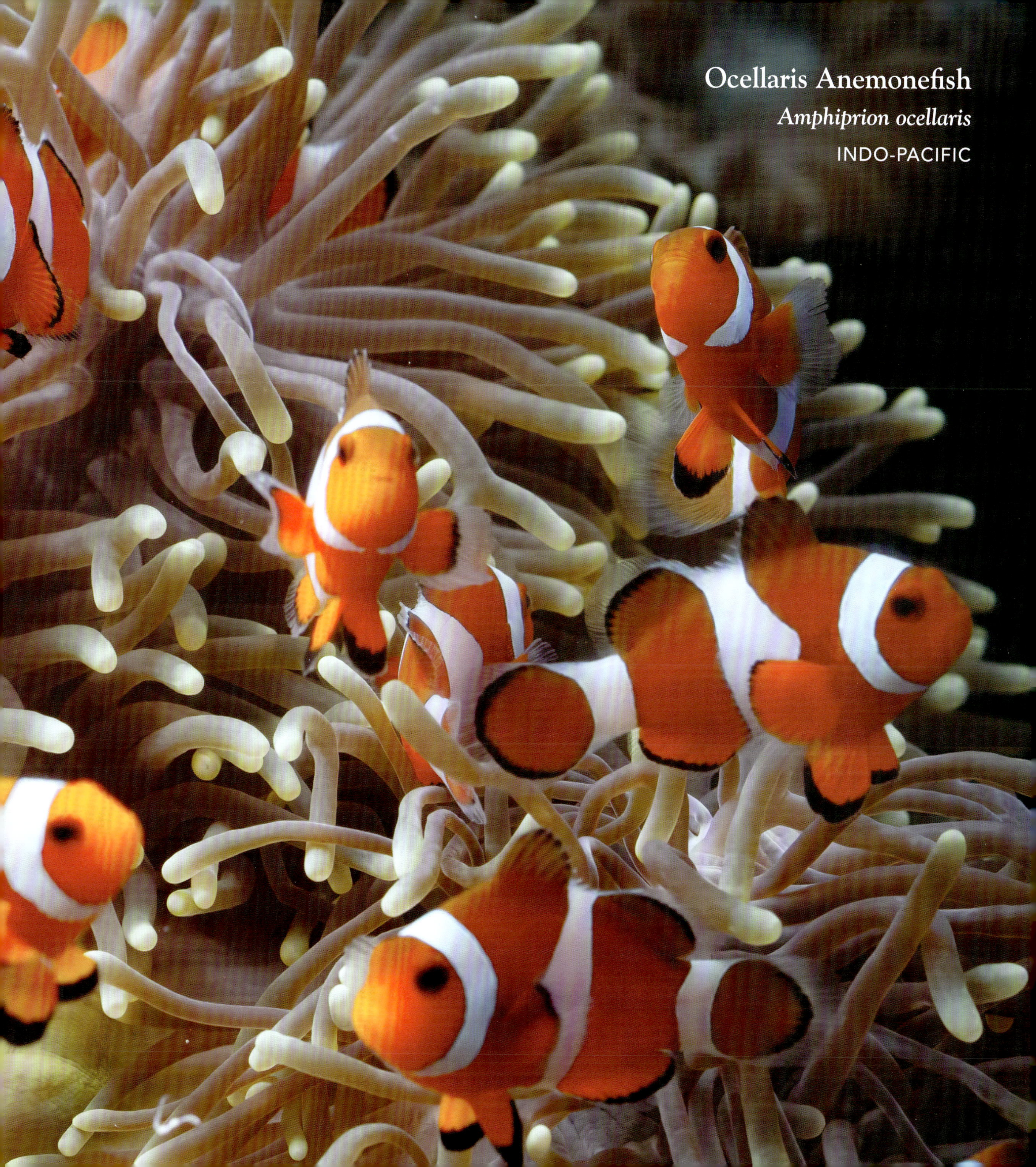

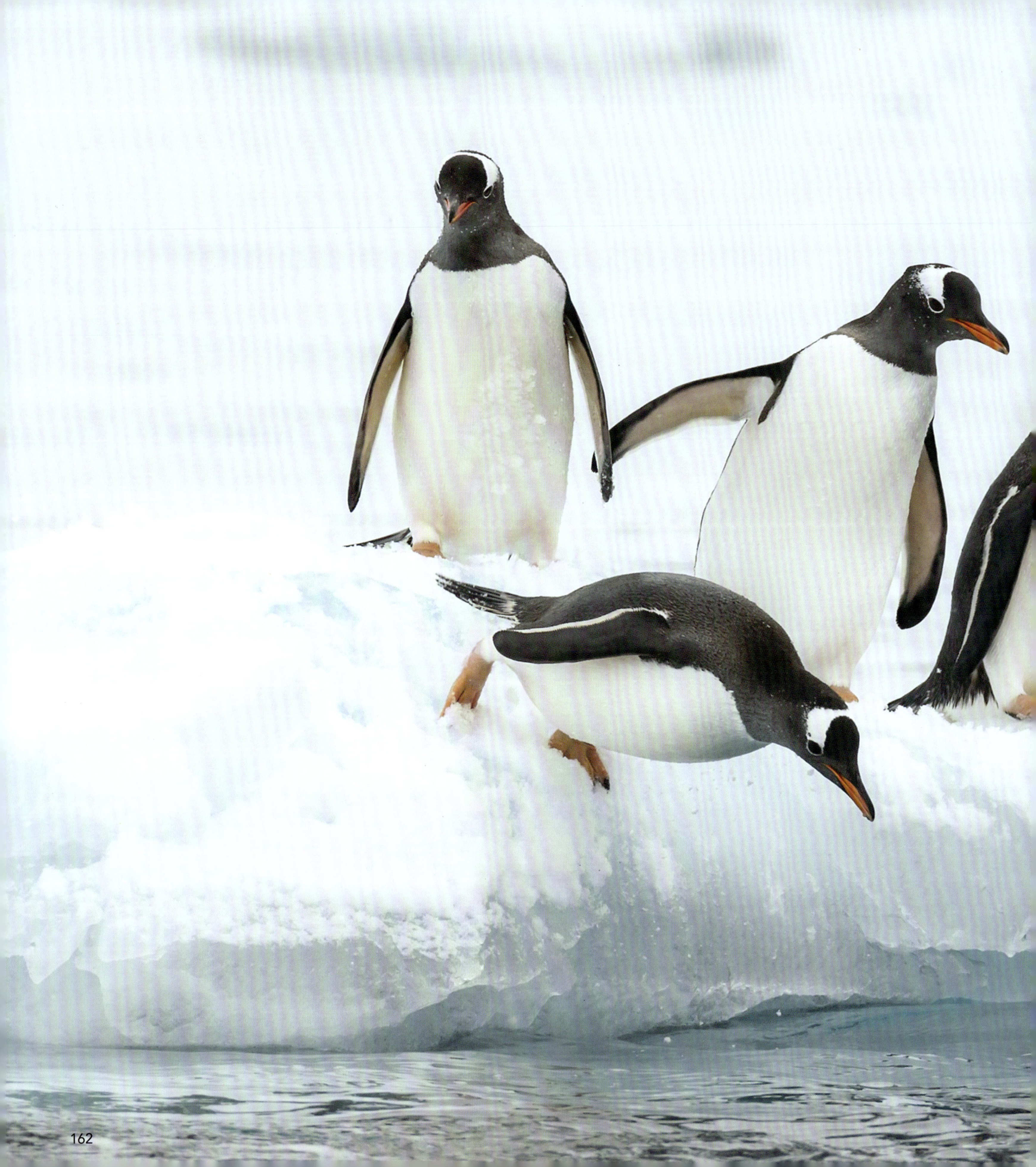

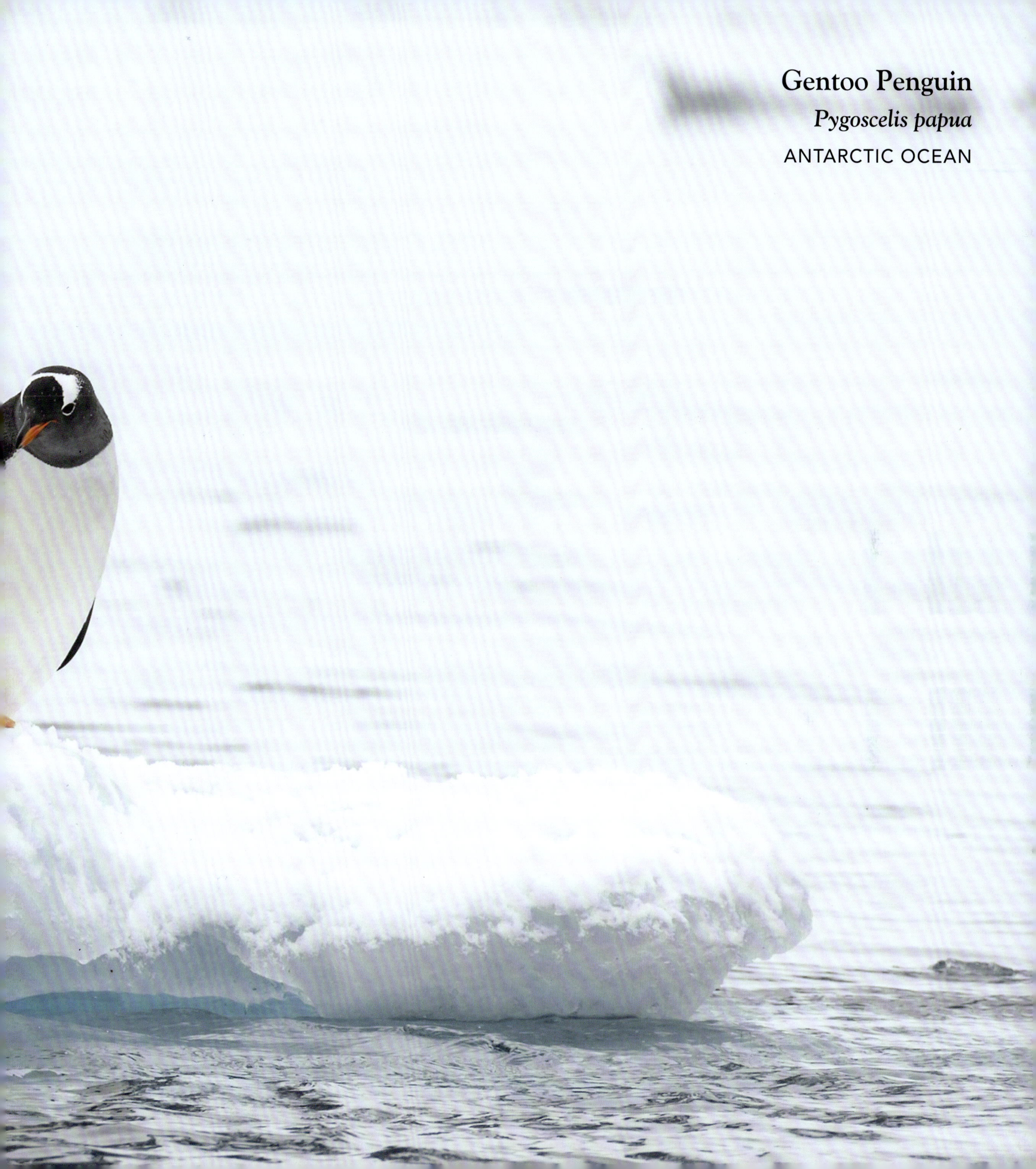

Gentoo Penguin

Pygoscelis papua

ANTARCTIC OCEAN

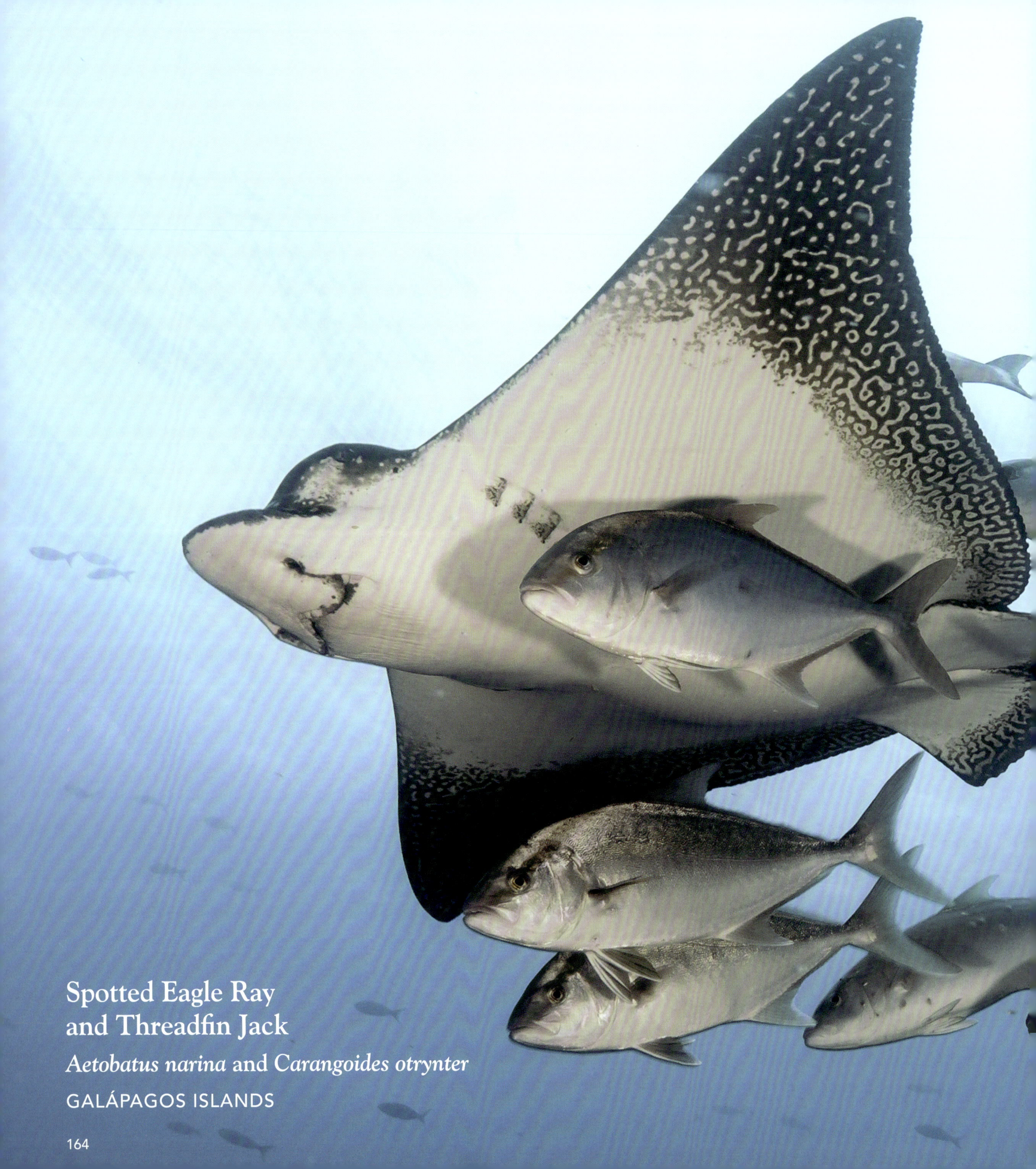

Spotted Eagle Ray and Threadfin Jack

Aetobatus narina and *Carangoides otrynter*

GALÁPAGOS ISLANDS

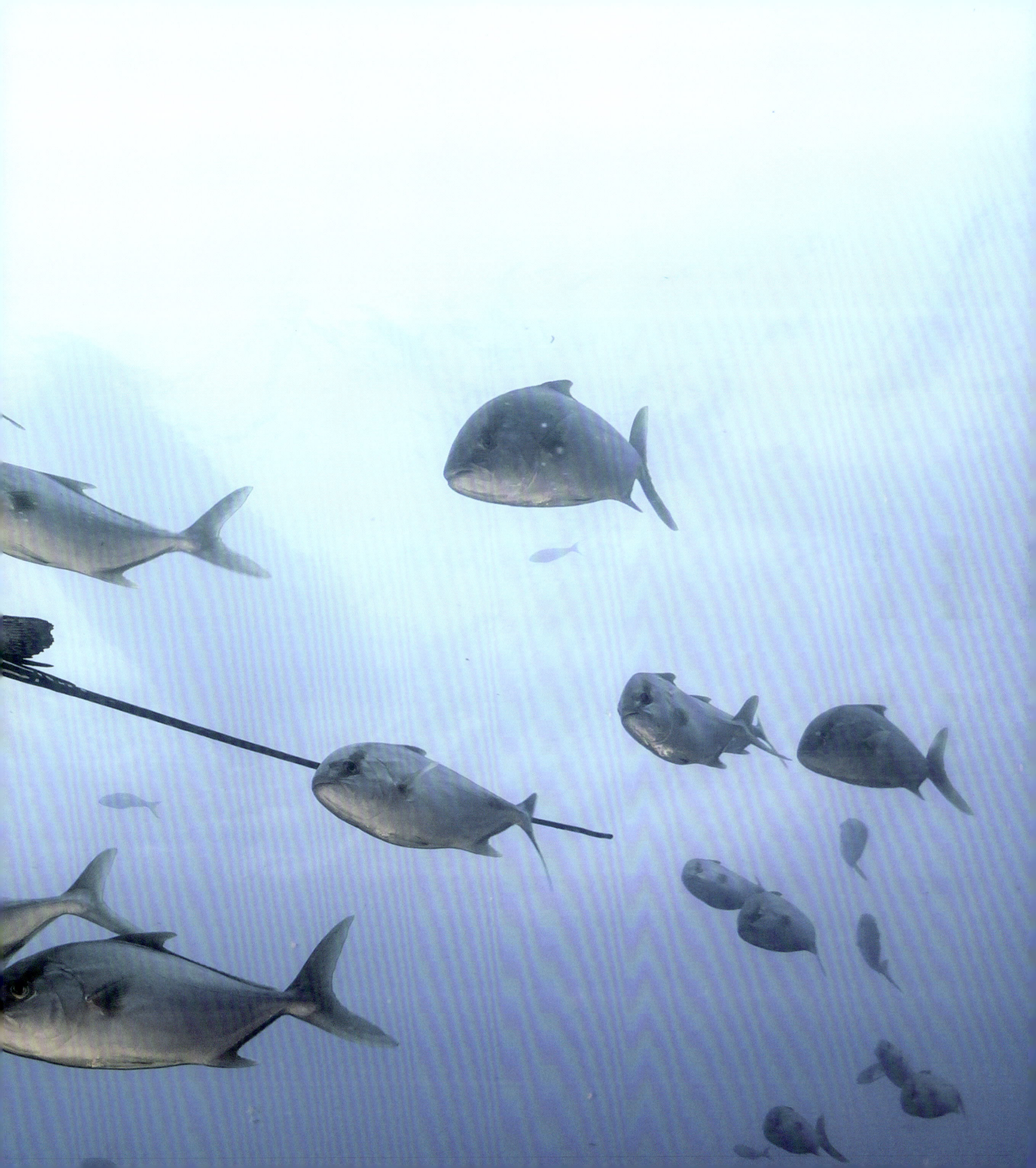

Graysby

Cephalopholis cruentata

WEST ATLANTIC AND CARIBBEAN

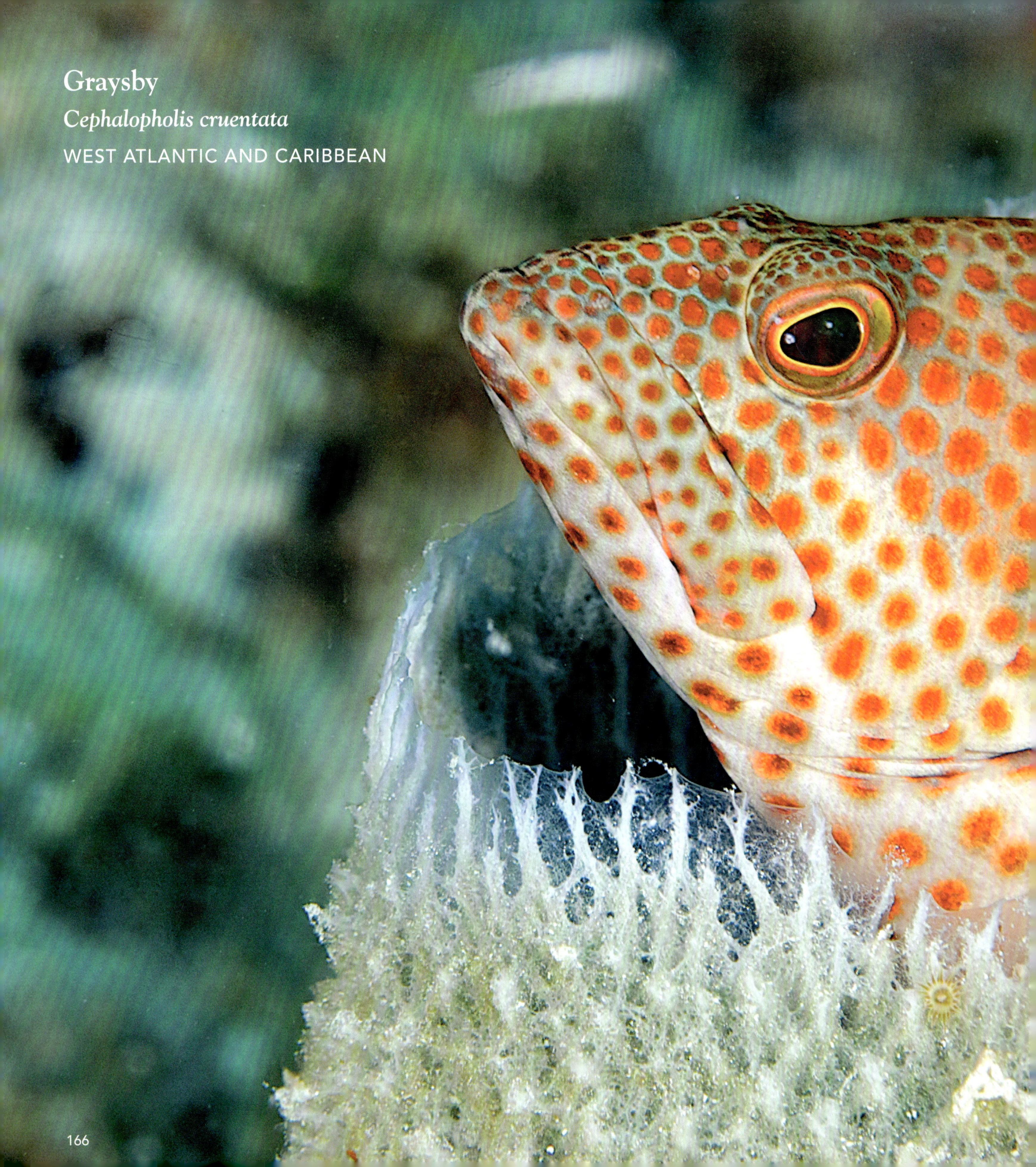

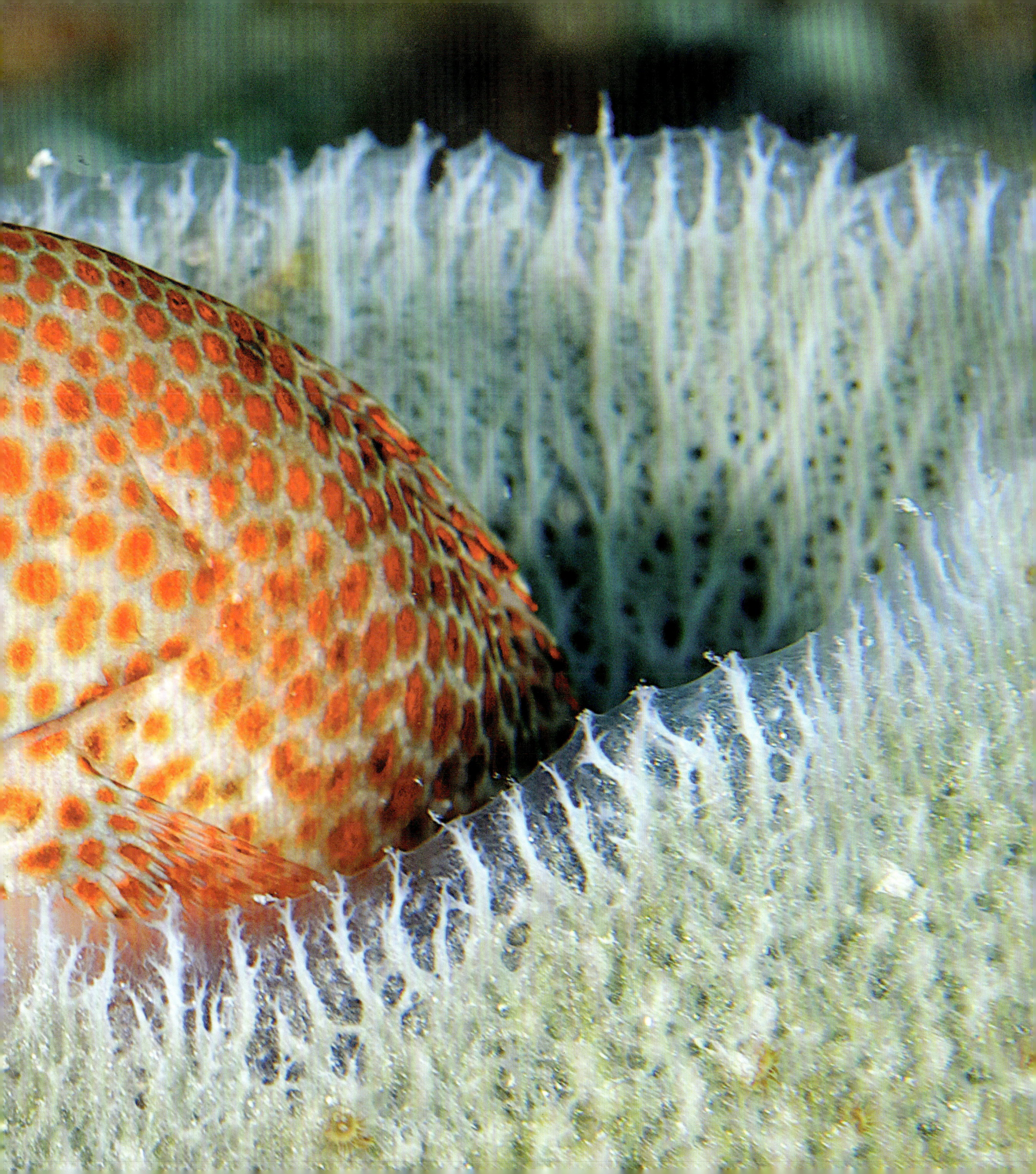

Nudibranch species

Nudibranchia

TROPICAL OCEANS

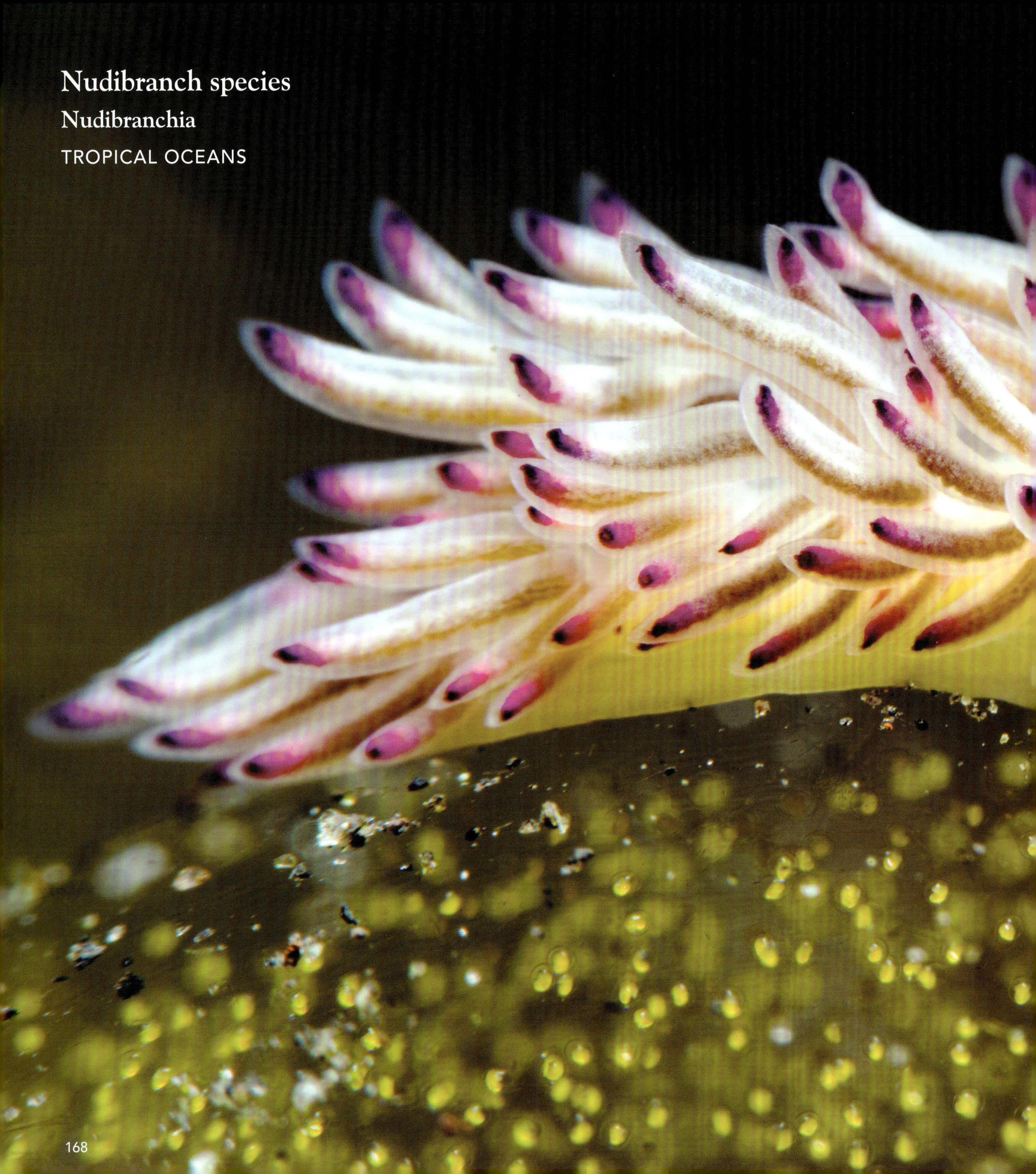

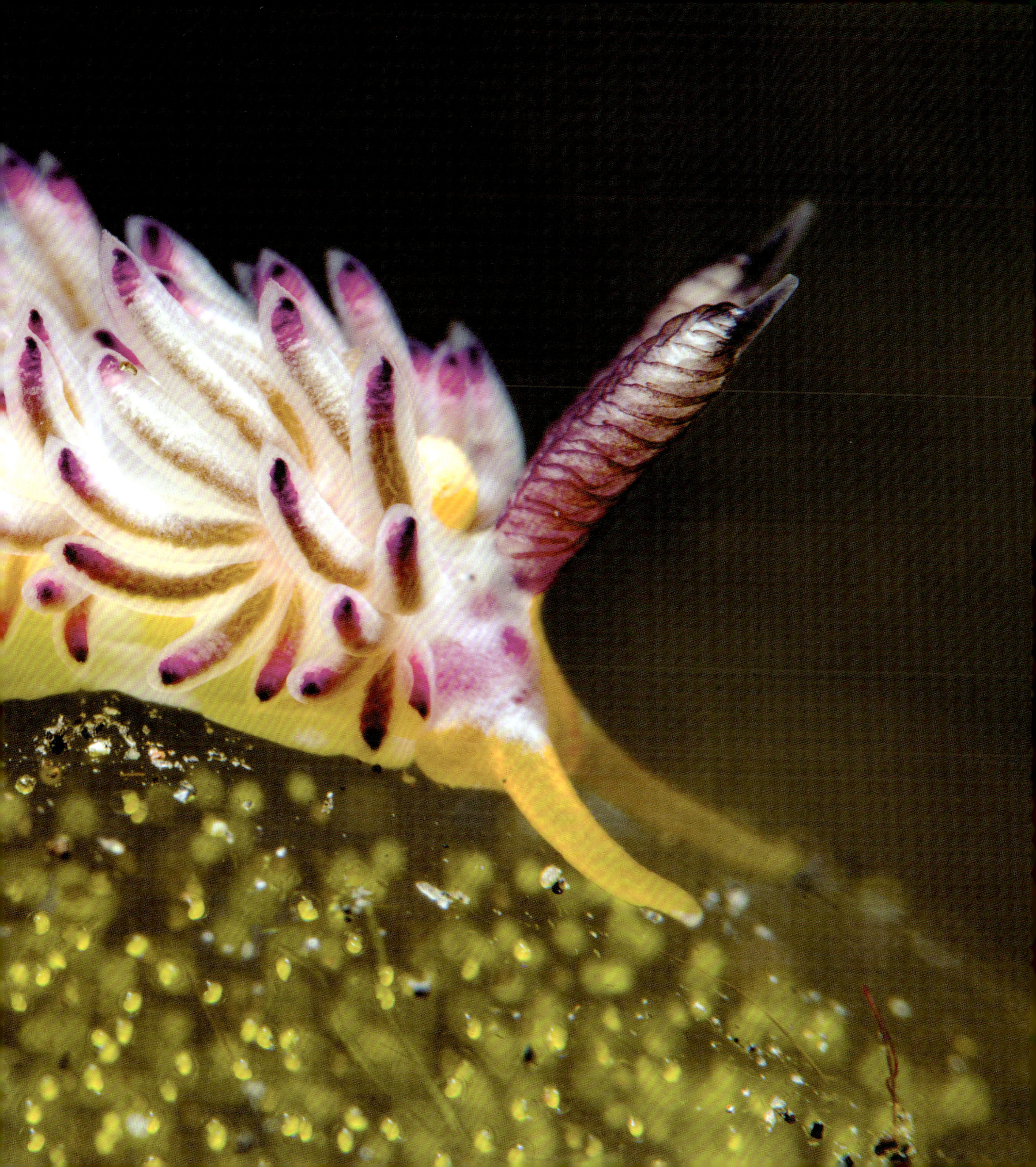

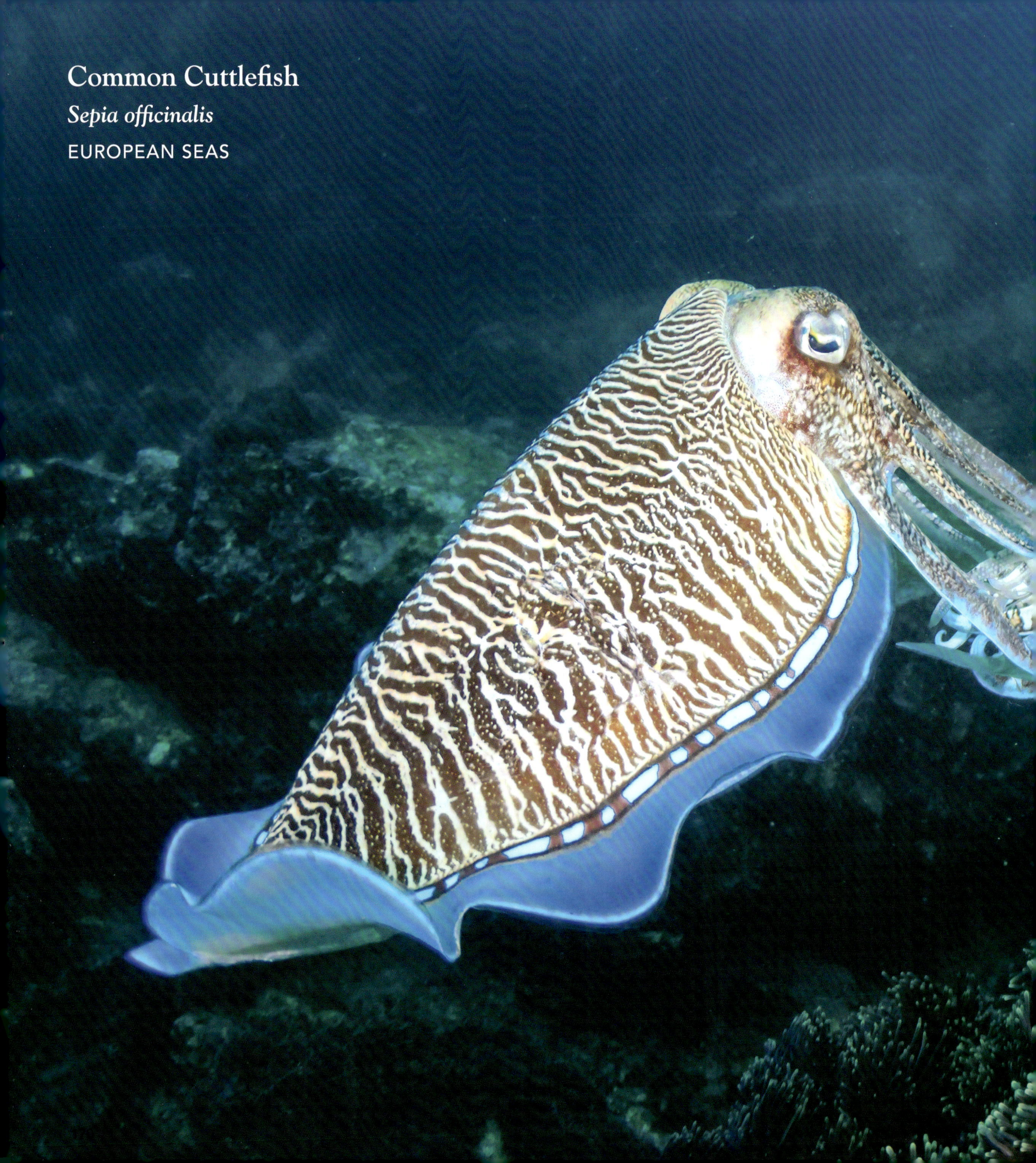

Common Cuttlefish

Sepia officinalis

EUROPEAN SEAS

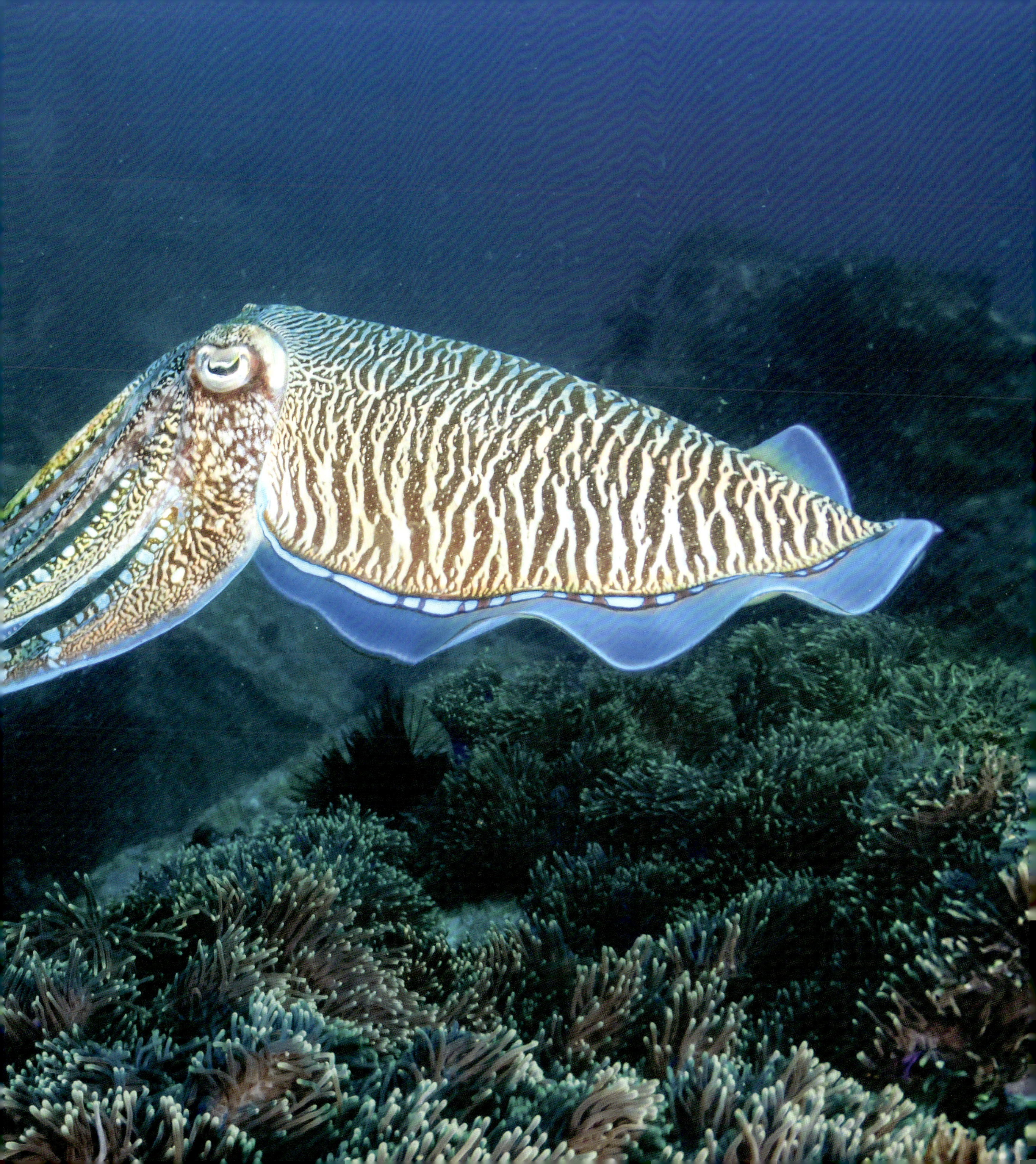

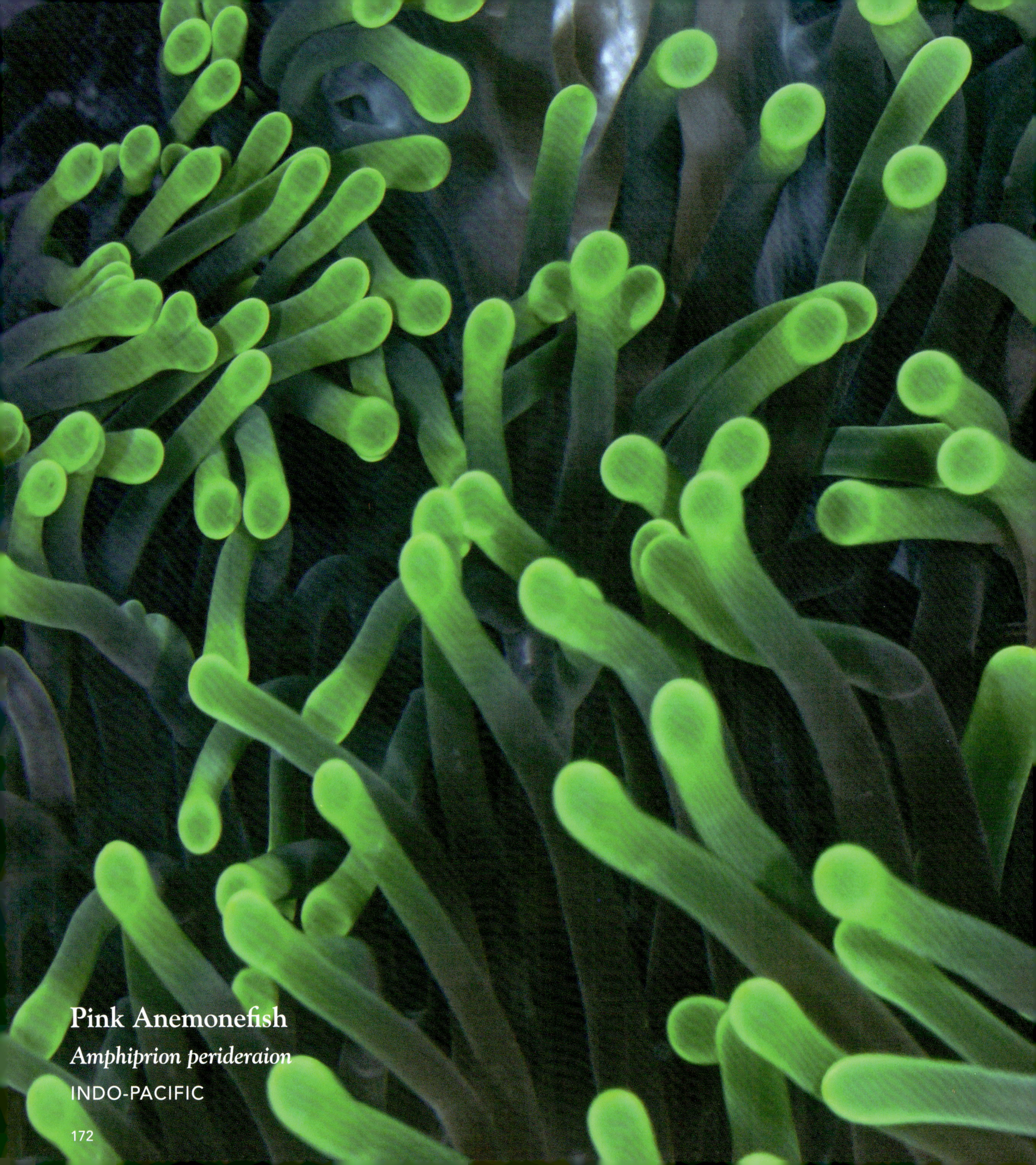

Pink Anemonefish

Amphiprion perideraion

INDO-PACIFIC

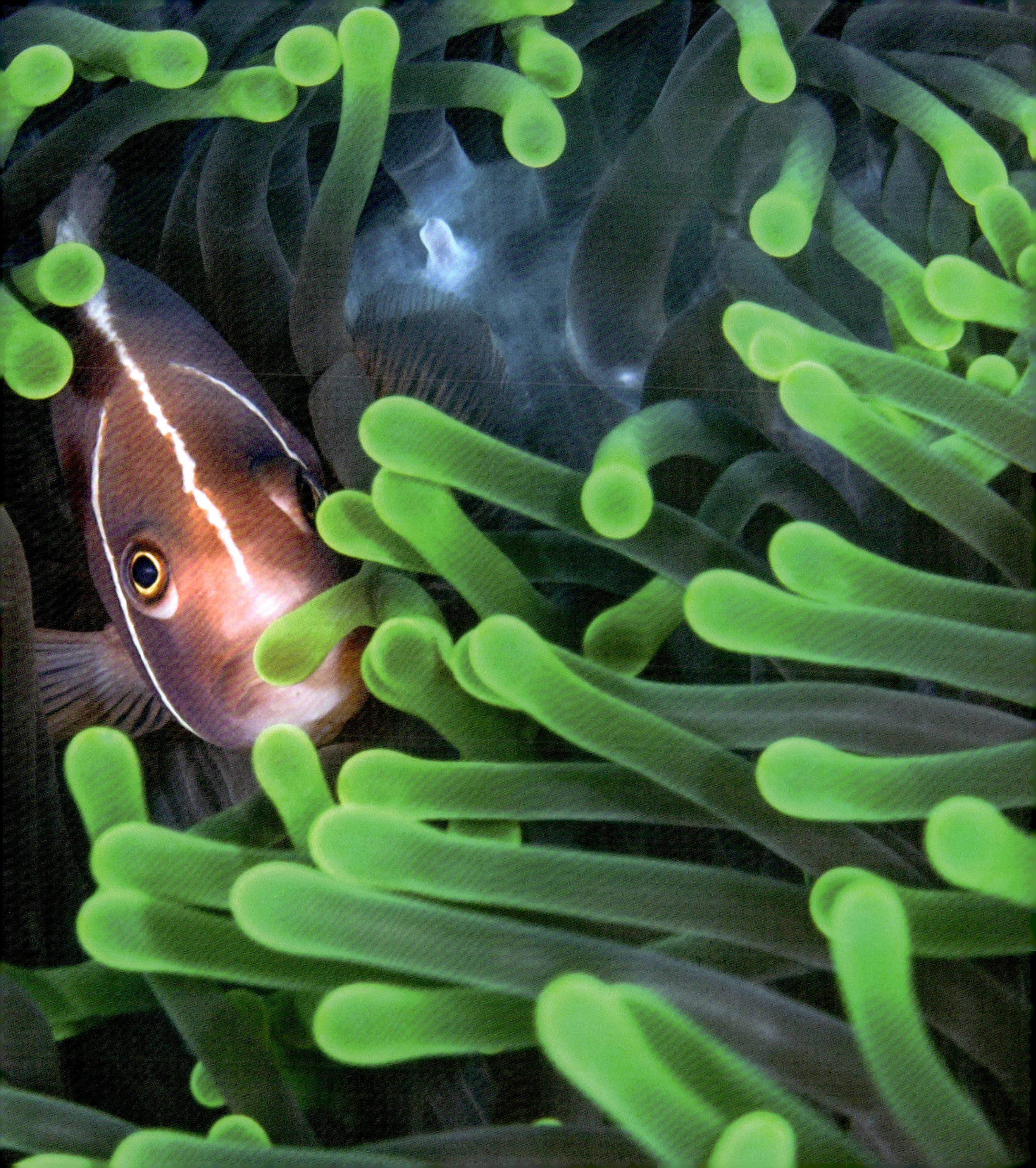

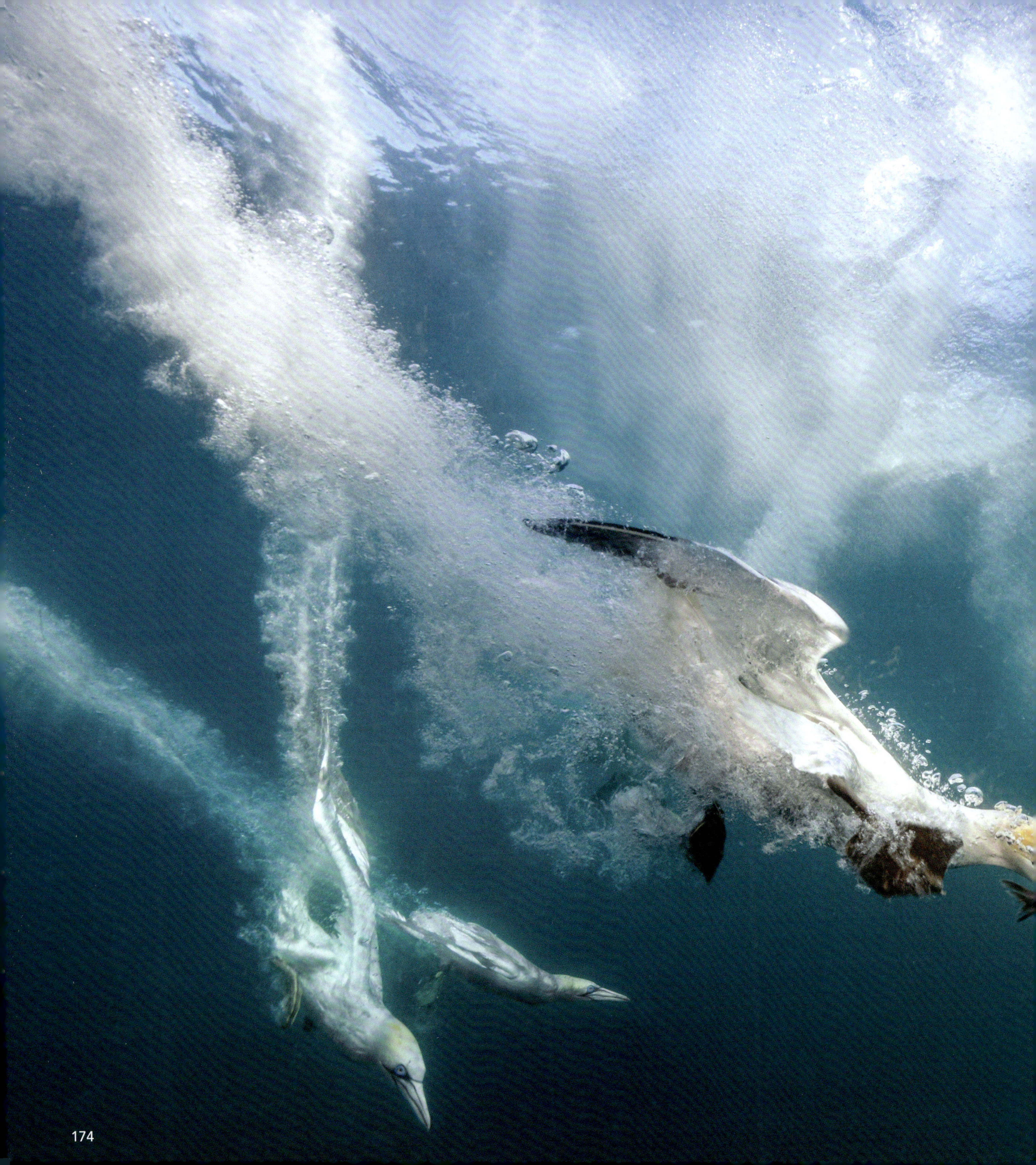

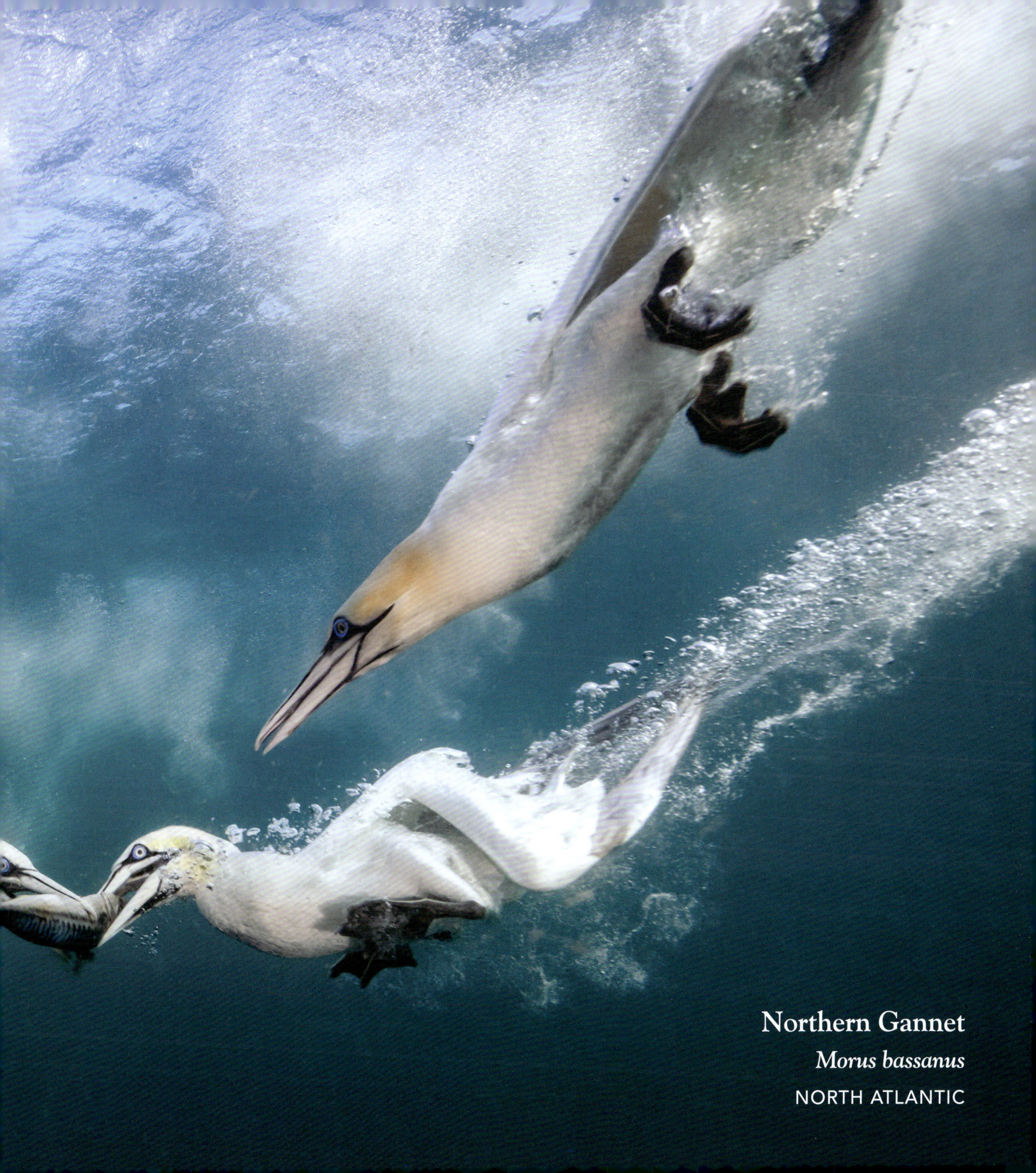

Northern Gannet

Morus bassanus

NORTH ATLANTIC

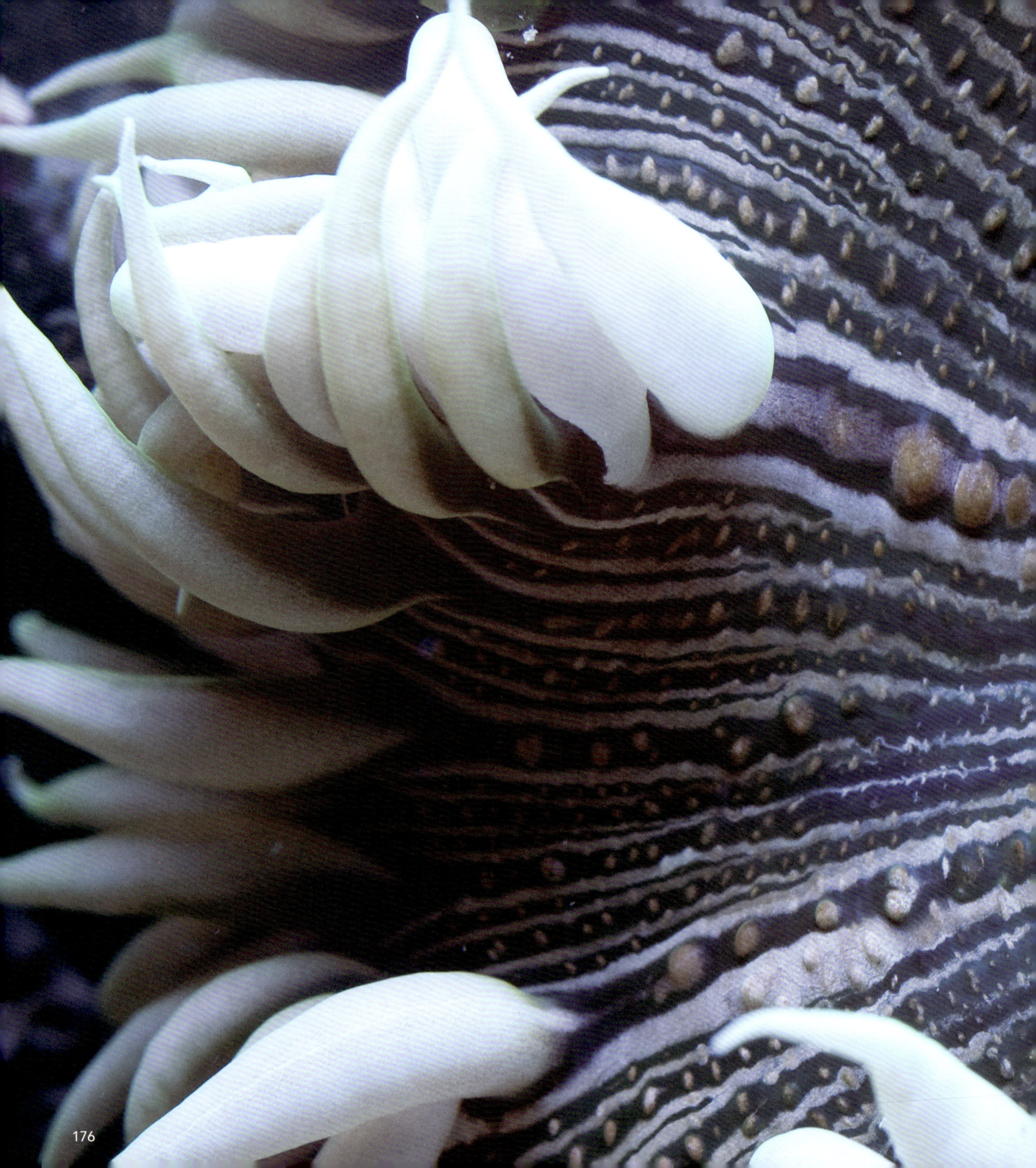

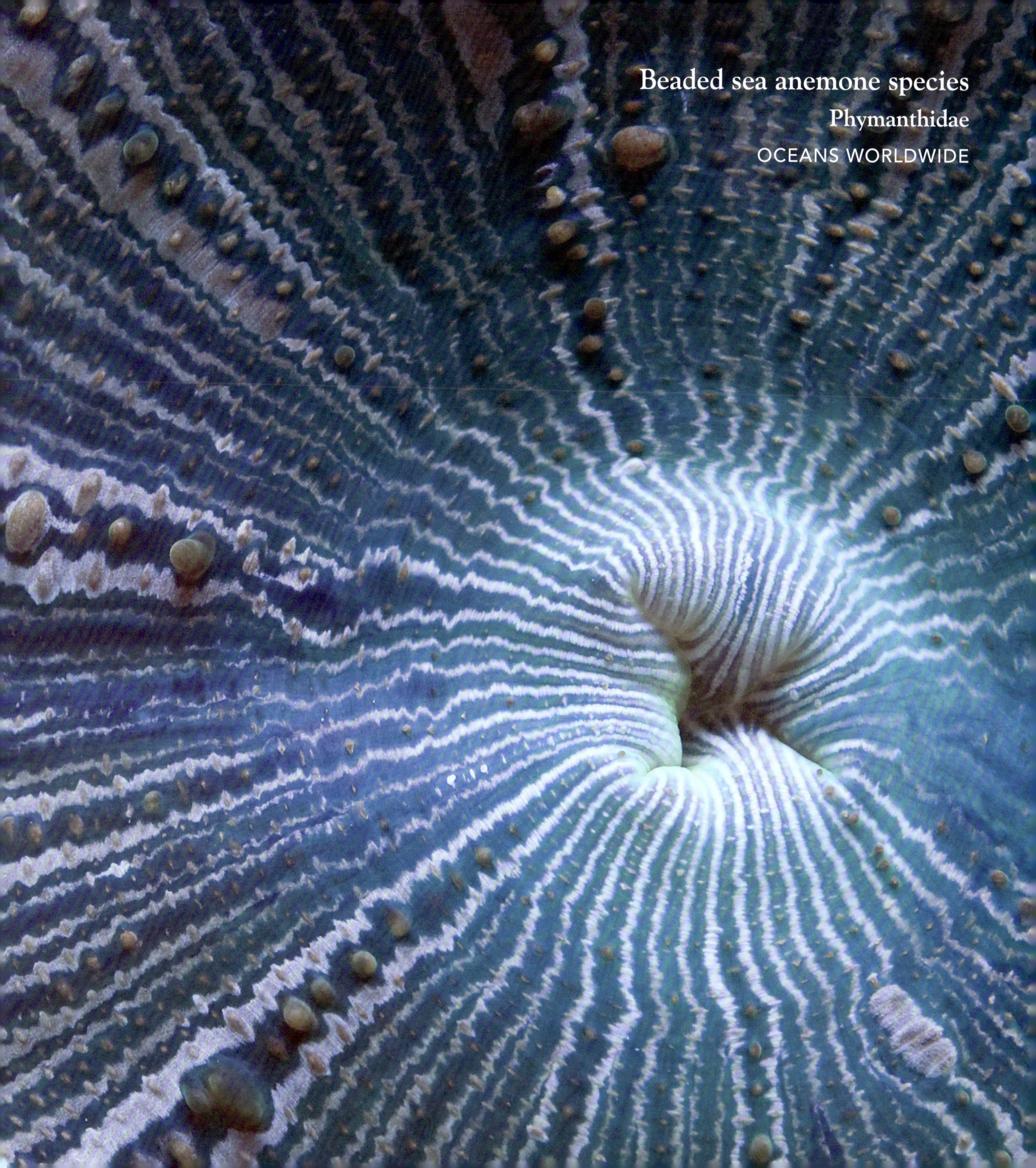

Beaded sea anemone species

Phymanthidae

OCEANS WORLDWIDE

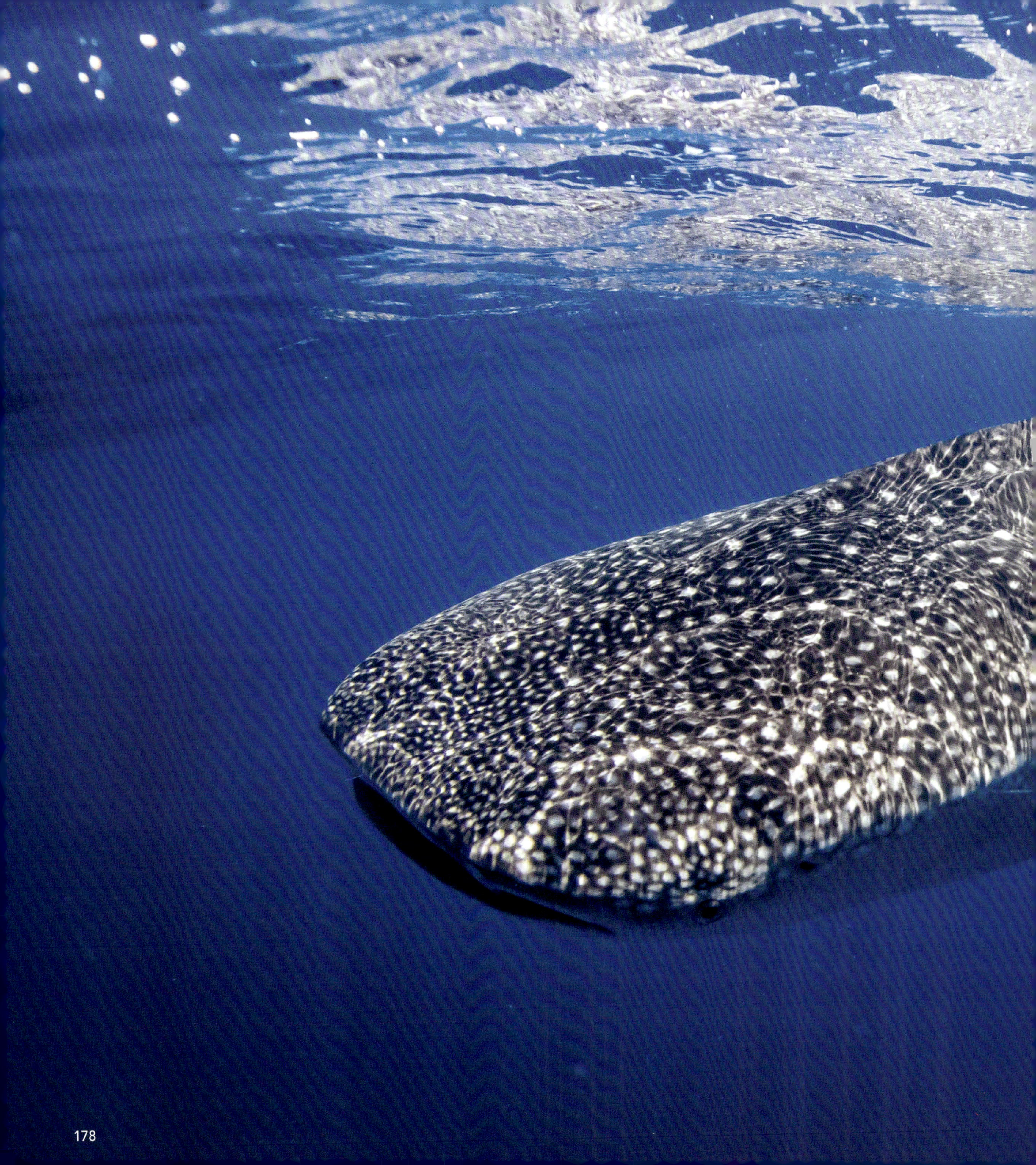

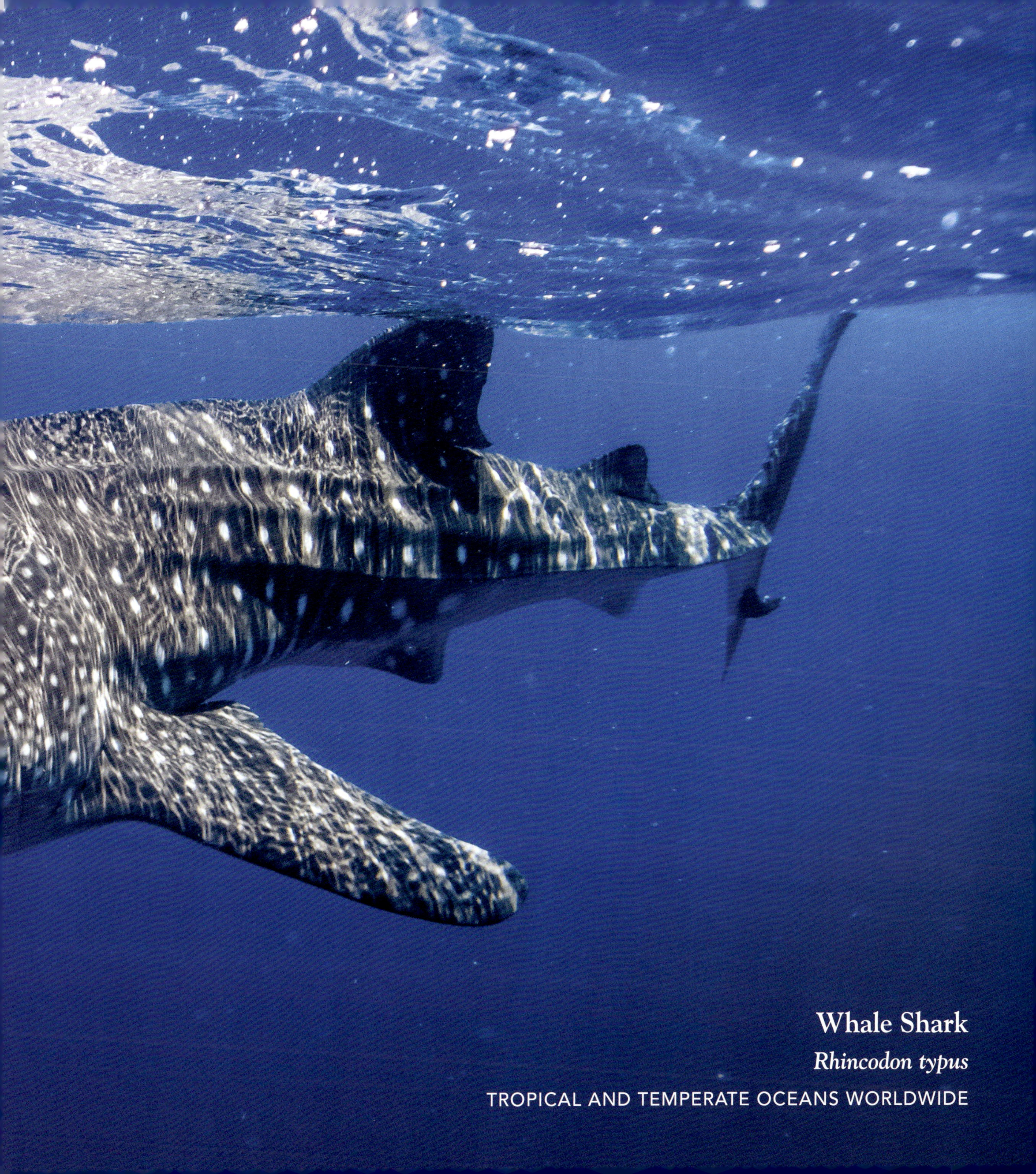

Whale Shark

Rhincodon typus

TROPICAL AND TEMPERATE OCEANS WORLDWIDE

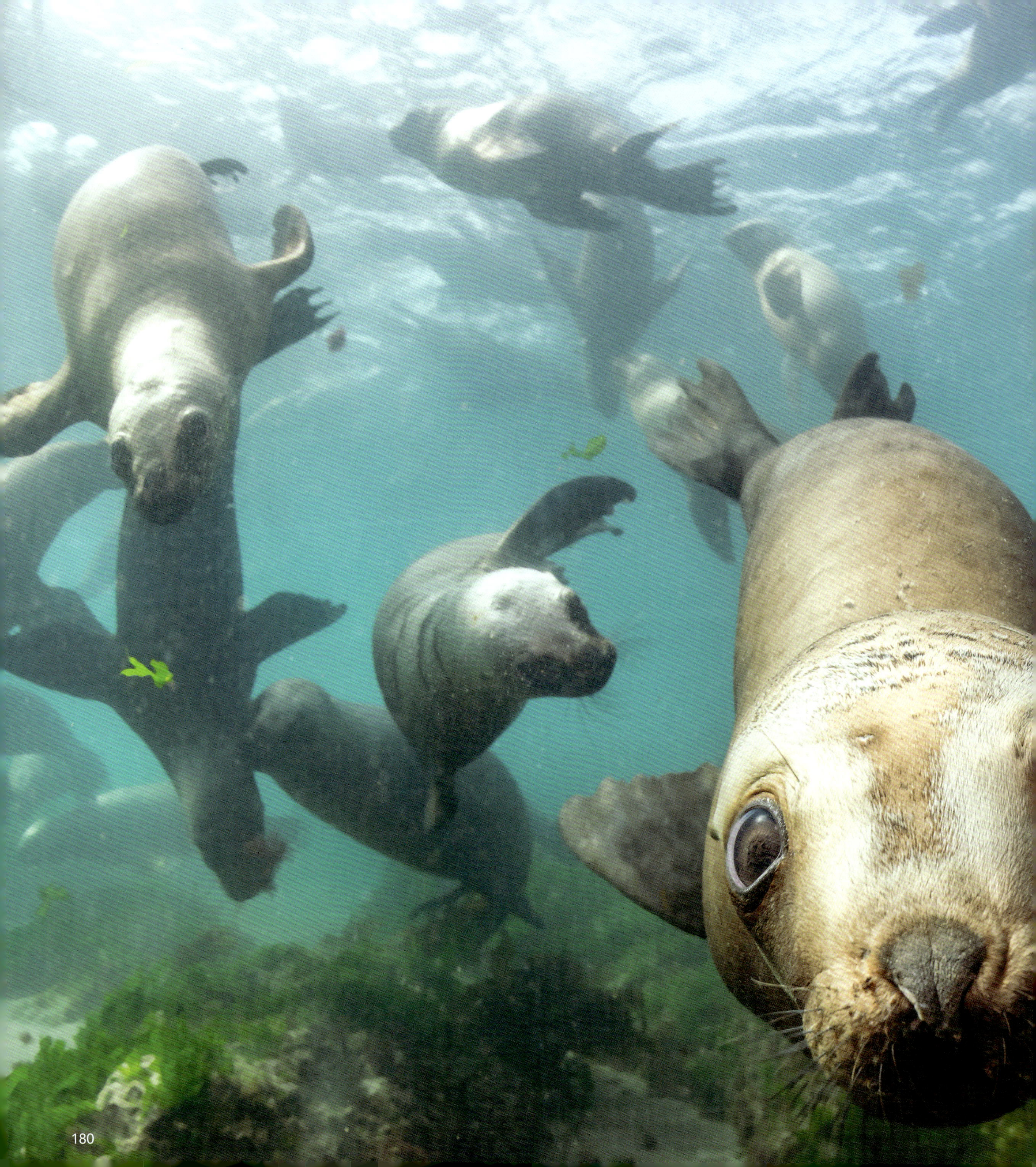

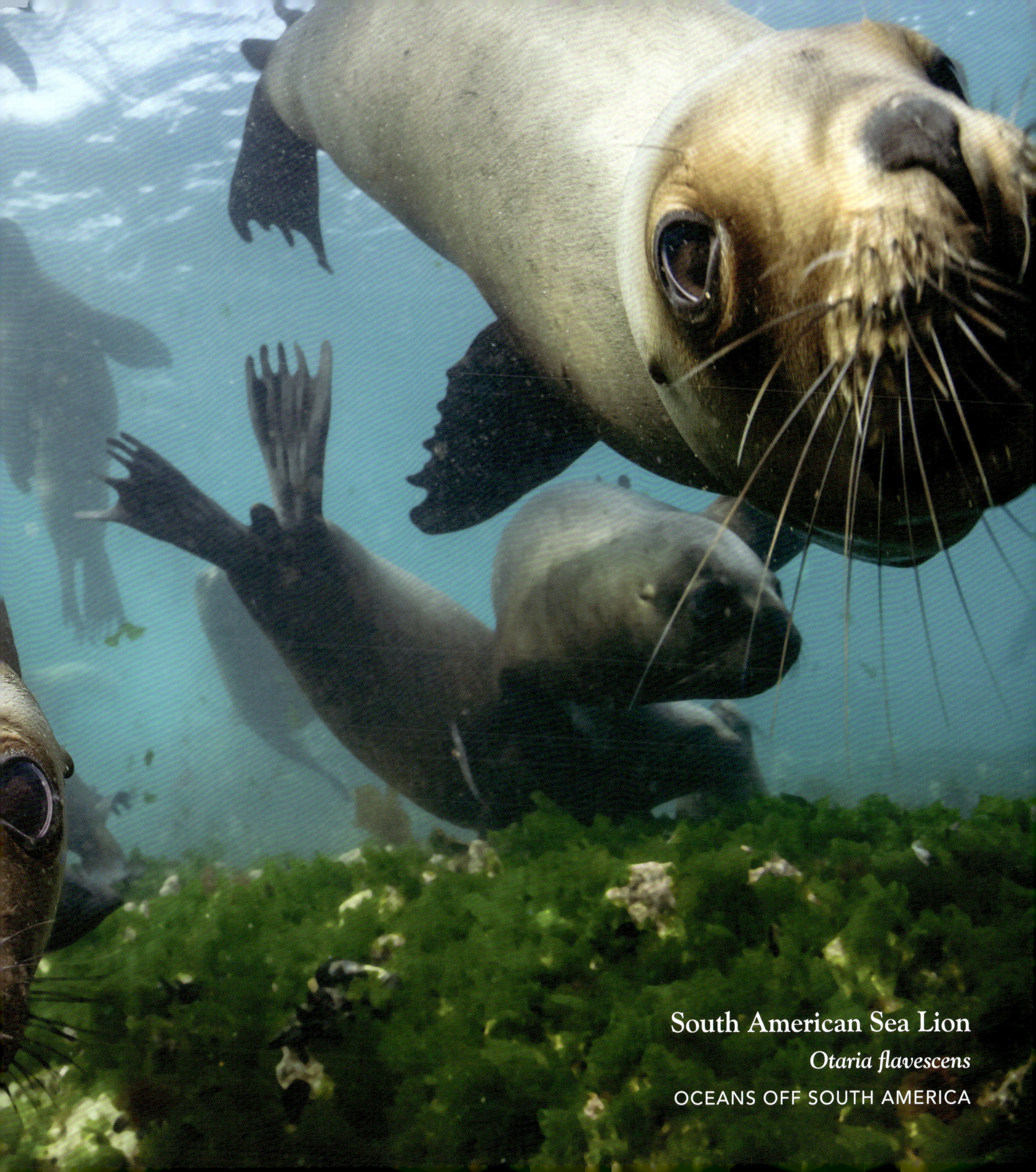

South American Sea Lion

Otaria flavescens

OCEANS OFF SOUTH AMERICA

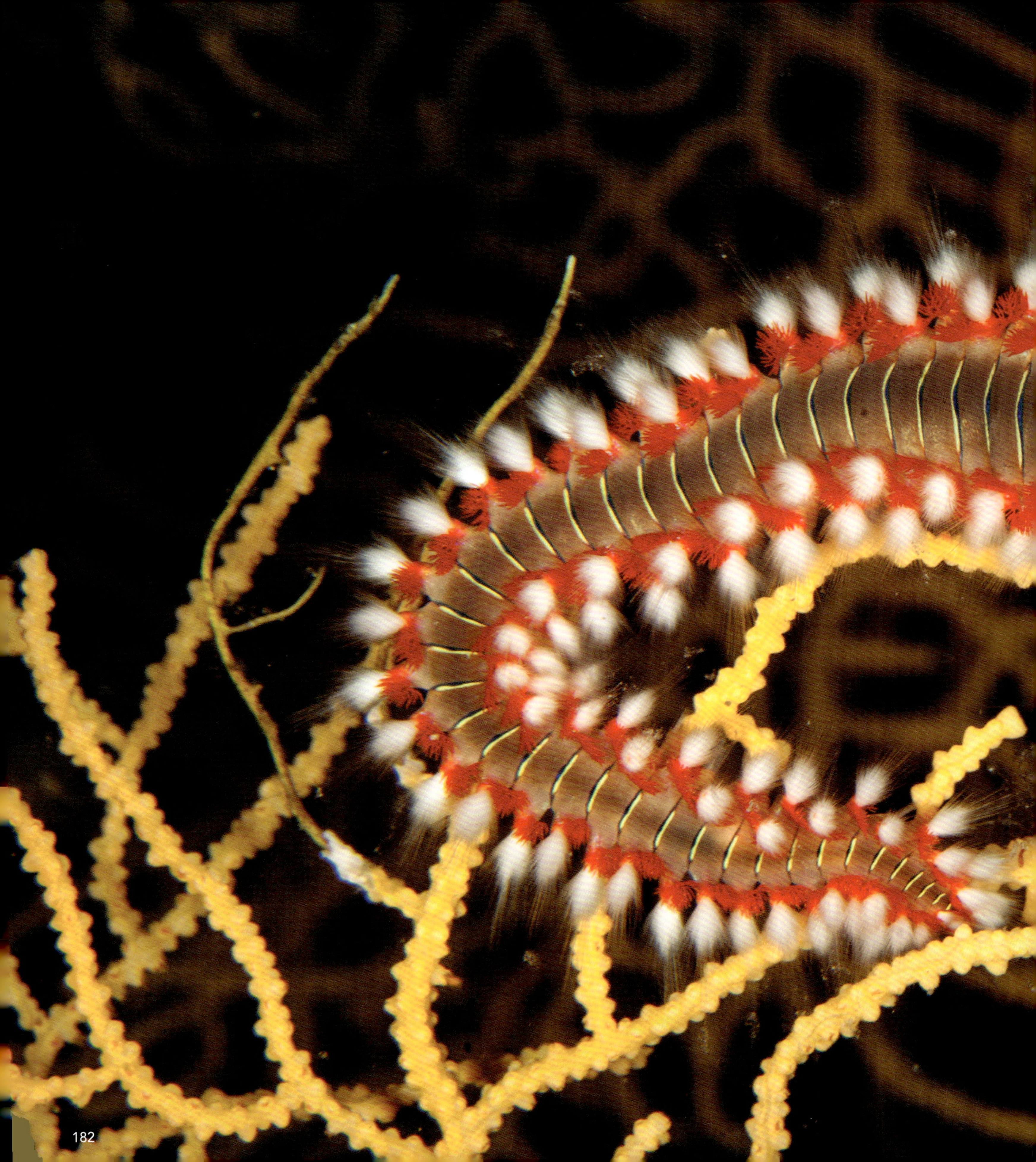

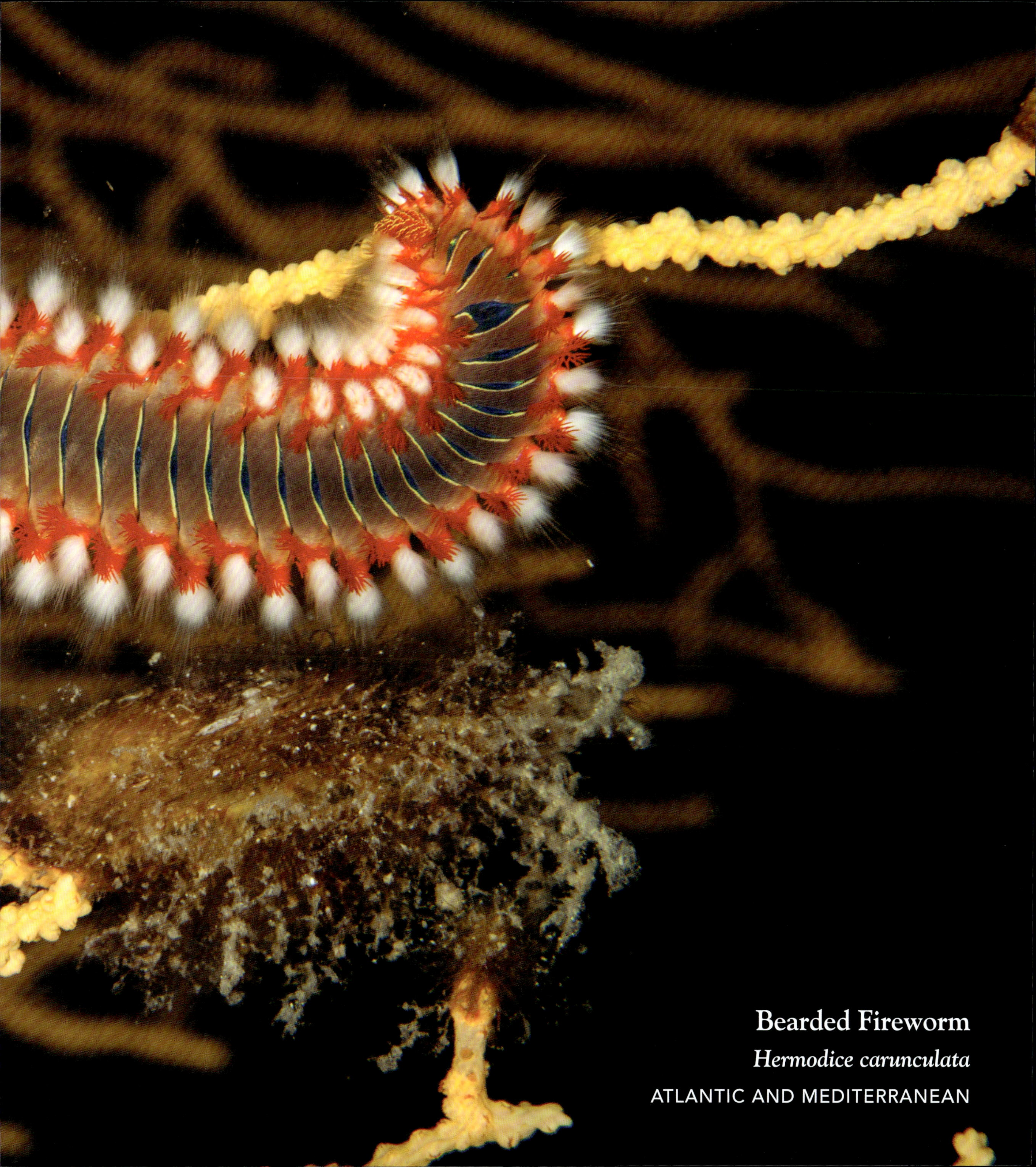

Bearded Fireworm

Hermodice carunculata

ATLANTIC AND MEDITERRANEAN

Ribboned Sweetlips

Plectorhinchus polytaenia

INDO-PACIFIC

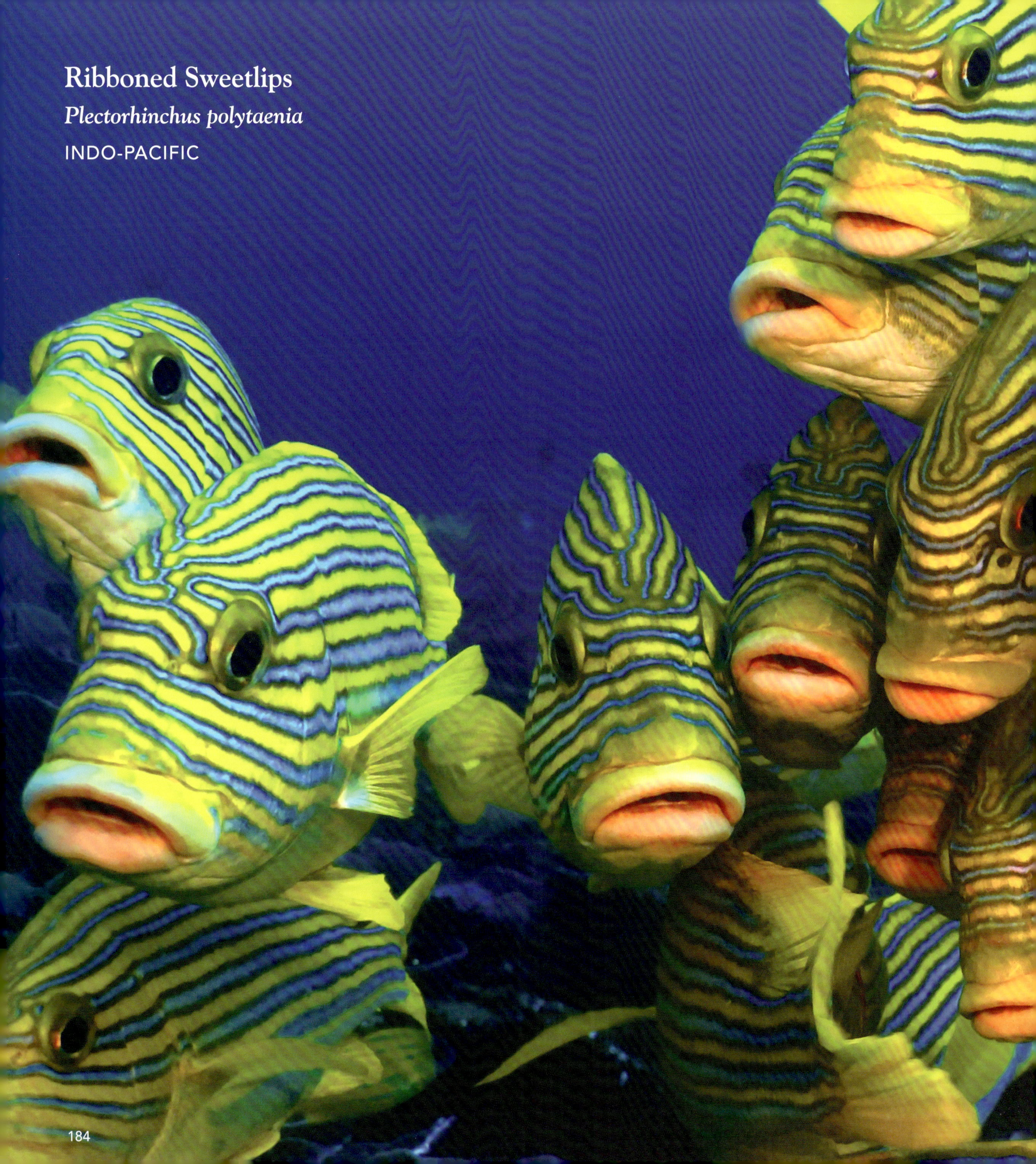

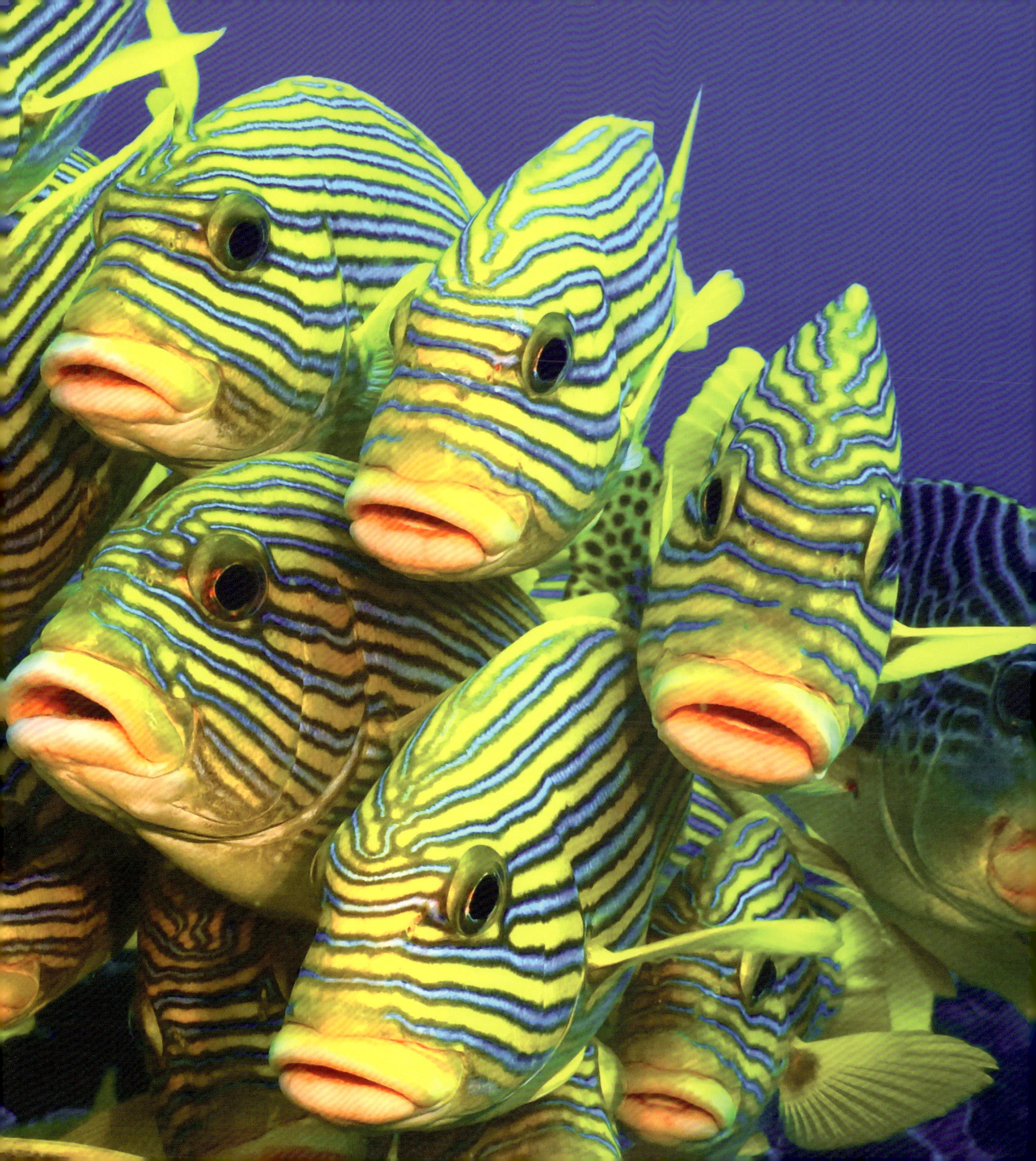

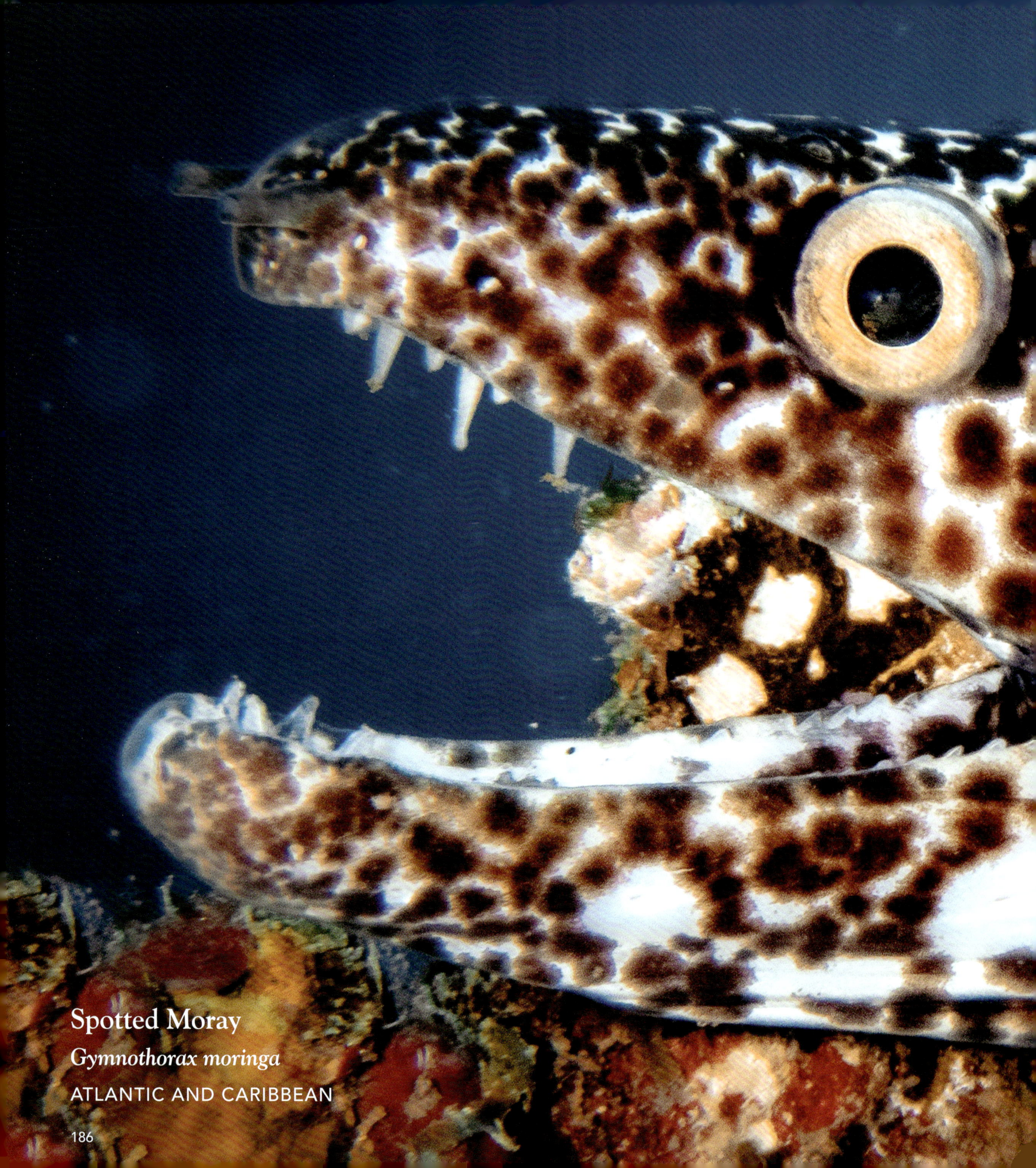

Spotted Moray

Gymnothorax moringa

ATLANTIC AND CARIBBEAN

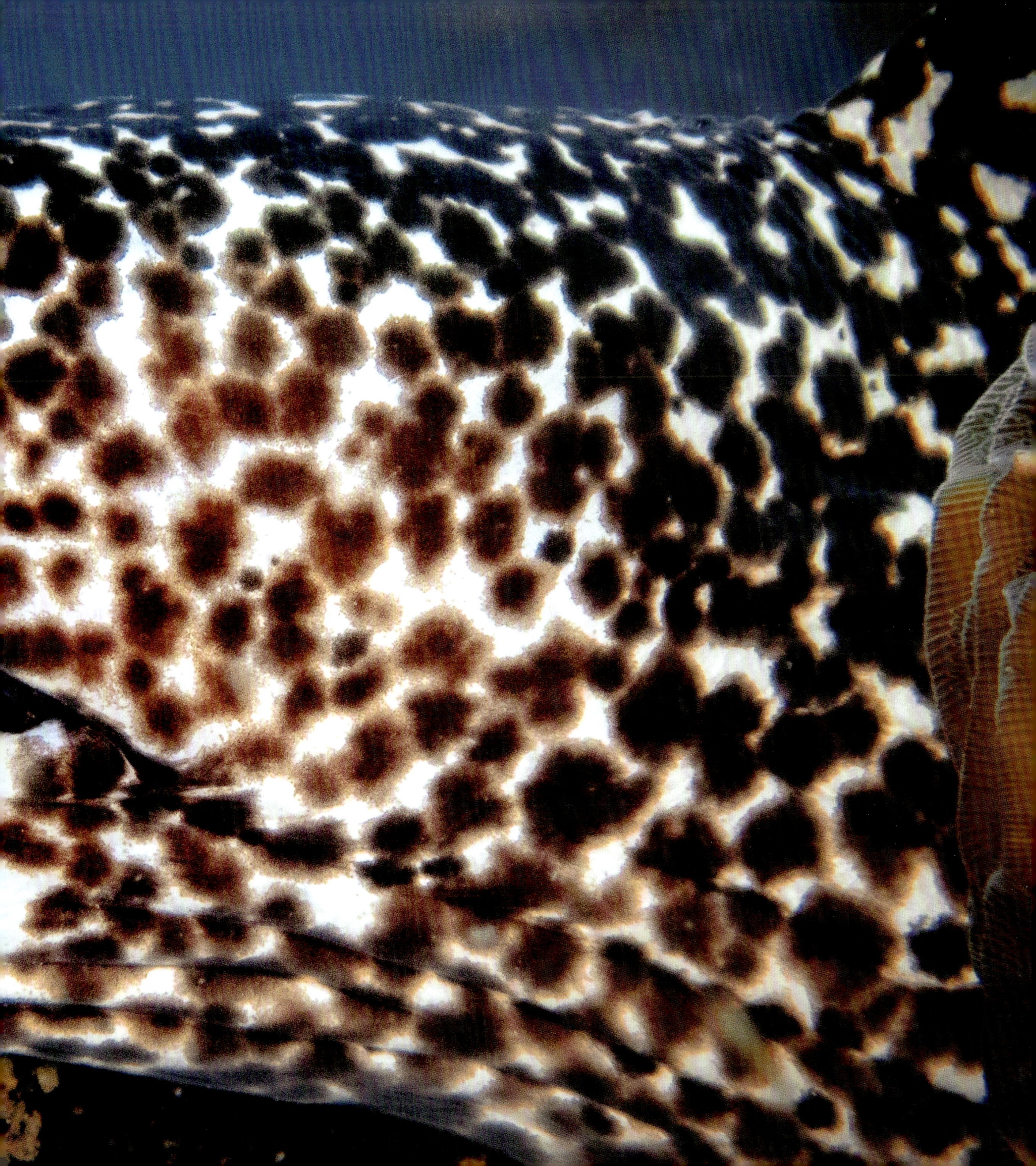

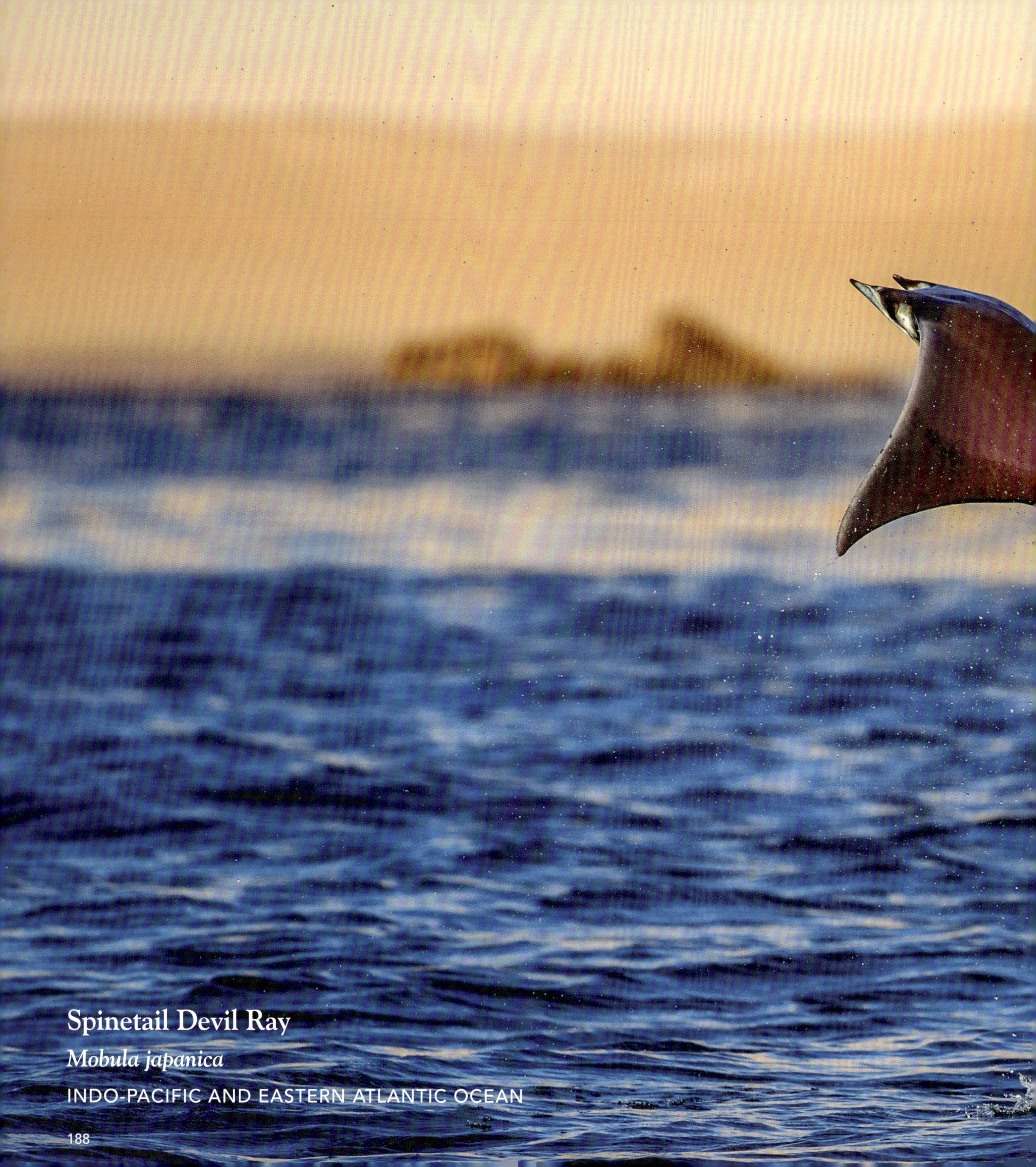

Spinetail Devil Ray

Mobula japanica

INDO-PACIFIC AND EASTERN ATLANTIC OCEAN

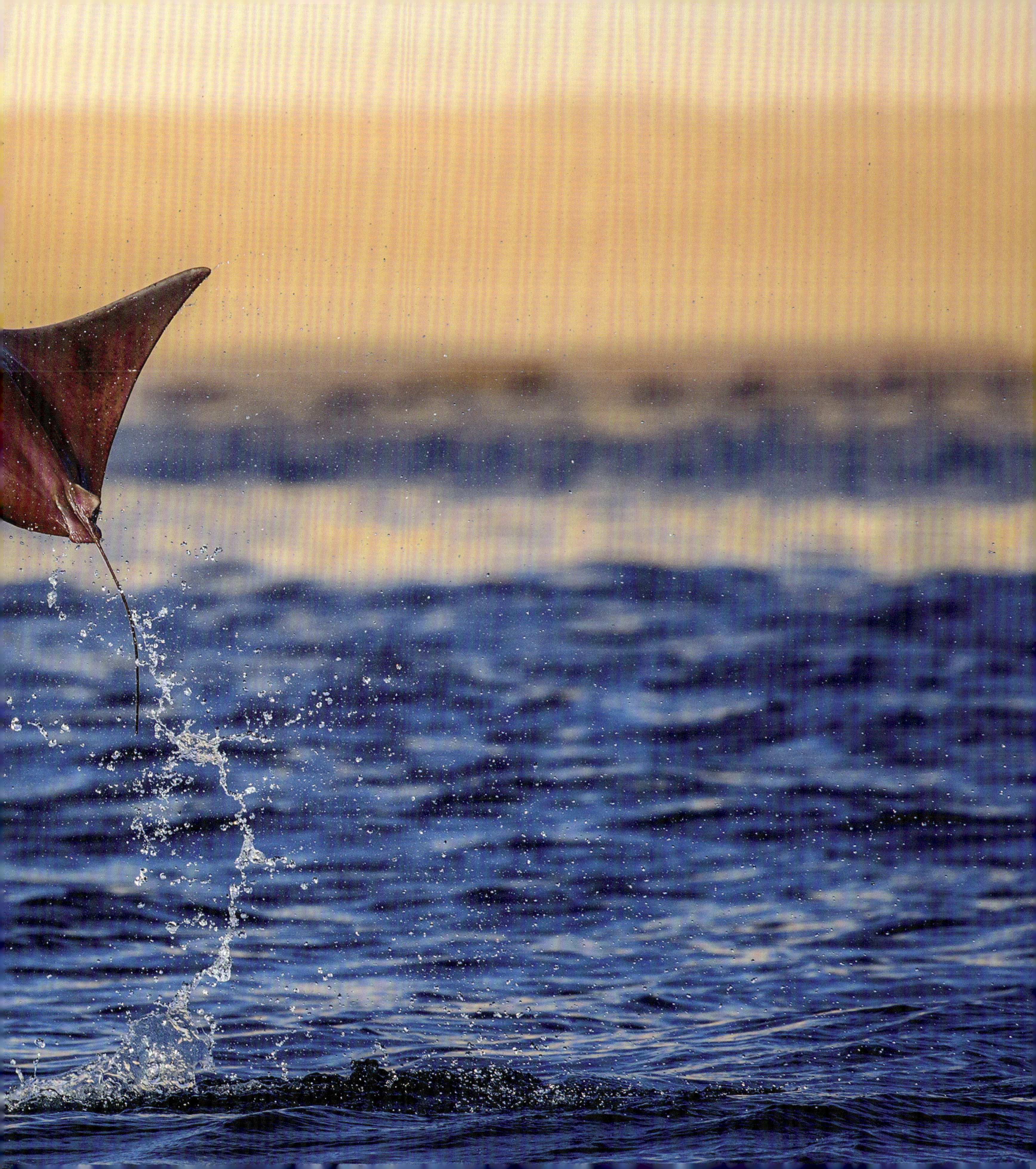

Bigeye Trevally

Caranx sexfasciatus

INDO-PACIFIC

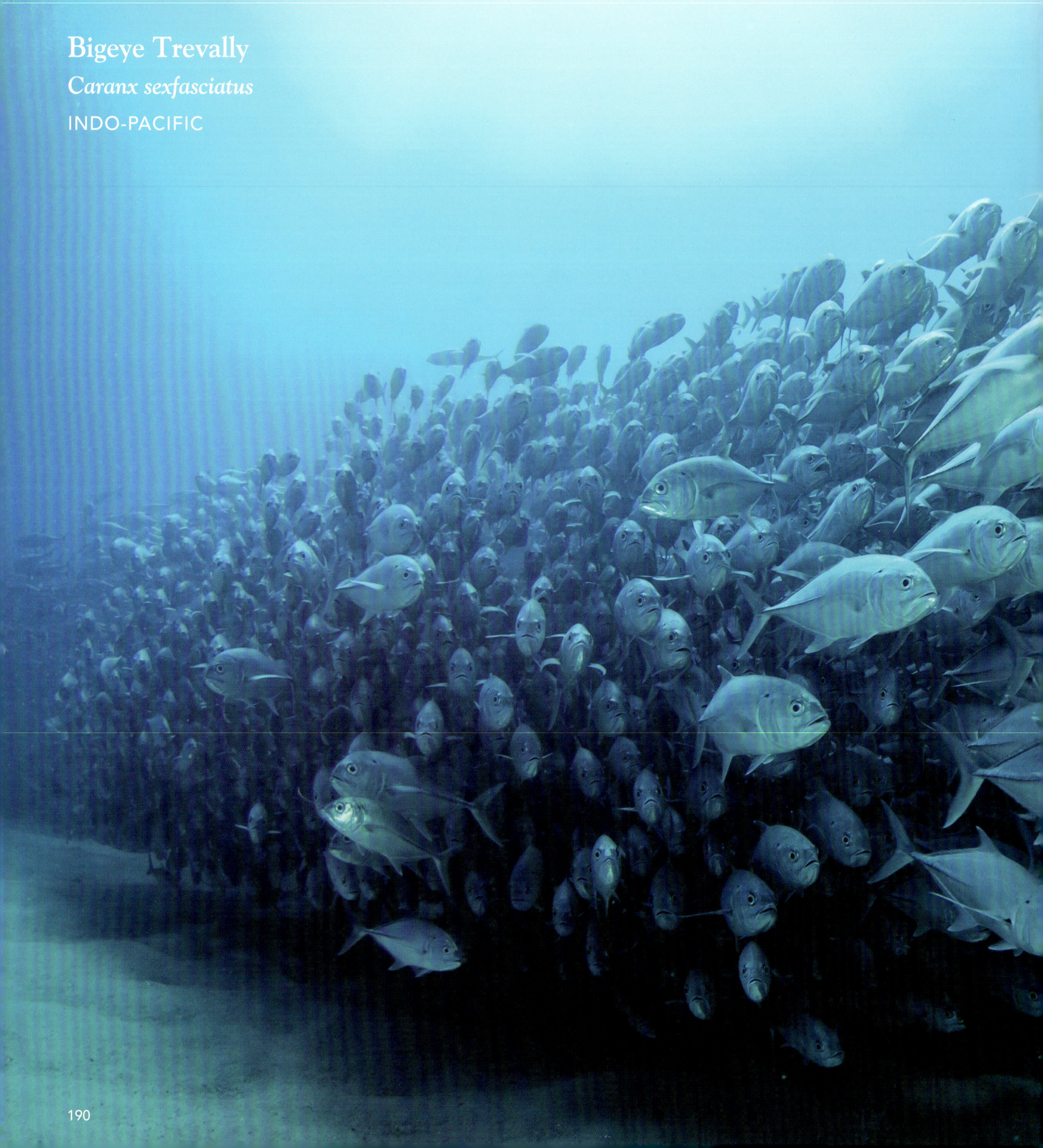

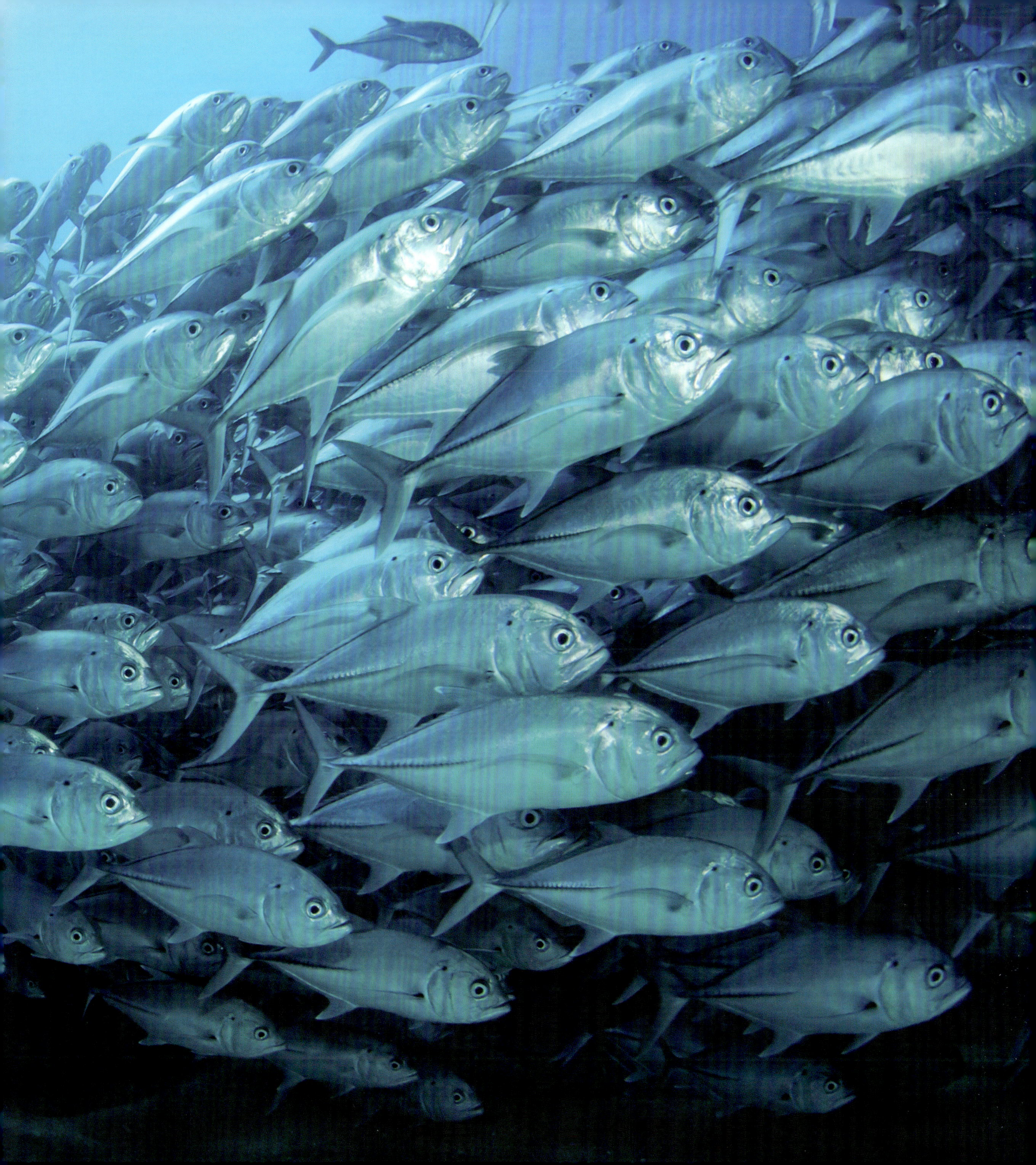

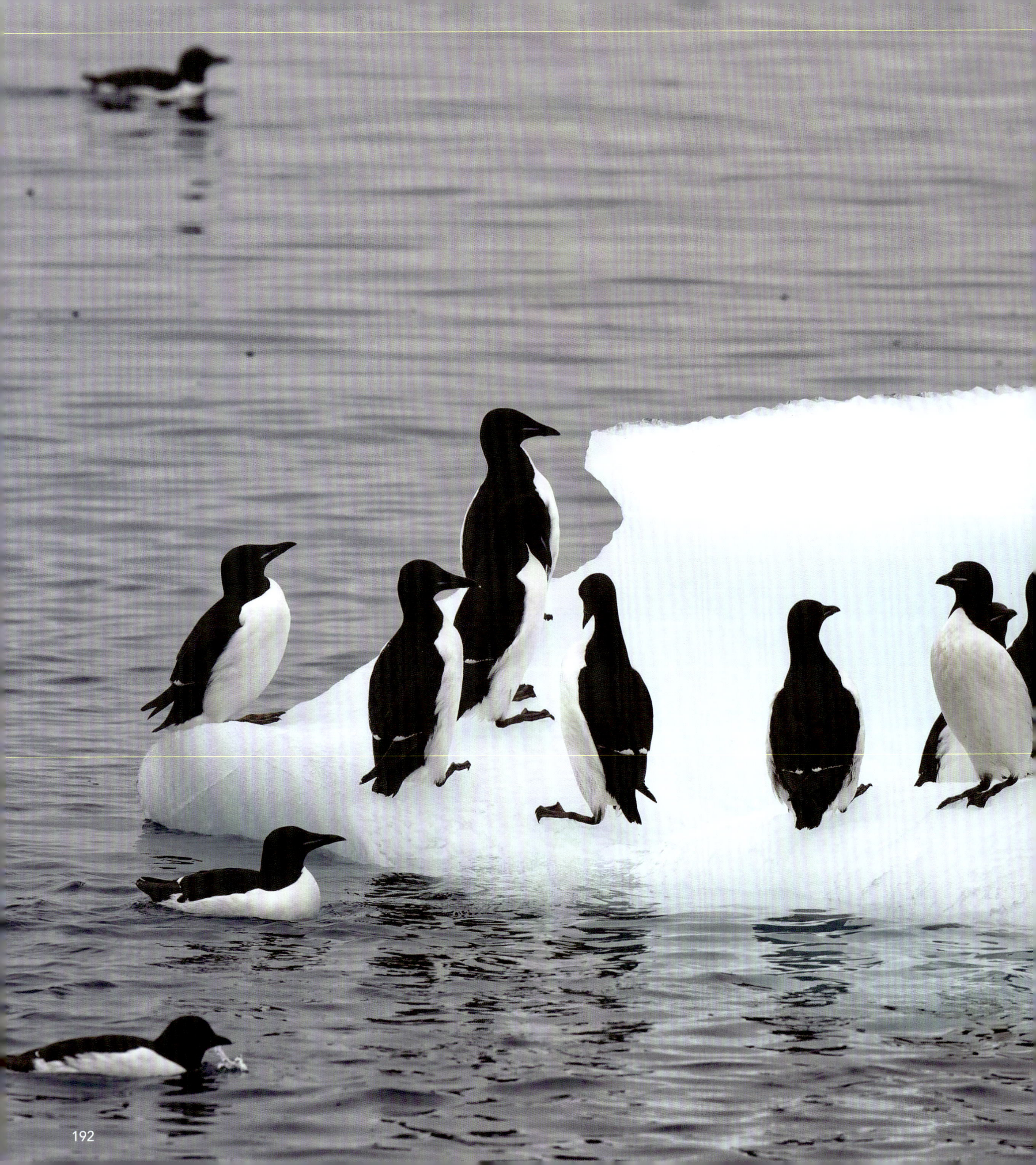

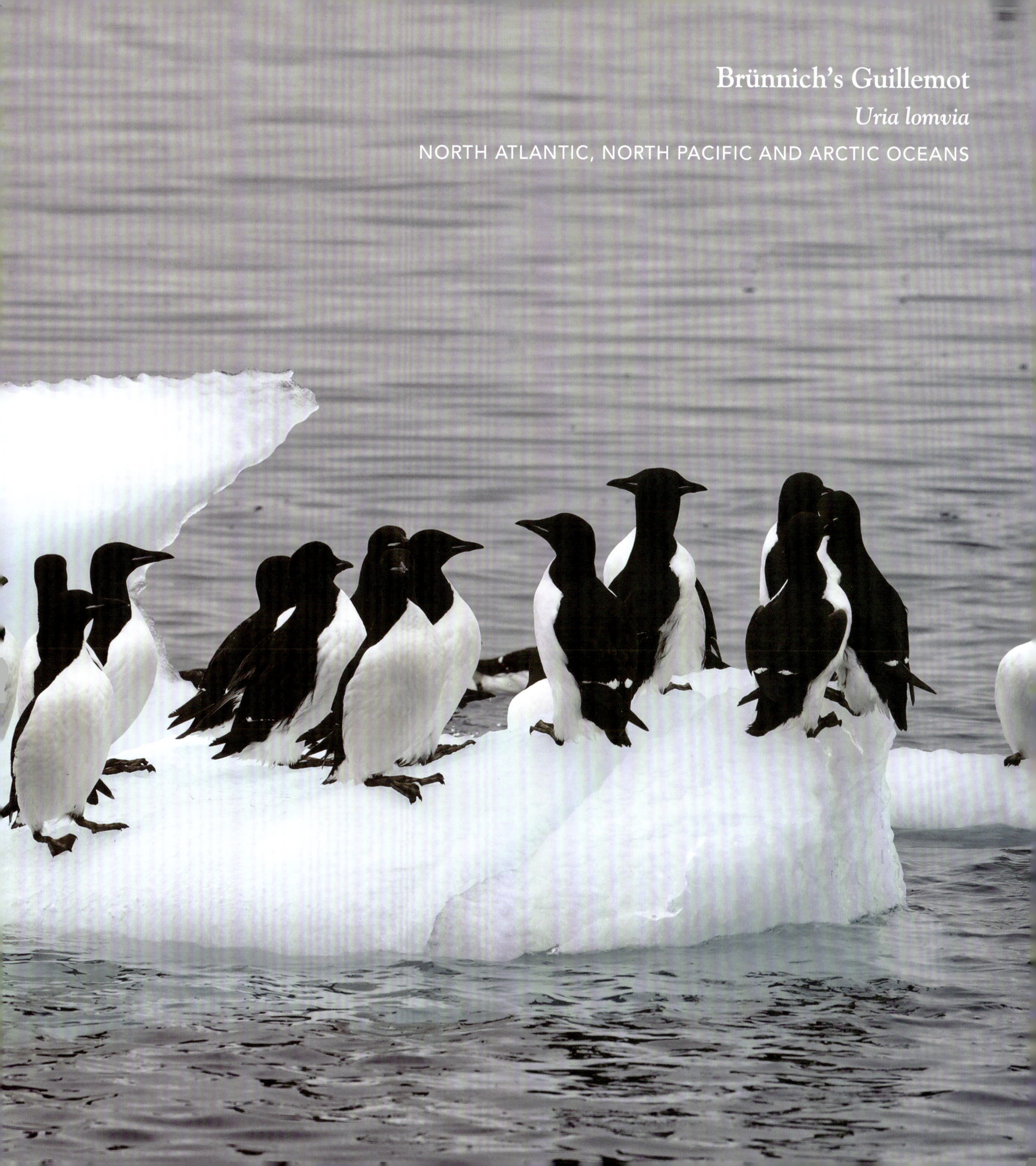

Brünnich's Guillemot

Uria lomvia

NORTH ATLANTIC, NORTH PACIFIC AND ARCTIC OCEANS

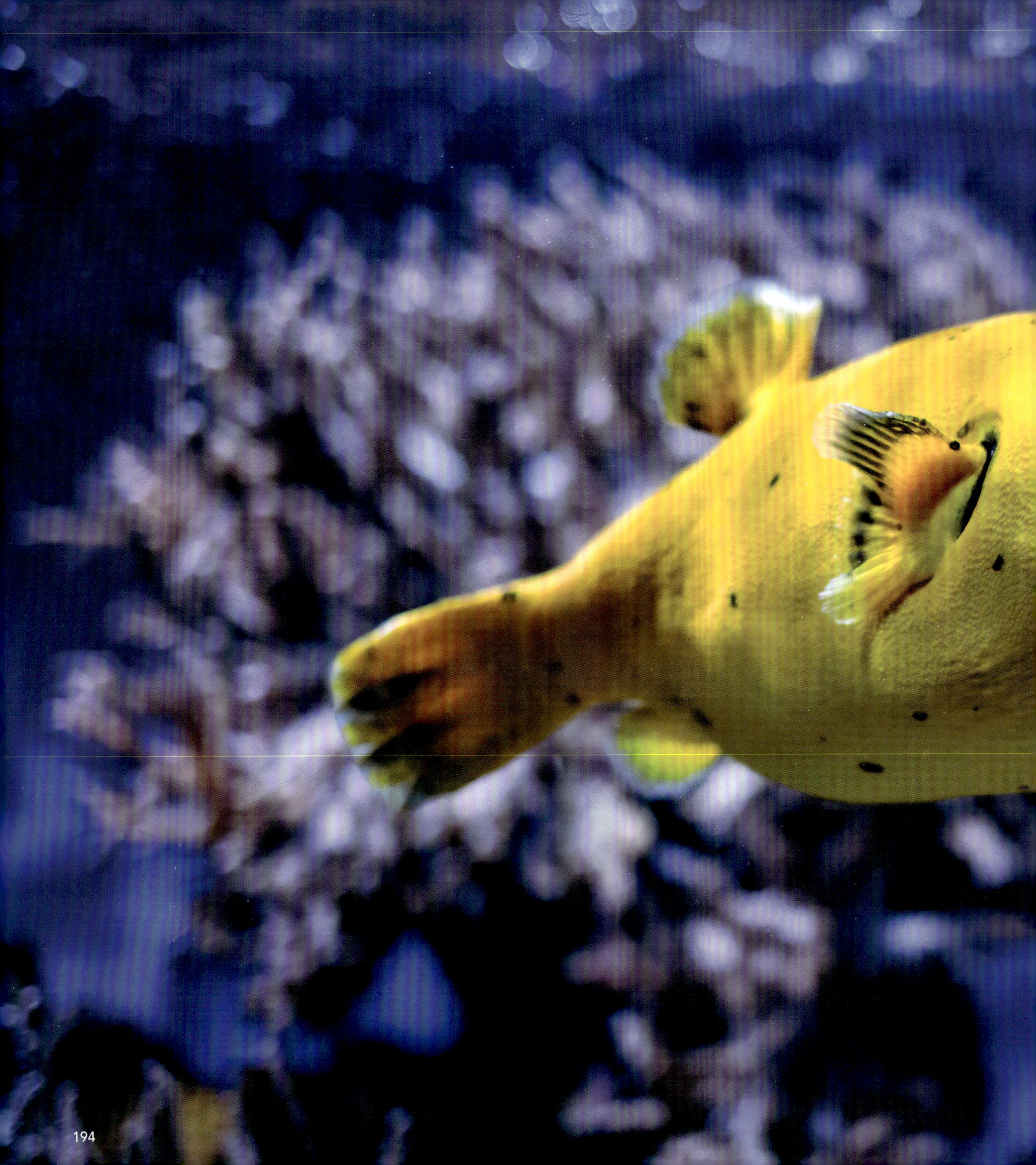

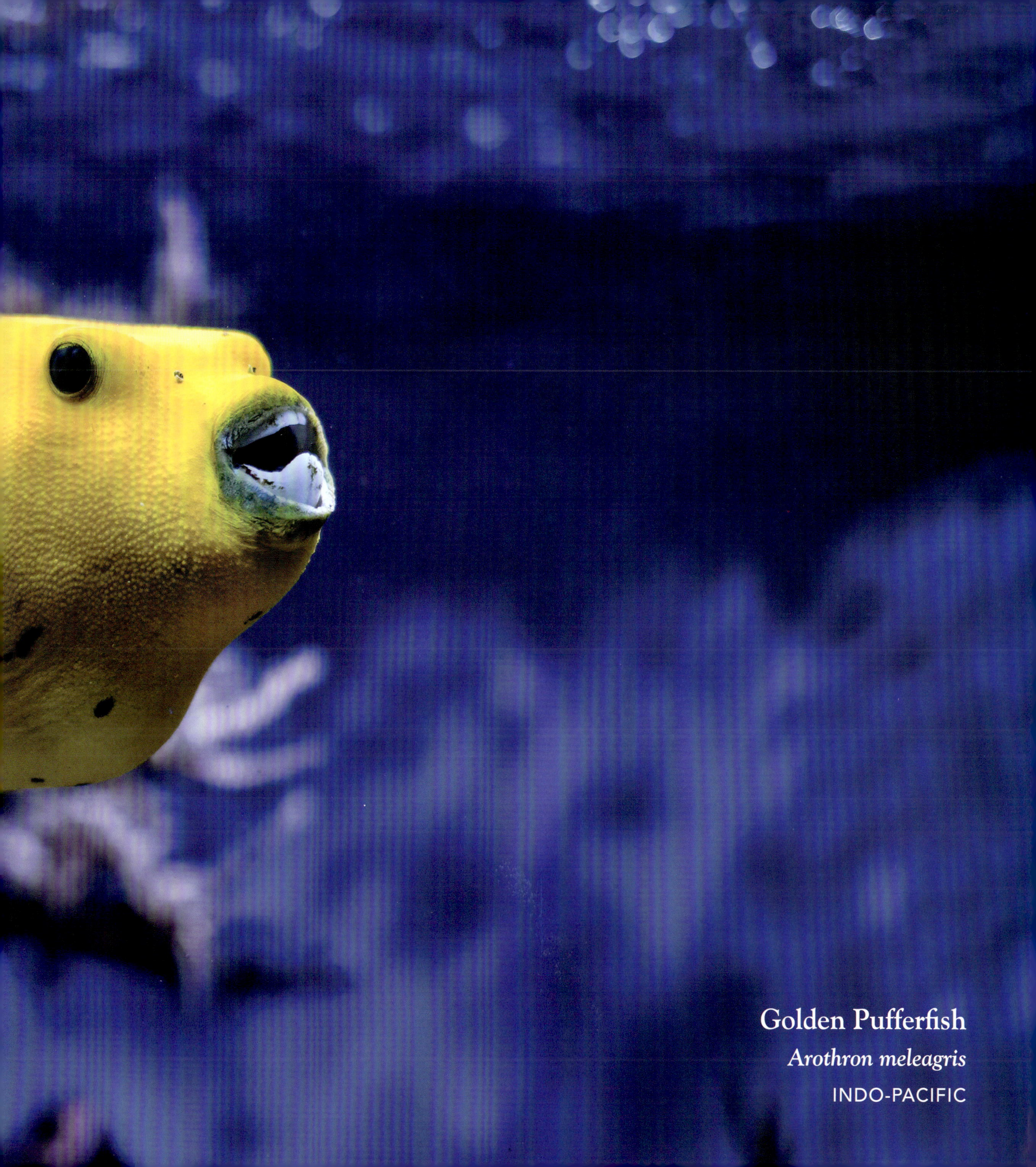

Golden Pufferfish
Arothron meleagris
INDO-PACIFIC

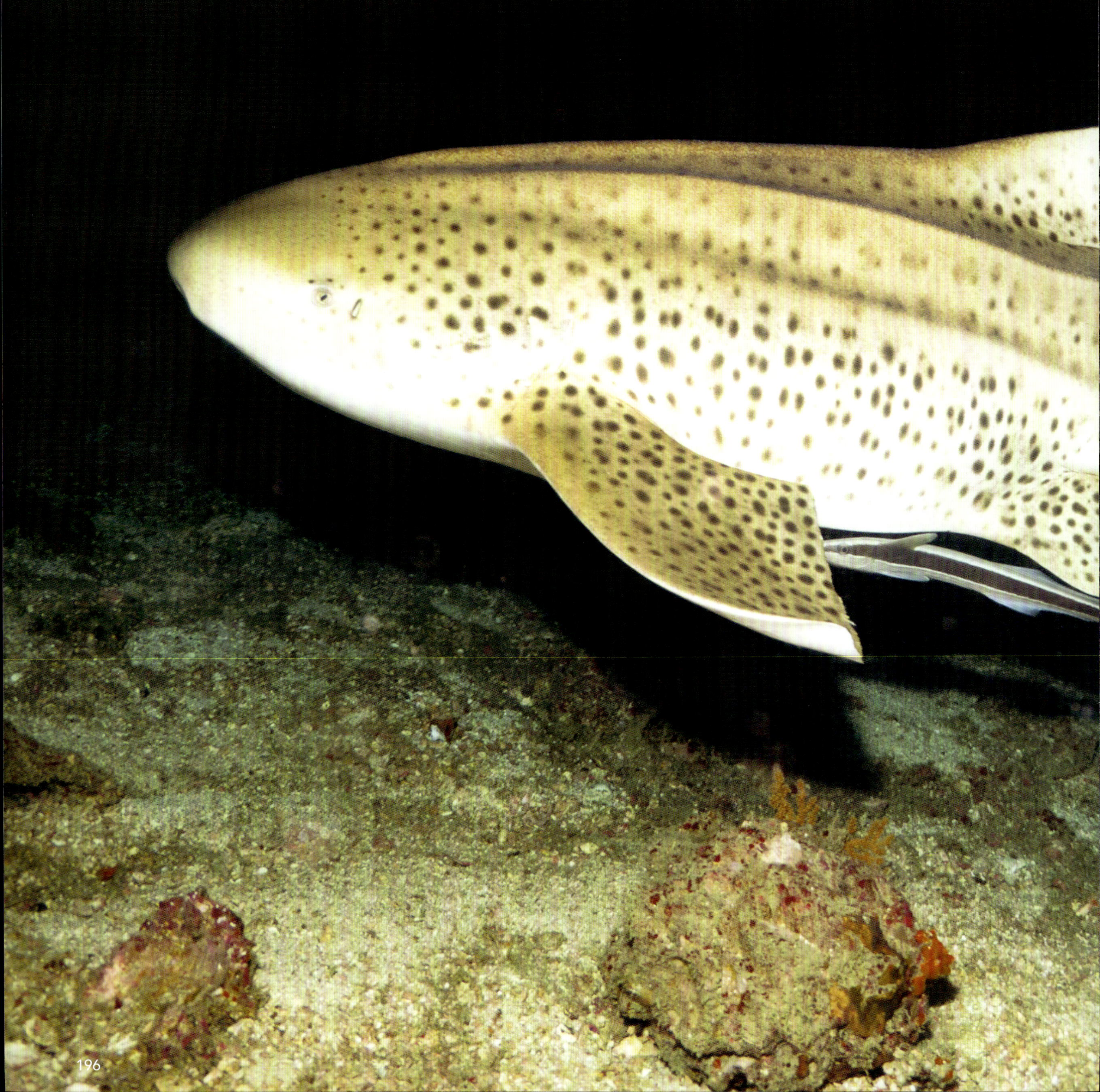

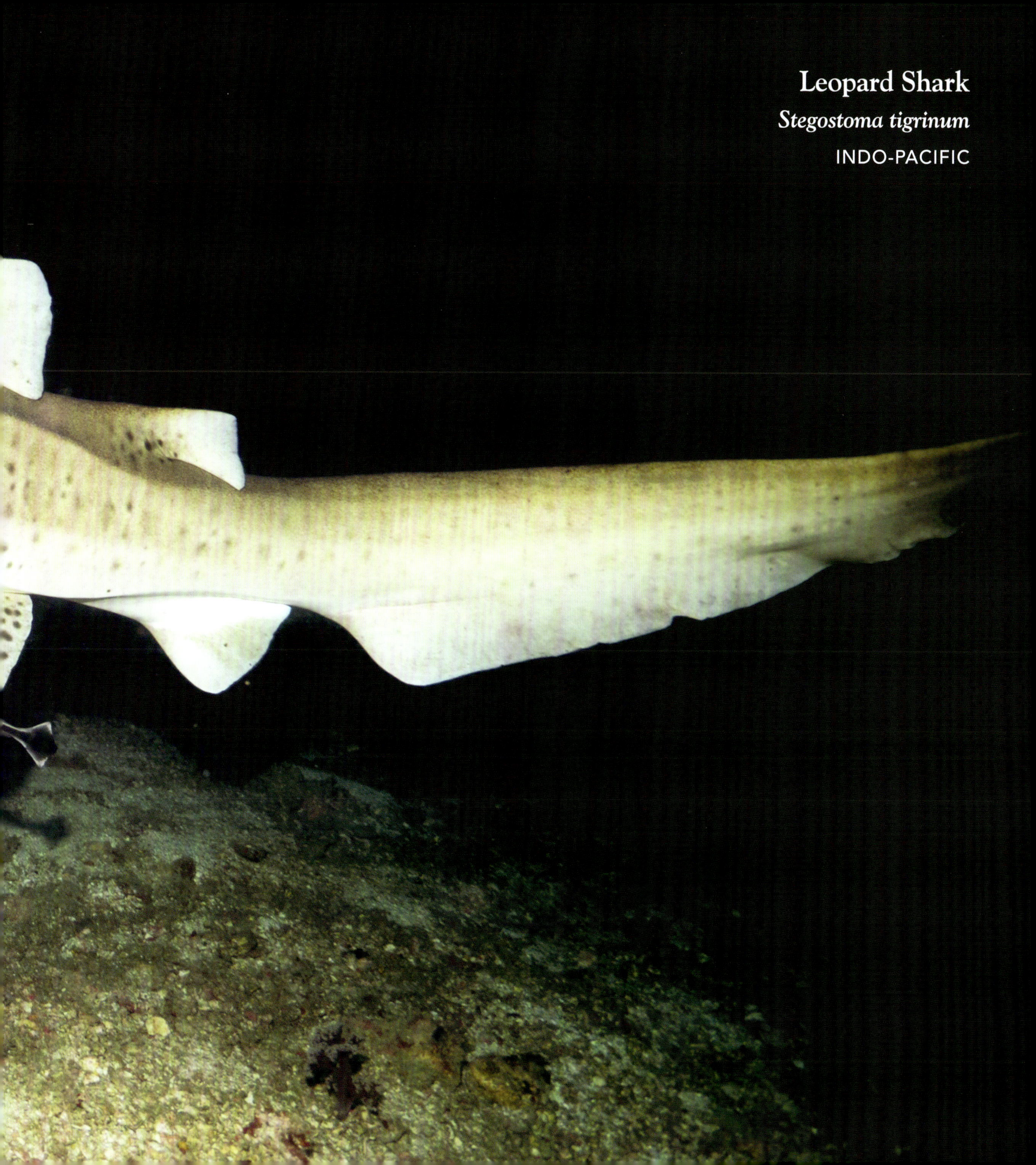

Leopard Shark

Stegostoma tigrinum

INDO-PACIFIC

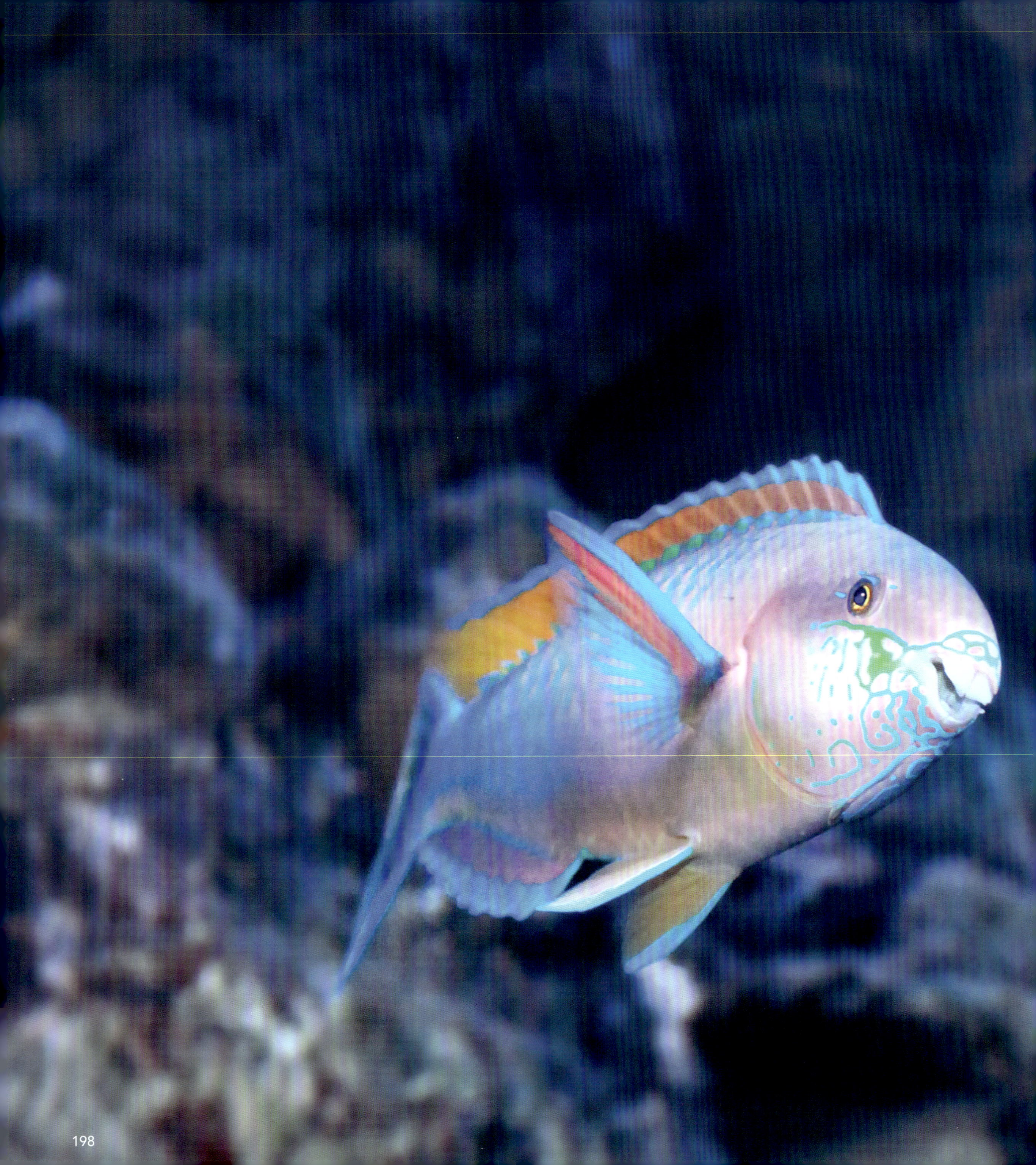

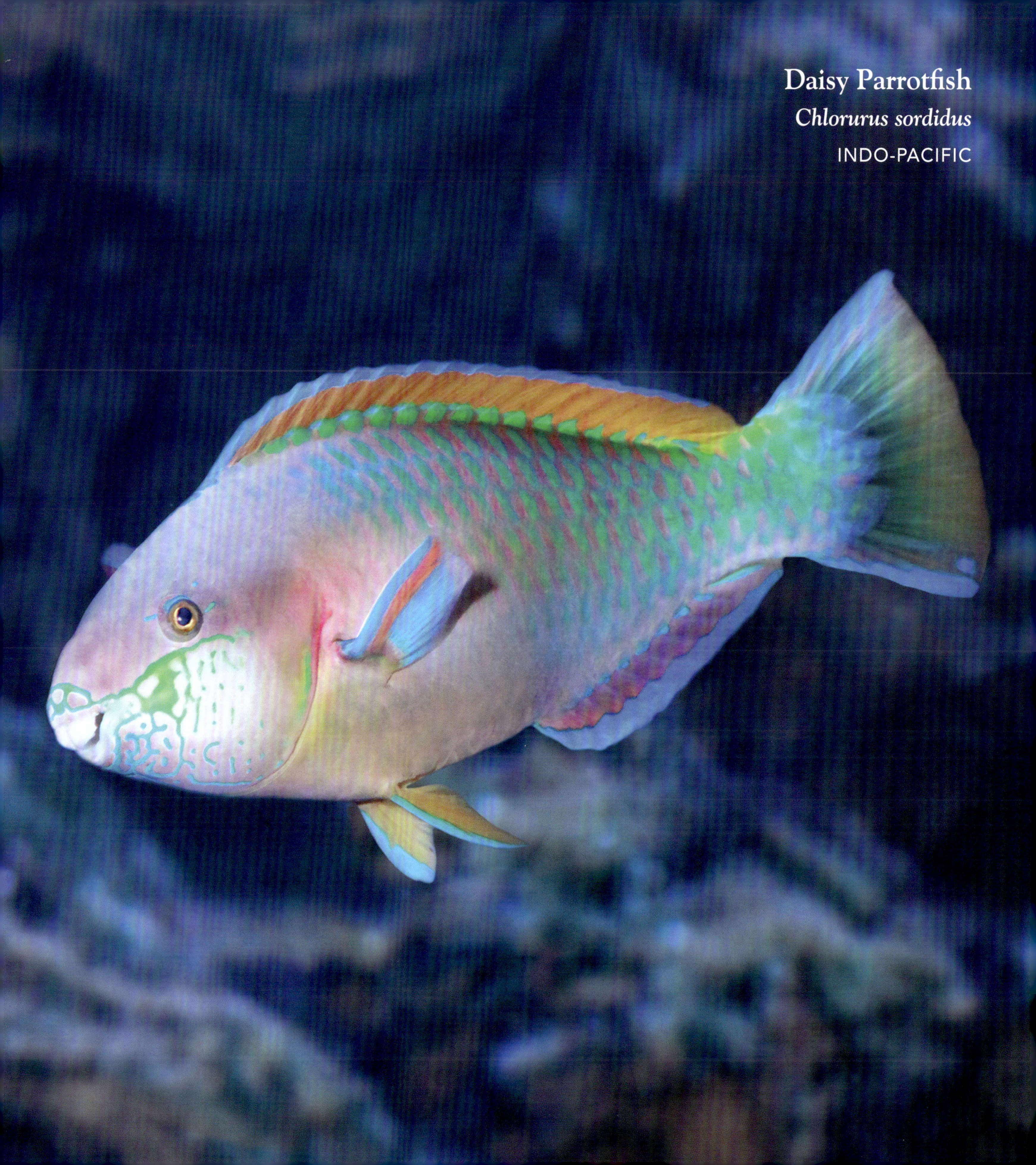

Daisy Parrotfish
Chlorurus sordidus
INDO-PACIFIC

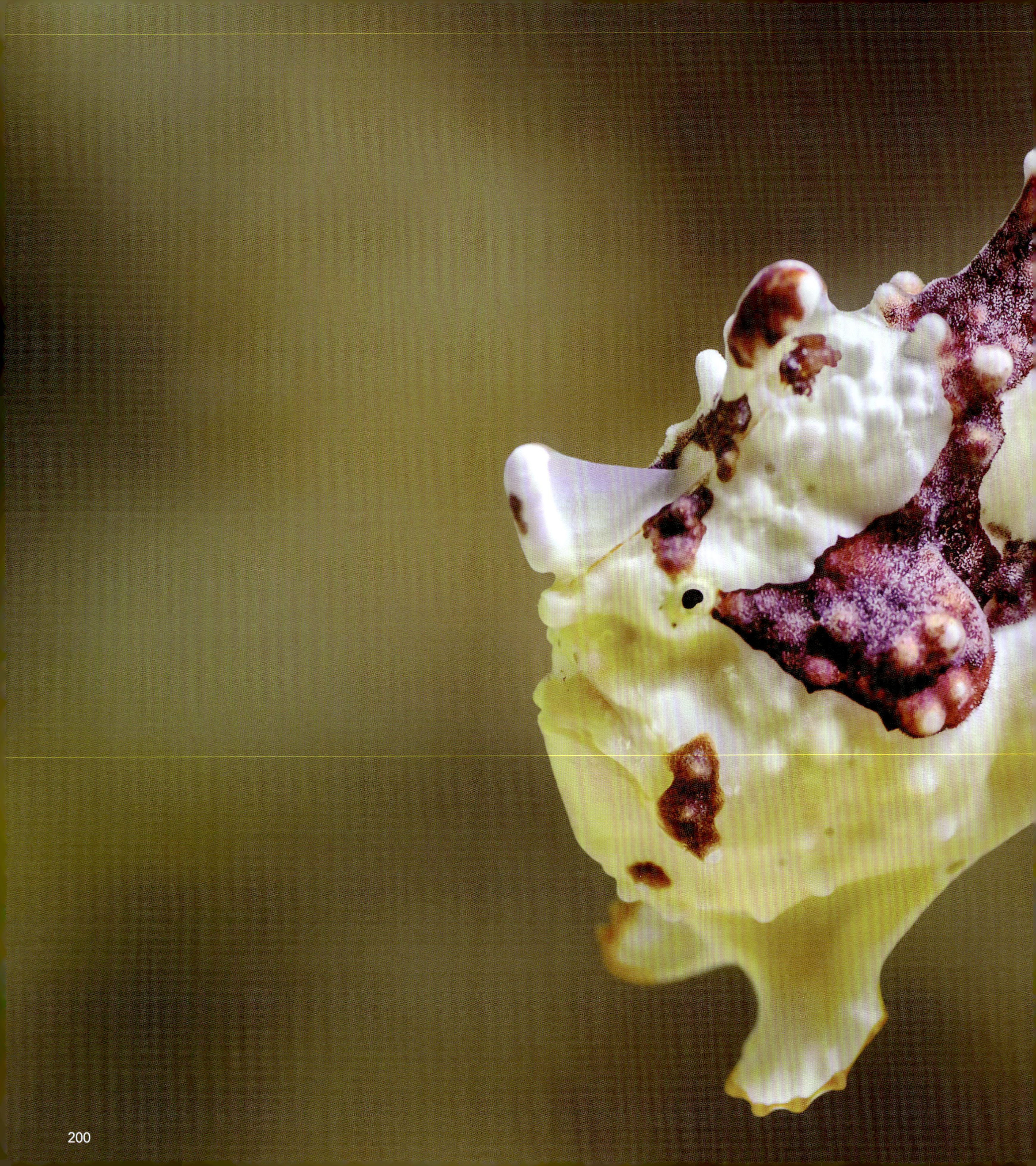

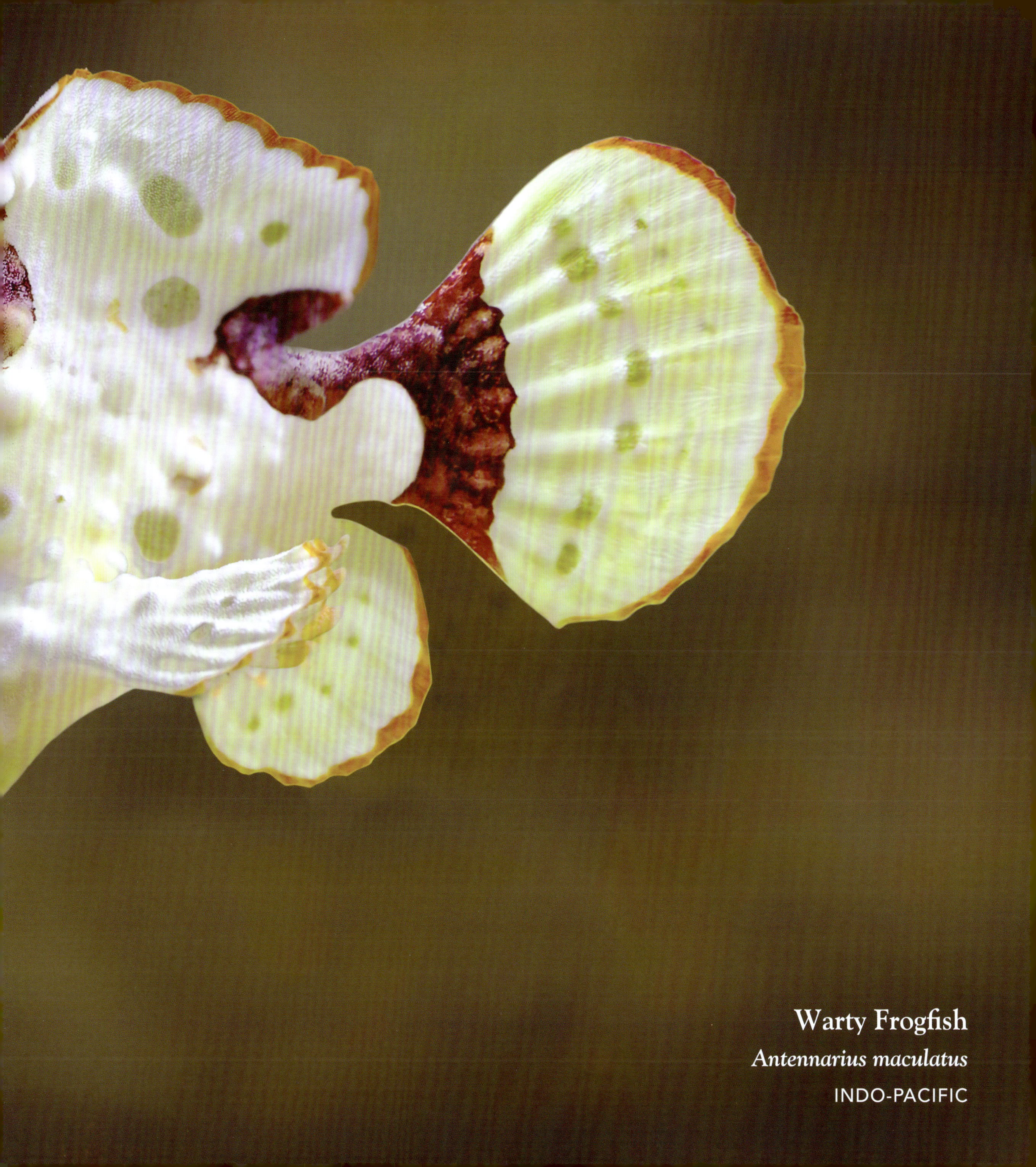

Warty Frogfish

Antennarius maculatus

INDO-PACIFIC

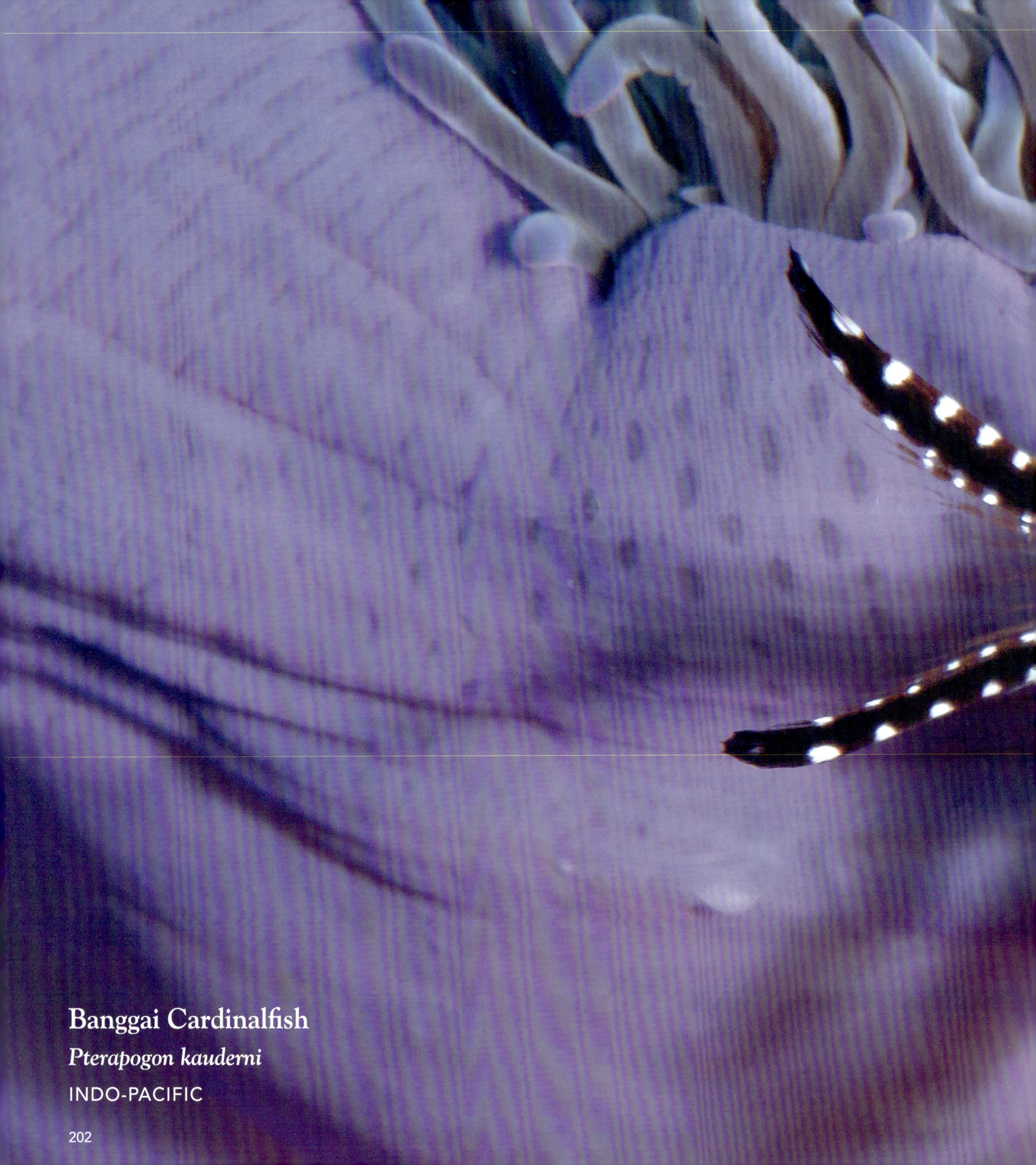

Banggai Cardinalfish

Pterapogon kauderni

INDO-PACIFIC

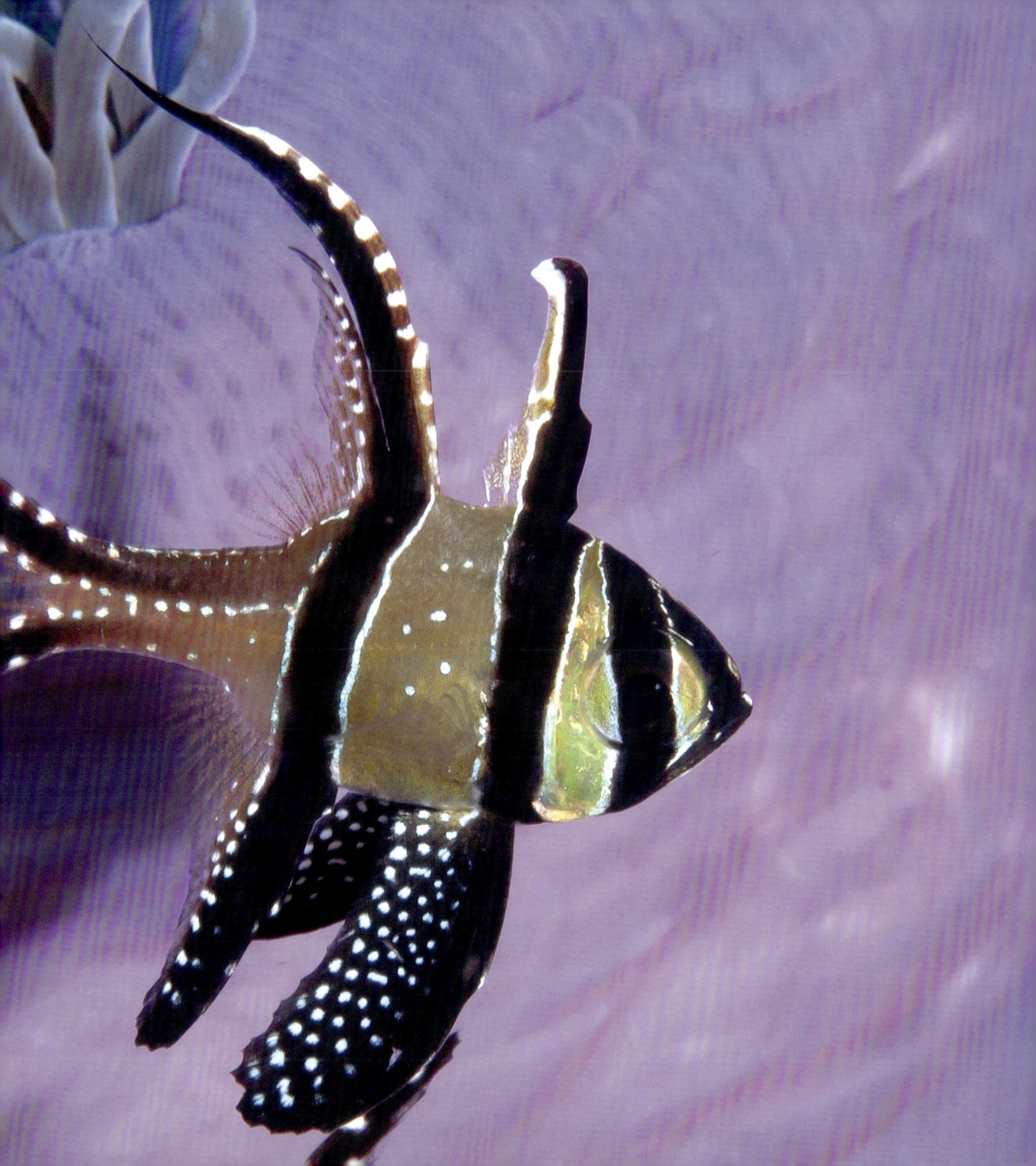

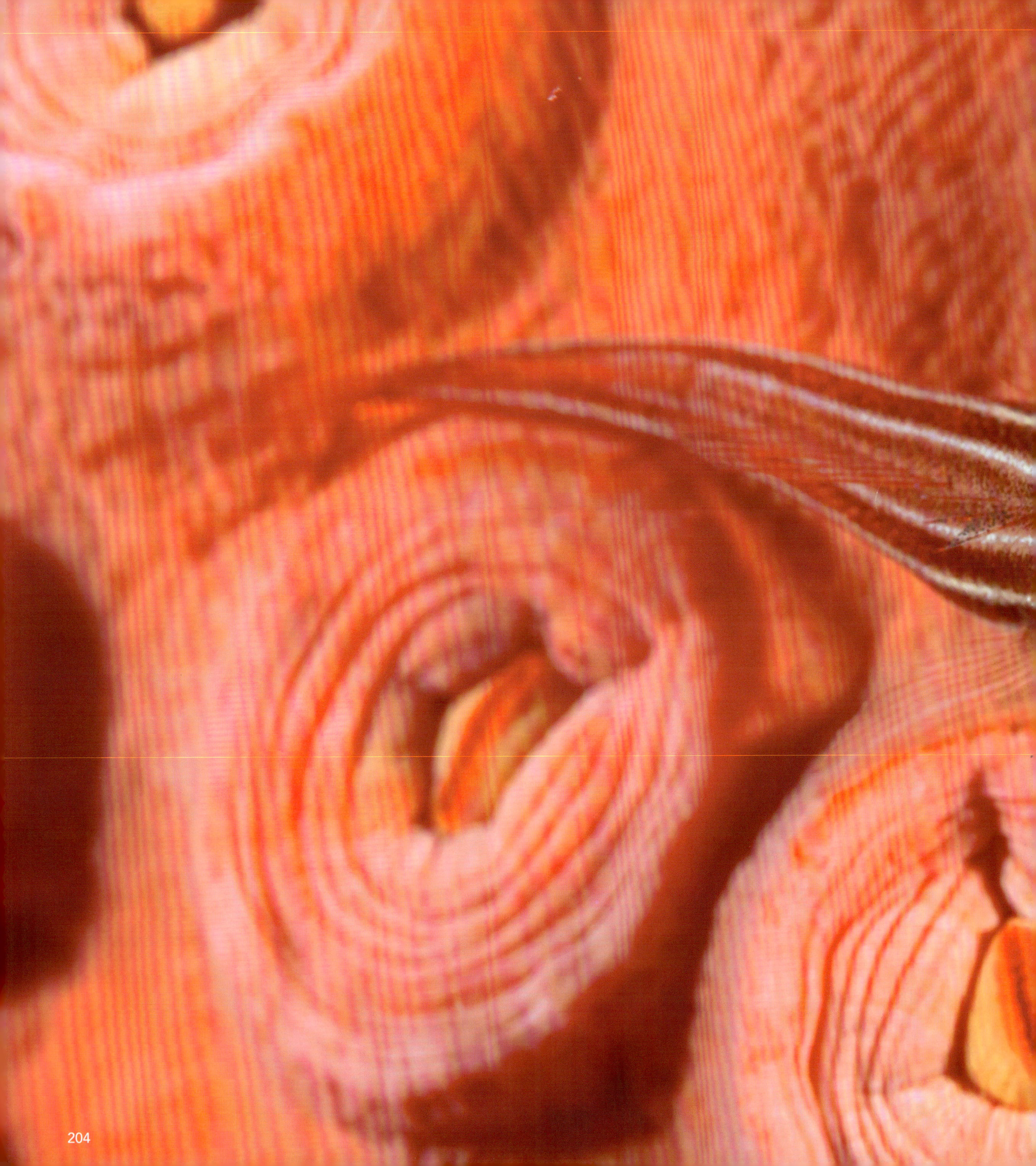

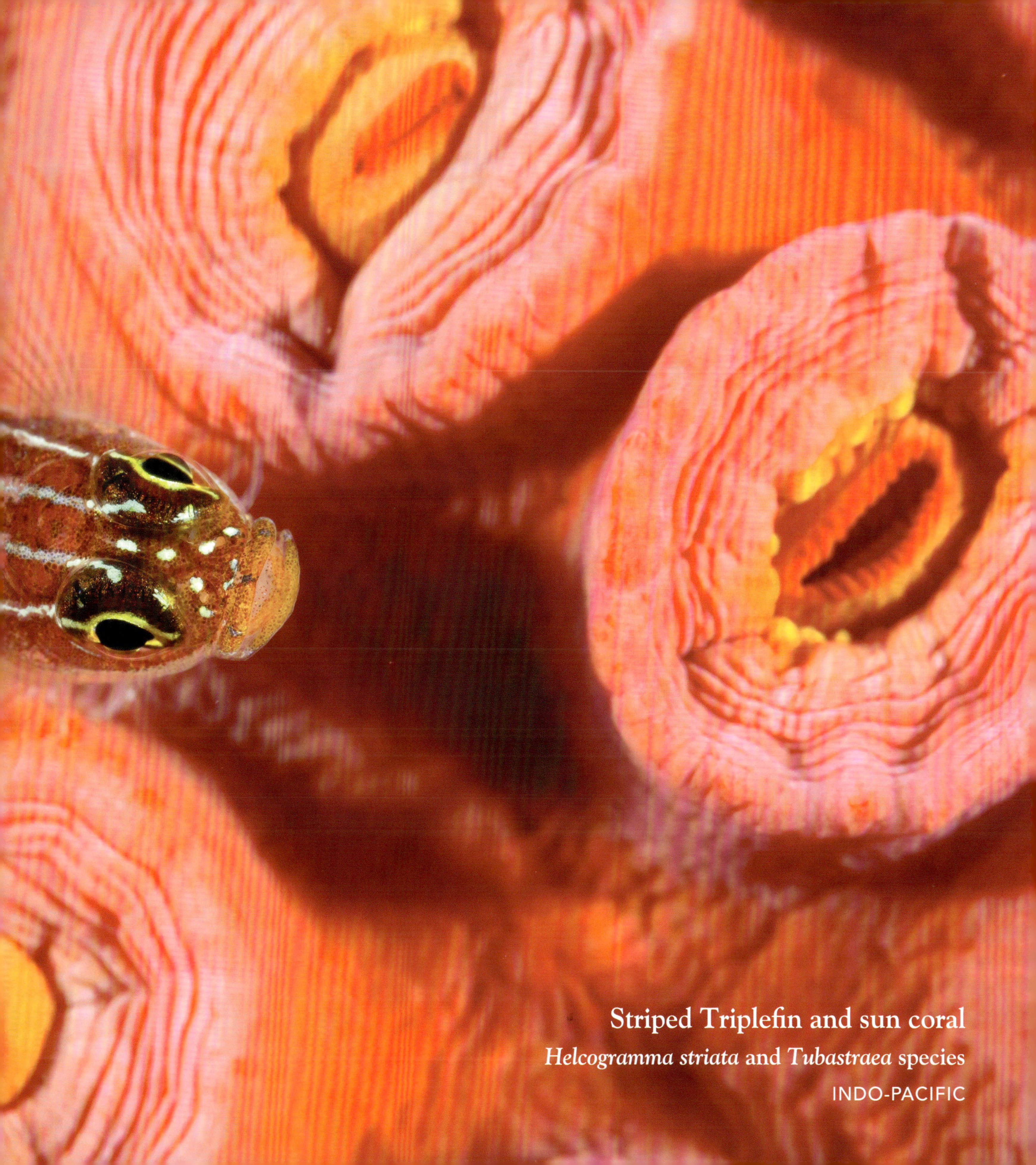

Striped Triplefin and sun coral
Helcogramma striata and *Tubastraea* species
INDO-PACIFIC

INDEX OF COMMON NAMES

INDEX OF SCIENTIFIC NAMES

First published in 2024 by Reed New Holland Publishers
Sydney

Level 1, 176 Fox Valley Road,
Wahroonga, NSW 2076, Australia

newhollandpublishers.com

A record of this book is held at the National Library of Australia.

ISBN 9781760796853

Managing Director: Fiona Schultz
Publisher and Project Editor: Simon Papps
Designer: Andrew Davies
Production Director: Arlene Gippert

Printed in China

FRONT COVER:

Mandarinfish
Synchiropus splendidus
PACIFIC OCEAN

ENDPAPERS

Hard coral species
Scleractinia
OCEANS WORLDWIDE

PAGE 1:

Star Horseshoe Worm
Pomatostegus stellatus
CARIBBEAN

PAGE 2–3:

Blue Whale
Balaenoptera musculus
OCEANS WORLDWIDE

RIGHT:

Tompot Blenny
Parablennius gattorugine
NORTH ATLANTIC

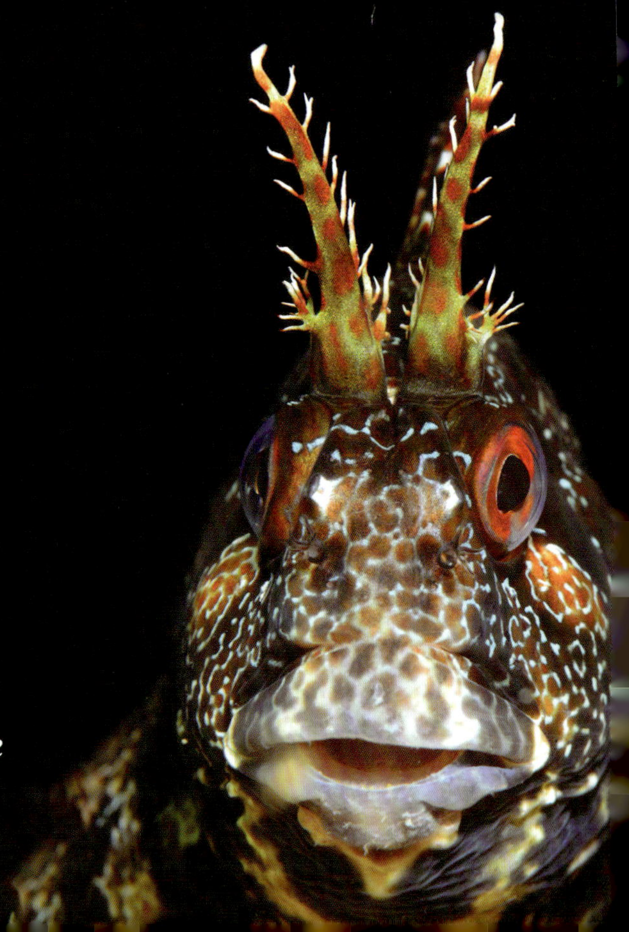

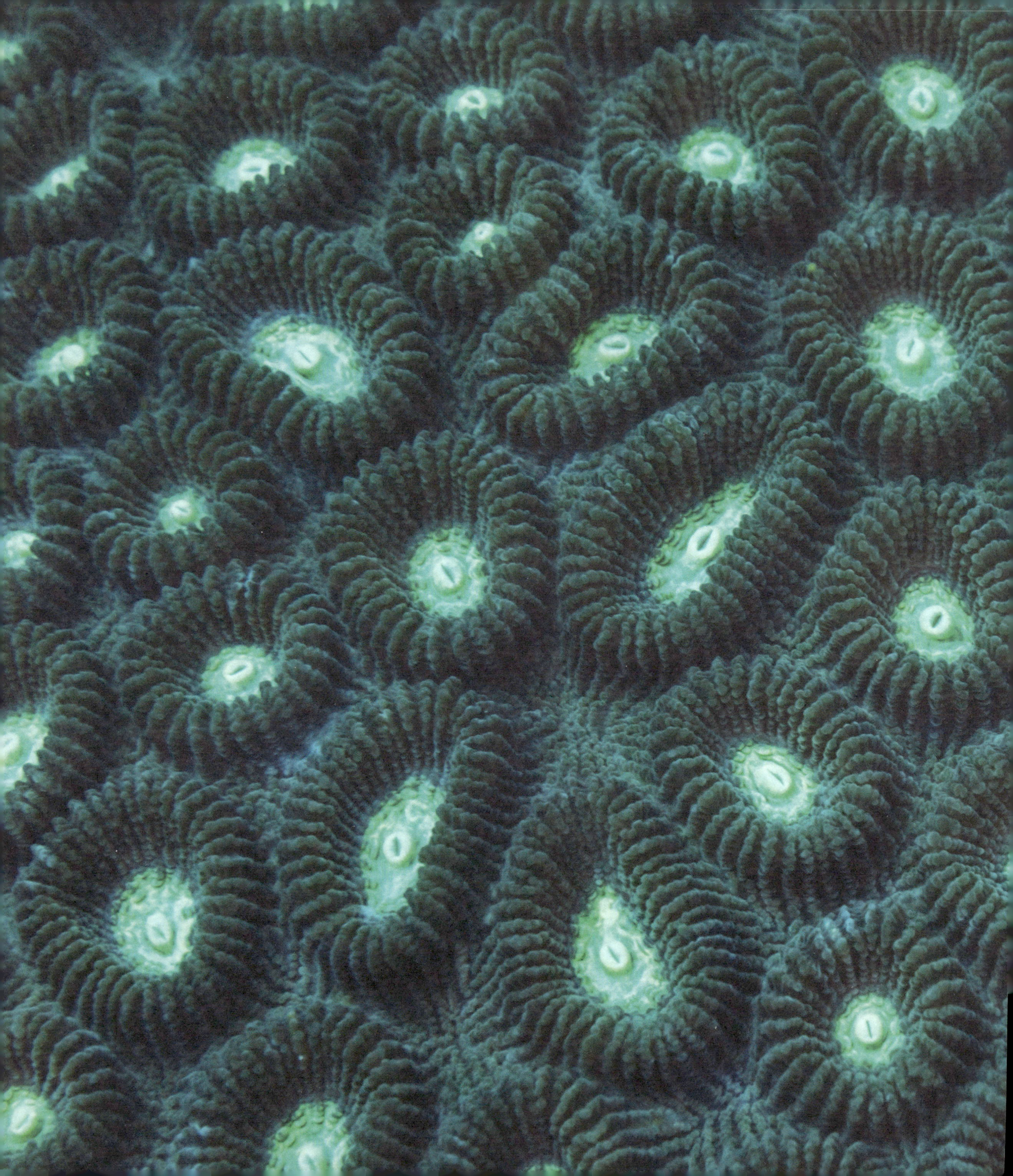